The Land Question in Britain, 1750–1950

Also by Matthew Cragoe

AN ANGLICAN ARISTOCRACY: The Moral Economy of the Landed Estate in Carmarthenshire 1832–1895

CULTURE, POLITICS AND NATIONAL IDENTITY IN WALES 1832–1886

ANTICLERICALISM: From the Reformation to the First World War (*Edited with Nigel Ashton*)

LONDON POLITICS, 1760–1914 (*Edited with Antony Taylor*)

WALES AND WAR: Society, Politics and Religion in the Nineteenth and Twentieth Centuries (*Edited with Chris Williams*)

Also by Paul Readman

LAND AND NATION IN ENGLAND: Patriotism, National Identity and the Politics of Land, 1880–1914

The Land Question in Britain, 1750–1950

Edited by

Matthew Cragoe
Professor of Modern British History, University of Sussex

and

Paul Readman
Head of Department and Senior Lecturer in Modern British History, King's College London

palgrave
macmillan

First published 2010 by
PALGRAVE MACMILLAN

Palgrave Macmillan in the UK is an imprint of Macmillan Publishers Limited, registered in England, company number 785998, of Houndmills, Basingstoke, Hampshire RG21 6XS.

Palgrave Macmillan in the US is a division of St Martin's Press LLC, 175 Fifth Avenue, New York, NY 10010.

Palgrave Macmillan is the global academic imprint of the above companies and has companies and representatives throughout the world.

Palgrave® and Macmillan® are registered trademarks in the United States, the United Kingdom, Europe and other countries.

ISBN-13: 978–0–230–20340–2 hardback

This book is printed on paper suitable for recycling and made from fully managed and sustained forest sources. Logging, pulping and manufacturing processes are expected to conform to the environmental regulations of the country of origin.

A catalogue record for this book is available from the British Library.

A catalog record for this book is available from the Library of Congress.

10 9 8 7 6 5 4 3 2 1
19 18 17 16 15 14 13 12 11 10

Printed and bound in Great Britain by
CPI Antony Rowe, Chippenham and Eastbourne

To Carol and Kristina

Contents

List of Figures and Tables ix

Acknowledgements x

List of Abbreviations xi

Contributors xii

Introduction 1
Matthew Cragoe and Paul Readman

1 The Common Field Landscape, Cultural Commemoration and the Impact of Enclosure, *c.* 1770–1850 19
Ian Waites

2 'Witnesses for the Defence': The Yeomen of Old England and the Land Question, *c.* 1815–1837 37
Kathryn Beresford

3 Chartism and the Land: 'The Mighty People's Question' 57
Malcolm Chase

4 The 'Manchester School' and the Landlords: The Failure of Land Reform in Early Victorian Britain 74
Anthony Howe

5 'A Contemptible Mimic of the Irish': The Land Question in Victorian Wales 92
Matthew Cragoe

6 Setting the Heather on Fire: The Land Question in Scotland, 1850–1914 109
Ewen A. Cameron

7 Irish Land and British Politics 126
Philip Bull

8 Richard Cobden, J. E. Thorold Rogers and Henry George 146
Antony Taylor

9 London and the Land Question, *c.* 1880–1914 167
Roland Quinault

10 The Edwardian Land Question 181
Paul Readman

11 Unemployment, Taxation and Housing: The Urban Land Question in Late Nineteenth- and Early Twentieth-Century Britain 201
Ian Packer

12 Land Reform and the English Land Market, 1880–1925 219
John Beckett and Michael Turner

13 Socialism and the Land Question: Public Ownership and Control in Labour Party Policy, 1918–1950s 237
Clare Griffiths

14 Epilogue: The Strange Death of the English Land Question 257
F. M. L. Thompson

Index 271

List of Figures and Tables

Figures

1.1 John Crome, *Mousehold Heath* (etching, *c.* 1810) 23
1.2 William Turner of Oxford, *Haymaking, Study from Nature, in Osney Meadow, near Oxford, looking towards Iffley* (Watercolour and Bodycolour, 1853–54). Private Collection 26
1.3 William Turner of Oxford, *Portmeadow, Oxford* (pencil, 1812) 28
1.4 William Turner of Oxford, *Whichwood Forest* (Watercolour, 1809) 32
8.1 Popular hostility to aristocratic landowners in a cartoon by 'Cynicus' (Martin Anderson), 1893 155
8.2 Henry George's proposals for land reform alarm the shade of William the Conqueror: *The Owl*, 19 March 1884 161
10.1 F. C. Gould, *The Tory Village: A Toy for Little Tories*, from F. C. Gould, *Cartoons of the Campaign* (London, 1895) 191

Tables

12.1 Land sales in England, 1896–1922 (in £s) 222
12.2 Hierarchy of buyers and sellers of land in England, 1918–21 228

Acknowledgements

This book stems from a conference on the land question held at the University of Hertfordshire in 2005. We would like to thank the University of Hertfordshire for hosting the conference, and King's College London for furnishing us with such handsome posters for the event; the Economic History Society and the Robert Shalkenbach Foundation for their generous support of the conference; the speakers and delegates for making the proceedings so interesting; and our co-organiser, Jeremy Burchardt, for all his input. The work of editing the volume has been made all the more straightforward by the efforts of our contributors: not only did almost everything come in to deadline, but subsequent editorial queries were turned round with the minimum of fuss. We can only hope the final volume does justice to the work everyone has put in.

Our own ideas about the land question have matured in a variety of contexts. We are grateful to the North American Conference on British Studies for allowing us to present a panel on the land question in Philadelphia in 2004, and to the many members of the British History 1815–1945 seminar at the Institute of Historical Research in London – especially our co-convenors F. M. L. Thompson and Roland Quinault – for their enduring interest in the problems raised by the land question. In pubs and curry houses around Bloomsbury, the legacy of Richard Cobden, J. E. Thorold Rogers and Jesse Collings has been ruminated upon at length and we would like to thank, in no special order, Ewen A. Cameron, Tony Taylor, Tony Howe, Dave Monger and John Price for their willingness to chew the fat with us.

Their burdens, of course, were made more bearable by the presence of alcohol. Our long-suffering spouses were often caught relatively unprepared in this respect by the sudden 3 AM flash of inspiration on the true import of a speech by Henry Richard or the Earl of Winchilsea. Kristina, Carol: by way of recompense, this volume is dedicated to you.

Matthew Cragoe and Paul Readman
London and Cambridge, May 2009

List of Abbreviations

ACLL	Anti-Corn Law League
BL	British Library
BLPES	British Library of Political and Economic Science
CDB	Congested Districts Board
CP	Cobden Papers
CUB	Central Unemployment Board
ELRL	English Land Restoration League
ILP	Independent Labour Party
LGB	Local Government Board
LNS	Land Nationalisation Society
MP	Member of Parliament
NAU	National Agricultural Union
NYPL	New York Public Library
NCA	National Charter Association
USRC	Unionist Social Reform Committee
WSRO	West Sussex Record Office

Contributors

John Beckett, Professor of English Regional History at the University of Nottingham, is currently seconded to the University of London as Director of the Victoria County History at the Institute of Historical Research. His publications include *The Aristocracy in England 1660–1914* (1986), *Agricultural Rent in England, 1690–1914* (with M. Turner and B. Afton, 1997) and *Farm Production in England, 1690–1914* (with M. Turner and B. Afton, 2001).

Kathryn Beresford has recently completed a PhD on regionalism and nationhood in England in the 1820s and 1830s at University College London. She is currently researching a book on news reporting in the twentieth century for the BBC World Affairs Correspondent, John Simpson.

Philip Bull is Associate Professor in History and Director of the Innovative Universities European Union Centre at LaTrobe University in Melbourne, Australia. He is author of *Land, Politics and Nationalism: A Study of the Irish Land Question* (1996) and of numerous articles on Irish nationalist politics in the late nineteenth and early twentieth centuries.

Ewen A. Cameron is Reader in Scottish History at the University of Edinburgh. He is author of *Land for the People? The British Government and the Scottish Highlands, c. 1880–1930* (1996), *Charles Fraser Mackintosh and Highland Politics, 1857 to 1892* (2000) and *Impaled upon the Thistle: Scotland since 1880* (2008). He is joint editor of the *Scottish Historical Review*.

Malcolm Chase is Professor of Social History at the University of Leeds and Chair of the Society of Labour History. His publications include *'The People's Farm': English Radical Agrarianism, 1775–1840* (1988), *Early Trade Unionism: Fraternity, Skill and the Politics of Labour* (2000), *Chartism: A New History* (2007) and articles relating to land reform in *Past & Present* and the *English Historical Review*.

Matthew Cragoe is Professor of Modern British History, University of Sussex. He has worked extensively on nineteenth-century politics and is the author of *An Anglican Aristocracy* (1996) and *Culture, Politics and*

National Identity in Wales, 1832–86 (2004) as well as articles in journals including *Past & Present, English Historical Review, Journal of British Studies* and *Rural History*.

Clare Griffiths is Senior Lecturer in Modern History at the University of Sheffield. She is the author of *Labour and the Countryside: The Politics of Rural Britain 1918–1939* (2007) and her publications on twentieth-century politics and rural history include contributions in *History Workshop Journal, Politix* and *Rural History*. She also reviews for the Arts pages in the *Times Literary Supplement*, and was awarded the Sir John Higgs fellowship for 2008–09 from the Museum of English Rural Life at the University of Reading to work on a project about visual representations of farmers and farming during the Second World War.

Anthony Howe is Professor of Modern History at the University of East Anglia. His books include *Free Trade and Liberal England, 1846–1946* (1998) and with Simon Morgan, he has edited *Rethinking Nineteenth-Century Liberalism: Richard Cobden Bicentenary Essays* (2006). He is editor of *The Letters of Richard Cobden, vol. I: 1815–1847* (Oxford, 2007), the first of a four volume edition, supported by an Arts and Humanities Council resource enhancement grant.

Ian Packer is Reader in History at the University of Lincoln. His publications include *Lloyd George, Liberalism and the Land* (2001), *Liberal Government and Politics*, 1905–15 (2006) and articles in the *English Historical Review, Journal of British Studies* and *Scottish Historical Review*.

Roland Quinault is Senior Research Fellow at the Institute of Historical Research, University of London, and a former Honorary Secretary of the Royal Historical Society. His publications include *The Industrial Revolution and British Society* (as editor, with P. K. O'Brien, 1993); *Land and Society in Britain 1700–1914* (as editor, with N. Harte, 1996); *Winston Churchill in the Twenty-First Century* (as editor, with D. Cannadine, 2004) as well as numerous articles on nineteenth- and twentieth-century British political and cultural history.

Paul Readman is Senior Lecturer in Modern British History, King's College London, where he is also Head of the History Department. He has published a number of articles on aspects of modern British political and cultural history in the *English Historical Review, Past & Present, Cultural and Social History, Journal of British Studies, Rural History* and elsewhere. He is author of *Land and Nation in England: Patriotism, National Identity and the Politics of Land* (2008).

Antony Taylor is Senior Lecturer in History at Sheffield Hallam University. His publications include *'Down with the Crown': British Anti-monarchism and Debates about Royalty since 1790* (1999), *Lords of Misrule: Hostility to Aristocracy in Late Nineteenth and Early Twentieth Century Britain* (2004) and many articles on nineteenth-century radicalism in *History, Historical Research, Historical Journal, Journal of British Studies* and elsewhere. He is currently writing a history of terrorism and insurgency in Britain as seen through the medium of pulp fiction.

F. M. L. Thompson is Emeritus Professor of History, University of London. A Fellow of the British Academy, he is former President of the Economic History Society, the British Agricultural History Society and the Royal Historical Society. He is also a former Director of the Institute of Historical Research. His first book was *English Landed Society in the Nineteenth Century* (1963) and his most recent was *Gentrification and the Enterprise Culture: Britain, 1780–1980* (2001).

Michael Turner is Professor of Economic History at the University of Hull. His publications include *After the Famine: Irish Agriculture 1850–1914* (1996), *Agricultural Rent in England, 1690–1914* (with J. V. Beckett and B. Afton, 1997) and *Farm Production in England 1700–1914* (with J. V. Beckett and B. Afton, 2001). His main current project is on *The Death of Copyhold Tenure, 1840–1940.*

Ian Waites is Senior Lecturer in the History of Art at the University of Lincoln. His research focuses on artistic depictions of the English landscape. He has contributed to John Lord (ed.), *Peter DeWint 1784–1849: For the Common Observer of Life and Art* (2007) and co-curated a major exhibition of DeWint's work at the Lincolnshire County Museum (2007).

Introduction

Matthew Cragoe and Paul Readman

Between the mid eighteenth and mid twentieth centuries, issues concerning the use, distribution and ownership of landed property generated considerable debate in Britain. By the mid-Victorian period, the 'land question', as it had become known, was preoccupying politicians and activists from all parts of the ideological spectrum and being hotly contested inside and outside parliament. Liberals and radicals launched crusades aimed at combating the claimed evils of 'landlordism', proposing measures to remedy everything from the pernicious effects of the game laws to the lack of decent wages for labourers. Conversely, political conservatives fought various rearguard actions to preserve the value and influence of landed property, resisting the schemes of reformers, while sponsoring legislation on matters such as smallholdings and agricultural rates to further their own cause. If the land question was never quite as important as franchise reform or Irish affairs (with both of which it could overlap at times), it was always there, in one form or another, a fixture in the political firmament throughout the period covered by this book.

Given its ubiquity across two centuries of British politics, it is perhaps surprising that the land question remains relatively neglected as a subject of historical inquiry. As Roy Douglas noted in his 1976 survey history of the politics of land between the late nineteenth and the mid twentieth centuries, the topic has too often been treated as an appendage of larger questions.[1] Since Douglas's book was published, a considerable volume of work on the land question has appeared, particularly in relation to Ireland and Highland Scotland,[2] yet much of this is necessarily specific in its scope. Now more than ever, therefore, the subject requires a comprehensive, pan-British treatment across the

200 or so years in which it was an issue of major importance. It is in the hope of beginning to fill this lacuna that the current volume is offered.

In doing so, the book seeks to move away from the tendency, much in evidence in the specialist literature, to define the land question either in terms of high political goings-on at Westminster, or in terms of the institutional history of extra-parliamentary organisations and pressure groups. It aims to do this in three ways. First, it emphasises the significance of language, rhetoric and ideas in the politics of land, which were informed by ideologies more sophisticated, and more powerful, than is sometimes assumed. Second, it recognises the multifaceted, protean character of the land question. As subsequent chapters will demonstrate, the land question manifested itself in distinctly different ways at different times and across the different nations of the British Isles; yet further variety was added when the land question mutated from a primarily rural to a largely urban issue in the early twentieth century. Third, the book acknowledges the relevance of the land question to social, cultural and economic history, so placing it in a wider context than typically found in much of the extant scholarship. Nevertheless, it does insist that at root, the land question was a political issue, debated across the ideological spectrum and yet holding a particular appeal to radicals, who saw in land reform a means to break the hold of the aristocracy over the destinies of the country.

The extent of the task facing them was made clear in 1876, when the government-sanctioned *Return of the Owners of Land* – or at least the re-workings of the data by the Essex squire John Bateman – revealed that approximately 75 per cent of the acreage of Britain belonged to about 5,000 people, 710 of whom owned one-quarter of the land area of England and Wales.[3] The wealth derived from these agglomerations of land was enormous: according to one estimate, by about 1880, sixteen titled families drew in gross incomes of over £100,000 from their holdings.[4] Modern scholarship has factored in the value of urban landholding, something omitted by the original return, to provide a more rounded picture. This reveals that the owners of the largest acreages were not necessarily the richest. Thus, although the Duke of Sutherland possessed over 1.3 m acres, he grossed only £142,000 per annum; by comparison, the Duke of Westminster, with just under 20,000 acres, benefited from his ownership of prime areas of London and earned almost £300,000 per annum. The Duke of Bedford, likewise, earned a substantial sum from his metropolitan estate: the annual value of his 83,000 acres was estimated at £225,000.[5]

Another feature revealed by the *Return* is worthy of note: the extent to which the great landowners held land across the British Isles. In this respect, the Dukes of Bedford and Westminster were unusual in that their holdings lay solely in England. Many owned land in two countries – the Duke of Buccleuch, for example, whose 460,000 acres embraced not only Scotland but substantial estates in Northamptonshire – and others in three: the Earls of Dudley and Ancaster, and the Marquess of Bute, for example, owned estates in England, Scotland and Wales, while the Marquess of Londonderry and Viscount Boyne had land in England, Ireland and Wales. The breadth as much as the scale of elite landholding ensured that radical politicians across the United Kingdom could find common cause in agitating the land question.

The agitation of the land question was particularly important at two points during the nineteenth century: during the 1840s and from the 1870s onwards. This is not to say that there was no feeling on the question beforehand – indeed, as Malcolm Chase notes, arguments were being made against the sheer waste of productive capacity occasioned by the emparkment of land around gentlemen's houses, sometimes in vast quantities, as early as the 1820s. The radical land reformer Thomas Spence, who had died in 1814, was a significant influence here. 'If there were no parks, and no pleasure grounds', averred the Spencean Allen Davenport in 1822, 'the whole face of the country would present to the eye cornfields, meadows, gardens, plantations of all kinds of fruit trees, etc., all in the highest state of cultivation.'[6] An unproductive landscape mirrored 'The Thing' – a political system based on jobbery, sinecures and privilege which cosseted the elite insiders and drained the wealth of the common people, and which was so excoriated by radical enemies of 'Old Corruption'.[7]

However, it was not until the 1840s that a genuinely concerted movement for agrarian reform came to the fore in England. At the heart of the new agitation lay the Chartists. In his contribution to this volume, Chase argues that Chartist interest in the land question went much deeper than mere subscription to Feargus O'Connor's famous 'Land Plan', which aimed to settle supporters on four-acre cottage holdings, located in a network of national colonies. He suggests that the Land Plan – which at its peak in 1847–48 had over 70,000 subscribers – cannot be understood in isolation from the broader skein of issues surrounding Chartist views of landed property. A powerful intertwining of the long-established ideologies of the Norman Yoke and Old Corruption provided the basis from which Chartists advanced arguments for, variously, forcible re-appropriation of land from the wealthy, the development of land and building societies, a free market in landed property, deeply radical taxation regimes and the moral necessity to maximise food production. Whatever differences of opinion existed among Chartists on other issues, he concludes, a consistently critical stance on private property in land was maintained.[8]

The Land Plan ultimately ended in humiliating failure. Only 234 subscribers were ever settled on the soil – a far cry from the dreams of its founder. One particularly acute problem faced by O'Connor and all Chartist advocates of land reform schemes was the revelation that they did not possess sole agitating rights on the question, as a consequence of which it was difficult to stake out and maintain a distinctive position. As Anthony Howe makes clear, the leaders of the middle-class Anti Corn Law League (ACLL), with more establishment influence and friends in parliament than their Chartist counterparts could ever hope to enjoy, were also enthusiastic advocates of land reform. The particular focus of their attention was the range of legal devices employed by the landowning classes to keep intact their estates across successive generations – primogeniture, entail and strict settlement. No one was more vociferous in this respect than Richard Cobden, who regarded such protectionism as a defining characteristic of aristocracy in England.

> By aristocracy, I mean that class whose families are sought to be sustained & perpetuated by the custom of primogeniture. That is, the landed class, high & low, rich & poor. I do not call a man, enriched by trade, however wealthy he may be, one of the aristocracy, until, like the Barings, & many others, he creates a family property in land, & seeks to perpetuate it by the law of entail – in a word, by the aristocracy, I mean, the feudal aristocracy.[9]

Staunch proponent of free trade as he was, Cobden was adamant that the same rules of free exchange must apply to the land as to other forms of property. This being the case, there was widespread surprise when, once the battle to abolish the Corn Laws had been brought to a successful conclusion in 1846, the leaders of the ACLL did not embark on a fresh crusade against the land laws. As it was, Cobden was beginning to recognise that the power of the aristocracy was not based on landownership alone, but relied on what Howe describes as 'the entwinement of landowners and the state'.[10] The solution to this difficulty required more than reform of the land laws alone could supply, and by the mid-1850s, Cobden and the rest of the Manchester School were looking to further financial and parliamentary reforms to undermine the position of the landed elite. British radicalism as a whole was to pay little attention to the land question until after the establishment of the Land Tenure Reform Association in 1869.[11]

Instead, Cobden seems to have placed his faith in the Freehold Land Societies that proliferated during the late 1840s.[12] Like many others, he saw in them a means of counteracting one of the chief effects of landlordism in Britain – the decline of the peasantry. However, he was obliged to recognise that these societies could not in themselves provide a new wave of Liberal voters capable of sweeping away the aristocracy. By no means all Freehold Land Societies were Liberal in political complexion: the Conservative party established their own society in 1852, though the conservative potential of free-holding had already been widely accepted before this point.[13] In 1850, for example, the staunchly Conservative *Blackwood's Magazine* highlighted the fact that twenty-acre farms in Flanders, Holstein and the Palatinate produced more food than equivalent holdings in England because the peasants cleaned the fields and dug into the corners where the ploughs did not reach: the land was, in effect, their savings bank.[14] 'The labourer is himself the owner of the soil, and to one so circumstanced work assumes quite a different aspect; the spade goes deeper, the scythe takes a wider sweep, and the muscles lift a heavier burden.' Recalling the agricultural reformer Arthur Young's famous claim that 'the magic of property turns sand into gold', the *Blackwood's* article concluded that 'No agricultural chemistry' was 'so potent as the sense of property'.[15]

In truth, the line dividing radical and conservative views of both the landscape and its occupants could be surprisingly fine, at least in some respects. Both sides gazed nostalgically at an idealised picture of a contented peasantry working their own plots – one seeing them as bastions for the security of the existing distribution of property, while the other as the building blocks of a virtuous republic of hardy and independent citizen cultivators. Kathryn Beresford demonstrates the way in which the rhetoric of the English 'yeoman' was self-consciously and sedulously mobilised by apologists for the landed elite throughout the early decades of the nineteenth century. The yeoman became, she says, the 'lynchpin of "old England" ', the cynosure of a timeless, paternalistic countryside where benevolent landlords flourished alongside prosperous farmers and contented labourers in a 'natural' hierarchy. Yet during the 1830s, the sturdy earthy qualities of the Kentish yeoman were equally attractive to those of a liberal disposition as they sought to mobilise the rural electorate against the landed aristocracy. As was also the case with a related cultural stereotype closely connected to patriotism – the figure of John Bull – that of the yeoman was never the preserve of one party alone.[16]

A similar array of tensions is captured from the opposite end of the political spectrum in the landscape studies explored by Ian Waites in the chapter with which this collection opens. Focussing on the work of two mid-nineteenth-century cultural figures, the artist William Turner of Oxford (1789–1862), and the working-class novelist and poet, Thomas Miller (1807–74), he explores how even radical perceptions of landscape were arbitrated by a new sense of nostalgia which emerged once it was realised that older modes of life were quickly disappearing. Both men remained psychologically wedded to a pre-enclosure landscape, their work confirming the remnants of this landscape as survivals from an almost lost age. For Turner, this took the form of paintings and drawings of the landscape around Oxford; for Miller, the evocation of an idealised Gainsborough. However, defiantly radical though the impulse behind these works may have been in intent, they appealed as much to conservative and bourgeois-liberal idealisations of the countryside as to those of a more radical orientation, and found institutional expression as much in bodies like the moderately progressive Commons Preservation Society founded in 1865 as in the Chartist Land Company or the Freehold Land Societies.[17]

By the 1860s, the land question had disappeared from the main currents of political debate in England. The heavy summer of mid-Victorian prosperity stilled the grumbling hive: work was plentiful in town and country, and few agitations made much headway in these conditions.[18] Cobden died in 1864; and though his last public speech included several lines that would later be construed by his brother in law, Thorold Rogers, as a clarion call for far-reaching land reform, the truth was that Cobden's actions had rarely matched his rhetoric on the subject of the land question. More significant in the campaign against the aristocracy was Cobden's implacable companion from the days of the League, John Bright. In the late 1840s, he went after the aristocracy in earnest, touring Ireland and laying the blame for the immiseration of the rural population firmly at the door of the elite, as well as agitating the vexed question of the game laws, which preserved the right of hunting, shooting and fishing to the aristocracy and their familiars.[19] In 1861, Bright made another important contribution to the development of the land question when he claimed to have established, on the basis of that year's population census, that there were only 30,000 landowners in England.[20] The compilation of the *Return of the Owners of Land* 15 years later was prompted in part by the Conservatives' desire to disprove this contention. This it did, suggesting that a million people owned land in the country, but any resultant triumph felt by the Conservatives was vitiated by the extraordinary concentration of property it revealed among the social elite. This concentration was especially marked in Scotland and Ireland. The data from the 1876 *Return* revealed that the level of aristocratic domination in these countries far exceeded that in England. In England, 56 per cent of the total area of land was held in estates of 1,000 acres or more; in Wales and Ireland, however, the equivalent figures were 61 and 78 per cent, respectively, and in Scotland, an extraordinary 93 per cent![21] For the rest of the century, those interested in land reform had access to hard data to underpin their claims.

The second peak of agitation regarding the land question was a more genuinely British phenomenon than the first, embracing the Celtic heartlands. If the English countryside slumbered in the high noon of mid-Victorian prosperity, the situation in Ireland was quite different. Here, the parliamentary campaign since the mid 1830s for legislation to recognise the claims of tenants to compensation for self-funded improvements on their properties fed into a new and more violent form of agitation. Philip Bull's analysis of the Irish land question sets out very clearly a key factor which also underpinned agitation of the issue in Wales and the Scottish Highlands: a basic difference in the approach of the owners and occupiers as to the terms on which land should be held. For most owners in these areas, whose social networks and cultural assumptions were tied closely into those of the English aristocracy, land was rented in the expectation that tenants would farm it for profit. However much the bulk of English tenants may have failed to live up to the principles espoused by the high farming lobby, and however powerful the 'moral economy' of shared identification between landlords and tenants on individual estates, this position was widely accepted. In Ireland, Wales and the Scottish highlands, however, tenants felt a primarily cultural identification with the soil they farmed and did not buy in to contemporary notions of 'improvement' and its associated rent rises. It was, perhaps, a 'peasant mentality', but it was strong enough to launch powerful agitations for reform in all three countries in the last 30 years of the nineteenth century, while also – in Ireland especially – feeding into developing discourses of national identity.

Gladstone, says Bull, recognised the basic problem in Ireland, and sought to provide restitution to the Irish farming community in his 1870 Land Act by allowing the principle that a tenant had a right to sell on his interest in a property to the next incumbent. Relatively limited in its actual effects, the act did little to pacify Ireland. The frustration that had built up at the lack of reformist legislation in the previous 30 years, the realisation that the Act of 1870 did not go far enough and the hardship caused by the failure of the potato crop at the end of the 1870s all combined to fan the flames of Irish agrarian radicalism. Under Charles Stewart Parnell, nationalist and agrarian politics came together in a campaign for the 'three Fs'. To the issue of 'fair sale' that had been addressed – if not quite resolved – in 1870, were added a demand for fixity of tenure and fair rents. Faced with unprecedented unrest in rural Ireland, particularly in the impoverished western counties, Gladstone responded once again. With his Land Act of 1881, a system of land courts was established to guarantee the 'three Fs': in Ireland, agrarian rents could now be fixed by judicial process. This was an extraordinary departure from *laissez-faire* principles, and one which many observers – not least a number of Whig magnates – saw as an inadmissible interference with the rights of private property.[22] But for the Irish, of course, it was a remarkable success, effectively ending the 'land war' that had raged since 1879 and allowing Parnell to channel the energies this agitation had unleashed into the home rule movement.

The Irish success encouraged the Welsh and Scots to like activity, although as it turned out in neither case did the same sense of urgency exist at the grass roots. In Wales, as Matthew Cragoe discusses, the nationalism of the radical politicians who agitated the land question did not find a sufficiently strong echo among tenants to force concessions from the government. For all the rhetoric, the situation in the Welsh countryside was much closer to that in England than that in Ireland. Despite the Welsh land question undeniably informing an emergent nationalist movement, there did not exist the same level of cultural alienation that animated Irish farmers, who harboured a smouldering resentment towards the Protestant ascendancy for their alleged appropriation of the (Catholic) people's land. In Wales, for all that the landlords were estranged from the general populace by denominational and linguistic differences, there was never any real sense of impending civil war: there were no guns behind hedges in the principality. And thus, while radical politicians and newspaper editors repeatedly put themselves in the van of agitations designed to topple the citadel of landlordism and liberate the oppressed *gwerin*, they failed with almost equal regularity to find the foot soldiers able to carry the fight to their enemies – not least because landlord–tenant relations were generally far better than many agitators claimed.[23] On the few occasions when some momentum was built up – as during the Tithe War in the late 1880s – the depressed state of the economy rather than political radicalism drove the tenantry into the field – and the apparent grant of economic concessions persuaded them to quit it. While Gladstone did concede, rather unwillingly, a Royal Commission to explore the whole issue of the land in Wales and Monmouthshire in 1892, he felt no need to extend the three Fs to Wales, let alone the complex machinery introduced in Ireland under the Ashbourne Act of 1885, which allowed tenants facilities to purchase their holdings and provided the template for the ultimate solution to the Irish land question. In the principality, neither the plight of the tenants nor the glue of nationalist idealism was sufficiently intense to bind together an enduring movement in favour of such fundamental concessions.

In Scotland, Liberal politicians were able to make much better use of the land question, and major concessions were secured. The situation was very different, of course, as Ewen A. Cameron makes clear. The Scottish Highlands shared with Ireland an experience of dispossession; even if the new landowners who bought into the region in the early nineteenth century were not alienated from the population in terms of religion or language (as in Ireland and Wales), they were nevertheless outsiders, the huge clearances of tenants conducted during the early nineteenth century remaining an enduringly powerful rallying cry. The depression of the later 1880s, which provoked the so-called Crofters' War, was sufficiently important for parliament to extend to farming tenants in the seven northernmost counties of Scotland the principal advantages granted to Ireland in 1881.[24] Moreover, the Conservatives introduced a scheme of land purchase in 1897. Yet, as Cameron concludes, although the plight of the crofting communities was a card that Liberal MPs from Scotland, lowland and highland alike, did not scruple to play throughout the late nineteenth century, the crofters themselves were effectively pacified by the recognition of their rights in 1886. Despite the presence of some crofter MPs in the Scottish Home Rule Association, it seems clear that, perhaps more in Scotland than Wales, the crucial identification of land with nationalism that typified the agitation in Ireland was lacking.

In England the agricultural depression that swept in on the back of cheap grain imports from America during the mid-1870s provided a context for a new interest in questions relating to the land. By the end of the decade, farmers had formed their own pressure group, the Farmers' Alliance, which endorsed candidates at the election of 1880. Although the movement was short-lived, the plight of the countryside had returned to the parliamentary agenda, and the Liberal Government was prepared to afford tenants new rights.[25] Under the Ground Game Act of 1880, farmers were permitted to destroy the vermin whose depredations could make the difference between bankruptcy and survival when margins were so tight; the Agricultural Holdings Act of 1883 allowed tenants to claim compensation for the improvements they had made to their holdings and funded themselves, and whose value was not exhausted at the time of their leaving. However imperfectly the legislation worked in practice, important limits had been placed on the freedom of the landowner to run his property on his own terms.

However, such concessions were far from satisfying radical critics of the land system, who, as Antony Taylor demonstrates, were much less concerned with the plight of the farming classes than with those who laboured beneath them. Building on the arguments of their mid-Victorian forebears, these individuals were convinced that 'landlord tyranny' remained a reality, particularly where entire villages were owned by single individuals (as was the case in large parts of Leicestershire and Norfolk, for example).[26] Because of their proprietorial control over the soil, landlords could deny labourers the opportunity of acquiring allotments or smallholdings, stifle religious freedom by refusing to permit the existence of nonconformist chapels and clamp down on uncongenial radicalism by preventing the use of village buildings for political meetings. Few English landlords were quite the ogres some of their critics made them out to be, but a quotidian, low-key oppression persisted in many places, acting as a powerful stimulus to reformist agitation.

One radical so stimulated was the remarkable J. E. Thorold Rogers, Drummond Professor of Political Economy at Oxford from 1862 to 1868, who vouchsafed the late Victorian land agitation a hero and a canonical text. The hero was his own brother-in-law, Richard Cobden. As noted earlier, Cobden had been rather longer on rhetoric than practical policies regarding land reform during his lifetime. Rogers, however, re-invented the great leader of the ACLL as a land reform crusader, largely on the basis of a short passage from his final public speech at Rochdale in 1864. Henceforth, Taylor maintains, the Cobden familiar to late Victorian radicals was an advocate of land reform first and a free trader second – the latest incarnation of the enduring 'yeoman' whose Sussex farming family had experience of dispossession and displacement at the hands of the enclosers. Alongside this re-inventing of Cobden, Rogers also opened up new perspectives for land reformers through his scholarly work. In 1884, his magnum opus, *Six Centuries of Work and Wages*, was published. This book provided a graphic re-interpretation of past wrongs and argued that the dispossession of the people should be traced not to the Norman Conquest, but to the 'New Conquest' following the Reformation: Ket's rebellion in Norfolk in 1549, Rogers claimed, marked the true death knell of the English peasantry. The volumes became required reading for land reformers, particularly those of a militant bent, and they were republished at least ten times before the First World War. Above all, they served to promote the ideas of the American radical, Henry George. In the context of Rogers's powerful argument that the dispossession of the poor was of relatively recent origin, George's contention that land should be made common property through the imposition of a single tax on its unimproved value seemed a timely and practical remedy. For members of the English Land Restoration League (ELRL), George's *Progress and Poverty* (1880) was the latest expression of a radical tradition that could be traced back through Rogers to Cobden himself.

To more conservative contemporaries, George's ideas seemed startlingly new and dangerous. The alarmingly wide circulation of Georgeite ideas became one of a number of factors engaging socially and politically conservative thinkers as the nineteenth century gave way to the twentieth. The downturn in the economy, the palpable 'emptying' of the countryside as agricultural labourers sought out better conditions in the towns and the shocking revelation that large numbers of urban inhabitants had been turned down for military service during the Boer War because they were physically unfit all added to the gathering sense of crisis. Paul Readman explores some of the tensions within the Conservative and Liberal Unionist coalition over these issues, and examines the way in which it came to adopt much of the analysis of Jesse Collings, who for years had campaigned for land reform to restore the 'yeomen' and peasant smallholders allegedly destroyed by enclosure.[27] Restoring the class of small proprietors, and engaging with their natural conservatism, seemed to offer Unionists a means not only of defending property of all types but of restoring the moral and physical character of the nation. On the eve of the First World War, such ideas had become inextricably entwined with Conservative patriotic discourse, pushing to one side older arguments which had centred on the defence of paternalist Tory landlordism.[28]

However, as Readman goes on to demonstrate, land also occupied a place in Liberal visions of the nation. As in the periods covered by Beresford and Waites, the land offered a vista broad enough for competing visions of patriotism to emerge. As for the Unionists, the stimulus to much Liberal concern was evidence of rural depopulation and the concomitant fear of moral and racial deterioration. In shaping their critique, Liberals drew on the idealised interpretations of the pre-enclosure countryside popularised by historians of the day such as Gilbert Slater and J. L. and Barbara Hammond. Their intimation that it was the commons that had provided the ordinary Englishman – the much-vaunted 'yeoman' farmer – with an independent way of life, free from the drudgery of wage-slavery and the tyranny of the squire, lay behind a stream of legislation passed in the period after 1880. A range of reforms were put forward to revive life in English villages, including measures to establish parish councils and allow the purchase of land for distribution as allotments to villagers. Such legislation, it was hoped, would help counter the petty tyranny still said to be exercised by some landowners over their communities.[29] In the years immediately before the First World War, a similar vision to that which had inspired these reformist efforts of the 1880s and 1890s provided the driving force behind Lloyd George's 'Land Campaign'. Drawing on roseate views of the pre-enclosure past, it sought to impose a minimum wage for agricultural labourers, further reforms of land tenure law, increased provision for the compulsory purchase of land for public purposes, leasehold enfranchisement and the institution of land value taxation as the basis of local rating.[30]

But long before the drums rolled in 1914, and the patriotic impulses of both parties were diverted into fresh channels, the land question had begun to change. In the first place, the long-term effects of economic depression, added to the social impact of various reforms made since the 1870s (notably the introduction of the secret ballot in 1872 and of County Councils in 1888), were making landownership a much less tempting investment than it once had been. John Beckett and Michael Turner note the way that the Settled Estates Act of 1881 allowed landowners to break entails on their property more easily and bring land to market. The land question was almost solving itself. Secondly, it had become clear that a new front had opened up in the land war: the urban. By the turn of the century, close to 80 per cent of British people lived in towns and cities,[31] and while this state of affairs certainly drove the 'back to the land' impulses of patriotic ruralists, the urban side of the land question seemed of increasingly greater relevance to the lived experiences of English men and women. It was a truism in Liberal discussions of the land question, of course, that landlordism had driven people off the land and into overcrowded and unsanitary slums, thus causing the 'race deterioration' or 'degeneration' revealed so starkly during the Boer War. However, as the political compass adjusted after the Third Reform Act and London began to assume an ever-larger role in setting the national political agenda, the urban land question became an increasingly important matter – more than an isolated skirmish in the nation's land war.

Often unduly neglected in the scholarship, the significance of the urban land question before 1914 is emphasised in the chapters by Roland Quinault and Ian Packer. For Liberal and radical reformers, many of the most pressing problems of city life could be attributed to the maldistribution of land, much of which, of course, remained firmly in the hands of aristocratic families. The speculative holding of land in and around large towns and cities led to bottlenecks in the supply of housing, thereby forcing up rents (to the benefit of landlords) and contributing to unhealthy slum conditions, which depressed the vitality of the race. In addition to this, Liberals argued, the urban land 'monopoly' stifled economic efficiency, causing property that could be developed to lie idle or underexploited: in this way, unemployment was stimulated and economic development retarded. And, Liberals contended, pity the poor businessman held at the mercy of the short leasehold. What incentive had he to invest in and develop his business when, on the expiry of his lease, the landlord might raise the price of its renewal, thereby penalising industry and effort and parasitically reaping the benefits of his labour? Those like Lloyd George who were animated by these apparent injustices felt urban land needed to be put on 'a business footing', exploited as a resource for the whole community rather than a privileged few, whose selfishness and greed acted as a handicap on the physical, moral and economical well-being of the nation.[32] For many, the preferred solution was fiscal: land ought to be 'taxed into use'. This would be done through the imposition of a tax on the base value of land – in other words, its value aside from that accruing from improvements made to it by its user or users. It was in preparation for just such a system of land value taxation that in autumn 1913 Lloyd George instituted his famous Land Campaign, the centrepiece of which was the comprehensive – and, as it turned out, enormously bureaucratic – valuation of all land in the country.[33]

By the Edwardian period, land value taxation was neither as novel nor as socialistic as it was portrayed by some contemporaries (and not a few historians since). Calls for the taxation of the 'unearned increment' in land had been current in Liberal-radical discourse for a long time, having appeared in the political argument of John Stuart Mill and the Mill-influenced Land Tenure Reform Association of the 1860s and 1870s, for example. They had also been a central element of Georgeite argument from the 1880s onwards. Yet, despite the amalgamation of old and new ideas in the Edwardian movement for land value taxation, it was certainly true that Liberal land taxers were typically to be found on the left of the party. This being the case, it is unsurprising that many such individuals – Josiah Wedgwood being one example – transferred their allegiances to Labour after World War One.

Indeed, many members of the pre-war Labour movement had been sympathetic to land value taxation, seeing it as the first step on the road to the ultimate goal of land nationalisation. As Clare Griffiths shows, this view survived the war, animating men like Wedgwood, but there was a tension between this perspective and that which simply envisaged the direct acquisition of the land by the state. This represented a longstanding ideological divide, having been precisely the issue over which the ELRL had split with the Land Nationalisation Society (LNS) in the early 1880s.[34] Like the LNS, the more radical land nationalisers of the interwar period were impatient with the idea that the nation could be restored to the land by means of a fiscal solution – better simply to rely on direct state intervention. Throughout the 1920s and 1930s, they probably had the upper hand in Labour's internal policy tussles over land nationalisation, which remained a significant issue for the party until the Second World War, not least because of its resonance with contemporary debates about nature conservation and landscape preservation.[35]

To people living through the interwar years, the question of the land was not without its drama. Indeed, in the immediate post-war period, it became both the cause and the consequence of collective anxiety. As Beckett and Turner discuss, although the years after 1918 saw no revival of Lloyd George's Land Campaign, a sense of cultural crisis nevertheless seems to have engulfed some contemporary commentators. More a function of the wider – and rapidly changing – social, economic and political context than a direct consequence of any legislative activity, it certainly had a significant effect, not least on the market for real property. As Beckett and Turner suggest in their chapter, a large amount of land came on to the market. While the acreage put up for sale was broadly in line with trends evident before 1914, in the changed social and economic circumstances of the peace it seemed to many contemporaries as though the established order was falling apart before their eyes. One-sixth of all the land in the kingdom was alleged to be on the market: it appeared that the great houses and the ancient families were being blown away like so much chaff before the icy winds of change.

Yet for all the alarm and speculation on the one hand, and argument and propaganda on the other, the land question gradually slipped down the order of the nation's priorities. Even in Labour circles the appeal of land nationalisation did not endure much beyond the Second

World War: by the 1950s, it had been despatched to the fringes of left-wing political discourse. As Michael Thompson makes clear in the epilogue, the British land question had ceased to be a live political issue. In some respects, Thompson's chapter can be seen as a companion piece – or codicil – to his Royal Historical Society paper of 1965, in which he noted historians' neglect of the nineteenth-century land question. The reason for this neglect, Thompson suggested, was that for all the extra- and intra-parliamentary debate on the land, very little in the way of socio-economic change had been effected by legislation.[36] The exception to this, of course, was Ireland, where landlordism was essentially dismantled by the pre-1914 acts of Conservative and Liberal governments. Elsewhere in the United Kingdom (with the possible exception of Scotland, where the Crofters' Act of 1886 undoubtedly had some impact), there was a great deal of political talk about land, but little legislative action which had any effect on the lived experiences of ordinary men and women. Social and economic change there certainly was – the landlordism complained of by nineteenth-century radicals did disappear – but to a large extent, the agents of change lay outside the narrowly political sphere.

There was thus no heroic political climax to the land question; it simply faded away under the impact of broader changes in the economy, society and culture of early twentieth-century Britain. Yet the land question's rather bathetic departure from the political scene makes it all the more important to understand why it loomed so large and for so long. Indeed, its prominence and persistence in contemporary discourse is reason enough for its study. What it signified, of course, is another matter – and there can be no single overarching interpretation. The land question was multifaceted and multivalent, engaging people of all ideological positions, and it was precisely for this reason that it occupied the prominent place it did. The chapters that follow recognise this, exploring the encounter between politicians of various shades with an issue which, as much as any other, represented one aspect of the struggle for power between the historical incumbents of that power, the landed elite, and those who sought to wrest it from them – a struggle which can be said to have defined the period between the late eighteenth and early twentieth centuries. In doing so, the land question also acted as a conduit for many of the key currents of radicalism, from the Chartists to Thorold Rogers to Josiah Wedgwood; it played an important role in the democratisation of late nineteenth-century Conservatism; it shaped conceptions of national identities in Britain as well as Ireland; and it energised political parties and mobilised support at election time.

Without neglecting the social and the economic, the chapters in this collection demonstrate an appreciation of this – of the crucial part played by the land question in shaping the vocabulary of modern British politics.

Notes

1. R. Douglas, *Land, People & Politics: A History of the Land Question in the United Kingdom, 1878–1952* (London, 1976), pp. 15–16.
2. On Ireland, see for example, J. S. Donnelly, *The Land and the People of Nineteenth-Century Cork: The Rural Economy and the Land Question* (London, 1975); P. Bew, *Land and the National Question in Ireland, 1858–82* (Dublin, 1978); D. E. Jordan, *Land and Popular Politics in Ireland: County Mayo from the Plantation to the Land War* (Cambridge, 1994); P. Bull, *Land, Politics and Nationalism: A Study of the Irish Land Question* (Dublin, 1996). On the Scottish Highlands, see for example, T. M. Devine, *The Great Highland Famine: Hunger, Emigration and the Scottish Highlands in the Nineteenth Century* (Edinburgh, 1988); E. A. Cameron, *Land for the People? The British Government and the Scottish Highlands, c. 1880–1925* (East Linton, 1996); E. Richards, *Debating the Highland Clearances* (Edinburgh, 2007).
3. D. Cannadine, *The Decline and Fall of the British Aristocracy* (revd edn, London, 1992), pp. 54–6; D. Spring, 'Introduction', to J. Bateman, *The Great Landowners of Great Britain and Ireland* (5th ed., Leicester, 1971, 4th ed., London, 1883), p. 12.
4. Cannadine, *Decline and Fall*, pp. 710–11.
5. Ibid.
6. See p. 62, below.
7. For which, see P. Harling, *The Waning of 'Old Corruption': The Politics of Economical Reform in Britain, 1779–1846* (Oxford, 1996).
8. For a comparative perspective on British land reform in the years of the Chartists, see J. L. Bronstein, *Land Reform and Working-Class Experience in Britain and the United States, 1800–1862* (Stanford, 1999).
9. Richard Cobden to Robertson Gladstone, 29 March 1851, Glynne-Gladstone Papers, 579, Clwyd (Flintshire) Record Office. The editors would like to thank Anthony Howe for this reference.
10. See below, p. 83.
11. M. C. Finn, *After Chartism: Class and Nation in English Radical Politics, 1848–1874* (Cambridge, 1993), pp. 265ff.
12. M. Chase, 'Out of Radicalism: The Mid-Victorian Freehold Land Movement', *English Historical Review*, 106 (1991), 319–45.
13. Ibid., 338.
14. G. Makgill, 'Laing's *Observations on Europe*', *Blackwood's Edinburgh Magazine*, 68 (December 1850), 675–8.
15. Ibid.; A. Young, *Travels in France during the Years 1787, 1788, 1784* (2 vols, Bury St. Edmunds, 1792), cited in *Dictionary of National Biography*, 63 (London, 1900), p. 363.
16. M. Taylor, 'John Bull and the Iconography of Political Opinion in England, c. 1712–1929', *Past & Present*, 134 (1992), 93–128: 'John Bull was accessible to a range of groups across the political spectrum at all times' (p. 98).

17. For the activities of the Commons Preservation Society, see Lord Eversley [G. J. Shaw-Lefevre], *Commons, Forests and Footpaths* (revd ed., London, 1910); for some comments on its moderate liberal ideology, see P. Readman, 'Preserving the English Landscape, *c.* 1870–1914', *Cultural and Social History*, 5 (2008), 197–218.
18. R. Quinault, 'Democracy and the Mid-Victorians', in M. Hewitt (ed.), *An Age of Equipoise: Reassessing Mid-Victorian Britain* (Aldershot, 2000), pp. 109–21.
19. G. M. Trevelyan, *The Life of John Bright* (London, 1913), pp. 162–5; R. A. J. Walling (ed.), *The Diaries of John Bright* (London, 1930), pp. 97–107.
20. Cannadine, *Decline and Fall*, p. 55.
21. Ibid., p. 9.
22. The duke of Argyll was perhaps the most prominent of the Whig dissentients, resigning from Gladstone's Cabinet over the 1881 Bill. See J. W. Mason, 'The Duke of Argyll and the Land Question in Late Nineteenth Century Britain', *Victorian Studies*, 21 (1978), 149–70.
23. D. Howell, *Land and People in Nineteenth Century Wales* (London, 1977); M. Cragoe, *An Anglican Aristocracy: The Moral Economy of the Landed Estate in Carmarthenshire, 1832–1895* (Oxford, 1996).
24. The main difference being that the 1886 Crofters Holdings (Scotland) Act did not permit free sale.
25. J. R. Fisher, 'The Farmers' Alliance: An Agricultural Protest Movement of the 1880s', *Agricultural History Review*, 26 (1978), 15–25.
26. In some counties, between one-third and one-half of all villages were 'closed': P. Horn, *Labouring Life in the Victorian Countryside* (Dublin, 1976), p. 8.
27. More detail on Collings's ideas and activities can be found in P. Readman, 'Jesse Collings and Land Reform, 1886–1914', *Historical Research*, 81 (2008), 292–314.
28. For the marginalisation of 'pure squire Conservatism' in the late nineteenth and early twentieth centuries, see P. Readman, 'Conservatives and the Politics of Land: Lord Winchilsea's National Agricultural Union, 1893–1900', *English Historical Review*, 121 (2006), 25–69 and idem, *Land and Nation in English Politics: Patriotism, National Identity and the Politics of Land, 1880–1914* (Woodbridge, 2008), pp. 238–9.
29. Where landlords did provide allotments or smallholdings, for example, they frequently imposed stringent terms and conditions of tenure on the labourers who rented them. The allotments on one Buckinghamshire landlord's estate in the 1890s were subject to a yearly tenancy that could be terminated at any time and for any reason, with no compensation for disturbance being offered. The landlord claimed all gaming and timber rights over the allotments, and tenants were not permitted to plough or till their allotments, nor were they permitted to sell any straw grown on their holdings. (*Terms and Conditions of Letting Garden Allotments, the Property of Lieut.-Colonel Herbert Edward Goodall, Situate in the Parish of Dinton in the County of Buckingham* [1893]: 'Allotments and Small Holdings', box 1, John Johnson Collection, Bodleian Library, Oxford). Such terms and conditions were very similar to those typically offered by landowners much earlier in the nineteenth century, as revealed by another document in the same collection, dating from 1833.

30. I. Packer, *Lloyd George, Liberalism and the Land: The Land Issue and Party Politics in England, 1906–14* (Woodbridge, 2001).
31. J. Saville, *Rural Depopulation in England and Wales 1851–1951* (London, 1957), p. 61.
32. Speeches of Lloyd George: *Times*, 1 February 1913, p. 8 and 7 July 1913, p. 5.
33. Packer, *Lloyd George, Liberalism and the Land*; B. Short, *Land and Society in Edwardian Britain* (Cambridge, 1997).
34. The best treatment of the ELRL and LNS remains A. J. Peacock, 'Land Reform 1880–1919: A Study of the Activities of the English Land Restoration Leagues and the Land Nationalisation Society' (MA thesis, Southampton, 1961).
35. C. Griffiths, *Labour and the countryside: The Politics of Rural Britain 1918–1939* (Oxford, 2007); D. Matless, *Landscape and Englishness* (London, 1998).
36. F. M. L. Thompson, 'Land and Politics in the Nineteenth Century', *Transactions of the Royal Historical Society*, 5th ser. 15 (1965), 23–44.

1

The Common Field Landscape, Cultural Commemoration and the Impact of Enclosure, *c.* 1770–1850

Ian Waites

Introduction

One 'traditional' image of the English landscape is that of a 'patchwork' of groups of small fields, enclosed and demarcated by verdant hedgerows. As Christopher Taylor pointed out many years ago however, the word 'traditional' has to be used advisedly in relation to any type of English landscape, since it has largely evolved in a constant state of flux, change and contradiction.[1] In much of midland and southern England at least, that patchwork landscape was largely created in the eighteenth and nineteenth centuries by the process historically known as parliamentary enclosure. As such, this 'traditional' landscape is 250 years old, at the very most. During the eighteenth and nineteenth centuries, Britain experienced a period of intense cultural, economic and industrial expansion which saw a cultural attachment to nature and the landscape begin to play a crucial role in the development of a strong sense of national identity.[2] Parliamentary enclosure was a component part of this expansion, producing a new landscape of small, divided and hedgerow-lined fields that, paradoxically, became emblematic of the 'English Countryside' and 'Englishness' for later generations. The subsequent cultural dominance of this type of countryside also reveals how the enclosed landscape's antithesis – the open or common field landscape – has been sidelined in key late twentieth-century historical studies of English agriculture and rural society. Chambers and Mingay's *The Agricultural Revolution, 1750–1880,* for instance, stressed the supposed problems with the open field system (the issues of scattered strips and 'bad' neighbours, the limits on expansion and innovation and the like) in order to show how 'necessary' and important parliamentary enclosure was at a time of a growing population and industrial change.[3] One consequence of this is that, in recent years, the open field landscape has generally been examined within the fields of archaeology or medieval history,[4] while the study of this landscape in the modern period has been dominated by parliamentary enclosure and its aftermath.

Equally, art historians have typically examined eighteenth- and nineteenth-century paintings of the English landscape in relation to ideologies of improvement in the countryside, and primarily within the context of parliamentary enclosure; very few seem to have displayed an interest in what was left behind. Generally, the common field landscape is referred to in passing, or as a brief preliminary context for the main business in hand. The most famous landscape paintings of Thomas Gainsborough and John Constable, for example, have been scrutinized for their semiotic traces of both the agricultural revolution itself, and the ideological and social struggles of the time.[5] Certainly, from the 1970s onward, art historians became aware that the idea of the artist as a romantic genius was flawed and incomplete, and that any depiction of the landscape was conditioned by its social and economic context. A major contribution to this shift in perception was John Barrell's *The Idea of Landscape and the Sense of Place* (Cambridge, 1972). While being specifically a study of the landscape poetry of John Clare, Barrell's methodology openly worked across several disciplinary boundaries, extending the study of the English landscape to include a combination of both literary and visual texts. Importantly, Barrell examined the central themes of Clare's poetry in relation to the physical and social changes brought about by the enclosure of Clare's native Helpston in Northamptonshire, and equated this with the coincident flowering of landscape aesthetics in England and the maturing of the landscape art genre. Essentially, Barrell's study of Clare established the idea that the examination of underlying contemporary social and economic evidence could be used to further extend our understanding of English landscape art.

In 1973, the Tate Gallery held a major exhibition entitled *Landscape in Britain 1750–1850*, which enhanced the possibilities of Barrell's approach. This exhibition extended our understanding of how the landscape could be artistically represented, for instance by showing drawings for landscape garden designs alongside the more traditional large-scale oils by the likes of Gainsborough and Richard Wilson. As such, this exhibition went some way towards dissolving the traditional artistic hierarchies of genre, technique and medium. Barrell further developed this trend in the scholarship with *The Dark Side of the Landscape: The Rural Poor in English Painting, 1730–1840* (Cambridge, 1980). This book argued that no landscape or figure in a landscape can ever be neutral, and must therefore be understood in relation to the class relationships and cultural ideologies of the time. One notable claim made by Barrell was his perhaps flawed argument that Constable deliberately reduced the presence of field labourers in his 1821 painting *Landscape: Noon* (more famously known as *The Hay Wain*) at a time when they were perceived by the landowning classes as a social 'problem'. Soon after Barrell's *Dark Side of the Landscape* was published, David Solkin reinforced this line of analysis by controversially arguing that the evocations of rural life and the countryside in English landscape art were mostly tailored to the tastes of patrons and their own view of their status. Solkin went on to establish the notion that while many of these patrons played an active role in the economic rationalization of the countryside, they also required compensatory and increasingly idealized artistic accounts of the landscape, created through carefully prescribed codes of representation.[6]

Because of the pre-eminence given to the examination of English landscape art in relation to the social and economic changes brought about by enclosure, scholars have eschewed serious examination of landscape art from the eighteenth or nineteenth centuries specifically in relation to the depiction of unenclosed open field and common land. Ann Bermingham's *Landscape and Ideology: The English Rustic Tradition, 1740–1860* (Berkeley, 1987) takes perhaps a more measured view of the prevailing cultural values linked with the accelerated man-made rationalization of the land than Barrell's *Dark Side of the Landscape* but it does not refer to any depictions of the common field landscape this process of rationalization eradicated. Michael Rosenthal's *British Landscape Painting* (Oxford, 1982) and *Constable: The Painter and his Landscape* (New Haven, 1983) paid some attention to common fields, as have a number of later works.[7] Indeed, Rosenthal has pointed out that in focusing on enclosed land, scholars 'have tended not to keep an eye open for its antithesis, the scenery of common ground'.[8] This observation remains valid: the common field landscape has yet to receive the attention it deserves from cultural historians.[9]

One reason for this is the very generally held view that depictions of the unenclosed landscape are few and far between. As the landscape historian Tom Williamson has commented, 'the pre-enclosure landscape of open fields and commons is poorly represented in visual art'.[10] Yet, given the presence of this type of landscape in central and southern England during the eighteenth century especially, and the general range of depictions of the countryside and rural society produced within the English landscape genre, it is surely apparent that a number of representations of the common field landscape exist, either as a coincidental detail or as a central subject of a painting. This chapter supports such a supposition, referring to nine paintings and drawings of common land by just one nineteenth-century artist, William Turner of Oxford. In addition to this, the literary work of Thomas Miller, the working-class novelist and poet, will also be examined in order to explore how artists and writers of the early nineteenth century were becoming aware of the social and cultural impact of enclosure, realizing that older, more traditional, modes of life were quickly disappearing in the face of rapid social and economic change. It will be seen how Turner and Miller responded to this by deliberately attempting to preserve in their work the memory of a disappearing landscape, or one that had already disappeared. More critically, this chapter will also demonstrate how they realized this by articulating a personal aesthetic view of the common field landscape – one which was opposed to the views and values of the prevailing pro-enclosure lobby. Finally, the chapter will demonstrate how this corpus of work was also shaped by an acute awareness of local associational detail and by a self-defining sense of place and belonging. While it is accepted that the work of Turner and Miller could never be entirely free of the contemporary social and cultural conventions of their time, it will be shown that the social attachment to the common field landscape could still be deep-rooted, and was more culturally and psychologically complex than has been previously allowed.

The commemoration of the common field landscape in Thomas Miller's 'Our Old Town'

The most notable and well-known literary evocations of the common field landscape are by the poet John Clare (1793–1864). Considerable historical attention has been paid to his anti-enclosure poems such as *Remembrances* and *The Mores*, both of which celebrate the common field landscape of his native Helpston and express the despair he felt when this landscape was eradicated after its enclosure from 1809. However, there are other writers from Clare's time who also commemorated the common field landscape in an affectionate and evocative manner. Thomas Miller (1807–74) came from a similar working-class literary background to Clare. His book *Our Old Town*, first published in 1857, is a recollection of his early life in Gainsborough, a small market town in Lincolnshire, during the first three decades of the nineteenth century. Gainsborough was an open field town and was not fully enclosed until 1804. Miller's vivid evocations of the countryside around Gainsborough seem to describe an unenclosed, common field landscape even though much of this countryside had been enclosed by the end of his infant years. This is not unusual amongst those writers and artists of the time who pay specific attention to the common field landscape in their work: between about 1812 and 1820, the painter John Crome (1768–1821) produced numerous studies of Mousehold Heath, near Norwich, a major part of which had been enclosed from 1799 onwards. Crome's pictures of Mousehold, painted over a decade later, give no hint of any enclosure having taken place. Instead, we have a visualization, as one historian recently put it, of 'a landscape as archaic and nostalgic as [Crome's] aesthetic conception is contemporary' (Figure 1.1).[11]

The very same could be said for Miller's sentimental, evocative, but essentially ahistorical descriptions of Gainsborough's open fields and commons.[12] The landscape of his childhood was one of 'flower-covered meadows and wide green open marshes that stretched far away in every

Figure 1.1 John Crome, *Mousehold Heath* (etching, *c.* 1810).
Source: Reproduced by permission of Norwich Castle Museum and Art Gallery.

direction'.[13] Elsewhere, Miller refers to the sense of freedom he felt in the 'immense stretches of country that faded in the sunshine or blended with the sky' where 'there was no boundary but the horizon to the distance'.[14] He also recalls the open fields having a 'number and variety of walks... like a network on a drawing, so often did they intersect one another.... It seemed to me that these old roads and walks had been laid out by our ancestors to suit every mood of mind, and state of health.'[15] The benefits of the common field landscape were not only couched in practical terms: this was a landscape that was lived in, experienced as well as worked, but it was also an obvious and important source of physical and psychological well-being for the people of Gainsborough.

Miller's recollections demonstrate a cultural immersion in the common field landscape that was defined by a very different attitude to those who wanted to impose both agricultural and *social* improvements via the enclosure process. Towards the end of *Our Old Town*, Miller refers to 'the wildest scenery in the suburbs of this Old-fashioned Town',[16] an expanse of land found four miles to the east of Gainsborough, which was known locally as 'Corringham Scroggs' – a notorious expanse of waste common not enclosed until 1852. The first *General View of the Agriculture of the County of Lincoln* in 1794 had opined that 'this large tract of county' was 'barbarous in the extreme' while in 1851, the Royal Agricultural Society stated that 'It is a sudden blow to the feelings of an agriculturalist when he enters upon this dreary region of unprofitableness.'[17] Local opinion concurred, with the *Stamford Mercury* speaking of the 'desolate wastes' of 'so large a tract of hitherto almost useless land'.[18] Miller, however, seemed to be in romantic awe of this land:

> Nowhere in broad England could any spot be found more primeval or rugged. If it had been cultivated, it was long centuries ago, for it bore no traces of being anything but what it was – a vast, tree-clad, thorn-covered, gorse-choked, fern-smothered wild... just as it was when the wolf howled in our island, and the early Britons dwelt in their huts.[19]

Later, Miller referred to the physical changes in the countryside around Gainsborough after enclosure, while quietly noting the social and economic consequences of the loss of the common land and its common rights that he saw as being passed down by the townspeople of previous generations: 'The crofts and garths, holms and holts they had left for the benefit of the poor "for ever", were no longer known.' The 'old landmarks were worn away', and the 'boundary-stones' (a common detail of open field organization, demarcating individual strips and areas for common grazing) were 'overthrown and lost'. 'In too many instances', Miller concluded, 'every trace of those old finger-marks of Charity [were] utterly erased'.[20] At a time when the upper classes prized 'sensibility' and intellectual sophistication while concurrently deriding those who lived off the common field system as 'barbaric', it is clear from books like *Our Old Town* that working-class writers such as Miller could express both their own personal and indelible attachment to this landscape, and their wider fears for the social and cultural costs of progress and change, in an articulate, subtle and sensitive manner.

'As it occasionally appeared before the enclosure': William Turner of Oxford's visualization of the common field landscape

At the beginning of the nineteenth century, the majority of open parishes in England had been enclosed, and only approximately 15 per cent of common arable remained.[21] Despite this, we can identify a new generation of landscape painters from the first half of the nineteenth century who, against all odds, intentionally depicted open fields and commons. At this time, these artists were beginning to carve out for themselves a certain amount of artistic and cultural autonomy, becoming less likely, for example, to shape a view according to the idealized classical criteria that had been imposed by aristocratic connoisseurs in the eighteenth century. The more idiosyncratic landscape artists of the early nineteenth century, such as John Crome, Peter DeWint and William Turner of Oxford began to choose scenes on the basis of their own, personal, artistic and aesthetic principles. The foundation of this was a new trend of 'Naturalism' that was emerging principally in reaction to the outmoded, idealized and prescriptive theories of 'The Picturesque'. Naturalism implied a style in which the artist tried to observe and then faithfully record the subject before him without deliberate idealization or stylization.[22] One way in which these artists aligned themselves with this emerging sensibility was to select as their subject matter the 'natural' but otherwise discredited and disappearing landscape of open arable fields, commons, heaths and wastes. Personal documentary evidence for how the nineteenth-century landscape artist might directly defend the unenclosed landscape and its way of life in the face of enclosure is scarce, but it has already been noted how Crome persisted in painting Mousehold Heath in its unenclosed and unimproved state years after enclosure had actually taken place.

By specifically looking at the work of William Turner of Oxford (1789–1862), a near contemporary of Crome's, we can examine such attitudes in more detail. Turner's work demonstrates how an artist could both respond to and help create a nostalgic sensibility for the common field landscape, by depicting it with a deliberate intent to record either what remained of it, or to recollect what had been lost.

We can begin with his *Haymaking, Study from Nature, in Osney Meadow, near Oxford, Looking Towards Iffley* of 1853–54 (Figure 1.2).[23] As Christiana Payne has rightly pointed out, this painting is an unusual and impressive depiction of an unenclosed hay meadow, and a prime example of how 'Artists sometimes chose to make studies of open fields which had not yet been enclosed'.[24] Turner of Oxford is an interesting artist because his work displays an aesthetic preference for the fast disappearing common field landscape. Several known works of his are of open arable fields or of common grazing land. One work

Figure 1.2 William Turner of Oxford, *Haymaking, Study from Nature, in Osney Meadow, near Oxford, looking towards Iffley* (Watercolour and Bodycolour, 1853–54). Private Collection.

Source: This image is taken from William T. Wilcox and C. Titterington, *William Turner of Oxford (1789–1862)* (Woodstock, 1984). Reproduced by permission of the publisher.

in particular, an 1822 view of Stanton Harcourt in Oxfordshire, is of note because it reveals how an early nineteenth-century artist 'sometimes... deliberately painted the landscape as it had been, rather than in its existing state.'[25] The field depicted in Turner's painting of Stanton Harcourt was actually enclosed in 1774, but it appears that the artist manipulated this landscape by ignoring post-enclosure hedgerows in order to show the field as being open.[26] Furthermore, Turner is also known to have produced a (now lost) watercolour with the intriguing title of *Ottmoor, as it Occasionally Appeared Before the Enclosure*. Ottmoor was a large expanse of unenclosed waste that was the centre of enclosure riots in 1830.[27] Given the title of his painting, and the fact that it was exhibited in 1831, the course of events surrounding Ottmoor's enclosure was obviously fresh in Turner's mind, to the point where it has been assumed that the painting was a deliberate protest against enclosure.[28] Within this suggested context of Turner's work, *Haymaking, Study from Nature, in Osney Meadow, near Oxford, Looking Towards Iffley* is especially interesting because of its depiction of common meadowland on the eve of enclosure. It was painted in the summer of 1853 and depicts the last crop of hay being taken from the meadow under the old system, before the field began to be physically enclosed in December of the same year.[29] As a painting of a soon-to-be-lost landscape, it is doubly significant because it depicts, quite clearly in the foreground, an old stone marker of the type that would be important to the organization of open fields such as these. It also calls to mind Thomas Miller's near contemporary account of a common field's boundary stones that were 'overthrown and lost' after enclosure.[30] *Haymaking, Study from Nature* demonstrates Turner's acute awareness of the loss of the physical traces of an old way of life, trenchantly summed up here in his deliberate, almost documentary, recording of a final event in a commonly farmed hayfield.

This painting is also interesting because it defies the conventional landscape-compositional rules of the time, which broadly demanded a gently undulating scene, featuring perhaps a winding track to lead the eye into the picture, and a number of trees and shrubs to add some variety and complexity.[31] No such factors are present in this painting, only a composition made up of two-thirds sky and one-third land, with a straight and virtually unbroken horizon-line. There is only a man on horseback to break the monotony of this otherwise flat and 'empty' landscape. Turner's numerous depictions of Portmeadow, Oxford – for example a pen, ink and wash study of *c.* 1818–20 and a watercolour *Portmeadow Under Flood: Sunset* (1847) – are also singular studies of flat and featureless common land. Portmeadow was never enclosed: at nearly 400 acres, it remains one of the largest pieces of extant common land in England today, and lies within parishes that were not enclosed themselves until the 1830s and 1840s. In his depictions of this common land, Turner repeatedly emphasizes the low, virtually empty horizon-line of the landscape, almost defiantly stressing the lack of any traditional 'picturesque' compositional attributes otherwise intended to lead the eye into the scene. An 1812 pencil sketch of Portmeadow (Figure 1.3) is so empty of conventional compositional factors that, as Wilcox and Titterington comment, 'it does not seem too impressionistic to sense the delight with which the "hungry" eye seizes upon such areas as, for example, the constellation of marks and lines that compose the small bridge'.[32]

When a commentator like John Byng in 1791 could write of a 'staring, black moor' being 'a wild, dreary prospect',[33] it is clear that the empty nature of common wastes in particular could provoke a sense of apprehension, even fear or danger. This is also reflected in Turner's work, for instance in his anxious and agitated *Scene near Woodstock* (1809), which shows a bleak, windswept and churned expanse of common waste on the Oxford to Banbury road near Tackley, where nearly 1,400 acres of common land was not fully enclosed until as late as 1873.[34] This painting represents the epitome of the enclosure propagandist's

Figure 1.3 William Turner of Oxford, *Portmeadow, Oxford* (pencil, 1812).
Source: Reproduced by permission of the Victoria & Albert Museum, © V & A Images/Victoria and Albert Museum, London.

aesthetically inclined idea of a 'barren' and 'barbaric' common field landscape, and of a distinctly un-picturesque landscape and painting. Another equally uncompromising painting of common grazing land by Turner is his *Bullingdon Green, Oxford* (*c.* 1840). Bullingdon Green was a common of approximately 100 acres that served the parishes of Cowley and Horspath south of Oxford. Horspath was enclosed in 1835 but Cowley was not enclosed until 1849, and much of Bullingdon Green remained as common land thereafter.[35] Once again, there is an absolute lack of visual or artistic 'picturesque' coordinates and features – only a vast, flat and empty expanse of churned up and rutted ground. It is clear that common wastes did challenge the mind to find or recover something beautiful or stirring in such a 'bleak' or 'barren' landscape populated by 'barbarians'. To painters such as Turner of Oxford however, the experience of the vastness and seeming infinity of such scenes appeared to be almost liberating, refreshing even, when set against the idealized, classicized compositional criteria imposed by the landowning classes. Indeed, Turner's persistent preference for common arable or grazing/waste as subject matter went directly against the grain of what many landowners considered to be agriculturally or aesthetically appropriate scenes to paint.

Turner's motivation for this can be further understood in relation to an emerging emphasis upon local associational factors and the tenets of Naturalism: the artist depicted a landscape as naturalistically as possible and without any deliberate idealization of the subject. This is clearly apparent in Turner of Oxford's uncompromising representation of Bullingdon Green. In literature, these new naturalistic tendencies were exemplified by William Wordsworth. In his preface to the third edition of *Lyrical Ballads* (1802), he contrasted his own writing with 'the gaudy and inane phraseology of many modern writers' and defined his purpose as being 'to choose incidents and situations from common life, and to relate or describe them throughout, as far as was possible, in a selection of language really used by men.'[36] At around the same time, Constable revealed a similar concern to depict the ordinary free from all idealization, describing his favoured subject matter as 'The sound of water escaping from mill-dams etc, willows, old rotten planks, slimy posts and brickwork. I love such things'.[37] Behind this lay a more widely read and understood source of new artistic thinking in relation to nature, and which increased the expressive potential of the painted landscape. Archibald Alison's *Essays on the Nature and Principles of Taste* (1790) extended the parameters of aesthetic appreciation by emphasizing the capacity of natural objects to arouse associations:

'Beauty of Forms arises altogether from the Associations we connect with them'.[38] To Alison, beauty was not inherent or necessarily achieved from any moral or metaphysical principles of the human mind. Instead it could be found in local situations, not from an 'essence' but from accidental or incidental associations.

Alison used passages from James Thomson's *The Seasons* (1730) to demonstrate how any description of the natural world could be 'undoubtedly beautiful in itself'. He then takes this further, however, by stating that this beauty can be increased by associating descriptions of the natural world with historical references and personal associations of memory, emotion and so on: 'how much more beautiful does it become by the new order of thought which circumstance awakens in the mind'.[39] The *Essays on the Nature and Principles of Taste* became very popular in the early nineteenth century after the second edition, published in 1810, received approving reviews: four more editions were produced by 1825. By this time, the cult of 'sensibility' and an increased antiquarian awareness of British history were giving support to the contemporary rediscovery of the past almost in terms of moral salvation in an increasingly industrialized and mechanistic present.[40] The associationist ideas of Alison and the notion of an almost preferable retreat into the past can also be read into the work of painters of common field landscapes such as Crome and Turner of Oxford.

It has been shown how Turner's work is important in that he depicted the common field landscape in a naturalistic and topographically specific manner while defying contemporary cultural conventions by taking advantage of the unfashionable and compositionally unconventional nature of this landscape. His work further exploited the potential of the common field landscape by using it to represent something symbolic or associational, in similar terms to those suggested by Alison. Turner's fascination with wide, open and featureless common field landscapes is also crucially supplemented by his consideration of the local circumstances of this landscape. As we have seen, his recording of the final communal haymaking on Osney Meadow, and of Ottmoor after anti-enclosure riots had taken place, demonstrated his awareness of local situations and concerns, particularly in relation to enclosure. Turner was a local man, living in the area throughout his life. The name he adopted as a practising artist was not only to distinguish himself from the more well-known J. M. W. Turner but also, it could be argued, to emphasize the distinctive nature of his local sphere of practice.[41] The historical and personal context to Turner's paintings, such as that of Osney Meadow, reinforces this. His numerous depictions of Portmeadow, for instance, indicate how Turner would have shared a local attachment to the common as a place of recreation – for sketching in his case, and for strolling and social gatherings, as one drawing from *c.* 1818 shows.

This resolutely local attitude clearly stimulated Turner's interest in exploring the potential for evoking a deeper sense of history and place in his paintings. Bullingdon Green was the site where the council for the Bullingdon Hundred had met in the Middle Ages. Portmeadow was also known to have an ancient history with evidence of Iron and Bronze Age forts. (Turner also painted Stonehenge several times, and is known to have painted the Oxfordshire Rollright Stones and the Nine Maidens in Cornwall.)[42] Demonstrably aware of Bullingdon's deeper history, Turner clearly sought out places where their use as 'common' land formed but one layer of their historical and social significance. Indeed, it is his willingness to see and record the remnants of more ancient uses that makes his depictions of nineteenth-century landscapes more poignant still, with their implicit denial of the next change that civilization would visit upon the countryside – enclosure. By painting the very last communal hay gathering before enclosure in his *Haymaking, Osney Meadow*, Turner recorded history already happening. But he even paid attention to places where common land was under the threat of enclosure and therefore on the verge of *becoming* history.

One striking example of this is provided by *Whichwood Forest* (1809), a painting of common woodland in Oxfordshire (Figure 1.4). The common rights afforded to this area of ancient woodland meant that Whichwood was home to the kind of traditional and unregulated activity that many landowners saw as being undesirable, such as an annual horse fair and pleasure fair that were constantly opposed by the landowner, the Duke of Marlborough. As a local man, born only a few miles away from Whichwood, Turner would have been aware of these issues and of the social, even cultural, context of Whichwood's common rights. Indeed, it can be seen that his work deliberately relates to what Turner clearly felt were important local traditions. On the reverse of this painting, Turner wrote 'Scene near where a pleasure fair was formerly held'. In 1808, the year before *Whichwood Forest* was exhibited, the Duke of Marlborough had some success in legally excluding the pleasure fair from the forest. A year later, Arthur Young strongly recommended the enclosure of Whichwood, stating that it was 'not in the view of productiveness alone, that such an enclosure be wished: the morals of the whole surrounding country demand it imperiously.'[43] The painting itself has been viewed in terms of evoking an underlying struggle for the common rights associated with the forest, via the depiction of the dense, writhing

Figure 1.4 William Turner of Oxford, *Whichwood Forest* (Watercolour, 1809).
Source: Reproduced by permission of the Victoria & Albert Museum, © V & A Images/Victoria and Albert Museum, London.

trees and the anxious, braying horse.[44] If nothing else, the painting can be associated with a certain sense of inevitability. Despite the historical and communal attachment to this particular piece of common land felt equally by those who exercised their common rights there and, it seems likely, by Turner himself, the process of improvement continued regardless. An act for the extinguishing of common rights and the disafforestation of Whichwood was passed in 1857 and by 1858, thousands of acres of this ancient landscape had been cleared.[45]

Conclusion

By the time of Turner of Oxford's death in 1862, both the English landscape and the manner in which it was depicted were changing in ways beyond even those wrought by enclosure. The railway, for instance, had made a profound impact upon the British countryside, and artists had already responded to this, most notably J. M. W. Turner with his *Rain, Steam and Speed* (1844). Against the sheer physical and visual impact of modernity that was so forcefully depicted in this painting, it is clear that the way in which the likes of Turner of Oxford viewed the English landscape was quickly becoming unsustainable and dated. The imaginative, artistic reconstructions of the common field landscape from the first half of the nineteenth century became depictions of an old world. By the mid-nineteenth century, a new notion of artistic realism had emerged, and it seemed that the mere naturalistic representation of landscape was not enough.

The one painting from the very end of the period covered in this chapter that fundamentally represents this new approach to the landscape is Ford Madox Brown's *An English Autumn Afternoon* (1852–55). Here, the idyll of nature is now seen firmly from a suburban perspective. John Ruskin asked Brown why he had painted such a 'very ugly subject', and Brown replied 'Because it lay out of a back window'.[46] Both the question and answer signal a new approach to the painting of nature. At this time, Ruskin noted two levels of landscape painting. The 'lower' was an artificial and idealized approach to the landscape which was defined by 'heartless surface', while the 'higher' was that in which the landscape painter had 'communion of heart with his subject.'[47] As an urbanite with a distinctly modern attitude towards nature, Brown went beyond both of Ruskin's 'levels' by stating that *An English Autumn Afternoon* was merely a 'literal transcript of the scenery round London.'[48] This embodied a new artistic approach towards the new human landscape that had almost superseded the old. In some parts of Turner's Oxford, the enclosure of the old open fields and commons permitted urban growth. The environment of *An English Autumn Afternoon* was Hampstead Heath – one of the initial pre-occupations of Britain's oldest national conservation body, the Commons Preservation Society (CPS). The CPS (later known as the Open Spaces Society) was founded in 1865 in order to preserve common land for the enjoyment of the public. From the late 1820s to his death in 1868, Sir Thomas Maryon-Wilson made many unsuccessful attempts to get parliament's permission to build on his land on Hampstead Heath. After his death, his successor reached a compromise with the Society and parliament to transfer all his rights as Lord of the Manor to the Metropolitan Board of Works. The result was a major first victory for the CPS in preserving green areas of common land in and around London, but the decision also signalled the final transformation of what was once a *living* landscape (where commoners once made a living by exercising their common rights) into one which had now become purely recreational.[49]

Thomas Miller's literary evocations of unenclosed Gainsborough, and William Turner of Oxford's visual representations of Oxfordshire's common land, signalled the beginning of such a transformation by confirming the remnants of this type of landscape as survivals from an almost lost age. Their work clearly reflected a new awareness of how an older environment and its way of life was being lost as a result of the enclosure process which, in itself, was but one component part of the change that seemed to be gripping all parts of English society. This chapter has demonstrated how an important, and perhaps underestimated, source of this awareness lay in the naturalistic manner in representing the English countryside that could be found in the literature and landscape painting of the first half of the nineteenth century. For Miller and Turner, the representation of life at this time of change tended to concentrate on local places, and on involving real people and real circumstances. Turner's work expresses a fascination for the 'natural', open and often quite extreme visual qualities of common field landscapes. This then becomes combined with a local and therefore more pressing awareness of loss, in relation to the enclosure of a landscape that would otherwise provide the artist with his preferred aesthetic qualities in abundance.

These paintings are remarkable because they depict the common field landscape either in its present existing, remnant state, or as a reconstruction or remembrance of a recent past before enclosure. Turner strove to depict bona fide unenclosed land if it still existed. He also recorded it just as it was about to disappear, and even attempted to reconstruct it as if it had never been enclosed. Such reconstructions of England's common land, by what are still relatively lesser-known writers and artists, deserve wider attention because they played a significant but generally underestimated role in English history. Their concentration on the local illuminated 'recent changes that implicate(d) local places in national systems'.[50] They also played their part in gradually determining a newer and ever more complex concept of national identity, because they focused attention on what are still highly sensitive issues of progress and loss, both across the English rural scene generally and – more incisively – within the English cultural psyche.

Notes

1. C. Taylor, *Fields in the English Landscape* (London, 1975).
2. See, for instance R. Porter, 'Nature', in his *Enlightenment: Britain and the Creation of the Modern World* (Harmondsworth, 2000), pp. 295–319.
3. J. D. Chambers and G. E. Mingay, *The Agricultural Revolution 1750–1880* (London, 1966).

4. See, for example, the excitement generated by the 2003 article, 'Earliest Evidence of Medieval Open Fields near Cambridge', *British Archaeology*, 69: http://www.britarch.ac.uk/BA/ba69/news.shtml.
5. M. Rosenthal, *Constable: The Painter and his Landscape* (New Haven, 1983); idem, *The Art of Thomas Gainsborough* (New Haven, 1999).
6. D. Solkin, *The Landscape of Reaction: Richard Wilson 1713–1782* (London, 1982).
7. See, for example, E. K. Helsinger, *Rural Scenes and National Representation: Britain, 1815–1850* (Princeton, 1996); M. Rosenthal, C. Payne and S. Wilcox (eds), *Prospects for the Nation: Recent Essays in British Landscape, 1750–1880* (New Haven, 1997).
8. M. Rosenthal, 'The Rough and the Smooth: Rural Subjects in Late-Eighteenth-Century Art', in M. Rosenthal, C. Payne and S. Wilcox (eds), *Prospects for the Nation*, p. 39.
9. Although see C. Payne, 'Boundless Harvests: Representations of Open Fields and Gleaning in Early Nineteenth Century England', *Turner Studies*, 2 (1991), 7–15; T. Fawcett, 'John Crome and the Idea of Mousehold', *Norfolk Archaeology*, 38 (1982), 168–81; I. Waites, 'Peter DeWint and the Lincolnshire Landscape' in John Lord (ed.), *Peter DeWint 1784–1849: 'For the Common Observer of Life and Nature'* (London, 2007), pp. 29–39.
10. T. Williamson, 'Enclosure and the English Hedgerow', in B. Ford (ed.), *The Cambridge Cultural History of Britain, vol. VI: The Romantic Age in Britain* (Cambridge, 1989), p. 264.
11. D. B. Brown, A. Hemingway and A. Lyles, *Romantic Landscape: The Norwich School of Painters* (London, 2000), p. 62.
12. The sentimentalism of *Our Old Town* is typical of the early Victorian period, similar in tone to Mary Russell Mitford's hugely popular *Our Village* (1832) which also eulogizes the life of 'the common'.
13. T. Miller, *Our Old Town* (London, 1857), p. 14.
14. Ibid., p. 59. This is comparable to lines found in Clare's poetry, where he writes of 'unbounded freedom' and of nature's 'wide and common sky'.
15. Ibid., p. 31. Again, Clare's descriptions of the ad hoc network of paths which traversed Helpston's open fields are reminiscent of Miller's: 'sheep tracks here and there; That lead a thousand ways' (*A Morning Walk, c.* 1831).
16. Ibid., p. 316.
17. *The Journal of the Royal Agricultural Society Volume Twelve* (London, 1851), p. 364.
18. *Stamford Mercury*, 26 May 1843 and 16 August 1850.
19. Miller, *Old Town*, p. 317.
20. Ibid., p. 32. Miller was also a close friend of the Chartist writer, Thomas Cooper, and so there may be a political undertone to how Miller 'prefers' to remember an unenclosed landscape of commons and common rights.
21. M. E. Turner, 'Enclosure Re-opened', *ReFresh (Recent Findings of Research in Economic and Social History)*, 26 (1998), 1–4.
22. The pioneering work on this is J. Gage, *A Decade of English Naturalism 1810–1820* (Norwich, 1969).
23. Aside from the works illustrated here, reproductions of the other paintings and drawings referred to in this chapter can be found in T. Wilcox and C. Titterington, *William Turner of Oxford (1789–1862)* (Woodstock, 1984).

24. Payne, 'Boundless Harvests', 14.
25. Ibid.
26. Ibid., 9.
27. See D. Eastwood, 'Communities, Protest and Police in Early Nineteenth-Century Oxfordshire: The Enclosure of Otmoor Reconsidered', *Agricultural History Review*, 44 (1996), 35–46.
28. Wilcox and Titterington, *Turner*, p. 10.
29. Payne, 'Boundless Harvests', 9.
30. Miller, *Old Town*, p. 32.
31. M. Andrews, *The Search for the Picturesque: Landscape Aesthetics and Tourism in Britain, 1760–1800* (Aldershot, 1989), p. 29.
32. Wilcox and Titterington, *Turner*, cat. no. 19, p. 38.
33. C. B. Andrews (ed.), *The Torrington Diaries: A Selection of the Tours of the Hon. John Byng between the Years of 1781 and 1794* (London, 1954), p. 346.
34. After an act passed back in 1836: W. E. Tate, *A Domesday of Enclosure Acts and Awards* (Reading, 1978), p. 218.
35. *Victoria County History of Oxford*, vol. 5, p. 3.
36. W. Wordsworth, *Lyrical Ballads* (London, 1802), p. vii.
37. R. B. Beckett (ed.), *John Constable's Correspondence* (Ipswich, 1962–1970), vi, p. 78.
38. A. Alison, *Essays on the Nature and Principles of Taste* (London, 1817 [1790]), i, pp. 317–18.
39. Ibid., pp. 30–1.
40. R. Sweet, *Antiquaries: The Discovery of the Past in 18th-Century Britain* (London, 2004); P. Levine, *The Amateur and the Professional: Antiquarians, Historians and Archaeologists in Victorian England 1838–1886* (Cambridge, 2003). Malcolm Andrews usefully points out that the natural scenery and ruins which Picturesque theory favoured increasingly became chief tourist attractions and high priority subjects for conservation as the nineteenth century progressed: Andrews, *Search for the Picturesque*, p. 240.
41. He did not appear to have any relationship with collectors in London and his patrons were exclusively local to Oxford and its environs: Wilcox and Titterington, *Turner*, p. 13.
42. Ibid., p. 9.
43. A. Young, *View of the Agriculture of Oxfordshire* (London, 1809), p. 239.
44. Wilcox and Titterington, *Turner*, p. 34.
45. Ibid.
46. V. Surtees (ed.), *The Diary of Ford Madox Brown* (New Haven, 1981), p. 144.
47. J. Ruskin, 'Of the Turnerian Picturesque', *Modern Painters* (London, 1987 [1856]), pp. 433–4.
48. Quoted in L. Parris (ed.), *The Pre-Raphaelites* (London, 1984), p. 111.
49. www.oss.org.uk/history/history.htm.
50. E. K. Helsinger, 'Land and National Representation in Britain', in Rosenthal, Payne and Wilcox, *Prospects for the Nation*, p. 24.

2

'Witnesses for the Defence': The Yeomen of Old England and the Land Question, *c.* 1815–1837

Kathryn Beresford

Introduction

In 1836, readers of Richard Barham's the *Ingoldsby Legends* were introduced to 'yeoman' Thomas Marsh, of Marston Hall near Folkestone. Marsh was a full six-foot in height, and in the prime of life. He is first encountered at the head of his 'well-furnished board' adorned with a 'cold sirloin... big enough to frighten a Frenchman', and 'ale strong enough to blow a man's beaver off', indicative of the English 'yeoman's' superior powers in the consumption of vitals and alcohol.[1] 'Yeoman' Marsh's abundant hospitality was matched by his literary contemporary, Mr. Wardle, from *The Pickwick Papers*. Mr. Wardle was the 'yeoman' of Manor Farm, Dingley Dell, of which it was said, 'There an't a better spot o' ground in all Kent'. A generous and convivial entertainer, he supported a very comfortable lifestyle and a dependent entourage of 'poor relations' and employees, who were well fed enough to include the infamous 'fat boy'. His 'best sitting room', was lit up by a 'crackling fire' and 'light-hearted laughter'. According to Dickens, it was just the place where, 'old English yeomen... would have held their revels' had they 'turned into fairies when they died'.[2]

Over the centuries, the English 'yeoman' has conjured up many images, often poetical and whimsical, or encumbered with political and cultural connotations that have made many historians wary of analysis.[3] Yet the dominant representations are identifiable enough. Like Wardle and Marsh, he was paternalistic and bountiful, fond of food and ale. He was possessed, if not of luxury and opulence, of the comforts that life in the countryside could bring. 'Yeomen' were self-sufficient farming men of middling status who owned and worked their own lands, ostensibly with at least 60 acres in their possession.[4] According to the codifying pen of William Blackstone, for example, 'A yeoman is he that hath free land of forty shillings by the year; who is thereby qualified to serve on juries, vote for knights of the shire, and do any other act, where the law requires one that is *probus et legalis homo*'.[5] Nevertheless, by the late eighteenth and early nineteenth centuries, 'yeomen' were not necessarily the freehold owners of the soil they tilled; rather, the security of a lease gave them sufficient independence and security to satisfy the requirements of the definition. This shift was noted by William Cobbett, who wrote in his *Rural Rides*: 'Those only who rent ... are properly speaking, farmers. Those who till their own land are yeomen: and when I was a boy, it was the common practice to call the former farmers and the latter yeoman-farmers'.[6]

Cobbett was, of course, one of the most resonant of many commentators on rural England in the early nineteenth century. As with practically every aspect of country life, he did not merely note this transition. The 'plight' of the 'yeoman' formed a prominent element in his critique of the governmental mismanagement and oppression that had destroyed the more equitable 'old England' of his boyhood, suggesting that when the 'yeomen' suffered, agricultural England and the nation, by extension, followed.[7] A tirade against paper money, for example, posited it as a 'system' that 'swallowed up' and 'bought out' 'yeomen', replacing them with the present race of 'renters'.[8] Likewise, in broadsides against the greediness of the church since the Reformation, it was the 'real' and 'independent' 'yeomen' that had been reduced to 'rack-renters' and 'dependants', leaving the land in the hands of 'squandering' landlords and the 'grinding land-valuer'.[9]

There is little doubt that smaller and medium sized owner-occupiers were facing great difficulties in the early nineteenth century. For at least a century, agricultural England had been undergoing a process of structural change, through which landlords and agricultural improvers sought to reorganize production along more efficient, profit-orientated lines, and many small farmers were compelled to sell up their lands, or saw their leases terminated.[10] This resulted in the creation of a large, landless proletariat, an increase in short-term contracts and a decline of live-in labour – all indicative of the widening social gap between farmers and their employees.[11] Nevertheless, regional variations were great, and small household producers endured in various forms, usually reliant on the labour of the whole family.[12] F. M. L. Thompson described the 'small landowners' who still cultivated their own land in the late eighteenth and early nineteenth century as the 'survivors of the true yeoman stock', who fitted 'somewhat uneasily into the structure of the landed interest'.[13]

This chapter explores how representations of the English 'yeoman' in the early nineteenth century formed a crucial element in the idealization of the rural community that underpinned opposition to the radical critique of landownership. As will be seen, the figure of the 'yeoman' functioned as a metaphor for the landed interest's fears for the national future and as a lynchpin of 'old England'.[14] A powerful and surprisingly complex vision of 'Englishness', 'old England' summed up how commentators as diverse as William Cobbett, crusading landlords such as Philip, fourth Earl Stanhope, and Tory newspaper editors understood the correct working of society. 'Yeomen' were placed at the heart of paternalistic societal structures, where they flourished alongside benevolent landlords and contented labourers. Such hierarchies, considered the 'natural' state of things, were believed to have been corrupted by recent changes in the social and agricultural landscape, and thus required reviving or reconfiguring for the future.

As a symbol of a correctly functioning nation, the 'yeomen's' utilization in political commentary reached beyond the boundaries of the land question. Besides being fondly commemorated in literature, their distinctive qualities were celebrated in newspapers and on the hustings as reasons for the countryman's power and influence: his reputation for plain-dealing, his strength, his much-lauded 'sturdiness' and 'stoutness', and his ability to work the land. Indeed, the 'yeomen' epitomized masculine virtues to which groups and individuals aspired. According to Ian Dyck, Cobbett, with his sturdy demeanour, straight-speaking ways, and round frock-coat, consciously embodied the image of the 'yeoman' and, once again, he was not alone.[15] The championing and embodiment of these qualities suggest another place for 'yeomen' in early nineteenth-century culture, as an agrarian symbol of national character whose attributes were aspired to, debated over, and which could give agency to political rhetoric.[16] As Helsinger has argued about wider representations of rural and agricultural England, the 'yeoman' was as fractured and contested as the countryside itself, where conflicting meanings were 'invoked in the struggle for cultural representation, which is also a struggle for political representation'.[17] As I will demonstrate, this became overtly true in the debates surrounding the 1832 Reform Act in Kent, when campaigners on many fronts sought to identify themselves with the earthy virtues of the 'yeomen'.

Land, nationhood, and identities

In the early decades of the nineteenth century, questions of nationhood, citizenship, and subjecthood were keenly contested. Although conflict in Europe ceased in 1815, British imperial expansion continued apace and, in an era which saw the massacre at 'Peterloo', the suspension of *Habeas Corpus*, and ongoing discontent in Ireland following the Act of Union, the domestic situation was far from stable. Campaigns surrounding parliamentary Reform and Catholic Emancipation provoked debates about who was 'manly' or 'English' enough to claim political rights, or on what grounds others should be denied. Coterminously, more socially inclusive political cultures emerged, located in the newspaper press and mass meetings as well as the intricacies of electoral politics.[18]

Many of the visible manifestations of domestic unrest, particularly those in the short time span of the later 1820s and early 1830s, were in provincial, and predominantly agrarian, southern and eastern England. The myriad of economic troubles included slumping produce prices, tithes, duties, monetary issues, and the malfunctioning Poor Law.[19] Population growth was perceptible, and increasingly an issue that small-scale schemes of emigration or tentative allotment projects could not redress. Ongoing popular protest and discontent peaked in 1830, with the 'Swing' unrest. This encompassed widespread rick-burning, machine breaking, demands for higher wages, and the leaving of threatening notes. The discontent was considerable, spreading from Kent throughout a large swathe of southern and eastern England and it was not restricted to the poorer classes of society. Fluctuating prices, the prospect of free trade measures passing through parliament, and very visible poverty amongst the so-called 'lower orders' induced provincial elites to organize petitioning campaigns and county meetings. Farmers and landlords were politically motivated by the 'protection' of agriculture, particularly the improvement and preservation of the Corn Laws, debates about which were to rage until the late 1840s.[20]

At first glance, however, this turmoil appears to be absent from contemporaries' representations of rural 'Englishness'. Indeed, by the early nineteenth century, links between 'Englishness', pastoral landscapes of prettily varied enclosures, and the 'rural idyll' were well established.[21] Landscapes of Kent, Surrey, and Sussex distinguished by their hop fields, market gardens, and scattered estates and villages were lauded for their distinctively 'English' beauty by writers as diverse as Cobbett, Dickens, and Surtees.[22] These small-scale, cultivated landscapes were seen to epitomize the counties, despite their recent origin in layout, and the fact that only a minority of the land was occupied in such a way.[23] In paintings and literature alike, from Constable and Turner through to Jane Austen, representations of rural people often perpetuated the historicist 'myth of old England', filling pastoral roles of 'peasant', 'yeoman', and 'squire' in peaceful, familial conceptions of hierarchical communities.[24] Idyllic descriptions in the novels of G. R. Gleig, incumbent of Ash near Sandwich, typified this neat tertiary structure, the human presence in the land signified by dwellings, if not by figures: amongst the 'undulating hills', 'luxuriant hop gardens', and 'fields... of yellow corn', he wrote, 'we find a farmhouse, a gentleman's seat, a cluster of cottages...'.[25]

These representations have played relatively little part in discussions of the reconfiguration of gendered identities in the era of Catholic Emancipation and Reform. According to Linda Colley, the years following 1815 saw the emergence of a 'British' identity, in which definitional factors were religious inclusion, imperial supremacy, and the abolition of slavery, superseding identities forged by the experiences of prolonged wars with France, and the unifying force of Protestantism, in the long eighteenth century.[26] Hall, Davidoff, and Tosh have demonstrated how the new gender roles of the post-war period, building on the ideologies of the mid to late eighteenth century, whilst always shifting and contested, were tied up in notions of domesticity, a strong work ethic, evangelical religion, and the dependence of women, children, and servants on independent middle-class men.[27] The masculine subject's definitional 'Others', however, could be found a long way beyond the 'domestic sphere'. He was constructed against the dependent poor, who were all the more 'unmanned' by the harsh terms of the New Poor Law in 1834, against slaves, and also against the effeminate and spendthrift aristocracy.[28] In these ways, the figure of the manufacturing or professional middle-class man became an embodiment of political citizenship and a cultural signifier of what it was to be an 'Englishman'.

Far from being primarily 'middle-class', such values had resonance throughout English culture.[29] Yet 'British' identities remained inherently fractured. Identifications with the 'four nations' persisted; those who saw themselves as 'English' could use the appellation interchangeably with 'Britishness', reinforcing cultural hegemony.[30] Gendered identities, moreover, were contingent upon the kind of public and regional cultures in which they were configured. Although the boundaries between 'rural' and 'urban' areas, the metropole and counties/provinces were often ambiguous, perceived differences between them, particularly the juxtaposition between industrial and agricultural England in this era of great change, provided crucial reference points in discourses of identity and nationhood.[31] In addition, the articulation of such identities had strong regional variations, which themselves could be contingent on the location and economy of the region.

The alleged 'martial prowess' that defined the masculinities of the 'Men of Kent', for example, was derived from Kent's strategic location, jutting out towards the continent, as England's first line of defence. Historical stories about their repelling enemies abounded, and were reproduced in newspapers and political speeches as well as songs and poetry. Their stolid 'yeoman' qualities were derived from perceptions of the peculiar prosperity and fertility of the 'garden of England'.[32] Whilst comparative work on the intersection of region, gender, and nationhood is still relatively limited, the masculinities of the 'Men of Kent' suggest the significance of the locally configured landscape in the articulation of identities, and of the 'yeomen' as a symbol of the 'virtues' of the land-working man, whose qualities, while not necessarily in direct conflict, clearly varied from those of the idealized middle-class urbanite. The latter part of this chapter, then, will show how representations of the 'yeomen' in this period functioned as symbols of agrarian masculinity.

Yeomen and the ideologies of 'old England'

The concept of 'old England' was intrinsic to understandings of nationhood amongst the 'landed interest'. Like many discourses of 'Englishness' and 'Britishness' in this era, it could have military connotations, inspired by the numerous conflicts of the eighteenth century: the 'wooden walls of old England' were, according to the popular song, the ships of the Royal Navy, and 'Hearts of Oak' fought for 'old England again and again'.[33] More pertinently, however, 'old England' found its expression in the press and at provincial political dinners and meetings, being a rallying cry for the traditionalist values of church, king, and constitution, the upholding of agricultural 'protection' with 'zeal', and an England where 'peasant, yeoman, and landlord' lived in harmony. Provincial newspapers extolled the cause of 'old England' with enthusiasm.[34] Indeed, an 'old English' scene was one of harmony, abundance, prosperity, and good food, where 'yeomen' sat down to eat the 'roast beef of old England', accompanied with veal pies, plum pudding, and bread.[35]

Representations of 'old England' were rarely complete without the 'yeomen', who summoned up images of a hardy, land-working, pure-blooded, and masculine 'race' which, in ideal circumstances, moved unaltered through time. William Woodbine, editor of *The British Yeoman, and Rural Gazette* and allegedly of 'labouring stock', saw their plain-dealing and generous virtues as having their origins in the 'old England' of King Alfred, although he feared that these 'pure' roots of 'Englishness' may be as lost as Alfred in the mists of time.[36] To Geoffrey Oldcastle, writer of *The Canterbury Magazine* in 1835, the 'race' of the 'Kentish yeomen' had emerged cultivating their fields at the dawn of antiquity. They had 'defied the foreign foeman' including the Romans and the Normans, and now, in the steps of their forefathers, and in an echo of Cobbett, resisted 'Scotch philosophers and Jews'. These 'plain', 'proud', and 'manly Kentish yeomen', like Marsh and Wardle, acted as the linchpins of patriarchal households, keeping all those around them 'safe and warm'.[37]

Representations of 'yeomen' betrayed contemporary preoccupations with race and ethnic origins. Sir Walter Scott's hugely successful novels of medieval heroism played a significant role in the 'reclaiming' of a racially pure Anglo-Saxon past and in producing related images of English masculinity.[38] As in the more overtly politicized works of Woodbine and Cobbett, Scott's 'yeomen' were his truest proponents of 'Englishness'. In *Ivanhoe* (1819), his most famous work, the hero's quest is enabled by the aid of fine specimens of 'stout, well-set yeomen, arrayed in Lincoln green'. Their plain-speaking personas and heroics are identified as 'Saxon' traits, revealed in a particularly positive light when compared to the duplicitous, although victimized Jew, Isaac, the invariably oleaginous Norman Knights, and evil Prince John. Ivanhoe's 'yeomen' resist the tyranny of French rule and fight boldly to help their masters to achieve victory, and a slight loosening of the 'Norman yoke'.[39]

Scott's influence has been discerned in the wave of literature that appeared in the 1840s discussing England's origins and dwelling on the current 'state of the nation' – notably Thomas Carlyle's *Past and Present* and Benjamin Disraeli's *Sybil*.[40] Indeed, Disraeli's reconfiguration of Conservatism, which emphasized the organic bonds of the nation and the importance of including the poor, was comparable with wider responses amongst the 'landed interest' to the problems of the 1820s and 1830s.[41] A character in *Sybil* (1845) suggests that it was the 'yeoman' that once provided the crucial middling ground between masters and slaves, luxury and misery, echoing Cobbett's lament for society prior to the Reformation: 'There were yeomen then, sir: the country was not divided into two classes, masters and slaves; there was some resting-place between luxury and misery. Comfort was an English habit then, not merely an English word.'[42] 'Yeomen', then, evoked images of a harmonious yet hierarchal society and of comfort: not of excess or luxury, but the hard-earned fruits of a man's labour upon the land. His lot was the antithesis of that represented by radical proponents of the land question discussed elsewhere in this volume.

What fuelled these emotive articulations of 'old England'? Beyond the domain of novelists and polemicists, conceptions of the 'comforts' of 'old England' were underpinned by ideas about cultural 'rights' which, drawing upon the resources of their own individual and collective memories, many poorer countrymen believed had been taken from them.[43] The loss of a symbolic daily meal of roast beef was particularly mourned alongside the decline of its 'yeoman' consumers: according to Cobbett, the true England of 'roast beef' had been transformed into a land of 'dry bread, or of oatmeal porridge'.[44] Indicating Cobbett's role as a 'mouthpiece of popular culture', plebian ballads likewise emphasized the loss of the 'roast beef of old England', no longer the daily diet of the English rural worker.[45] In addition, Cobbett's and Woodbine's championing of the 'yeomen' functioned as a thinly veiled criticism of perceived new gender roles, apparently brought about by the transition from patriarchal households in which, in theory at least, the patriarch wielded his power and benevolence over women, children, and 'servants in husbandry', to the less clearly structured world of wage-labour. The bountiful, paternal 'yeoman' was arguably the symbol of a perceived 'golden age' in gender roles, in which a prosperous, tranquil social order enabled male supremacy in the household as well as the community.[46] For the 'landed elite', however, the conflicts and priorities could be rather different: inherent in 'old England' were conceptions of a despised 'new England' built on industry, free trade, and the breakdown of traditional hierarchies in which their lands were unthreatened by unruly rioters, to be replaced by discipline- and structure-free communities. As J. Benet, MP for Wiltshire, told the Commons in 1822, the import of foreign grain would render England a land purely of manufacturers and would 'reduce and deprave the yeomanry'.[47]

Comparable understandings of 'old England' underpinned the 'practical paternalism' that was selectively enforced with great passion by landlords throughout Great Britain in the face of challenges to their authority.[48] English landlords, particularly in the post-Swing and New Poor Law era, provided congenial moments of contact between themselves and their underlings, including the annual labourers' dinners, and organized festivities and ploughing matches that became the practice of the Labourers' Friend Society.[49] At the Great Ploughing Match at Cottesmere, Rutland, in 1833, the familial structures of society were firmly on display, with the middling class of 'yeomen' intact: 'the day was ushered in by the ringing of bells and congregating "yeoman" farmers, their families and husbandmen in their best attire'. The aims of the organizer, Sir Gerard Noel, were to encourage industry and 'manly spirits' by bringing 'back the good old breed of English peasants' and 'promote the welfare of old England'.[50] The revival of a 'yeoman' class was seen as a way of cultivating motivated and obedient subjects for the future. Early support for the Labourers' Friend Society in the *Maidstone Gazette*, for example, suggested that by helping the labourer to 'win for himself an honest independence' landlords would be moving towards the restoration of 'that important branch of the community, the ancient yeomanry or small farmer' who 'would again recover his long lost energy, and almost forgotten manliness of character'.[51]

The enforcement of neo-feudal bonds between rich, middling, and poor was far from the only ideological underpinning of these paternalistic practices. Jeremy Burchardt, historian of the allotment movement that became increasingly widespread in the 1830s, argues that 'paternalism' – in the sense of 'attempts to revert to a society based on difference and hierarchy' – was only a 'minor and eccentric strand', secondary to the 'progressive' ideals of improved morality and self-help.[52] Nevertheless, the two ideologies were not mutually exclusive. Earl Stanhope campaigned tirelessly for an improvement in the condition of labourers and tried out many practical schemes, including the creation of allotments on his Devon estates as early as 1821.[53] While he rejected any desire to create a land of 'peasant owner-occupiers', condemning any truly 'radical' restructuring of landholding as 'evil' republicanism and 'un-English', his belief in a lost 'golden age' fuelled his mission for the future.[54] In letters to like-minded agricultural 'improvers', he declared that the destruction of small farms and farmers, apparent since 1792, had led to 'a very unnatural and disordered state of the body politic', and hence he would 'hail with pleasure' a 'return to the former system'.[55]

'Old England', indeed, was underpinned with very contemporary fears about declining morality and the value of the 'yeomen' as an independent middle class. For example, G. R. Gleig, whose books bewailed the current state of morality at terrifying length, regretted the demise of the 'brace of petty farmers ... one of the finest and most virtuous classes of society' whose 'homes were the nurseries of good and faithful servants ...'. His 'yeomen' of yesteryear, unlike the labourers and tenants of his own day, did not apparently share their descendants' predilection for the pub and the weekly newspaper![56] More pertinently, commentators on the riots in 1830 saw the decline of the 'yeomen' as one of the underlying causes of the unrest: a Kentish 'freeholder' lamented that the corruption of the societal order had transformed once happy, prosperous smallholders into that distinctly un-English category of 'slaves'.[57] The fate of the 'yeomen' was also lamented in emotive broadsides against free trade. A letter from 'a farmer' to the *Maidstone Journal* in 1831 complained that the looming Reform Act was wanted only by free-traders such as the Birmingham Political Union, and spelled doom for the countryman: '...should this measure be carried to the extent proposed', the writer argued, 'a Yeomen of Kent may hereafter be found on the page of history, but he will be sought in vain upon the surface of the soil'.[58]

This focus on the decline of a 'natural' and inherently English social order was further mobilized by the presence of 'outsiders', notably Irish itinerant labourers, who became particularly visible in the fiercely competitive labour market of the south-eastern counties in the late 1820s and 1830s. An 1831 pamphlet, for example, was typical in suggesting that the lifestyle of the 'respectable yeoman...to whom a decent coat, meat diet, malt liquor and a comfortable house are, from habit and feeling indispensable' was threatened when he was not only stripped of his land but placed in competition with 'savage barbarians' who would work for next to nothing and who were contented with a 'bare hovel...potatoes and water'.[59] Swing, nevertheless, highlighted the tensions between the paternalistic bonds of 'old England' and the needs of the capitalist market. Whilst Stanhope, amongst others, called for both Irish and English landholders to look after 'their own', emotive laments for the 'peasant' and 'yeomen' did not, as Cobbett noted, prevent landlords employing cheap, imported labour.[60] Nevertheless, discourses of 'old England' provide a valuable glimpse into the complex ways in which the 'nation' was articulated against the backdrop of agrarian conflict and change.

Yeomen, identity, and politics

As a fundamental element in conceptions of 'old England', then, the 'yeoman' had a significant presence in debates about the land question. Yet not all representations of 'yeomen' emphasized their decline. Indeed, the 'yeomen's' much-lauded virtues were also celebrated as reasons for the countryman's power and influence, providing competing images of English masculinity in the light of the growing influence of urban, middle-class values.

Cobbett famously eulogized the poor countryman's 'hardness' and bravery as the true virtues of English 'manhood', compared to the 'soft' masses of the manufacturing cities in the north, and his defence of 'manly' and rough rural sports against the moralistic onslaught of evangelicals is well documented.[61] Similarly, Woodbine contrasted specifically 'yeoman' virtues against the indolent habits of town-dwellers:

> Whatever the idle and vain may think of you – yowkals... chow bacons, chopsticks, or country bumpkin... however they may ascribe your plain dealing to rudeness, your rural pursuits to want of taste... and intellect... your calling is the most honourable, the most conducive to the blessings of health and confidence, and the one best calculated to produce independence of mind, benevolence of heart, and purity of morals.[62]

Independence and morality were, of course, classic components of masculinity in early nineteenth-century middle-class 'domestic ideology'; Woodbine clearly believed countrymen to be the *more* moral and independent, and indeed domestic.[63] Nevertheless, this was also a defence of attributes that did not always fit neatly into middle-class ideals. Large appetites, even large waistlines, were attributes of which such 'Englishmen' as Woodbine and Oldcastle were certainly not ashamed. Like John Bull, the 'yeoman's' purported paunchiness could be used to denigrate him.[64] Yet his 'stoutness' could equally be a symbol of strength, affluence, and prosperity, and mobilized emotively in political rhetoric. This was the case with regard to 'yeomen' identities in Kent.

The articulation of 'yeomen' identities often had regional leanings, and was understandably most conspicuous in areas considered to have a tradition of self-sufficient smallholders, such as Kent and Norfolk.[65] In Kent, 'yeomen' virtues were integral to manifestations of regional identity, whether regionally specific expressions of 'Englishness' or the more county-specific 'Men of Kent'. Although this identity could be articulated in varying ways, those who wielded it usually advocated quasi-militaristic forms of behaviour, speech, and appearance associated with bearing arms for one's country, with physical prowess, and with loyalty. Like the economy of the county, they were also predominantly agrarian. The quintessential 'Men of Kent' were sturdy 'yeomen': brawny, brave, and ready to defend to the death the land they tilled.[66] Like the landscape, the 'Kentish yeomen' were symbolic of the heightened virtues of rural 'Englishness' in which Kent apparently excelled. As this well-known jingle illustrates, the prosperous 'yeoman' stood alongside the 'apples, hops and cherries' as a symbol of the fertility and affluence of the region compared to other areas of Britain:[67]

A Knight of Cales,
A Gentleman of Wales,
And a Laird of the North Countree:
A Yeoman of Kent,
With his yearly rent,
Will buy them out all three!

This particular poem predates the period, but was quoted by Barham and Scott.[68] In Kent, then, the appellation 'yeoman' was popular with men of all levels of society, from town-dwelling tradesmen to the aristocratic owners of vast estates.[69] Being a 'yeoman of Kent' certainly had resonance among the humbler members of the 'landed interest'. Robert Stapely, a farmer of Tunbridge Wells, who held his lands by copyhold and leasehold, declared, in his will of 1836, that he was proud to be a 'stout yeoman' of a 'county of stout yeomen', further suggesting that those who lived on annual tenancies and leaseholds were happy to embrace the identity of the 'yeoman', with its reassuring connotations of independence and security, as their own.[70]

The 'pride' felt by individuals such as Stapely became visible in the 1820s and early 1830s, when public debates over citizenship helped stimulate a reconfiguration of political culture and new articulations of the 'nation' and the 'people'.[71] Kentish Tories and their supporters continued to utilize the 'yeomen' to appeal to their 'rank and file' supporters, and underline the strength of traditional societal bonds. The 'yeomen' were 'the strength, the very sinews of the country', who harboured 'strong feelings of attachment to Church and King', rhetoric appropriated throughout the English provinces.[72] Nevertheless, in 1831 and 1832, it was Reformers who most successfully seized upon the rural, middling classes' 'yeoman' qualities to stake claims for the widening of the franchise. For Sir William Cosway, addressing supporters at a Reform Dinner in Dover, the 'Yeomen of Kent' deserved the vote, not just because of their 'reason' or 'religiousness', but because they 'talked little, did much' and were stolid, dependable, farmers.[73]

The appearance and 'yeomen'-like qualities of a politician and his supporters could even be a factor in his success. At the 1828 mass meeting on Penenden Heath, near Maidstone, organized to address the issue of Catholic Emancipation, both sides appealed to their followers as solid, dependable 'Yeomen of Kent'. They were described as powerfully built men of the fields, close to the landscape and nature. The ubiquitous Cobbett, in attendance to oppose both sides and promote the use of his Indian Corn, was unexpectedly won over to the anti-Catholic cause of the 10th Earl of Winchilsea, apparently swayed more by their demeanour than their political stance. He was impressed by Winchilsea's bluff oratory and 'stout' manly appearance, which he set against the 'effeminacy' of 'liberal' Lord Darnley. In even starker contrast, he described the Catholic Association's Richard Lalor Shiel, in strongly racialized language, as using 'wild' gesticulations and foaming at the mouth in an animalistic manner. His highest praise was nevertheless reserved for Winchilsea's following of 'yeomen', rendered 'conspicuous' by their 'sturdy appearance', and whom he later robustly defended in the metropolitan press against accusations of bigotry.[74] The embodiment of 'yeomen'-like qualities was not restricted to the election ground. Kentish 'Knights of the Shire', notably Sir Edward Knatchbull and Thomas Law Hodges, were lauded by their supporters as typifying the solid 'English yeoman', an image bolstered by expensive rounds of election dinners and numerous drinking songs written in their names.[75]

Yet, maybe the most powerful representations of the 'yeomen' were located in representations of people and landscape. On Penenden Heath in 1828, Cobbett was particularly struck by the harmony of people within the market-garden landscape near Maidstone, which he considered one of the finest in England: the '2,000 men on horseback' were mingled with the cultivated hills of Kent creating an image which he saw as 'an honour to the county and an honour to the country'.[76] Similarly emotive descriptions enhanced newspaper reporting of the elections and festivities of 1831 and 1832, where ruddy-faced 'yeomen' and 'farmers' celebrated their newly won rights against the backdrop of crop-abundant fields and village greens decorated with their produce.[77] At the May 1832 election, the *Maidstone Gazette* reported upon a scene of exclusive, hierarchical yet interdependent Kentish 'yeomanry', once again located on the picturesque backdrop of Penenden Heath, whose distinctive virtues justified their claims to power: 'twenty thousand of the respectable and sturdy yeomanry of Kent, consisting one grand assemblage, affording to the spectator a proud specimen of Britain's wealth and power, in the most valuable of her possessions – her hardy sons'.[78] Women were not entirely absent from these scenes, yet their labours in county politics were done little justice by decorous descriptions of them on the peripheries of the fields.[79] The all-pervasive 'yeomen', then, provided a strikingly masculine vision of landed 'Englishness'.

What, however, were the political implications of these patriotic celebrations of the 'yeomen'? The 1832 Reform Act extended the county franchise to £10 copyholders and leaseholders, as well as tenants paying rent of over £50 per year.[80] The medium-sized tenants, the chief constituency appealed to as 'yeomen' on election grounds and at county meetings, thus joined the ranks of the political citizenry. Genuine smallholders, in terms of the struggling cottager who, far from embodying the image of the benevolent paternalist, survived off the labour of the whole family and juggled waged-work with small-scale cultivation, did not.[81] Women, of course, were formally excluded for the first time.[82] Nevertheless, county politics, in terms of those elected and who spoke at public meetings, remained dominated by the large landholder for at least the next three decades. At a meeting in 1830 that addressed the 'deplorable' state of agriculture, William Cobbett, eliding the 'yeomen' with the classical radical notion of the 'people', triumphantly claimed that a petition for Reform moved by Mr Bradley, 'a yeoman', was carried 'in spite of all the efforts of the aristocracy'. Mr Francis Bradley Esquire, was a substantial landowner, with parcels of land in at least 11 Kentish parishes, most of which was leased to tenants.[83] Yet what Bradley embodied for Cobbett at that moment was not his genuine economic situation but an idea: a vision of the stolid, independent, and 'unpurchasable' small landowner, whose perceived value came sharply into focus in an era when the real smallholding 'yeomen' was fast ceasing to exist. By Cobbett's own classification, Bradley was not a *real* 'yeoman'.[84] Nevertheless, he empowered him and his cause in the eyes of his readers by branding him as such.

Conclusion

In the early nineteenth century, the English 'yeoman' was mythologized through literature, songs, and political polemic, embodying rural elements of the national character. 'Yeomen' lay at the heart of idyllic images of landscapes of pastoral harmony and plenty, imbued with apparently timeless qualities that signified the racial and ethnic origins of 'Englishness'. Nevertheless, the yeoman's utilization in debates surrounding the land question, at a time when the agricultural economy in general and the position of smaller landholders in particular was extremely unstable, raises interesting questions about intersections of land, gender, and nationhood. Images of the imperilled 'yeomen' became symbolic of the fate of the nation, and an intrinsic part of discourses of 'old England'. For the landed elite, the dominant impulses in national thinking, towards specific conceptions of 'the people' and 'the nation', were configured in a climate of fear about upheaval, made all the more pressing by serious outbreaks of domestic unrest, and a deeply felt nostalgia for the social hierarchies of rural England's 'golden age' pasts. William Cobbett's 'old England', articulated through his demands for a more benign, patriarchal social structure, shared many attributes with elite 'old Englanders' such as Stanhope. Nevertheless, the latter asserted the correctness of the 'natural', racially pure bonds of 'old England' in order to defend their hegemony within the provinces and at Westminster. In contrast, Cobbett and the poorer classes of countrymen he arguably represented wielded it in attempts to regain rights and needs recently lost: food and land.

'Yeoman' virtues also came to symbolize rurally and regionally specific conceptions of English masculinity and were consciously embodied by public figures as diverse as Cobbett and the 10th Earl of Winchilsea. Political campaigners in the English provinces drew upon the rugged, sturdy qualities of the 'yeoman', their physicality and relationship with the land justifying their claims to power. The qualities of masculinity emphasized in public life suggest that discourses of manhood in Kent, and possibly throughout rural and provincial England, contrasted with the domestic, evangelical, and 'civilizing' masculinities that were in the ascendancy in metropolitan and industrial areas in the post-war era. A new look at the 'yeomen' of 'old England', then, adds new elements to debates on gendered identities and suggests intimate links between cultural perspectives on land, gender, and nationhood in this highly turbulent period.

Notes

1. R. H. Barham, *The Ingoldsby Legends; or, Mirth and Marvels, by Thomas Ingoldsby, Esquire* (London, 1840 [1836]), p. 371.
2. C. Dickens, *The Pickwick Papers* (London, 1999 [1837]), pp. 81, 372.
3. G. E. Mingay, *Enclosure and the Small Farmer in the Age of the Industrial Revolution* (London, 1968), p. 10; B. Reay, *Rural Englands* (Basingstoke, 2004), pp. 3–8.
4. Bateman's survey of 1883, as analyzed by F. M. L. Thompson, describes the 'lesser yeomen' as owning between 100 and 300 acres and the 'greater yeomen' as owning 300–1,000 acres. Thompson observes that few of these owners were 'yeomen' in the 'farming sense' as, by this time, only 10 per cent of the land was farmed by owner-occupiers: F. M. L. Thompson, *English Landed Society in the Nineteenth Century* (London, 1963), pp. 116–17.
5. W. Blackstone, *Commentaries on the Laws of England. The Rights of Persons, Book 1* (Oxford, 1765), p. 394.
6. W. Cobbett, *Rural Rides* (London, 1953), i, p. 14 [5 November 1821].
7. I. Dyck, *William Cobbett and Rural Popular Culture* (Cambridge, 1992), p. 138. See also R. Williams, *Cobbett* (London, 1983), pp. 55–6.
8. *Cobbett's Political Register*, 17 November 1821.

9. W. Cobbett, *History of the Regency and Reign of King George IV* (London, 1830), p. 13.
10. G. E. Mingay and J. Chambers, *The Agricultural Revolution, 1750–1880* (London, 1966), pp. 127–8; R. C. Allan, *Enclosure and the Yeoman, 1450–1850* (Oxford, 1992), pp. 1–14.
11. The literature on these changes is extensive, but three overall summaries from contrasting perspectives are J. E. Archer, *Social Unrest and Popular Protest in England, 1780–1840* (Cambridge, 2000), pp. 8–27; Mingay, *Enclosure*, p. 10. See also A. Howkins and I. Dyck, '"The Time's Alteration": Popular Ballads, Rural Radicalism and William Cobbett', *History Workshop Journal*, 23 (1987), 20–38.
12. Reay, *Rural Englands*, esp. chs 3–4. For regional variation, see J. Wordie, 'Social Change on the Levesson Gower Estate 1714–1832', *Economic History Review*, 27 (1972), 593–4.
13. Thompson, *English Landed Society*, pp. 7–8.
14. According to Thompson, the broadly defined 'landed interest', comprised the landed aristocracy and gentry and 'the great body of the agricultural community, the farmers and labourers ... and the blacksmiths, wheelwrights and publicans who provided them with services': *English Landed Society*, pp. 4–5.
15. Dyck, *William Cobbett*, pp. 14–15.
16. For some discussion of the other figures and symbols that have embodied British national character and patriotism including John Bull, see R. Samuel (ed.), *Patriotism: The Making and Unmaking of British Identity* (London, 1989), iii. In his analysis of the post-1815 years, Peter Mandler draws attention to the work of Henry Hallam, who argued that Englishness found its roots in the independent Saxon yeomanry. In keeping with the argument of the book, Mandler emphasizes their institutional origins (such as socage tenancies, for example) rather than racial underpinnings, and says relatively little about rurally derived conceptions of national character at this early stage: P. Mandler, *The English National Character: The History of an Idea from Edmund Burke to Tony Blair* (New Haven, 2006), p. 37.
17. E. K. Helsinger, *Rural Scenes and National Representation, 1815–1830* (Princeton, 1997), p. 6.
18. J. Vernon, *Politics and the People: A Study in English Political Culture, 1815–1867* (Cambridge, 1993), p. 39; F. O'Gorman, *Voters, Patrons and Parties: The Unreformed Electoral System of Hanoverian England 1734–1832* (Oxford, 1989); J. A. Phillips, *Electoral Behavior in Unreformed England: Plumpers, Splitters, and Straights* (Princeton, 1982); P. Langford, 'Property and "Virtual Representation" in Eighteenth-Century England', *Historical Journal*, 31 (1988), 83–115.
19. B. Hilton, *A Mad, Bad and Dangerous People: England 1783–1846* (Oxford, 2006), pp. 251–64.
20. J. Wordie, 'Perceptions and Reality: The Effects of the Corn Laws and the Repeal in England, 1815–1906', in Wordie (ed.), *Agriculture and Politics in England, 1815–1939* (New York, 2000), pp. 33–59; T. L. Crosby, *English Farmers and the Politics of Protection, 1815–1852* (Hassocks, 1977).
21. A. Bermingham, *Landscape and Ideology: The English Rustic Tradition, 1740–1860* (London, 1987); J. Barrell, *The Dark Side of the Landscape: The Rural*

Poor in English painting 1730–1840 (Cambridge, 1980), p. 5; J. Brewer, *The Pleasures of the Imagination: English Culture in the Eighteenth Century* (London, 1997), pp. 625–6.

22. Dickens, *Pickwick Papers*, p. 280; R. S. Surtees, *Jorrocks' Jaunts and Jollities* (London, 1869 [1843]), pp. 2, 281–2.
23. G. Mingay, 'Agriculture', in A. Armstrong (ed.), *The Economy of Kent, 1640–1914* (Woodbridge, 1995), p. 53.
24. Reay, *Rural Englands*, p. 3; Barrell, *Dark Side of the Landscape*, p. 6; L. Nead, *Myths of Sexuality: Representations of Women in Victorian Britain* (Oxford, 1988), p. 42. According to Helsinger, representations of the rural poor in the work of J. M. W. Turner, for example, facilitated complex systems of 'misrepresentation', which depicted poverty and posed challenges to idealized images of landscapes, but ultimately reflected the 'expectations and fears of the upper classes': Helsinger, *Rural Scenes and National Representation*, pp. 173–4.
25. G. R. Gleig, *The Chronicles of Waltham* (Paris, 1835), p. 1.
26. L. Colley, *Britons: Forging the Nation 1707–1837* (London, 1996), p. 351.
27. J. Tosh, *A Man's Place: Masculinity and the Middle-Class Home in Victorian England* (New Haven, 1999), pp. 17–30; C. Hall, *Civilising Subjects: Metropole and Colony in the English Imagination, 1830–1867* (Cambridge, 2002), pp. 27–8; C. Hall and L. Davidoff, *Family Fortunes: Men and Women of the Middle Classes 1780–1850* (London, 2002 edn), pp. xiv–xv.
28. For depictions of the aristocracy, see P. Corfield, 'The Rivals: Landed and other Gentlemen', in N. Harte and R. Quinault (eds), *Land and Society in Britain, 1700–1914* (Manchester, 1996), pp. 11–14.
29. Davidoff and Hall, *Family Fortunes*, pp. xxx–xxxi.
30. Colley, *Britons*, pp. 13–18, 308–14, 393.
31. The development of culturally specific imaginings of the differences between town and country was explored in R. Williams, *The Country and the City* (London, 1973).
32. *Times*, 24 October 1828, *Kentish Gazette*, 14 October 1828; *Maidstone Journal and Kentish Advertiser*, 28 October 1828.
33. H. Green, 'The Wooden Walls of Old England. An Ode', *c.* 1790. For an example of it being sung at political meetings, see *Berkshire Chronicle*, 25 October 1828. 'Hearts of Oak' (1759), was written by W. Boyce with words by D. Garrick; for an example of its use, see *Maidstone Journal and Kentish Advertiser*, 28 October 1828.
34. *Berkshire Chronicle*, 20 October 1828, 5 November 1831; *Kentish Observer*, 11 October 1832.
35. *Hampshire Chronicle*, 2 July 1832. Mandler has argued that 'romantic' visions of 'English' history had a prominent place in popular conceptions of nationhood in the later part of this period. However, Tory or 'Cobbettite' imaginings of 'old England' and medievalism are given relatively little prominence in his discussion, which focuses instead upon the growing popularity of 'Merrie England' and potentially 'levelling' visions of pre-1688 England, and locates creative impulses within the rising middling classes, rather than the 'agricultural interest' and their economic fortunes. See P. Mandler, ' "In the Olden Time": Romantic History and English National Identity', in L. Brockliss and D. Eastwood (eds), *A Union of Multiple Identities: The British Isles,*

c. 1750–c. 1850 (Manchester, 1996), pp. 78–92; P. Mandler, *The Fall and Rise of the Stately Home* (New Haven, 1997), pp. 22–33.

36. *The British Yeoman, and Rural Gazette*, 1 (July 1832).
37. *The Canterbury Magazine*, 2 (January 1835).
38. B. Melman, 'Claiming the Nation's Past: The Reinvention of an Anglo-Saxon Tradition', *Journal of Contemporary History*, 26 (1991), 575–95.
39. Sir W. Scott, *Ivanhoe* (Harmondsworth, 1994 [1819]).
40. Melman, 'Claiming the Nation's Past', 579–81; C. A. Simmons, *Reversing the Conquest: History and Myth in Nineteenth-century British Literature* (New Brunswick, 1990).
41. S. Borgstede, ' "All is Race": Inclusion and Exclusion in Disraeli's Discourses of Race and Nation', paper given at the conference on 'Inclusion and Exclusion in the Long Nineteenth Century', University of Hamburg, 5–7 May 2006.
42. B. Disraeli, *Sybil* (Oxford, 1986 [1845]), p. 61; cf. W. Cobbett, *A History of the Protestant Reformation in a Series of Letters* (London, 1824–5), letter 5.
43. Dyck, *William Cobbett*, p. 138.
44. Cobbett, *History of the Protestant Reformation*, letter 6; *Cobbett's Political Register*, 20 February 1830. For more on beef as a symbol of 'Britishness' or 'Englishness', see B. Rogers, *Beef and Liberty: Roast Beef, John Bull and the English Nation* (London, 2003).
45. Dyck, *William Cobbett*, pp. 132–5. See also P. Jones, 'Captain Swing and Rural Popular Culture' (PhD thesis, Southampton, 2004), pp. 54, 67.
46. *Cobbett's Political Register*, 22 December 1832; *The British Yeoman, and Rural Gazette*, 2 (June 1832). This critique of the breakdown of the patriarchal household arguably foreshadows the gendered discourse of the Chartists, who developed the rhetoric of 'family breakdown' and the 'breadwinner' wage in order to exclude women and children from the factory and mine: A. Clark, *The Struggle for the Breeches: Gender and the Making of the English Working Class* (London, 1995), p. 267.
47. *Times*, 8 May 1822. Much of the pro-Corn Law literature in the Wellington Pamphlets also supports this stance. See, for example, *General Remarks on the State of the Poor and Poor Laws, and the Circumstances Affecting their Condition viz. Game Laws, Currency, Free-Trade, Tithes, Corn Laws, Alehouses, &c* (London, 1832): Wellington Pamphlets, Univ. of Southampton Special Collections, 980/1.
48. M. Cragoe, *An Anglican Aristocracy: The Moral Economy of the Landed Estate in Carmarthenshire, 1832–1895* (Oxford, 1996), p. 73; D. Roberts, *Paternalism in Early Victorian England* (London, 1979), pp. 271–3. For contrasting accounts see R. Wells, 'Poor Law Reform in the Rural South East: The Impact of the "Sterne Bourne Acts" during the Agricultural Depression, 1815–1835', *Southern History*, 23 (2001), 57; P. Mandler, 'The Making of the New Poor Law Redivivus', *Past and Present*, 117 (1997), 131–57.
49. For accounts of labourers' dinners in Kent and Sussex, see Sir Edward Knatchbull to Norton Knatchbull, 17 June 1831, Knatchbull Papers, Centre for Kentish Studies U951 C26/11; C. Greville, *The Greville Diary*, ed. P. W. Wilson (London, 1927), pp. 469–70 [23 May 1834].
50. *An Address to the Nobility and Landed Proprietors of Great Britain and Ireland by a London Merchant* (London, 1834), p. 74: Wellington Papers, Univ. of Southampton Special Collections, 1150/2.

51. *Maidstone Gazette and Kentish Courier*, 1 September 1832.
52. J. Burchardt, *The Allotment Movement in England, 1793–1873* (Woodbridge, 2002), p. 127.
53. A. Newman, *The Stanhopes of Chevening* (London, 1869), pp. 228–32, 234–6.
54. Lord Stanhope, printed address on 'The State of the Country', 1821, Stanhope Papers, Centre for Kentish Studies U1590 C196/1. For the 'foreignness' of radical land plans, see also Lord Teynham, 'Plans for Amelioration and Observations on the Condition of the Labouring Classes': paper sent to the Duke of Wellington, April 1830: Wellington Papers, Univ. of Southampton Special Collections, WP1/1108/24.
55. Stanhope to T. French, 18 September 1820, Stanhope Papers, Centre for Kentish Studies, U1590 C196/6; Lord Stanhope, printed address on 'The State of the Country', 1821, U1590 C196/1; Stanhope to M. Wright, 22 April 1821, U1590 C196/6.
56. G. R. Gleig, *Country Curate* (London, 1830), p. 63; *Chronicles of Waltham*, p. 5.
57. A letter to Sir Edward Knatchbull baronet MP from 'A Freeholder', November 1830: Knatchbull Papers, Centre for Kentish Studies, U951 C14/2.
58. *Maidstone Journal and Kentish Advertiser*, 25 October 1831.
59. G. P. Scrope, *A Letter to the Magnates of Southeast England* (London, 1831).
60. Lord Stanhope, *Hansard*, new ser., 25 (9 July 1830), col. 1121; *Maidstone Gazette and Kentish Courier*, 28 September 1830 and subsequent issues; *Cobbett's Political Register*, 22 January 1831.
61. *Cobbett's Political Register*, 20 February 1830.
62. *The British Yeoman, and Rural Gazette*, 1 (July 1832).
63. For domestic ideology, see Hall and Davidoff, *Family Fortunes*, part 1.
64. J. Surrel, 'John Bull', in Samuel, *Patriotism*, iii, pp. 8, 23. See also M. Taylor, 'John Bull and the Iconography of Public Opinion in England, 1712 to circa 1929', *Past and Present*, 134 (1992), 93–128.
65. Numerous pamphlets and journals were aimed at the 'Norfolk Yeoman'. For example, *The Norfolk Yeoman's Gazette and Eastern Advertiser* ran for 13 issues in 1823: E. Hasted, *The History and Topographical Survey of the County of Kent* (Canterbury, 1797), i, p. 300.
66. K. Beresford, 'Men of Kent: Gender and Nationhood in Regional Perspective' (PhD thesis, University College London, 2007).
67. Dickens, *Pickwick Papers*, p. 28.
68. Barham, *Ingoldsby Legends*, p. 370; Scott, *Ivanhoe*, p. 457; *Kentish Gazette*, 17 October 1828.
69. See for example, *Maidstone Journal and Kentish Advertiser*, 23 September 1828.
70. Prerogative Court of Canterbury Wills, Robert Stapley, Yeomen of Tunbridge Wells, 10 March 1829, PROB 11/1753.
71. Vernon, *Politics and the People*; P. Joyce, *Visions of the People: Industrial England and the Question of Class, 1840–1914* (Cambridge, 1991), pp. 9–13.
72. *Kent Observer*, 20 December 1832; *Times*, 9 May 1835. See also the following accounts, all from *The Times*: Worcester Conservative Meeting, 30 September 1835; South Warwickshire Election, 27 June 1835; Grand Conservative Dinner at Framlingham, East Suffolk, 3 October 1836; North Lancashire Conservative Anniversary Dinner, 24 October 1836.
73. Reform Dinner at Dover, 1831, *Kent Herald*, 20 May 1831.
74. *Maidstone Journal and Kentish Advertiser*, 4 November 1828. For an analysis of manifestations of regional and national identity at the Penenden

Heath meeting, see K. Beresford, 'The Men of Kent and the Penenden Heath Meeting', *Archaeologia Cantiana*, 125 (2005), 151–71.

75. *Maidstone Journal and Kentish Advertiser*, 17 November 1829, 9 August 1831; *Kent Gazette*, 29 April 1831, 15 July 1831, 5 August 1831; *Times*, 14 November 1829, 21 November 1834; 'A song to be sung upon the occasion of the dinner to be given for Sir Edward Knatchbull, baronet, by his friends, 3 August 1831, at Sittingbourne', repr. in R. De Vaynes (ed.), *A Kentish Garland* (Hertford, 1880), p. 344.
76. Cobbett, *Rural Rides*, i, p. 252 [5 September 1823]; letter to editor of the *Morning Chronicle*, repr. *Maidstone Journal and Kentish Advertiser*, 11 November 1828.
77. *Maidstone Gazette and Kentish Courier*, 28 August 1832, 31 July 1832.
78. Ibid., 17 May 1831.
79. Horn, *Ladies of the Manor*; K. Gleadle, 'Charlotte Elizabeth Tonna and the Mobilisation of Tory Women in Early Victorian England', *Historical Journal*, 50 (2007), 108; *Kent Gazette*, 28 October 1828, 5 July 1832; *Maidstone Journal and Kentish Advertiser*, 4 November 1828.
80. N. Gash, *Politics in the Age of Peel* (New York, 1953), p. 86.
81. Reay, *Rural Englands*, esp. chs 3–4.
82. C. Hall, 'The Rule of Difference: Gender, Class and Empire in the Making of the 1832 Reform Acts', in I. Blom, K. Hagemann and C. Hall (eds), *Gendered Nations: Nationalisms and Gender Order in the Long Nineteenth Century* (Oxford, 2000), p. 107.
83. *Cobbett's Political Register*, 20 March 1830.
84. See note 6, above.

3

Chartism and the Land: 'The Mighty People's Question'

Malcolm Chase

Introduction

> Patronage, which is a consequence of, and springs from, the Large Farm System, *withholds the land from you*; while the law of primogeniture, and the barbarous law of settlement and entail, prevents such as are able from buying small allotments of land. To break through these barriers is easy and simple, and should be the great national object. By its accomplishment alone can you now set up the principle of individualism against that of centralization... [T]he land of a country belongs to society; and... society, according to its wants has the same right to impose fresh conditions on the lessees, that the landlord has to impose fresh conditions upon a tenant at the expiration of his tenure. Society is the landlord: and as society never dies, the existing government are the trustees... Society looks on the performance of all requisite duties as the only condition on which its lessees can make good that title. (Feargus O'Connor, 'The Land! Its Value: And How to Get It', *Northern Star* 9 November 1844.)

Between 1838 and 1848, Chartism held a place at the centre of British domestic politics. Then, for a further decade, it exercised an intermittent influence on the trajectory of radical politics. As a political movement its concerns extended far beyond the six points for parliamentary reform, embodied in the People's Charter from which it took its name.[1] Studies of the movement in relation to landed property, however, have overwhelmingly focused upon the Chartist land plan. This scheme to settle its supporters on four-acre cottage holdings, located in a network of national colonies, attracted over 70,000 subscribers at its peak in 1847–48. Its inelegant and protracted demise, after only 234 subscribers had been located on the land, tarnished the subsequent reputation of Chartism. The movement's greatest leader, Feargus O'Connor (whose personal investment in the scheme – financially, politically and emotionally – was considerable) was similarly blighted. It is tempting to explain both the appeal and failure of the land plan by reference to naïve nostalgia for a pre-industrial society. Yet, the sentiments underpinning its appeal were far from simple 'back to the land' platitudes, as O'Connor's attack – quoted above – on the way private property and political patronage were mutually sustaining reveals.

Until recently, the tendency among historians of the movement has been to view this sprawling (and, organizationally, deeply flawed) edifice as a scheme of O'Connor's invention alone.[2] Early studies largely analyzed it as a *sui generis* phenomenon, linked to the Chartist movement for practical and promotional purposes, whilst being intellectually and politically somewhat detached from it. Yet paradoxically, this near-exclusive historiographical focus on the Plan has prevented a fully rounded understanding of it. This chapter will argue first that the land plan cannot be understood in isolation from the broader issue of how Chartists regarded landed property; and second, that despite widespread differences of opinion among Chartists throughout the movement's history, a consistently critical stance on private property in land was maintained.

The land plan, launched in April 1845, was the object of unalloyed negativity from early historians of the movement: For Robert Gammage, himself a Chartist, the scheme was patently a 'fallacy'. 'illegal in its very foundation' and a 'great folly which was to contribute to the disgrace of the Chartist movement'.[3] Mark Hovell, whose influential 1918 study set the historiographical tone for half a century, even went so far as to assert that the plan 'was not a real Chartist scheme.'[4] The only favourable response to the land plan among early historians came from continental European authors, un-encumbered with the baggage of Fabian socialism (which viewed the leadership of O'Connor with distaste and land reform generally as a distraction from the central purposes of working-class politics in an industrializing society).[5] Since the 1970s, however, the interpretive pendulum within the historiography of Chartism has swung decisively in O'Connor's favour, and in parallel to this there has occurred a surge of interest in the land plan.[6] So decisive has this been that the National Trust was moved in 1997 to acquire the only remaining un-modernized cottage holding on the former Chartist estates, 'because of its national importance and historical significance'.[7]

However, the historiographical renaissance enjoyed by the land plan has obscured the extent to which agrarian ideas were central to all currents within Chartism. A powerful intertwining of the long-established ideologies of the Norman Yoke and Old Corruption provided the basis from which Chartists advanced arguments for, variously, forcible re-appropriation, land and building societies, a free market in landed property, deeply radical taxation regimes, the moral imperative of agricultural reform to maximize food production and, from 1851, 'the Charter and something more', a social democratic programme with land nationalization at its heart. Three elements underpinned them all. First was an outright hostility to large accumulations of landed property, irrespective of the legal form in which they might be held. Thus, secondly, Chartism was suspicious of central government as the putative owner or manager of the national estate. Thirdly, all Chartist conceptions of the reform of landed property shared a 'way of seeing' land that was shaped by ideas of shared access, usage and control rather than by possessive individualism.

Land and the Norman Yoke

At their heart, most if not all Chartist ideas about landed property derived from the concept of the Norman Yoke. Chartism was rooted in the tradition of earlier radicalism, especially the conviction that Old Corruption determined both the tone and fiscal character of government.[8] Thus Chartists were naturally inclined to endorse the view that, as the Tyneside Chartist weekly *Northern Liberator* put it, 'the illegitimate William had legitimated usurpation'.[9] However, Chartist usage of the concept was as much connotative as denotative. The extent to which Chartists actually believed in the Norman Yoke's historical veracity is debatable; but it was a powerful tool to think with, and the concept was freighted with critical judgments about the institution of landed property. It was in this manner, rather than as part of a factual account of the evolution of private property in land, that Chartist speakers and authors deployed the language of the Norman Yoke. For example, according to a Derby police informer Jonathan Bairstow, a National Charter Association (NCA) missionary, depicted England 'in the days of Alfred the Great' thus:

> There was no Factorys, no mill owners, the manufacture and farming was about Equal and the price and food and Labour was Regulated by the King and parliament and all lived happy and Comfortable; things went on this way for several Centurys until Wm the Conqueror came over with his hired tools to make you subservient to [h]is will . . . the

> Land was the property of all and was only now held by the few from the share of power they held in the Government of the country.[10]

This trope in Chartist thought was equally appealing to the movement's Irish and Scottish supporters. Indeed, Alfred the Great was potentially a figure in admiration of whom both English and Irish, and Catholic and Protestant, could combine. Blessed with a clean pair of hands as far as Ireland was concerned, he stood for a different concept of English authority, untainted by landlordism. 'England became *feudalised*', explained the leader of Irish Chartism, as a result of the 'Norman banditti – the great progenitors of England's boasted barons, with William the Illegitimate – founder of the present illustrious dynasty! – at their head'.[11] Following the death of Daniel O'Connell, a growing rapprochement with Irish nationalists saw Liverpool Chartists seek to overcome the sectarian divisions that undermined the movement on Merseyside through the formation of 'the Alfred League'. Described by its promoters as 'a National Co-operative Cheap Justice Association', the League was dedicated to the 'recovery of property *Stolen from the People*, including the plunderings of the Norman Robbers.'[12] Behind this rhetorical smokescreen, the League actually operated as a friendly society. (More familiarly known by its later title, the Loyal Order of Alfred, it was one of many fraternal initiatives that emerged from Chartism.)

The Norman Yoke endured as a trope in English radical thought far longer and pervasively than Christopher Hill suggested in his prescient and pioneering essay on the subject.[13] As late as 1856, Ernest Jones, O'Connor's former lieutenant, who had assumed the latter's mantle from 1850, opined that 'the seizure of the Saxon land by the Norman robber' was 'the parent wound, from which we bleed to-day':

> Join with me for the re-conquest of the land. It is the task of the age – the mission of the century. You talk of unchaining yourselves: unchain the land, and your own chains will fall. The franchise is the bond that binds your hands; but land monopoly is the dungeon that surrounds your bodies.[14]

The Norman Yoke reinforced the radical assault upon the landed aristocracy. Successive imitations of John Wade's *Black Book*, the Ur-text of the fight against 'Old Corruption', argued that the reformed House of Commons was still dominated by Britain's landed elite.[15] Monopoly of political power and monopoly of land were decidedly not coincidental.

It was political monopoly that had made possible the consolidation of the land monopoly through parliamentary enclosure: 'Robbery', according to the *Northern Liberator*, 'by means of Enclosure Bills, of the COMMON LANDS, consisting of MILLIONS OF ACRES, from the industrious and poorer part of the population ... under colour of legislation, *filched*, in the most barefaced manner.'[16] Bronterre O'Brien, one of the most articulate and thoughtful of the Chartist leadership, put it bluntly: 'Knaves will tell you that it is because you have no property that you are unrepresented. I tell you, on the contrary, it is because you are unrepresented that you have no property.'[17] Thus the Norman Yoke also licensed the notion that social reformation might not be entirely peaceable. Land which had been forcibly appropriated might, morally and necessarily, be the legitimate object of draconian measures for its re-appropriation. William Hill, a former handloom weaver, Swedenborgian minister and the founding editor of the greatest of the Chartist newspapers, *Northern Star*, argued in a leader on the law of primogeniture:

> The thousand modes of plunder by which the nation's bones are being constantly picked, arise, in the first instance, out of the determination of those whose ancestors first obtained a monopoly of the soil, by what is called 'right of conquest'; that is to say, by robbery and murder, not only to retain all the ill-gotten spoil of their fathers; but, under colour of the letter, though in defiance of the spirit, of this law of primogeniture, to make the people from whom the land was originally stolen, support, at least, five-sixths of the whole number of thieves and thieves' descendents by extraordinary labour, independent of the land.[18]

Yet this coruscating attack went on to propose simply that 'by Universal Suffrage, the people [will] get the power to annihilate the law of primogeniture, along with every other relic of the barbarous ages.'[19] As so often in Chartism, the language of Hill's editorial projected not just truculence but violence, even though the underlying objective for which it argued was a legal reform of relatively limited extent (and we might note, had it ever been implemented, of limited effectiveness).[20]

However, the supposedly forcible nature of the Norman land grab did justify draconian remedies in the minds of many Chartists, including those typically associated with its 'moral force' (as opposed to 'physical force') tendency. For example, in 1849, the poet and engraver William J. Linton called for the confiscation of that year's harvest. This, he argued, should then be re-allocated to paupers, to the unemployed and to the labourers who had produced it, as the first instalment of what Linton termed a 'national rent'. Linton's national rent would have been almost identical to the single tax of later Georgeite land reformers: levied at the rate of 20 shillings per acre it would encourage the maximization of agricultural production, render unnecessary all other forms of taxation, and along the way assist the formation of a national estate since the property of defaulting landowners would be surrendered to the state.[21]

Chartism and agriculture

Linton's argument crystallizes a further dimension of Chartist views of land reform, namely that it was a practical and moral imperative, necessary to maximize agricultural production and alleviate poverty, as well as a means to right a political injustice. The argument that thoroughgoing land reform alone could maximize the productive capacities of the soil was well established long before Chartism. It can be traced to radical opposition to Malthusianism and, beyond that, to the view that parks and landscaped gardens were a facet of effeminizing luxury, a physical manifestation of corruption that constituted the ultimate affront to the poor. 'Why are huge forests still allowed to stretch with idle pomp and all the opulence of eastern grandeur?' Mary Wollstonecraft had demanded in 1792. 'Why does the brown waste meet the travellers view when men want work?'[22] This theme had particularly been developed during the Regency years by the Spencean Philanthropists.[23] Three Spenceans – Allen Davenport, Charles Neesom and Thomas Preston – lived long enough to exercise a significant influence on metropolitan Chartism.[24] 'If there were no parks, and no pleasure grounds', Davenport claimed in 1822, 'the whole face of the country would present to the eye cornfields, meadows, gardens, plantations of all kinds of fruit trees, etc., all in the highest state of cultivation.' The Spencean tradition was a vital part of London Chartism. Through George Julian Harney, the principal guiding hand on *Northern Star* from 1843 to 1850, it came to shape Chartist ideology more widely. 'His creed was – and Thomas Spence had taught it him – that "the Land is the people's farm" ', Harney declared in 1845, 'and that it belongs to the entire nation, not to individuals or classes.'[25]

The view that landed estates had been siphoned off from the nation at large paralleled the notion that Old Corruption continually annexed the income government derived from taxation. Similarly, an unproductive landscape mirrored 'The Thing' – idle, parasitic and bloated in luxury.

These ideas were given wide voice by Chartists, including those without any connection to the Spencean tradition. In a speech from the pulpit of a Methodist meeting room at Charlestown, Ashton-under-Lyne, in 1848, Scottish-born surgeon Peter McDouall declaimed that:

> Population has now so fast increased that every part of the land that has hitherto remained unproductive must be broken into tillage; that gentlemen's parks, as well as commons, must be divided into pastures, to feed the people – that is a proposition in which a great many of you must agree ... everything tells us that no portion of this land can any longer lie idle; and ere long, the aristocracy will find themselves obliged to cut up their parks, and enclose the forests, and render them productive for the rest of the community.[26]

This argument was mutually reinforcing with the abiding radical belief that – of all the possible methods of organizing the cultivation of the land – smallholding maximized productivity returns relative to the input of labour. It could thus alleviate poverty both by widening employment opportunities and facilitating the production of plentiful food, countering the Malthusian spectre. 'When I see a man with his foot upon his spade', declared O'Connor in his seminal *Practical Work on the Management of Small Farms*, 'I think I recognize the image of his God, and see him in that character which even the Malthusian deigns to assign him – A MAN STANDING ON HIS OWN RESOURCES.'[27] This notion was itself powerfully reinforced by contemporary idealization of spade husbandry (perhaps the only principle held consistently and unanimously by the three commanding personalities of early nineteenth-century radicalism, William Cobbett, Robert Owen and Feargus O'Connor). Even Bronterre O'Brien, one of the fiercest critics of O'Connor from within the Chartist movement, eulogized smallholding. 'The hope of individual reward', he explained, 'is the most natural incentive to labour.' Though he strongly favoured free trade, O'Brien rejected the notion that the leaders of the Anti-Corn Law League 'mean to give you as cheap bread as O'Connor's four acres would give you. Mind, I am no admirer of Feargus O'Connor – it's quite otherwise I assure you. But truth is truth, come from whom it may.'[28]

The long-established radical call for small farms was widely configured as the means through which both to reform agricultural production and alleviate poverty. In the words of Christopher Doyle, a Manchester powerloom weaver and NCA activist who became a full-time official for the land plan,

> It was the duty of the government of the country to cause the waste lands to be cultivated so as to give employment and food to those who were willing to labour, but were too often, as at the present time, in consequence of the artificial state of the labour market, thrown out of employment in large masses, to the great injury of society at large.[29]

To argue for collectivized agriculture was an ideological Rubicon no Chartist ever crossed. Land nationalizers and land planners alike favoured small-scale cultivation. Ernest Jones consistently espoused smallholdings, even as he abandoned the tenets of the land plan in favour of land nationalization. Hostility against centralization, a consistent trope in O'Connor's argument for the land plan, featured prominently in Jones's case for nationalization of the land. 'By the state retaining for ever as national property the land once purchased, the centralisation of the land in the hands of a few rich individuals becomes impossible . . . the occupiers of the land are to be *tenants*'.[30] This concept meshed well with post-Chartist radical Liberalism, of which Jones was an exemplary exponent after the demise of the NCA in 1858. 'England's wealthiest Ballarat is England. Our goldfields are golden fields of wheat . . . Give us a million peasant farmers.'[31]

For Chartists, therefore, the first duties of a reformed parliament would necessarily include legislation to reform landed property, as a critical part of righting injustice, fighting poverty, producing cheap foodstuffs and eliminating unemployment. 'Behold *cause* and *effect* at once presented to view! Behold evil and remedy. Down with . . . landed monopolists! Restore the wages-slaves to those lands of which their forefathers were plundered. And behold the means in political power, and in that alone.'[32] Chartism consistently argued that land reform would be an imperative once the Charter was law. For example in September 1839, in virtually its last act before it dissolved, the Chartist National Convention adopted a *Declaration of the Rights of the People* that committed the movement to an elected magistracy, to the abolition of the standing army and to taking into public ownership any land that had once been 'appropriated to public and general use'.[33] Historians, distracted by the heat and fury of 1839, have usually overlooked this detailed exposition of the policies that a parliament, elected on the basis of the People's Charter, would have sought to enact. The immediate colonization of Crown lands even found its way into some strike resolutions during the 1842 strike wave, alongside a call for the Charter to be made the law of the land.[34] Subsequently, the NCA briefly adopted (1843–44) a constitution in which all mention of the Charter was expunged from NCA objectives, but provision 'for the unemployed, and means of support for those who are desirous to locate upon the land' was explicitly avowed.[35] The emergence of the Chartist land plan in 1844–45 is only explicable within the context of the commitment to agrarian reform that had been central to Chartism almost from its inception.

Chartism and landed property

Private landed property's place at the heart, as Chartists saw it, of a chain of political and social oppression justified calls for its reform both as a matter of both pressing urgency and irrefutable moral rectitude. However, Chartism faced a dilemma in that the arguments it advanced often appeared to favour the spoliation and destruction of private property. There were moments in 1839 when the equation appeared absolute, for example when *The Times* reported the Dukinfield Chartist Abraham Lee producing bullets from his pocket as he declared, 'it was every man's right to have a piece of land, and every man should never rest 'till everyone had his own right'.[36] Generally, however, Chartists drew clear distinctions between various categories of land and the reforms that should be applied to each. Calls for the immediate confiscation of private property were usually confined to common land enclosed by parliamentary act, for 'upwards of six millions of acres of commons lands have been taken from the working classes'.[37] In addition, economic necessity was often advanced as justifying the cultivation of so-called waste over the heads, if necessary, of whoever held it. Crown and Church of England lands were to be released for intensive cultivation as soon as feasible. For the rest, Chartists projected a gradualist reformation in land holding, to be achieved by the introduction of free trade in land, usually reinforced by state acquisition of freeholds at the death of owners 'by surrender, or by any means concordant with justice and a generous treatment of all classes'.[38]

> Perhaps no more vile falsehood was ever invented than that laid to the charge of the Chartists, asserting that they require a spoliation and division of property.... They merely ask for the old mode of dividing and leasing land, in small portions, so that the same measure which now supports one, may support hundreds.... For most assuredly, when the laws are made by UNIVERSAL SUFFRAGE, as ere

> long they must be, though no one will be robbed of the property which he has now acquired, means will be taken to prevent the future acquisition and accumulation, in individual hands, of large heaps of wealth and property by the oppression and starvation of the people. The 'classes' know this, and hence the bitterness of their animosity against the people, whom they perceive to be rising to their due station in society; hence their anxiety to put down the charter agitation; and hence the lying absurdities about equalising property which they have so industriously propagated.[39]

After 1848 Chartism matured as a political movement and its leading figures began to think in more sophisticated terms than the surge of reactive reforms that, it had hitherto been anticipated, the enactment of the People's Charter would initiate. Critical awareness grew that even the simultaneous repeal of the laws of primogeniture, strict settlement and entail would not immediately force large quantities of land onto the market; and such land as did become available might not be in the form of small parcels. Such small acreages as were flushed onto the market might not be readily affordable, even through the mechanism of lotteries or mutualist strategies such as loan or land clubs. Furthermore, the increasing interest taken by former Anti-Corn Law Leaguers after 1846 in land redistribution (via the rapidly expanding Freehold Land Society Movement) and land law reform (on a gradualist basis) suggested that as a specifically Chartist tactic, the repeal of primogeniture, strict settlement and entail was deficient.[40] Harney neatly encapsulated this problem in February 1850:

> The people are promised wonderful felicity by the repeal of the laws of primogeniture and entail, bringing the land to the public market. Mr. Bright and others desire to have the land as free to traffic in as labour is now. What would be the effect of such a 'reform'? Those who had the money to buy land would become landlords, and every landlord, whether lord of five or of fifty-thousand acres, would be a conservative – the sworn enemy to further change. Moreover, monopolising the soil, and commanding the sources of toil in the manufacturing districts, the new aristocracy would possess a power over the lives of both agricultural and manufacturing workers unexampled in the world's history.
>
> The proletarians need another sort of reform. The feudal aristocracy being doomed to expire, care should be taken that no new aristocracy

be allowed to take their place. With that view THE LAND MUST BE MADE NATIONAL PROPERTY.

Harney was the pivotal figure in re-orientating Chartism explicitly to embrace a social programme that was incapable of confusion with liberalism: 'push forward a propaganda of social democracy. Let them struggle for *the Charter and something more* – THE CHARTER, THE LAND, AND THE ORGANISATION OF LABOUR!'[41]

'The Charter and something more', an adaptation of the traditional Chartist slogan 'the Charter and nothing less', was the basis on which the NCA adopted a social democratic programme in March 1851. Features of this programme included proposals to settle the unemployed on the land via 'the restoration of poor, common, church and crown lands to the people. Such lands to be divided among the poor in suitable proportions. Those located to be tenants of the state, paying a proportionate rent-charge for their holdings.' Nationalization of other land was to be achieved gradually through purchase. Taxation would be levied on land and accumulated wealth only.[42]

It should be noted that arguments for nationalized ownership, however, had circulated within Chartism prior to 1851. The 1848 programme of the National Association for the Organization of Trade (a metropolitan Chartist trades' initiative, promoting producer co-operatives) began with this first principle: 'That the land, being the gift of the Almighty to the people universally, ought to be held in sacred trust by the state for their benefit, and not be exclusively possessed by a fractional part of the community.'[43] Harney, influenced as we have seen by the Spenceans, had espoused analogous arguments in 1845. Feargus O'Connor's sentiments, in the quotation that heads this chapter, offered a similar radical interpretation of the rights and responsibilities of private property and the State. O'Connor did not promote the land plan with the intention of creating a socially conservative alternative to, or deviation from, Chartism. Rather, he conceived its estates as a practical demonstration of how society would be reconstituted under the Charter, and he dared to hope that in time these estates might be so successful that even an unreformed government might be persuaded of the desirability of a small farm system. In this respect he found support from the unlikely quarter of John Stuart Mill, the first edition of whose *Principles of Political Economy* praised O'Connor's 'well-conceived arrangements' as offering a model for land reform in Ireland.[44]

Bronterre O'Brien's interest in land nationalization pre-dated Chartism and had first been aired in the pages of the great unstamped paper

Poor Man's Guardian which he edited from November 1832 until it closed in 1835. O'Brien first hinted polemically at the case for land nationalization in December 1833 ('to attack property is... to attack a robbery'). By 1835, his argument was well refined:

> What the Irish want... are what nature requires, and justice entitles them to;... they want their rents lowered to one-half or one-third their present amount; or if they are to pay competition prices for the use of the land, they want that ALL shall profit by these prices. They require that the fee-simple of the land shall revert to the rightful owner, viz. THE NATION, from which it could never be alienated without the general consent expressed by the majority – that the nation shall therefore resume its proper position as grand landlord of the whole country, and receive the rent henceforward in behalf of the people, to be divided share and share alike among every inhabitant, rich and poor, after defraying the expenses of government, this is the only just way of holding land.[45]

Even O'Brien, however, was cautious about applying comprehensive land nationalization in the English context. This is particularly apparent in his support for Thomas Bowkett, an active Chartist and secularist, in the promotion of building societies.[46] Plebeian land and building clubs had existed since the 1790s. From the 1820s, practical interest in the agrarian ideal led to the formation of a small but growing number of land societies. In Bowkett Building Societies members' subscriptions were pooled to make an interest-free loan to each member in turn to enable them to buy a property, 'turns' being decided by ballot. In legal and actuarial terms, there was absolutely nothing to distinguish Bowkett's initiative from that of O'Connor in the Chartist Land Plan, except for one key difference: Bowkett Building Societies were restricted to between 50 and 100 members. Bowkett's scheme grew in effect by cloning societies rather than engorging the sole original. They were far from immune from failure and, like O'Connor's land scheme, they were denied the protection of the Friendly Societies Act because they operated as a lottery. Yet the Bowkett principle endured into the 1930s.[47] The emergence of this associational form out of the Chartist movement (and from O'Brien's circle at that) further alerts us to how closely associated Chartism was, in all its varied facets, with the idealization of small property ownership. Some Chartist localities were contemplating the launch of societies through which their members could acquire smallholdings as early as 1840, the same year that there was a revival of interest in London in the land reform plans of the veteran Spencean Thomas Preston.[48] And from the late 1840s, significant numbers of Chartists became involved in building societies.[49]

The projected organization of land holding within a Chartist polity also turned on Chartists' view of the State. Hostility to the centralization of State power was a strong underlying current in Chartist ideology.[50] Like the promotion of the smallholding ideal, this was one of the elements that bound together O'Connor and his critics in the movement. Reformed government should facilitate and guarantee access to the land, but no more. Prioritizing land redistribution therefore curtailed enthusiasm for land nationalization. The mechanism needed at a national level to administer what (following Spenceanism) was often conceptualized as 'the people's farm' was arguably incompatible with the Chartist concept of light national government and significant local autarchy. The London Working Men's Association's journal, *The Charter*, argued control should be vested in democratically elected local commissioners.[51] O'Brien's response to this, at least in his Chartist phase, was to argue (much as Thomas Spence had done at the turn of the eighteenth century) in favour of parochial control. *Lloyds' Weekly London Newspaper* even alleged that O'Brien 'was the most distinguished... plagiarist' of Spence.[52] But the concept of the parish as the primary mechanism for both government and regulation of property carried diminished conviction in a rapidly industrializing and urbanizing society. Spence remained an authority to whom Chartists favouring outright public ownership continued to appeal.[53] However, it is arguable that the Spencean ideal survived in its purest form in the colonies of the Chartist Land Plan. 'By its accomplishment alone can you now set-up the principle of individualism against that of centralisation.' Chartism's estates were structured round individual land holdings, the only centralized facility being a schoolhouse, and they were promoted as being free of 'NATIONAL EXCISE PARSONS', and having none of the features of 'the present Labour system of England [which] is one huge system of communism; the wealthy idle director living upon the ignorance and dependence of aggregate struggle.'[54]

Conclusion

All Chartists agreed that land reform would be a political, economic and social imperative for a reformed parliament. They were unanimous that the basis on which land should be held for cultivation must be that of smallholdings and small farms. The emergence of arguments in favour of land nationalization was attenuated by a continued disposition in favour of small-scale ownership and suspicion of the State and its centralizing tendencies. This strongly inclined Chartists towards friendly societies and other mutualist organizations in their later careers. It also eased the passage for those ex-Chartists (and they were legion) who wished to secure a place in the Liberal sun.

Was there a single defining feature of the various Chartist positions on land reform? It is a commonplace of Chartist historiography that it appealed particularly to small producers, typically domestic outworkers such as handloom weavers. A disposition towards small-scale production is evident too in Chartist agrarian ideology. It is a disposition that the Land Plan did not create but rather shared with an over-arching political outlook that privileged issues of equity and access over ones of equality and ownership. Access to – and control of – the land, rather than the democratization of ownership itself, was the essential basis from which all Chartist land reform emerged. Once this is understood, then we can see that Harney was not being disingenuous in espousing Spencean ideals while editing a paper which was vociferous in its support of the land plan; nor was there any inherent inconsistency between the land plan and land nationalization, or between the latter and building societies. The ostensibly Janus-headed stance of the Chartists, at once critical of private ownership of the soil and yet jealous for rights of property in land, ceases to be problematic once we register that the key issue for all Chartist land reformers was access to, rather than ownership of, the land.[55]

Notes

1. The literature on Chartism is extensive. The most substantial histories are D. Thompson, *The Chartists: Popular Politics in the Industrial Revolution* (London, 1984), and M. Chase, *Chartism: A New History* (Manchester, 2007).
2. J. MacAskill, 'The Chartist Land Plan', in A. Briggs (ed.), *Chartist Studies* (London, 1959), pp. 304–41; A. M. Hadfield, *The Chartist Land Company* (Newton Abbott, 1970); M. Chase, 'We Wish Only to Work for Ourselves: The Chartist Land Plan', in M. Chase and I. Dyck (eds), *Living and Learning* (Aldershot, 1996), pp. 133–48.
3. R. G. Gammage, *History of the Chartist Movement, 1837–1854* (Newcastle, 1894 [1854]), pp. 249, 268.
4. M. Hovell, *The Chartist Movement* (Manchester, 1918), p. 32. A second edition of Hovell's seminal book was issued in 1925 and the third in 1966. It remained in print until the 1970s.
5. E. Dolleans, *Le Chartisme* (Paris, 1913), ii, pp. 278–301, 328–36, 348–54, 367–86; F. Bachmann, *Die Agrarreform in der Chartistenbewegung* (Bern, 1928);

H. Niehuus, *Geschichte der Englischen Bodenreformtheorien* (Leipzig, 1910), pp. 91–9.

6. J. Saville, introduction to reprint edition of Gammage, *History of the Chartist Movement* (New York, 1969); D. J. V. Jones, *Chartism and the Chartists* (London, 1975), pp. 130–7; Chase, 'We Wish Only to Work for Ourselves'; J. Bronstein, *Land Reform and Working-class Experience in Britain and the United States, 1800–1862* (Stanford, 1999); A. Messner, 'Land, Leadership, Culture and Emigration: Some Problems in Chartist Historiography', *Historical Journal*, 42 (1999), 1093–1109; A. M. Hadfield, *The Chartist Land Company* (new edn, Aylesbury, 2000); M. Chase, ' "Wholesome Object Lessons": The Chartist Land Plan in Retrospect', *English Historical Review*, 118 (2003), 59–85.
7. National Trust, *Rosedene: An Appeal for Restoration* (leaflet issued 1997).
8. For the classic exploration of the extent of Chartism's debt to earlier radical tropes and its consequences see G. Stedman Jones, 'Rethinking Chartism', in his *Languages of Class: Studies in English Working Class History, 1832–1982* (Cambridge, 1983), pp. 90–178.
9. *Northern Liberator*, 11 April 1840.
10. Derby Local Studies Library, MS BA/909/16186, items 10 and 11 (Jonathan Bairstow, 14 June 1841).
11. [P. O'Higgins], *Chartism and Repeal: An Address to the Repealers of Ireland, by a Member of the Irish Universal Suffrage Association* (Dublin, 1842), p. 5. See also 'On the Law of Primogeniture', [Scottish] *Chartist Circular*, 21 December 1839.
12. Alfred League advertisement on back cover of 'Effiax', *The Tax-Payer's Catechism, or Dialogues between Mentor and Telemachus on the Causes of Chartism* (Liverpool, 1848).
13. C. Hill, 'The Norman Yoke', in J. Saville (ed.), *Democracy and the Labour Movement* (London, 1954). See also A. Briggs, 'Saxons, Normans and Victorians', in *The Collected Essays of Asa Briggs* (Hassocks, 1985), ii, pp. 215–35.
14. E. Jones, *Evenings with the People 2: The Hereditary Landed Aristocracy* (London, 1856), p. 4. M. Taylor, *Ernest Jones, Chartism and the Romance of Politics, 1819–69* (Oxford, 2003) identifies land reform as a consistent trope in Jones's political career, stretching from Chartism to the cusp of selection as a Liberal parliamentary candidate shortly before he died.
15. Re-issues and pirated editions of John Wade's classic *Black Book* (first published 1820) were frequent during the Chartist period. The leading Lancashire Chartist Reginald Richardson published successive editions of his *Popular Black Book and Almanac*, along with *The Black Book, or Annual Tell Tale* (Salford, 1839), *The Red Book; or A Peep into the Peerage* (London, 1841) and *The Blue Book of the Commons* (Manchester, 1848). See also *The Black Book of England; Exhibiting the Existing State, Policy and Administration of the United Kingdom* (London, 1847); *The Black Book of the British Aristocracy* (London, 1848); *Court Jobbery: Or, the Black Book of the Palace* (London, 1848).
16. 'To the Landlords of North England', *Northern Liberator*, 15 June 1839.
17. *Bronterre's National Reformer*, 15 January 1837. For O'Brien see A. Plummer, *Bronterre* (London, 1971).
18. Editorial, 'Primogeniture', *Northern Star*, 25 April 1840.
19. *Northern Star*, 2 May 1840.

20. Chartists reinforced their case against primogeniture by arguing that it drove the younger sons of the aristocracy 'like so many devouring locusts' into military and naval service, the law and the Church: *The Speech Delivered by William Dixon, the People's Candidate, at the Moot Hall, Wigan, 1841* (Wigan, 1841), p. 12. See also P. McDouall, 'Land', *English Chartist Circular*, 46 (December 1841); 'Primogeniture', *Northern Star*, 25 April and 2 May 1840.
21. W. J. Linton, *The People's Land, and an Easy Way to Recover It* (London, 1850), p. 6; cf. F. B. Smith, *Radical Artisan: William James Linton, 1812–97* (Manchester, 1973), p. 68.
22. M. Wollstonecraft, *A Vindication of the Rights of Men, in a Letter to the Right Honourable Edmund Burke, Occasioned by his Reflections on the Revolution in France* (1790), repr. in J. Todd (ed.), *Mary Wollstonecraft: Political Writings* (London, 1993), pp. 60–1.
23. M. Chase, *'The People's Farm': English Radical Agrarianism, 1775–1840* (Oxford, 1988), pp. 45–120.
24. Ibid.; see also J. Bellamy and J. Saville (eds), *Dictionary of Labour Biography* (London, 1988), viii, pp. 38–45, 177–81, 192–8, and (for Neesom) Chase, *Chartism*, pp. 184–91.
25. *Northern Star*, 30 August 1845.
26. *An Authentic Report of the Trial of Doctor Peter Murray McDouall* (Manchester, 1848). For McDouall, a figure of considerable influence on northern Chartism, see Chase, *Chartism*, passim.
27. F. O'Connor, *A Practical Work on the Management of Small Farms* (7th edn, Manchester, 1845), p. 40.
28. [B. O'Brien], *A Brief Inquiry into the Natural Rights of Man* (London, 1852), p. 45; *The Poor Man's Guardian and Repealer's Friend*, 1 [3 June 1843].
29. C. Doyle, *Northern Star*, 1 January 1848. For Doyle see P. Pickering, *Chartism and the Chartists in Manchester and Salford* (London, 1995), esp. pp. 194–5.
30. E. Jones, 'Letters on the Chartist Programme', *Notes to the People*, 1, 3 (May 1851), 55–6. See also idem, 'Our Land: Its Lords and Serfs. A Tract for Labourers and Farmers', *Notes to the People*, 1, 5 (June 1851), 103–14.
31. *Birmingham Daily Post*, 27 November 1867; cf. *Labour and Capital: A Lecture* (1867), quoted in J. Saville, *Ernest Jones: Chartist* (London, 1952), p. 230.
32. E. Jones, 'Monopoly and its Effects', *Notes to the People*, 1, 23 (September 1851), 444.
33. *Northern Star*, 14 September 1839; *Charter*, 15 September 1839. For the Declaration, see Chase, *Chartism*, p. 106.
34. For example at Bolton, The National Archives, Home Office Papers, HO 45/249, fol. 127 [15 August 1842].
35. Report on the 1843 Convention, *Northern Star*, 16 September 1843; see also Chase, *Chartism*, p. 248.
36. *Times*, 29 March 1839.
37. J. Mason, *A Letter to Mr Macaulay, MP, in Reply to the Charges Made by that Gentleman against the Chartists* (Birmingham, 1842), p. 11.
38. Quotation from the programme adopted by the 1851 Chartist Convention, quoted in Jones, 'Letters on the Chartist Programme', p. 55.
39. Editorial, 'Equalisation of Property', *Northern Star*, 2 May 1840.
40. M. Chase, '"Out of Radicalism": The mid-Victorian Freehold Land Movement', *English Historical Review*, 106 (1991), 319–45.

41. G. J. Harney, 'The Charter, and Something More!', *Democratic Review*, February 1850, 351–2.
42. 'Plan of Agitation Adopted by the Chartist Convention', *Friend of the People*, 18 (12 April 1851). The 1851 programme is also analyzed in Chase, *Chartism*, p. 339.
43. *Power of the Pence*, 2 (18 November 1848). For the National Association for the Organization of Trade, see J. Belchem, 'Chartism and the Trades, 1848–50', *English Historical Review*, 98 (1983), 558–87.
44. J. S. Mill, *Principles of Political Economy* [book 2, ch. 10], ed. J. M. Robson (Toronto, 1965), ii, p. 1001.
45. 'O'Connell and the Irish', *Poor Man's Guardian*, 13 June 1835.
46. *National Reformer*, 14 November 1846, 6 February 1847, 1 and 15 May 1847.
47. S. Newens, 'Thomas Edward Bowkett', *History Workshop Journal*, 9 (1980), 143–8; E. J. Cleary, 'Starr, Richard Benjamin (1813–1892)', *Oxford Dictionary of National Biography* (Oxford, 2004).
48. *Northern Star*, 16 May, 29 August, 12 September and 31 October 1840. See also Pickering, *Chartism and the Chartists*, 117–19.
49. J. West, *History of the Chartist Movement* (London, 1920), pp. 282–3; Chase, *Chartism*, pp. 26, 245, 349, 353–7. See also 'James Maw', in J. Bellamy and J. Saville (eds), *Dictionary of Labour Biography* (London, 2000), x, p. 139. For convergences between late Chartism, building societies and other forms of mutualism, see J. Saville, *1848: The British State and the Chartist Movement* (Cambridge, 1987), pp. 208–11.
50. F. C. Mather, *Chartism and Society* (London, 1980), pp. 26, 58–9, 83–5; E. Yeo, 'Some Problems and Practices of Chartist Democracy', in J. Epstein and D. Thompson (eds), *The Chartist Experience* (London, 1982), pp. 345–80.
51. 'The Land of England Belongs to the People of England', *The Charter*, 1 December 1839.
52. *Lloyds' Weekly London Newspaper*, 5 October 1845. On O'Brien as a land reformer, see esp. Plummer, *Bronterre*, pp. 179–84.
53. For examples of appeals to Spence's authority, see *London Dispatch*, 18 June 1837 and *Northern Liberator*, 30 December 1837 (Place); *Northern Star*, 16 June 1838 (calls for increased 'Spencean knowledge'); *Operative*, 25 November 1838 and *Northern Star*, 8 December 1849 (O'Brien); *Northern Star*, 3 February 1849 (Nottingham Chartists), 30 August 1845 and 31 August 1850 (Harney).
54. *Northern Star*, 9 November 1844, 16 October 1847, 18 November 1848.
55. On this point within English agrarian radicalism generally see Chase, *'The People's Farm'*, pp. 183–4; Iorwerth Prothero makes the same point with reference to English and French artisan radicalism in his *Radical Artisans in England and France, 1830–70* (Cambridge, 1997), pp. 140–1.

4
The 'Manchester School' and the Landlords: The Failure of Land Reform in Early Victorian Britain

Anthony Howe

The League and the 'Landocracy'

From the late 1830s, the Anti-Corn Law League launched a blistering attack on the landed classes in Britain which was unparalleled in scale and intensity, at least until its lineal descendant, the Land Campaign of Lloyd George in Edwardian Britain.[1] Not only were the aristocracy held up as a rapacious set of tyrants who deprived the people of food, but they were also depicted as an oppressive class of landlords, who shirked their share of national taxation, whilst demanding excessive rents from their tenants, and held the agricultural labourers in near feudal bondage. In part, this rhetoric was designed simply to undermine the Corn Laws as the most obvious and objectionable sign of aristocratic self-interest but for many opponents of the League, and some of its supporters, repeal of the Corn Laws was simply the prelude to a wide-ranging attack on 'the interests, the revenue, and the political power of the land owners'.[2] Within this wider anti-aristocratic carapace, the League attack on the landlords also contained its own programme of rural reform. At its most extreme this was based on an alternative model of agrarian organization, that of continental peasant proprietorship, with the eventual goal of 'the division of the land among the body of the people'. For as Richard Cobden, the leader of the League, affirmed, 'If the land be held by a few nobles, the people are destitute of energy, self-respect, & intelligence – where on the other hand the soil is shared by the population at large, as in Switzerland, I found a thriving, frugal, & intelligent community.'[3] But contrary to the fears of many landlords, repeal of the Corn Laws did not act as the curtain-call to a Jacobin-style expropriation of the landed aristocracy and for the Manchester radicals, the primary means towards any such division of the land rested upon the less dramatic achievement of 'free trade in land', through the reform of the laws of entail and inheritance, especially the abolition of primogeniture.

Nevertheless, as is well-established, even this moderate aim of land reform became one of the many issues which gently petered out in the 'Age of Equipoise'. In accounting for its failure, historians have emphasized the heterogeneity of land reform as a cause, with different analyses of the problem and widely differing solutions. Where the Anti-Corn Law League with its clear goal of repeal had acted as the magnet for a widely diffused hostility to the Corn Laws, land reformers remained fragmented, seeking diverse goals, whether cottage gardens and allotments, peasant proprietorship, utopian village communities, or even land nationalization. For example, however much Chartists and Leaguers might agree on the desirability of undermining the power of the landed interest, they entirely disagreed on the best solution to the land question. On the one hand, O'Connor's Land Plan met the derision of the League as utopian while few individualistically minded Leaguers had any stomach for O'Brien – style land nationalization. On the other, Chartists saw reform of the land laws simply as the means to creating a new money-based aristocracy.[4] Other critics of the aristocracy such as William Howitt or even John Stuart Mill were unwilling to join forces with the League, however much they might stigmatize the evils of primogeniture or praise the virtues of peasant proprietorship.[5] In the longer term, as is familiar, the radical voice of the League itself fell silent, compromised by the willingness of its wealthy supporters to buy up landed estates, join hunts, acquire heraldic arms, and in general succumb to the embrace of 'feudal values'. At the same time, as Cobden often pointed out, the prosperity of trade and industry created sufficient outlet for labour and capital so that scarcity of land did not arise as an economic issue. Culturally too, as Peter Mandler has shown, popular fascination with aristocratic mansions grew into a boom in Victorian country-house visiting, itself a sign of reduced class tension.[6] In this context, the land question flared up only occasionally and the challenge to the landed monopoly proved impotent against what Cobden deemed the 'landlord spirit', whose prevalence was quite at variance with his experience of continental Europe.[7]

The failure of land reform may therefore be explained both in terms of its internal weaknesses and the strengths of the opposition to it but its failure must also be related to the nature of the critique of the landed interest voiced by the League, and the wider contextual reasons which explain the inability of the League model of rural reform to acquire a wider audience. This is an aspect of the history of the League which has recently been neglected, for historians exploring the League's impact as a self-sufficient middle-class social and cultural institution have played down the class animus which drove its leaders.[8] Cobden has typically been portrayed as the voice of calm rational criticism of the aristocracy, but beneath this veneer lay the bitter resentment of a dispossessed son of a Sussex yeoman:

> [N]o one will accuse me of favoring the landowning class – My earliest predilections were *for* the tenant & *against* the receiver of rent. I was brought up in a farm house, & the recollections of my childhood are associated with the terrors of the rent-day, & the mischief of game preserves.[9]

Among other League orators, Bright's passion derived more clearly from his religious background as a Quaker as well as from the entrepreneurial values he upheld, while William J. Fox, an erstwhile Unitarian minister, voiced perhaps the League's most powerful class invective against the aristocracy.[10] The Benthamite Thomas Perronet Thompson had been in the forefront of the attack on the landlords and the Corn Laws since the 1820s,[11] while the most aristocratic of the League's leaders by birth, C. P. Villiers, readily posed the Corn Law issue as one of justice between 'the owner of the soil and every other consumer in the community'.[12] The hitherto under-explored language of the League, therefore, embodied a powerful anti-aristocratic rhetoric creating a central element in a populist vision of the masses versus the classes which lasted into the Edwardian period.[13]

Given this undoubtedly powerful critique of the landed interest, why was the League unable to shape a more effective campaign in favour of land reform? Here the League's attack was weakened by its confused epistemological foundations. In part, it upheld a Ricardian critique of a 'parasitic' aristocracy, in which rent was a surplus drawn from the people over and above the necessary costs of production, with the interests of landlords always at variance with those of all other classes. However, as Donald Winch notes, the League was 'disinclined to use the more divisive Ricardian formulation' since this also meant that the landowners would be the only class to suffer from free trade in corn.[14] Albeit highly qualified, Ricardo's support for exceptional treatment for the land in view of the unequal tax burdens it bore also reduced his usefulness for propaganda purposes, and as a result he was rarely cited by the League. Much of the case for free trade was therefore based on the authority of

Smith, whose recognition of 'rent' as a cost of production, or in effect a reward for the services rendered by the landlord, necessarily undermined the 'parasitic' critique, although providing grounds for disputing the efficiency with which the aristocracy fulfilled its 'service' function.[15] This theoretical confusion even marred Cobden's own rhetoric, for however opposed he was to the 'landlord spirit', intellectually he remained a Smithian, holding out the possibility that 'landlord spirit' might be modified, not only by repeal but also by improved relations with the tenantry, technical change in agriculture, and political reforms which would undermine the power of the aristocracy. He consistently denied that he attacked landowners as a class, however much he pursued the injustice of the Corn Laws: 'Our lecturers shall continue to haunt them in their agricultural fastnesses, & our Circular shall proclaim their legislative robbery to the ends of the earth. There shall be no peace for the landlords but in their return to the ways of justice.'[16]

The ways of justice were defined for Cobden by the removal of the hand of the state and the re-establishment of 'market principles'. Hence, although occasionally tempted to discuss the 'Rent' question, he insisted his aim was not lower rents:

> I could never conscientiously in public or private urge the farmers to look to a reduction of rent as an accompaniment of Free-trade – I believe that with an entire removal of all 'protection' as it is called, farming would be as good an investment of capital, *at present English rents*, as any other trade, – provided only that the land was held on *mercantile principles* – viz a long lease, no restrictive covenants, & no game preserves – Get rid of *protection*, & you will bring the landlords to these mercantile principles, for they will then have no excuse for letting their land for more than it is worth, & tenants will no longer concur in mystifying themselves about elections & act-of-parliament.[17]

The essence of the League critique thus emphasized that the same rules of free exchange must be applied to the land as to other forms of property. This required the abolition of primogeniture, easing the conditions of transfer of land, and the reform of the laws of entail and strict settlement. Hence by the time of Repeal, there was a widespread expectation that former Leaguers would now campaign for free trade in land as the next logical step after free trade in corn, a case typically endorsed by *The Economist* and the newly formed *Daily News*.[18] But the radical critique, like that of the Benthamites, did not extend beyond the application of economic laws and the removal of artificial props supporting the landed interest.[19] The League model was simply one of 'free trade' between landlord and tenant.

Within the constraints of this radical critique, the Anti-Corn Law League sought by various strategies to undermine what it saw as the legal privileges of the aristocracy. For example, in a campaign, whose impetus was soon undermined by Peel's re-introduction of income tax, it devoted considerable energy to investigating the issue of land taxation, convinced of the existence of what it called the 'Land Tax Fraud'. This was first exposed by Adam Scott in his *Plea for the Total and Immediate Repeal of the Corn Laws* (1842). Cobden roundly pronounced in the House of Commons that 'the people were taxed in order to exempt the landowners', and the League's case centred on the claim that while rents had risen some 2000 per cent, land was still taxed on a historic valuation from the 1690s. One League lecturer calculated that on the basis of rental increases, the land tax should in 1842 have produced annually £11,400,000 as opposed to the £1.4 million it had raised in 1841.[20] The League set its lawyers to work, publishing *The Constitutional Right to a Revision of the Land Tax* in 1842, but this search for historic injustice was rarely highlighted subsequently in a campaign focused clearly on the present evils of the 'Bread Tax'.[21] Nevertheless, Cobden himself sometimes stressed what would come to be called the 'unearned increment', pointing out that land values increased 'without any help from the owners' while taxation of land was by no means commensurate with the increase in value.[22] Here the League's case, while little developed in the 1850s and 1860s, fed naturally into the ideas of Henry George, whereas in the People's Budget Lloyd George, Offer has claimed, borrowed not only Cobden's terms but also 'acted out Cobden's fantasies'.[23]

In fact, raising the issue of land taxation was a response to the landlords' attempts to resist repeal on the grounds of the peculiar burdens on landed property and formed part of the League's wider campaign to undermine the case that such burdens on land justified the retention of the Corn Laws. Its activists R. H. Greg and Henry Ashworth were deputed to give evidence to the 1846 select committee, seeking to show that personal (including manufacturing) property bore burdens at least as high – if not higher-than those on land.[24] Typically too Archibald Prentice, the later chronicler of the League, rejected the special burdens plea on the grounds that the land tax was not 'an exclusive burthen requiring an equivalent, but a commutation, which, in common justice, ought to have advanced with the advance of the rent of land, and the increase of other public burthens'.[25]

However there were clear limits to the League campaign against the landlords, for arguably it sought more to improve agrarian practice than to attack the structure of landed society. It is evident that the League fought shy of directly taking up contentious issues such as rent or primogeniture, although it was ready occasionally to evoke the events of 1830 as a warning of potential rural revolution.[26] But in general its rural campaigns were inspired by the propagandist desire to emphasize aristocratic mismanagement of the land, for example by its use of journalists to investigate rural conditions. The League also did much to make known what it considered good practice on the part of landlords, with the improving efforts of League-supporting aristocrats such as Ducie, Radnor, and Kinnaird being publicized, and the East Lothian example of the farmer George Hope being given special emphasis. In addition, the League built up an important range of contacts with improving farmers, for example Charles Lattimore, pointing out his eviction by his landlord.[27] By this emphasis on the improving landlord and the progressive tenant, the League sought to undermine the argument that the Corn Laws were essential to agrarian productivity; more polemically it claimed that the League itself had 'conferred the greatest benefit upon the Country, and in nothing more so than in the Stimulus they have supplied to improving the cultivation of Land'.[28]

Where however the League failed was in detaching the farmers from their allegiance to an 'oppressive' landlord class. This became Cobden's central goal in 1843, misapprehending the degree of support he could expect in the countryside, and misled by the view that the 'rational' case for progressive agriculture on the basis of free trade would win over the English tenantry as it showed some evidence of doing in Scotland. In fact, Cobden's campaign proved counter-productive as he unleashed the Anti-League and intensified class warfare in rural England.[29] Even so, Cobden continued to believe that tenant farmers were educable as to their own interests, and in late 1845 put much energy into publicizing the agrarian experts Trimmer and Morton's findings demonstrating that '"protection" is merely a system of reciprocal robbery for the farmers'.[30] Arguably, the League's attempt to show that the Corn Laws were unnecessary for agricultural prosperity together with the 'class warfare' it had unleashed in the countryside were powerful educative forces on the thinking of Sir Robert Peel on the Repeal issue.[31] Nevertheless, when those laws were repealed in 1846 the question for the future was whether repeal might prove, as many Protectionists purported to fear, 'the first step to an agrarian revolution', with the application of Jacobin-style policies to the English landed interest.[32]

The Manchester School and the English peasantry

If the attack on 'landlordism' was central to the Anti-Corn Law League, what became of the League's rural radicalism after 1846? In part, it remained an element in various radical campaigns designed to improve the position of the English tenantry – that aimed at compensation for tenants' improvements for example – although in Scotland there was a far more vigorous movement for farmer's rights including the abolition of the Game Laws.[33] Cobden, while declining to take the lead on the reform of the Scottish law of entail,[34] was prepared to take up the issue of malt tax repeal as a boon to farmers, as part of a general readjustment of taxation and reduction of government expenditure. In addition, while the protectionist threat remained a live one, the 'Manchester School', in countering it, prepared to maintain and even extend its attack on landlordism. Girding his loins to visit the protectionist stronghold of Buckinghamshire, Cobden wrote to his Lincolnshire friend John Norton: 'Our only way of putting an end to this controversy is by going directly to the sore place, and attacking rent – I never took that line in the anti corn law agitation, but shall do so from henceforth – The landlords & farmers must be separated from each other –... [I] shall unmask landlordism, both here & in Ireland, without mercy'.[35] This renewed attack on the aristocracy proved short-lived, however, and as the protectionist revival ebbed away, the Manchester radicals, especially Cobden, devoted their main efforts to the freehold land societies spawned by the League but whose aim was more to break the political power of the aristocracy in the counties, and not the subdivision of Britain into peasant holdings.[36]

Nevertheless, it seems clear that Cobden's own prescriptions for the land went well beyond the idea of tenant farmers renting large farms from improving landlords, and did emphatically embrace the radical vision which emphasized the desirability of structural reform in English agriculture and the creation of a multiplicity of peasant proprietors in place of a small group of aristocratic owners.[37] For there is no doubt that Cobden wished to address what a growing number of radicals saw as the central anomaly of British history, the disappearance of the peasant proprietor, and his replacement by the combination of rent-receiving landowners, 'capitalist' tenant farmers, and 'proletarian' agricultural labourers. Cobden saw this change as responsible for the decline in public spirit, 'for we shall find that in all ages and countries the moral and political status of the people depends more on the distribution of landed property than any other cause'.[38] On the basis of the 1861 census, Cobden calculated that England and Wales comprised 15,100 landed proprietors, 220,000 tenant farmers, and 1,100,000 agricultural labourers.[39] His own origins, as we have already seen, predisposed him to this model, and he succumbed in part to the radical myth of the English peasantry dispossessed by ruthless landowners during the Napoleonic Wars. His native prejudices were strengthened by travel abroad in the 1830s and early 1840s. Above all, his post-Repeal European tour of 1846–47 reinforced Cobden in his belief that subdivision of the land was crucial to peaceful political and social progress, a view he hoped to elaborate in an unwritten study of the condition of Europe *c.* 1846/47.[40] But such a study, with Cobden's encouragement, was published by Joseph Kay, brother of the educationalist Kay-Shuttleworth, and the son of a Lancashire cotton merchant.[41] Kay's book coincided remarkably closely with Cobden's own views and he went on to become a leading advocate of free trade in land, although his views only made a real mark in the 1870s.

The continental model of peasant proprietorship was one whose virtues the radicals – not least Cobden – for the most part continued to uphold. In 1848, Cobden wrote to the phrenologist George Combe:

> I have not had good opportunities of *seeing* the condition of the small proprietors in France – but I have talked a good deal with very able men about it, & never met with any body whose opinion was worth having who did not express a favorable view of the present division of landed property in France, as compared to the state in which it was prior to the first revolution & in which it is in England now – For myself I must confess that all my sympathies are in favor of the subdivision of property – The possession of a piece of land has a tendency to create self-respect, prudence, & self-control – & these are at the root of all wisdom & virtue.[42]

Cobden found support for his views in the works of Hippolyte Passy, and later in the comprehensive surveys of Léoncé de Lavergne, who, while prepared to admit some weaknesses in the French system of *morcellement,* attributed French inferiority to English agriculture not to small French farms but to the enduring legacy of 22 years of warfare against Britain.[43] As Britain succumbed to successive invasion scares, Cobden attributed to the subdivision of land the pacific tendencies of the French people, keen to avoid both the expense and disruption which war caused; in part, his tract *1793 and 1853* (1853) was designed to make the British public 'acquainted with the state of the French people, the division of land, the absence of privileges, equality of churches &c, & if it make their mouths water, it will be far better than the contempt & hatred which are now being fostered against their neighbours'.[44] As a result, in early 1853, he was attacked in *The Times* for praising the subdivision of estates in France, and the controversy he had provoked[45] obliged him to elaborate his position, for if peasant proprietorship were desirable, how did he propose to achieve in England the subdivision of land which in France had been achieved by revolution? Here the disparity between ends and means became apparent, for while upholding the desirability of small farms, Cobden disowned compulsion: 'I am for *freedom*, & not for the French law. – I go with Adam Smith & Stuart Mill, with however a strong conviction that the more landed property can be diffused amongst the people without injuring Economical laws (which are moral laws) the better for the interests of *all*.'[46]

What solution did the political economy of Smith and Mill offer? Smith had condemned primogeniture and approved small farms (without defining small), while Mill's views included approval of the Chartist settlement at Rickmansworth, advocacy of peasant proprietorship, especially in Ireland, but only in 1869, when he became the prime mover in the Land Tenure Reform Association, did Mill become an advocate of more interventionist policies.[47] From this Cobden was left to contemplate what he saw as the inevitable failure in an unreformed parliament of the attack on primogeniture which had been taken up by Locke King in the House of Commons, although he had slightly greater hopes that conditions for land sale might be improved in England.

The radical analysis of the land question was further complicated by the condition of rural Ireland. From the time of his first tract, *England, Ireland and America* (1835), Cobden was convinced that any solution to the land question had to begin in Ireland. For 'landlordism' was not a uniform British problem but assumed far greater urgency as a problem of Irish rural society. Interestingly therefore it was the 'Condition of Ireland' which in many ways preoccupied the Manchester School after Corn Law repeal; this was especially true of John Bright, who undertook a tour of Ireland in 1849 and called for a new League against the 'wide and silent cruelty' of a 'demoralising' landlordism.[48] Yet, while Cobden was not ready to rise to the call for a new anti-landlord League, he did frequently urge the importance of land reform in Ireland and was keen to ally the Manchester School with the Irish Tenant Right League. As a result, both Cobden and Bright took a strong interest in the fortunes of the Irish Freehold Land Society set up in 1850, and gave support to the efforts of the Irish Tenant Right League both in parliament and in Ireland. This alliance in some ways stemmed naturally from the Anti-Corn Law League, whose ranks had included the Irish tenant right campaigner Sharman Crawford, while urban merchants such as the Quaker Jonathan Pim were keen to promote free trade in land in Ireland, with the support of economists such as Neilson Hancock.[49] Nevertheless, the Irish land reform movement soon ran into the sands of English obstruction, while the growing division among the Irish land reformers themselves removed the possibility of legislative action. Reform of the land laws in England proved equally problematic, as Liberals such as Philip Pusey found, so that by 1853, despite the occasional attempts to portray Cobden as the advocate of the forcible break-up of landed estates, fears that the repeal of the Corn Laws would lead to agrarian revolution in England had all but disappeared.

The land question and the aristocracy

Given therefore the failure of land reform in Ireland and the constraints of 'economical laws' in England, land reform was effectively removed from the radical agenda. For the Manchester School, the priority became financial and parliamentary reform to undermine the power of the aristocracy, which as Cobden realized was not simply based on landownership but on the entwinement of landowners and the state. Among other things, this campaign aimed to cut down government expenditure, a good deal of which the radicals believed simply went into the pockets of the aristocracy. Much of this campaigning was designed to mobilize the forces of urban liberalism but the radicals also sought persistently to reduce the power of the landowners in ways they believed would benefit the distinctive interests of rural society. As we have seen, this was the primary purpose of the freehold land societies, but Cobden was also determined to separate landlords and farmers, not least by promoting the abolition of the malt tax. In this way, he aimed to show that retrenchment would benefit farmers directly while simultaneously weaning them away from Tory attempts to revive Protectionism. He sought therefore to work with those like Charles Lattimore who advocated the independent interests of the farmers, whether through the Farmers' Club, the *Mark Lane Express*, or the Total Repeal Malt Tax Association. Yet the move against the Malt Tax faltered in 1849–50, and although Cobden returned to the issue in 1864, even suggesting an Anti-Malt Tax League, his advocacy of this cause ultimately came to little.[50]

In any case, arguably much more congenial to Cobden in these immediate post-Repeal years was the campaign for the ballot.[51] For he saw the ballot, perhaps even more than the freehold land societies, as a blow to aristocratic power, including of course the political direction of the tenant farmers. Hence he urged his agricultural ally Lattimore that it was 'the vital question for the counties – no man should be deemed worth fighting for as a liberal who is not for the ballot'. Yet on this issue, as with the abolition of primogeniture, Cobden found that the very aristocratic power he hoped to undermine was, through its parliamentary dominance, sufficient to prevent the reform he sought.

Thirdly, among the campaigns which for Cobden had a particular rural resonance was that for the repeal of the Taxes on Knowledge, a campaign which had successfully brought together former Chartists and anti-Corn Law Leaguers under the leadership of Thomas Milner Gibson. While much of this movement was metropolitan in emphasis, for Cobden the leading issue was the diffusion of knowledge in rural England, knowledge which he believed was crucial for the emancipation of the agricultural labourer. His return to his native Sussex in 1850 had alerted Cobden to conditions of rural society barely changed since 1815. Thus he wrote to Brougham about 'the mental inaccessibility and dullness of the laboring agriculturalists':

> I have frequently asked myself, whilst perambulating the Duke of Richmond's villages, – in what do these peasants differ from their Saxon forefathers? – The range of their ideas is about the same; bounded by their daily occupations, which have not much varied in a thousand years. – Their knowledge of the world does not extend much beyond their own parish. – No light penetrates their minds beyond their hamlets.[52]

The repeal of the taxes on knowledge facilitating the sale of cheap newspapers came therefore to have crucial importance for Cobden as the instrument of rural enlightenment and in time emancipation from aristocratic mental thrall.

Nevertheless, Cobden remained well aware that issues such as the malt tax, ballot, and newspapers did not affect the underlying question which his removal back to the Sussex countryside made insistent – that of the landless condition of the rural labourers and the concentration of land ownership. He became fond of taking visitors to the top of the Sussex Downs and displaying vast territories owned by three peers – 'I see', he wrote, 'the evils of the system perhaps more closely from living here at the junction of the properties of three noblemen on whose land I could ride from the sea to Surrey right across Sussex'.[53] As the Crimean

War began, Cobden contemplated the similarity of conditions in Russia and England, believing that in both countries changes in the laws of succession would effect fundamental changes in social organization; in private, he claimed Russian serfs were better off than Sussex peasants.[54] But while the forces of English radicalism became largely fixated with war, the Eastern Question, and the constitution, Cobden remained keenly exercised by rural England, concerned with the impact of the War on prices and rural conditions, but also seeking to engage with the larger issue of ownership. As he wrote to W. W. Mitchell editor of the *West Sussex Gazette*:

> It [the land question] requires delicate handling, but must be dealt with.– The danger is, with ignorant people, of encouraging the notion of Communism, when one speaks of the division of landed property [.] The question must be discussed on *Economical* grounds, leaving aside the political tendencies of primogeniture &c.– The subject is indissolubly bound up with the condition of the rural population [.] You cannot ameliorate the fate of our peasantry so long as they are divorced from the ownership of the land.[55]

Yet the ability to organize a campaign around this issue still eluded Cobden. Former allies in the anti-Corn Law cause such as Parkes warned him that the land was not a question amenable to extra-parliamentary pressure, and was one on which Liberals themselves were too divided for effective action.[56] Occasional radical voices were heard, especially that of James Beal, the metropolitan radical auctioneer, who argued in 1855 that primogeniture was an 'infinitely greater evil than a Corn-law', while some provincial radicals urged Cobden to take up a League-style campaign.[57] Nevertheless, even Cobden himself by the later 1850s seemed more inclined to promote emigration as the most immediate way for the rural poor to improve their condition, an interest which brought him into regular contact with the agrarian reformer James Caird, who also took an interest in the opening up of the American prairies.[58]

Re-opening the land question in the 1860s

British radicalism as a whole was to pay little attention to the land question after 1856 but it was testimony to the persistence of Cobden's rural ideas that he returned to this issue in the 1860s, seeking for the first time to create an effective extra-parliamentary campaign for 'free trade in land'. Michael Thompson has suggested that Cobden's recurrence to land reform in 1864 may be seen simply as an opportunistic gesture, provoked by the suggestion of J. T. Delane, editor of the *Times*, that he had favoured the break-up of large estates in his Rochdale speech of 1863.[59] Nevertheless, there are grounds for thinking that a wider, more principled explanation is possible. Firstly, Cobden's own interest in the land question had been sharpened by the course of the American Civil War, and it was now the condition of the American South and what he saw as aristocratic sympathy with the slave-owning class which revived Cobden's belief that the land question had to be tackled. Secondly, Cobden remained very much alive to the unsolved problem of Ireland, and while he realized the political impossibility of the compulsory break-up of great estates in Ireland, in theory he saw this as unobjectionable and indeed the best solution.[60] Thirdly, Cobden was aware that land reform remained an issue of considerable interest to many groups of radicals. Significantly, when Bright became MP for Birmingham in 1859, he found an audience keener than that in Manchester to support land reform, an issue which Joseph Chamberlain himself would soon take up.[61] The coming Liberal W. E. Forster had also shown a growing interest in Bright's old issue, the game laws, seeking, unsuccessfully, to set up a select committee in 1863.[62] There was also a continuing interest in the Land Question among London's radical artisans and the secularist movement, with George Drysdale, better known as the prophet of sexual licence, being also an exponent of the land question (on Cobdenite lines).[63] Fourthly, Cobden himself was in close touch with a new generation of liberals whom he hoped would take up the unfinished business of the Anti-Corn Law League, and educate public opinion as to the dangers of the English land system. They included the future founder of the Cobden Club, Thomas B. Potter, as well as Cobden's friend, William Hargreaves, a man who cherished with the ardour of the League's heyday the vision of aristocratic mansions turned into hotels for the masses.[64] Above all, Cobden was close to the university liberal J. Thorold Rogers, a relative by marriage. Rogers, as Tony Taylor explores later in this volume, was a pioneer of economic history whose researches had provided the empirical foundation for the view that the territorial aristocracy had usurped the lands of the English yeomanry. Rogers fully identified with the Cobdenite case for free trade in land as the means to the break-up of large estates and the only solution to rural poverty.[65]

This wider background of a revived interest in land reform provides the context in which Cobden famously urged in 1864 the creation of 'a League for free trade in Land'.[66] Nevertheless, the aim of any such League was to be confined to creating an opinion in favour of reform rather than to put forward any specific remedy. For, as Cobden warned,

'You must be very careful in dealing with this question not to shock & frighten people with its political aspect, because *that* in the eyes of comfortable & substantial people looks like revolution. – You must keep as much as possible to the politico-economical view.'[67] Cobden's aim was simply to arouse middle-class opinion: 'What we want is a clearer public opinion as to the mischiefs & *dangers* of the present system. – Depend on it, there is danger in a course of policy which tends to throw the land of a country into fewer & fewer hands.'[68] The actual reforms he had in mind still extended to no more than 'dividing real estate between all the children equally in the case of intestacy, instead of as at present giving it to the eldest heir male', the motion on which Locke King had been regularly and decisively defeated.

The 'Free Trade in Land' league remained a Cobdenite vision, placed temptingly before the coming generation of Liberals, but soon obscured by the shadow of parliamentary reform. In 1865 as in 1848 and, as again in the 1880s, parliamentary reform came to be seen as the precondition for successful land reform. To some extent this proved true and, as is well-established, the Second Reform Act did provide the impetus for the partial fulfilment of Cobden's 'League'. This took two forms. First, the Land Tenure Reform Association, influenced largely by J. S. Mill, was explicitly Cobdenite in that invitations to its inaugural conference quoted Cobden on the need for a 'League for Free Trade in Land', although the Association's subsequent endorsement of taxing the unearned increment was repudiated by many of those who considered themselves orthodox Cobdenites.[69] Second, however, the more orthodox radicals ranged in the Cobden Club sought to revitalize public opinion on the land question with a series of influential publications as well as the endorsement of economists such as Henry Fawcett.[70] Third, as Matthew Cragoe suggests later in this volume, the 1868 election in Wales seemed to furnish a new raft of well-documented cases of landlords evicting tenants for political reasons – cases which Welsh Liberal MPs brought before both parliament and the court of public opinion in a variety of guises.[71]

The early 1870s were therefore to see a widespread revival of interest in the land question, with Chamberlain claiming that had Gladstone taken up Bright and Cobden's ideas on land tenure reform, the Liberals would have won the 1874 election.[72] Most segments of opinion on this issue worked broadly within the parameters of free trade in land, with even plebeian radicals, guided by Bright, for the most part, adopting this goal.[73] In many ways therefore it was the Manchester School attack on the landlords which lent the greatest continuity to land reform between the 1840s and the 1870s, but the later generation of radicals inspired by Mill was to prove no more able to overcome the obstacles to land reform which had frustrated the campaign which Cobden and Bright had somewhat sporadically attempted to mobilize.

Notes

1. See below, chs 9–11.
2. G. R. Porter to Cobden, 22 December 1845, Cobden Papers, West Sussex Record Office [hereafter CP] 1, fo. 114; F. M. L. Thompson, *English Landed Society in the Nineteenth Century* (London, 1963), p. 283.
3. Cobden to John Roberton, 6 June 1851, British Library [hereafter BL], Add. MS 43655 fos. 261–3.
4. See above, ch. 3.
5. J. Hampden Jnr [W. Howitt], *The Aristocracy of England: A History for the People* (London, 1846); cf. D. Martin, 'Land Reform', in P. Hollis (ed.), *Pressure from Without in Early Victorian England* (London, 1973), pp. 140–1, 146; idem, *John Stuart Mill and the Land Question* (Hull, 1981).
6. P. Mandler, *The Fall and Rise of the Stately Home* (New Haven, 1997), pp. 51–64.
7. Cobden to J. E. T. Rogers, 15 October 1864, Rogers Papers, Bodleian Library, Oxford; Cobden to Bright, 30 March 1864, BL Add. MS 43652 fos. 166–9.
8. See especially P. Pickering and A. Tyrrell, *The People's Bread: A History of the Anti-Corn Law League* (Leicester, 2000).
9. Cobden to John Morton, 4 October 1845, Morton Papers, Gloucestershire Archives, D1021 4/12.
10. For Fox's 'blister to the aristocracy', see R. Garnett, *The Life of W. J. Fox, Teacher and Social Reformer, 1786–1864* (London, 1910), pp. 259–61; for typical speeches, see *The League*, 27 January, 9 March and 10 August 1844.
11. M. E. Turner, *Independent Radicalism in Early Victorian Britain* (Westport: CT, 2004), esp. pp. 27–73.
12. 'A Member of the Cobden Club', *The Free Trade Speeches of the Rt Hon. Charles Pelham Villiers* (London, 1883), ii, p. 309.
13. For the persistence of anti-aristocratic rhetoric see A. Taylor, *Lords of Misrule: Hostility to Aristocracy in Late Nineteenth- and Early Twentieth-Century Britain* (Basingstoke, 2004).
14. D. Winch, *Riches and Poverty: An Intellectual History of Political Economy in Britain, 1750–1834* (Cambridge, 1996), p. 353.
15. M. Blaug, *Ricardian Economics* (New Haven, 1958), pp. 202–9; D. Winch, 'Between Feudalists and Communists: Louis Mallet and the Cobden Creed', in A. Howe and S. Morgan (eds), *Rethinking Nineteenth-Century Liberalism: Richard Cobden Bicentenary Essays* (Aldershot, 2006), pp. 247–63.
16. Cobden to C. P. Villiers, 4 February 1840, A. Howe (ed.), *The Letters of Richard Cobden Volume One 1815–1847* (Oxford, 2007), p. 179.
17. Cobden to Morton, 4 October 1845, above note 9.
18. F. M. L. Thompson, 'Changing Perceptions of Land Tenure in Britain, 1750–1914', in D. Winch and P. K. O'Brien (eds), *The Political Economy of British*

Historical Experience, 1688–1914 (Oxford, 2002), p. 130, n. 21; *Daily News*, 16 March 1846, p. 6 and 6 November 1846, p. 2.

19. A. Offer, *Property and Politics, 1870–1914* (Cambridge, 1981), pp. 23–34; J. E. T. Rogers, *Cobden and Modern Political Opinion* (London, 1873), ch. 3.
20. *Hansard*, 3rd ser., 61 (14 March 1842), cols. 558–63; A. Prentice, *History of the Anti-Corn Law League* (London, 1853), i, pp. 264–7. See also Howe, *Letters of Richard Cobden*, pp. 250–1.
21. Cf. R. Hilditch [a Manchester barrister], *Aristocratic Taxation: Its Present State, Origin, and Progress, with Proposals for Reform* (London, 1842).
22. See, for example, Cobden's Covent Garden speech, 17 December 1845: *Speeches*, p. 177.
23. Offer, *Property and Politics*, p. 363.
24. Select Committee of House of Lords on Burdens Affecting Real Property, Parl. Papers 1846, VI, qq. 3743–4156 (Ashworth), qq. 4192–545, 7463–619; R. Boyson, *The Ashworth Cotton Enterprise* (Oxford, 1970), p. 208. Cobden's election agent Henry Coppock also gave evidence as town clerk of Stockport.
25. *League*, i, p. 420.
26. 'The Landowners in Danger', *Anti-Bread Tax Circular*, 22 September 1842.
27. See A. Kadish (ed.), *The Corn Laws* (London, 1996), i, esp. pp. xxxix–xlv, vi.
28. *Burdens Affecting Real Property*, Parl. Papers 1846, VI, Greg, q. 4356. For the League's comparable efforts to stir up the Game Law question, see C. Kirby, 'The Attack on the English Game Laws in the Forties', *Journal of Modern History*, 4 (1932), 18–37.
29. See Howe, *Letters of Richard Cobden*, pp. xlvii–xlix and passim.
30. To Morton, 1 October 1845: *Letters*, pp. 395–6.
31. It was Cobden's speech (13 March 1845) on the impact of protection on the farmers and labourers which Peel famously asked Sidney Herbert to answer, 'for I cannot': J. Morley, *The Life of Richard Cobden* (London, 1881), i, p. 318.
32. [J. W. Croker], 'Agriculture – France – Division of Properties', *Quarterly Review*, 79 (December 1846), 237.
33. I. G. C. Hutchison, *A Political History of Scotland, 1832–1914* (Edinburgh, 1986), pp. 87, 104–8.
34. Cobden to David Monro, 4 January 1848, NAS GD71/334.
35. 2 January 1850 (copy), CP 43. Cobden's speech produced a strong counter-attack, esp. from his old antagonist George Game Day: see for example *North Wales Chronicle*, 29 January 1850, p. 4; *Derby Mercury*, 30 January 1850, p. 3; *Trewman's Exeter Flying Post*, 31 January 1850, p. 4; *Ipswich Journal*, 2 Februay 1850, p. 3.
36. See esp. F. M. L. Thompson, 'Cobden, Free Trade in Land, and the Road to the Abbey National' in Howe and Morgan, *Liberalism*, pp. 68–79.
37. Cf. C. Dewey, 'The Rehabilitation of the Peasant Proprietor in English Political Economy', *History of Political Economy*, 6 (1974), 17–47, esp. 19–21.
38. To J. Waylen, 24 January 1855 (copy), CP 108.
39. 'R. S. T.', *Morning Star*, 22 January 1864, repr. *Times*, 7 January 1873, p. 10.
40. M. Taylor (ed.), *The European Diaries of Richard Cobden, 1846–49* (Aldershot, 1994), p. 25.

41. *The Social Condition and Education of the People in England and Europe: Shewing the Results of the Primary Schools, and of the Division of Landed Property, in Foreign Countries* (London, 1850).
42. 29 February 1848: BL Add. MS 43660 fos. 103–106; Morley, *Cobden* ii, p. 17.
43. H. Passy, *On large and Small Farms, and their Influence on the Social Economy: Including a View of the Progress of the Division of the Soil in France since 1815* (London, 1848). De Lavergne's works included *Essai sur L'économie de l'Angleterre, de l'Ecosse et de l'Irlande* (Paris, 1854), and *L'Economie Rurale depuis 1789* (Paris, 1860).
44. Cobden to Parkes, 31 January 1853, Parkes Papers, University College London.
45. 'France according to Mr Cobden' (letter): *Times*, 2 February 1853, p. 3.
46. Cobden to Parkes, 8 February 1853, Parkes Papers, University College London.
47. See especially Martin, 'Land Reform' and *John Stuart Mill.*
48. Bright to Cobden, Add MS.43383 fos 207–10, 25 September 1851. G. M. Trevelyan, *The Life of John Bright* (London, 1913), p. 164.
49. *Anti-Bread Tax Circular*, 24 January 1843; R. D. Collison Black, *Economic Thought and the Irish Question, 1817–1870* (Cambridge, 1960), pp. 33–44.
50. See Cobden to E. T. Simpson, 5 February 1864, widely reported in the press, for example *Leeds Mercury*, 3 March 1864, p. 4.
51. B. Kinzer, 'The Failure of "Pressure from Without": Richard Cobden, the Ballot Society, and the Coming of the Ballot Act in England', *Canadian Journal of History*, 13 (1978), 399–422; idem, *The Ballot Question in Nineteenth-Century English Politics* (New York, 1982).
52. 27 October 1852, Brougham Papers, 833, University College London.
53. To J. O. Halliwell, 12 December 1863, Halliwell-Phillipps Papers, Edinburgh University Library, L.O.A.86/55.
54. M. Taylor, *The Decline of British Radicalism, 1847–1860* (Oxford, 1995), p. 230; Cobden to W. W. Mitchell, 13 December 1855, West Sussex Record Office (WSRO), Add. MS 13886/23.
55. 11 May 1855, WSRO, Add MS 13886/21.
56. Parkes to Cobden, 28 January, 4 February 1853, CP 11; 9 February 1853, Parkes Papers, University College London.
57. Beal, *Free Trade in Land*, p. 64. John Middleton of Hull, inviting Cobden to speak on secular education, also urged him to take up free trade in land as he had done in corn: Lancashire Public School Association Archives, M136/2/3/2354: Manchester Archives and Local Studies (5 November 1850).
58. Cobden to Caird, 23 September 1858, CP 54, fos. 5–8 (copy), cf. Caird, *Prairie Farming in America* (London, 1859). Cobden's interest had been prompted by his misguided investments in the Illinois Railway.
59. Thompson, 'Cobden', esp. pp. 69–70.
60. Cobden to Hargeaves, 21 February 1864, Add MS. 43655, fos. 347–50.
61. J. E. T. Rogers (ed.), *Speeches by John Bright* (London, 1869), pp. 445–58. Chamberlain added 'free land' to the programme of the National Education League in 1872: P. Marsh, *Joseph Chamberlain* (New Haven, 1994), p. 53.
62. *Hansard*, 3rd ser., 169 (3 March 1863), cols 1544ff.
63. 'G. R.', *The Land Question* (London, 1863). In this work (p. 50) Drysdale held the abolition of primogeniture and entail to be a far more important

application of the 'beneficent principle of Free Trade' than even the abolition of the Corn Laws.

64. Cobden warned the editor of the *Morning Star* that Hargreaves 'has such a righteous indignation against the landed system of this Country that he is not to be trusted to write on it': to Samuel Lucas, 12 January 1864, WSRO CP 135.
65. See ch. 8, below.
66. Speech at Rochdale, 23 November 1864: J. Bright and J. E. T. Rogers (eds), *Speeches by Richard Cobden* (London, 1878), pp. 479–96, at 493.
67. Cobden to Lucas, 12 January 1864 (copy), WSRO CP 135.
68. To Halliwell, 12 December 1863, see above, note 53.
69. See esp. Martin, *Mill*, and 'Land Reform and Class Conflict in Victorian Britain' in H. Perkin (ed.), *The Structured Crowd* (Hassocks, 1981), pp. 100–35; M. Finn, *After Chartism* (Cambridge, 1993), pp. 267–71; Winch, 'Between Feudalists and Communists'.
70. A. Howe, *Free Trade and Liberal England, 1846–1946* (Oxford, 1997), pp. 124, 128.
71. See below, pp. 95, 100–2.
72. R. Quinault, 'John Bright and Joseph Chamberlain', *Historical Journal*, 28 (1985), 632.
73. E. Biagini, *Liberty, Retrenchment and Reform* (Cambridge, 1992), p. 190.

5

'A Contemptible Mimic of the Irish': The Land Question in Victorian Wales

Matthew Cragoe

Introduction

The 'Welsh Land Question' became an important factor in British politics in the last 20 years of the nineteenth century.[1] The campaign orchestrated by the young Tom Ellis, Liberal MP for Merioneth – often designated 'the Member for Wales' by his many admirers – to secure for Wales the famous 'three Fs' granted to Ireland in 1881 – Fair rents, Fixity of tenure and Free sale – has an established place in the history books. Yet Ellis's activities represented the culmination of a much longer agitation by Welsh radicals, and in this chapter, the ways in which the land question came to be politicized in Wales will be explored. In particular, the radicals' frequent invocation of the Irish experience as a way of explaining what was going in the Welsh countryside will be examined. For all that the parallel outraged landowners of all political persuasions – one Gladstonian supporter condemned the Welsh radicals' land campaign as 'a contemptible mimic of the Irish... like a poor travesty of a tragedy'[2] – its persistent use is suggestive.

The chapter begins by attempting to establish the true nature of conditions in the Welsh countryside and offering a critical comparison with the situation in Ireland. In the second section, attention turns to the origins and development of the Welsh land question, and the ways it was agitated in the second half of the nineteenth century. As will become clear, there was a marked difference between the real difficulties which beset the relationship between landlord and tenant in Wales and the critique offered by Welsh radical MPs such as Ellis.

Landlord and tenant in the Welsh countryside

The Welsh countryside was – and is – a place of contrasting landscapes and agricultural opportunities. On the higher ground in the west and north of the country, small-holding tenant farmers on annual leases scraped a precarious livelihood from the thin soil; in the lowland vales, by contrast, prosperous tenants on large holdings were able to experiment with advanced agricultural techniques, especially in Glamorganshire, where their investment was protected by a well-established custom of tenant right.[3] Wales, like Scotland, had not one, but several farming systems. However, it was with Ireland that Welsh radicals sought to compare the principality, and it is to the validity of that comparison that this section will be devoted.[4]

The landholding structure of the two countries was similar. In Wales, some 60 per cent of the land was owned in estates of over 1,000 acres by 571 families in 1873; in Ireland, half the land was held in similar estates belonging to approximately 750 families.[5] The role of the landowners in local society, however, was very different. Landlord absenteeism, for example, was a particular problem of the Irish countryside: half of all landowners were said to live away from their estates in the first half of the nineteenth century.[6] As Cormac Ó'Gráda has remarked, 'had *phytophthora infestans* destroyed landlords instead of potatoes in 1845, agricultural output [in Ireland] would have been only marginally affected'.[7] Levels of absenteeism undoubtedly declined after the Famine, the Encumbered Estates Act of 1849 facilitating the transfer of land into new hands: one survey of 1870 suggested that only 24 per cent of estates were then affected.[8] Nevertheless, the consequence of the pre-Famine absences was that the Ireland could not match the long habits of mutuality that marked relations between the resident landlord and his tenantry on Welsh estates.[9] During the sittings of the Royal Commission on Land in Wales and Monmouthshire in the 1890s, numerous instances of tenants having been associated with the same farm for several hundred years were brought forward – one witness found a tenant whose family had been on the same farm for 500 years![10] The Commission Report – a document not famous for its bias towards the landlords – accepted that tenancies were essentially hereditary and added: 'There is certainly a much larger number of tenants who can boast of an uninterrupted family connection with the same holdings extended over several centuries than there is of estate owners or of occupying freeholders whose families have succeeded each other in the ownership of their respective properties for an equal period'.[11] There were undoubtedly other cultural forces pushing landlord and tenant apart in Wales, as will be discussed below, but Welsh landowners generally spent a significant proportion of their time on their estates.

They also managed the business of letting out their farms differently. In the principality, land was let directly to the tenants of the estate. Welsh farm sizes were small, to be sure, averaging only 47 acres in 1875, a legacy of the system of partible inheritance that prevailed in the principality before the Tudor period.[12] In Ireland, however, a quite different system was in operation: landowners let their land in large holdings to middlemen who then sublet it, often in ruinously small holdings. The famous analysis of the Trinity College Estate in 1843 bears repeating: there were 12,529 tenants on the estate, yet only 1 per cent paid rents directly to the estate; 45 per cent were sub-tenants to the 1 per cent, and a further 52 per cent sub-tenants to the 45 per cent![13] The whole precarious edifice, facilitated by long leases to middlemen, meant it was difficult to rationalize and modernize agriculture even where landowners had the will to do so.[14] Wales never experienced the problem of middlemen and its concomitant of extensive sub-division; the feeling of identity between landowners, their tenants and the estate was much closer as a result.[15]

Insecurity of tenure was a complaint made by politicians in both countries: however, evidence suggests that Wales emerges well from the comparison. David Howell has dismissed as 'a gross exaggeration' the radical claim that tenants were too worried by the threat of insecure tenure to invest in their holdings.[16] Evidence is plentiful that even after the widespread switch to annual tenancies in the early nineteenth century, tenants in Wales enjoyed *de facto* security of tenure. Indeed by the end of the century, it was considered by one prominent commentator that changes of tenancy – the best evidence of insecure tenancy – were far more frequent in England than they were in Wales.[17]

In Ireland, modern scholarship has offered reassurance that tenants there also enjoyed greater levels of security than was once allowed. Paul Bew and William E. Vaughan, for example, have both disputed the extent of tenants' insecurity, pointing out that levels of eviction were no different in Ireland from those anywhere else in the United Kingdom in normal years.[18] Yet the situation of the tenant remained far more precarious in Ireland than it did in Wales. Welsh landowners, for example, seem largely to have resisted the urge to amalgamate smaller holdings (thereby dispossessing incumbent tenants) in order to create the larger units beloved of high farming advocates;[19] in Ireland, by contrast, the period around the Famine witnessed a major upheaval in land-distribution as landlords took the opportunity to amalgamate holdings and create larger, viable farms.[20] Larger holdings of 15 acres and more represented one-third of the total in 1845; by 1851, they represented one-half;[21] only in the West – north Connacht, south Ulster – did the old, pre-famine pattern of land holding survive.[22] Equally, though Irish landlords have now been exonerated from the charges of perpetual, capricious eviction levelled at them by contemporaries, the number of families turned from their holdings between the late 1840s and the 1880s was huge: the constabulary recorded the eviction of 68,767 families in this period, and noted at least 200 instances in which wholesale clearances of tenants were made from an estate in the years 1850–53 alone.[23] Even if most evictions occurred during the severe economic downturns in the later 1840s and the later 1870s, the numbers remain staggering. They dwarf into insignificance the roll-call of political evictions recorded in Wales – a dozen or so in Merioneth after the election of 1859; 69 in Carmarthenshire, Carnarvonshire and Cardiganshire after the election of 1868; and four during the tithe disturbances of the late 1880s – which formed the principal evidential basis for the radicals' claims that tenants in the principality lacked proper security of tenure.[24]

Therefore, in terms of landlord absenteeism, the terms upon which property was let and the tenant's security in his holding, conditions in Wales compared well with those in Ireland. The real problems of the Welsh countryside lay elsewhere. Perhaps the most important characteristic of rural society in Wales was the low standard of agriculture. As John Hervey, an experienced Pembrokeshire land surveyor, told a Royal Commission in 1844: 'In no part of the country are the first principles of agriculture at so low an ebb'.[25] Several causes can be identified. Perhaps the most important factor was what Howell has dubbed the 'peasant mentality' of the farmers, who held land primarily for the cultural status it bestowed and eschewed contact with the money economy as far as possible.[26] The contemporary rule of thumb was that landlords looked for a return of 3 per cent on their capital investment in land through rents, and tenants for 10 per cent on the capital they invested in the business of farming their holdings, but this broke down in the principality.[27] Farms were worked with family labour wherever possible, and children often stayed on the holding until their thirties, earning little more than pocket money in this time.[28] Such habits undoubtedly intensified the Welsh farmer's passionate attachment to the family holding. Every farming family felt it a priority to ensure transmission of the farm to the next generation: anything which imperilled that transition – risky experimentation with new farming methods, for example – was discouraged.

The consequence of this peasant outlook was a self-perpetuating crisis of under-funding. All observers agreed that the chief evil besetting

Welsh agriculture was the farmer's lack of capital.[29] Thomas Mousley, agent to the vast Cawdor estate in West Wales, identified the farmers' 'want of capital' as one of the three great deficiencies afflicting agriculture, alongside their lack of agricultural education and enterprise. However, this problem was aggravated by the fact that farms were often so small, and the capital generally expected of incoming tenants so low, that many of those who took farms 'really belong to the labouring class'.[30] The strong competition for farms – fuelled by the ambitions of both thrifty labourers and the grown-up children of existing tenants, combined to create the 'land hunger' that marked the Welsh countryside and played a part in keeping rent levels high.[31]

Under such conditions, agriculture could not flourish. Whether all the blame for this state of affairs belongs to the farming class, however, is debatable. In many ways, Welsh landowners abetted the 'peasant' character of agriculture in the principality.[32] While many patronized the various agencies of 'improvement' that sprang up periodically in the countryside, subscribing to agricultural societies or making prize bulls available for their tenants' herds, they also ran their estates within a 'moral' framework that prioritized non-financial imperatives.[33] As noted earlier, farms were not amalgamated to produce larger holdings, and were not in any case let at their full valuation in most cases; moreover, many landowners preferred to let vacant holdings to the relations of an existing tenant, schooled in the customs of the estate, rather than risk introducing a new tenant from outside, however well-capitalized. Welsh landowners were as un-attuned to the pursuit of high farming as their tenants and largely content to run their estates 'with the grain' of tradition.[34]

This shared outlook was a significant force for stability in the Welsh countryside. However, there were also important cultural elements pushing in the opposite direction and widening the gap between landlord and tenant. Kate Jenkins, vice chair of the Llangadock School Board, put it thus to the Welsh Land Commission in 1894: 'There is a great lack of human brotherhood between landlord and tenant in Wales. They are of separate language, religion, politics, often nationality'.[35] The language division was certainly deep-rooted. Even though many landowners could trace impressive Welsh lineages, they invariably spoke English and had no knowledge of Welsh; the farmer, for his part, had sufficient English to conduct business on market day, but at his fireside, in the bosom of his family, the native tongue prevailed.[36] The landowner was thus shut out from the cultural life of the community in which he lived, and in no sphere was this more important than the religious.[37] The Religious Census of 1851 revealed that 80 per cent of those attending a place of worship did so under the auspices of the dissenting chapels, where services were in Welsh: the largely English-speaking Church of England, the church of the landowners, had lost its following in the Welsh countryside. Such division translated easily into the sphere of politics. The majority of landowners supported Conservative candidates, while their nonconformist tenants favoured more progressive politics, increasingly putting their weight behind the Liberal party in the period after 1867.[38]

However, the cultural separation between landowners and occupiers was also visible in all sorts of other ways. The circumstances of early childhood, for example, did not allow the formation of sympathetic bonds between those who would one day own the soil and those who would tenant it. A report on the condition of the agricultural labourer in Wales in the 1890s noted that whereas the son of the laird and the son of the labourer might attend elementary school together in Scotland, such a crossing of class lines would never happen in the principality, though the children of farmers and labourers would sit side by side.[39] Even in their recreations, the owners and occupiers lived parallel lives. Lord Penrhyn, for example, told the Welsh Land Commission that he regretted the absence of foxhounds in Carnarvonshire, saying 'We meet upon business perhaps [already]; but it [the Hunt] would bring us together out-doors; we should have one common source of amusement, which would be good for all of us.'[40] However, the truth was, as Mr Jeffreys, tenant of Brook Farm, Raglan, said: 'I do not think the Welsh farmers go much to hounds'.[41]

In a sense, the owners and occupiers of the soil in Wales lived parallel existences. If the landowners were not in the habit of crossing this divide to mete out cruel and unusual punishments, nor were they well informed about the lives of their tenants; equally, the tenants lived in ignorance of the cultural milieu in which the landowners moved. It was on this basis of mutual ignorance that radicals built their political land question in the second half of the nineteenth century.

The Welsh land question

The Welsh land question may be said to have started between February and May, 1866. A series of letters appeared in the Cobdenite *Morning Star*, analyzing the social condition of Wales. Penned by the eminent Welsh radical, Henry Richard, they re-cast the problem in such a way that the relationship between landlord and tenant became a key battleground in the fight to secure recognition of Wales's status as a nation. Earlier writers had tended to see the issue as part of a wider British agitation.[42] In the early 1850s, for example, the Reverend Samuel Roberts of Llanbrynmair had provided a Welsh echo to Philip Pusey's nationwide campaign for Tenant Right.[43] Roberts detailed the experience of his father in taking over an overgrown hill farm in Montgomeryshire: having spent both his life savings and his wife's dowry on bringing it back into cultivation and repairing all the roads and fences, his rent was summarily (and ruinously) raised by 35 per cent, his tithe doubled and the rateable value of the farm to the parish likewise increased.[44] The literal truth of the story may be doubted as it was the universal custom in Wales, unlike Ireland, for the landowner rather than the tenant to fund the building of roads, houses and barns which seem to have eaten up most of Roberts senior's capital.[45] Either way, the pamphlet was designed to indicate that the lack of compensation for unexhausted improvements affected tenants in Wales as grievously as it did their counterparts in England, rather than to suggest that the principality had some special affliction. Similarly, when the leading Welsh language newspaper, *Baner Ac Amserau Cymru*, devoted a leading article to 'The Rights of the Tenant' in 1860, it scarcely mentioned Wales, focussing instead on Henry Corbett's 4-year-old book on tenant right.[46]

Richard's approach was quite different. For him, the Welsh people's peculiar destiny was bound up specifically in the issue of land. His letters dwelt on the deep-rooted religiosity of the Welsh *gwerin*, akin to the German 'Volk', and their almost elemental connection with the distinctive landscape of Wales.[47] He recalled attending religious meetings near the seashore, 'the softened murmur of the ocean mingling with, as if it bore burden to, the sound of sacred song that came from the assembled multitude'. On other occasions, he continued, the spot selected would be

> an open glade amid rich woodland scenery . . . where the green sward sloped up gradually from the stage on which the ministers stood, forming a sort of ascending natural gallery. And as the surrounding trees, gently swayed by the wind, bent and rustled, it might almost seem, amid the solemn associations of the scene, to the excited feelings of the people, 'As if the forest leaves were stirred with prayer'.

As the sermon developed, 'Wave after wave of emotion would pass over and thrill through the vast congregation, until it was seen to move and sway to and fro, "as the trees of the wood are moved with the wind".' Elsewhere in the letters, he described how the harvest fields in Wales would 'often ring with the sound of song and psalm', and 'the voice of prayer' be 'lifted in thanksgiving to the great Giver, while the workers stand or kneel amid the fragrant hay-swaths they have just cut, or under the golden sheaves of corn they have bound and stacked.'[48] Land and people were one.

This sense of an organic bond between the Welsh people and their landscape underpinned Richard's critique of relationships in the Welsh countryside. To him, the landowners had forsaken the right to the rule over the land by their estrangement from the people's culture: they were alienated in language and religion from those around them, and their position as the principality's political representatives was thus deeply anomalous.[49] Richard urged electors to return to parliament men who shared their own national and religious outlook, but he did not shy from acknowledging the perils that such a course of action would entail.[50] The aristocracy were jealous of their power, and were known to evict tenants who flouted their direction at election time. At Merioneth in 1859, for example, tenants on the Rhiwlas and Wynnstay estates in the county were allegedly turned off for their Liberal votes.[51] If sufficient resolve were shown, however, the shackles could be broken and the spirit of the nation freed. He closed by repeating the old Welsh proverb: 'Trech Gwlad Nag Arglwydd', – 'a land is mightier than its Lord'. In the context of Richard's world view, it was a summons not to the people alone, but to the very hills and valleys to rise against their alien oppressors.

Richard thus re-defined the land question in Wales. The tenant's security of tenure was identified as primarily a political and cultural rather than an economic problem, something that must be resolved if the champions of the nonconformist middle class were to displace the aristocracy as the legitimate political voice of the principality. That middle class, radical and wedded to nonconformity, sought legislation which recognized the distinctiveness of Wales – its nonconformist culture, its claims to national status. The consequence was that the Welsh land question was separated from the strict facts of economic life in rural Wales; enthusiasm for the movement ebbed and flowed as its proponents saw opportunities to advance their wider political agenda. And, overwhelmingly, this meant that agitation of the land question in Wales was tied to the rhythm of politics in Ireland.

In an insightful article, Paul O'Leary has remarked upon the peculiarity of Welsh Liberals responding so enthusiastically to the lead given by events in Ireland from mid-century.[52] In particular, he notes how surprising it was that Welsh nonconformists should respond so positively to the Catholics' campaign for the disestablishment of the Church in Ireland in 1868. In fact, from a political perspective, the Welsh radicals' willingness to 'play the Irish card' throughout this period is readily explicable. Ireland provided a context easily understood by contemporaries; the trick was to convince English opinion that unless parliament began to pay attention to the range of Welsh grievances, especially relating to religion, popular disillusion would propel the principality down the same violent and rebellious road. Establishing a *prima facie* case that the potential for disaffection existed, that relations in the Welsh countryside were so strained as to make such a denouement conceivable, was a key part of the strategy.

The crucial interlinking of the situations in Wales and Ireland grew rapidly in the months surrounding the general election of 1868. When Gladstone announced his plan to disestablish the Church of England in Ireland, Welsh nonconformists immediately demanded a similar boon for Wales: 80 per cent of the population, they pointed out, worshipped in the chapels.[53] 'Justice for Ireland' in the matter of the Anglican Church became a call for similar justice to be meted out to Wales, and when Gladstone introduced his Land Bill in 1869, the same easy elision of Irish and Welsh grievances occurred.

By this time, the radicals were able to adduce fresh evidence of the critical state of landlord–tenant relations in the Welsh countryside. Following the general election of 1868, it appeared that 'hundreds' of tenants had been turned from their farms for their Liberal votes by vengeful Tory landowners.[54] A campaign was launched to bring the scandal to public attention, and to raise a fund from which the evictees might be compensated for the losses they had suffered in conscience's cause. Henry Richard, now MP for Merthyr Tydfil, led a debate on the issue in the House of Commons, while the evidence of Welsh witnesses to the Select Committee on Municipal and Parliamentary Elections caused uproar.[55] The campaign 'out of doors' to raise the compensation fund was even more dramatic. The large public meetings held in Aberystwyth, Liverpool, London and Manchester coincided with the beginnings of a sharp rise in the number of agrarian outrages committed in Ireland, several landowners and large farmers being murdered.[56] Against this background, the Welsh radicals' willingness to play the Irish card had a decided air of menace. Typical was the comment made by the land reformer, Humphrey Sandwith, at Aberystwyth in December 1869, that but for the dissenting ministers, 'he sincerely believed that some of these petty tyrants of landowners would frequently be shot from behind a hedge'.[57]

The landed members of the Welsh Liberal party were not prepared to subscribe to this kind of talk and many refused to attend the meetings called on behalf of the evicted tenants. One who sent a letter explaining his absence from the gathering at Aberystwyth was William Owen Stanley, MP for Beaumaris in Anglesey, who wrote

> Nothing can be more injurious to a country than setting landlord and tenant at variance. We must be warned by the example of Ireland. Wales, although at one time oppressed by penal laws as savage as those in Ireland, has from her highly religious and Protestant feeling, remained happy, loyal and contented ... She has no wrongs to redress like Ireland, but enjoys to the full equal laws with England.[58]

Laughter and groaning apparently greeted the reading out of this letter to the conference, and in his column for *Baner Ac Amserau Cymru* the following week, the radical journalist John Griffith, 'Y Gohebydd', simply exploded: '*HAPPY WALES!*', he wrote: '*No wrongs to redress like Ireland!* Would it be too much, I wonder, to ask the Honourable William Owen Stanley to make clear to us though the BANER ... the difference between a tenant in Cardigan and a tenant in Kildare, except that one pays his *rent* in clean money – whilst the other pays his in lead?'[59] At the somewhat less excitable meeting in favour of the evictees held at Liverpool the following month, Richard presented the same truth in slightly more moderate form: 'They wanted a tenant right [in Wales] nearly as much as they did in Ireland, and he thought if the Welsh landlords did not take warning, there would arise an agitation in Wales, as there was in Ireland, to demand protection against the capricious exercise of their authority (hear, hear and cheers)'.[60]

Contemporary newspapers were in no doubt about the moral to be drawn from the material presented by the Welsh radicals. The demand for fixity of tenure became a common theme in the columns of radical Welsh newspapers,[61] but perhaps more interesting is the reaction of leading Liberal newspapers in England. In May 1869, the *Daily News* stated: 'It is very well to talk about the ballot, which of course must come; but if this kind of dealing with tenants goes on there will be a Welsh as well as an Irish Land Question.'[62] And after the Commons debate on the issue in July, the *Newcastle Chronicle* said: 'It would seem that in Wales the tenant is at much at the mercy of the landlord as he is in Ireland', and suggested that ballot and better land laws were clearly required in both countries.[63]

There is no doubt that the radicals' campaign on behalf of the evicted tenants, with its clever positioning of Wales as a version of Ireland that could yet be saved by parliamentary intervention, was highly successful in alerting a wider British audience to the existence of a new 'nation' in their midst. But while secret voting arrived in 1872, no land legislation was forthcoming for Wales. In any case, it was not at all clear that farmers were as keen on the land question as their self-appointed champions in parliament and the press. After several coat-trailing articles on landlord–tenant relations in 1870, for example, at the height of the agitation over the evicted tenants, the *Baner's* editor openly expressed his disappointment that not one person had written to the paper on the theme.[64] And, indeed, once the immediate crisis had passed, the Welsh land question dropped off the political radar for a decade.

It was not until the mid-1880s that it re-emerged with any force. While the campaigns surrounding the Irish Land Act (1881) naturally created some excitement – *Baner* ran a 4-month educational campaign on the virtues of the 3 Fs – there was no deep-rooted appetite for the cause in Wales. In keeping with the fundamentally political nature of the Welsh land question, it was in the immediate aftermath of the Third Reform Act that the new campaign arose. To be sure, these were hard years in the Welsh countryside, as profit margins on beef and mutton collapsed; however, the response of the farmers was to seek a reduction in their outgoings – notably in a campaign against the payment of tithe.[65] Attempts by Thomas Gee, veteran editor of *Baner*, to transform the tithe agitation into the kind of movement that might force land reform were strikingly unsuccessful.[66] As the landlords' leading late-century apologist J. E. Vincent revealed, Gee's Land League managed to attract subscriptions of only £62 in the course of its 3-year existence: 'that', as he said, 'is the enthusiastic desire of the Welsh farmer for the reform of the law of tenancy converted into pounds, shillings and pence'.[67]

As noted earlier, however, the Welsh land question was not fundamentally an economic issue: it was political. Moreover, it was, as always, taken more seriously when conditions in Ireland were volatile – the growth of Michael Davitt's 'plan of campaign' formed the background to a new upsurge of political activity in Wales.[68] The Third Reform Act had witnessed the return to parliament of a new group of MPs, many from strikingly modest social backgrounds. None was more important or talismanic than the young MP for Merioneth, Tom Ellis. The son of a local tenant farmer, educated at Aberystwyth and then at Oxford, he had first-hand experience of the Welsh countryside and drew the attention of parliament to the condition of Welsh rural society at regular intervals between 1887 and 1893.[69] In 1888, he unsuccessfully moved a resolution in the House of Commons, highlighting the antipathy between the owners and occupiers of land in Wales, and the economic hardships faced by the farmers; the following year he was a member of the Select Committee on Small Holdings which received evidence from four Welshmen; and then in 1892, he introduced a Land Tenure Bill with a full Land Court on the Irish pattern. The Bill was rejected by a large majority, but in the history of the Welsh land question, Gladstone's intervention in the debate, and his unexpected comment that there was a clear case for 'a thorough, searching, impartial and dispassionate inquiry' was a defining moment. Within a year, a Royal Commission had been established to investigate the question.

The composition of the Commission, which featured a majority who favoured radical action on the land question and a small Conservative minority who did not, made it inevitable that its researches, while undoubtedly 'thorough' and 'searching', would be neither 'impartial' nor 'dispassionate'. Nevertheless, by and large, the landowners emerged remarkably well from the Commission's investigation. Armed with able legal counsel and a huge volume of detailed archival evidence from their own estate offices, they proved more than a match for their tenant assailants, many of whom did not even keep a farming diary or notebook.[70] While the bland conclusion of the Commission's Report was that the Agricultural Holdings Act (1883) might usefully be extended in certain ways to benefit landlord and tenant alike, a group of six Commissioners put their names to a resolution urging 'the creation of a judicial tenancy and the constitution of a Land Court (whether by the erection of a new organisation or the extension of the existing County Courts), having power to fix rents and reasonable conditions of tenancy, coupled with provisions giving tenants security in their holdings as long as they observe the conditions and pay the judicial rent'.[71] This was twinned with the rather curious recommendation that the new laws only apply to 'agricultural holdings of such a size as is sufficient for the maintenance of a tenant farmer without other employment or other sources of income': how the existence of such eligibility was to be established was left unexplored.

By the time the Commission's recommendations were published in 1896, the Conservatives were once again in power, and no action was taken. The great saga of the land question in Victorian Wales was played out. The Commission had allowed everyone their 'day in court' and so eased tensions all round. Equally, however, the political context now changed. The steady growth of nationalist feeling among Wales's parliamentary representatives, which had been so important a factor in their pursuit of the land question, foundered in opposition.[72] With it went the political logic which had buoyed agitation of a specifically 'Welsh' land question for the past 40 years.

Conclusion

The speed with which the Welsh land question disappeared from the radar of British politics, without any need for the kind of government-backed scheme of land purchase used in Ireland to solve it, reinforces the notion that there were essentially two distinct land 'questions' in Victorian Wales: the social and economic version that existed in the countryside and the cultural–political version that animated the leaders of Welsh opinion. The former had much in common with the wider British debate concerning tenant right, while the latter was designed to illustrate Welsh national distinctiveness. In championing the 'political' land question, Welsh propagandists sought to obtain both impact and leverage by drawing comparisons between the situations of Wales and Ireland. In reality, there were few such parallels. As K. T. Hoppen has written, 'however much the Welsh Land War may have tried to dress itself in garments first tailored in Ireland ... it always remained comparatively modest in both degree and extent.'[73] There was certainly little appetite in the principality for the violence associated with the 'plan of campaign' either, and though Davitt was provided with a Welsh platform by the Reverend Michael D. Jones in 1887, this action was roundly denounced by more mainstream figures both at the time and later.[74] It was, said R. A. Jones, arranged by 'two or three gentlemen ... entirely upon their own authority' and was 'almost universally condemned by Welsh farmers and politicians'.[75] The 'Irish card' had to be played with caution. The game was to suggest the potential for Wales to become a second Ireland, not to that it already was. As there were two land questions in Wales, so were there two possible solutions. For Welsh radicals from the 1860s onwards, nothing less than legislation to limit the political power of the aristocracy could be acceptable; only their own return to parliament would prove that the corrupting influence of the alienated landowning aristocracy really had been laid to rest. In the countryside itself, however, things were rather different. There were doubtless tenants who suffered economic hardship and could have benefited from some legislative protection. The Welsh Land Commissioners concluded that while the large estates generally treated their tenants very well, and old families long associated with smaller estates did likewise, there could be a problem when those who had made money in industry bought a landed estate and expected to 'make it pay'.[76] On such estates, rents could be driven up very quickly with scant disregard for the older, easy understanding of what landlord owed to tenant and vice versa. Nevertheless, the historical consensus is that for most of the tenants, most of the time, the system worked reasonably well. As the Liberal chairman of the Carmarthenshire County Council told the Commission, the chief benefit tenants would derive from any new legislation would be to ensure '*that they get as a right* what they now obtain as a *favour*.'[77]

Notes

1. D. W. Howell, *Land and People in Nineteenth-Century Wales* (London, 1977), p. 85; K. O. Morgan, *Rebirth of a Nation: Wales 1880–1980* (Oxford, 1981), pp. 38–9.
2. J. K. Chapman (ed.), 'A Political Correspondence of the Gladstonian Era', *Transactions of the American Philosophical Society*, 61 (1971), 46.
3. A. W. Jones, 'Glamorgan Custom and Tenant Right', *Agricultural History Review*, 31 (1983), 1–14.
4. For a thoughtful comparison of prevailing ideas of land tenure in the English countryside and Ireland, see P. Bull, *Land, Politics and Nationalism: A Study of the Irish Land Question* (Dublin, 1996), pp. 5–26.
5. M. J. Winstanley, *Ireland and the Land Question 1800–1922* (London, 1984), p. 11; Howell, *Land and People*, pp. 20–1, 87. For the social consequences of absenteeism, see, for example, M. Edgeworth, *Castle Rackrent* (London, 1828).
6. Winstanley, *Ireland and the Land Question*, p. 11.
7. C. Ó'Gráda, 'Poverty, Population, and Agriculture, 1801–45', in W. E. Vaughan (ed.), *A New History of Ireland V: Ireland under the Union, 1 – 1800–1870* (Oxford, 1989), pp. 128–9.
8. W. E. Vaughan, *Landlords and Tenants in Mid-Victorian Ireland* (Oxford, 1994), pp. 3–4.
9. Howell, *Land and People*, pp. 20–1, 87.
10. J. E. Vincent, *The Land Question in North Wales* (London, 1896), p. 161.
11. J. E. Vincent, *The Land Question in South Wales* (London, 1897), pp. 81–2.
12. Howell, *Land and People*, p. 70.
13. Winstanley, *Ireland and the Land Question*, p. 16.
14. J. S. Donnelly, Jr., 'The Journals of Sir John Benn-Walsh Relating to the Management of his Irish Estates, 1823–64', *Journal of the Cork Historical and Archaeological Society*, 79 (1974), 86–123.
15. D. Williams, *The Rebecca Riots* (Cardiff, 1986), p. 67. Rare examples of subletting can be found: *Royal Commission of Inquiry for South Wales*, Parl. Papers 1844, XVI, qq. 5230–5241 (James Evans).
16. Howell, *Land and People*, p. 87.
17. Vincent, *Land Question in South Wales*, p. 89.
18. P. Bew, *Land and the National Question in Ireland, 1858–82* (Dublin, 1978), p. 19.

19. The absence of allegations in the Welsh radical press is telling: *Baner*, 20 Tachwedd 1872, p. 13, letter of Tyddynwr; cf. *Royal Commission on Land in Wales and Monmouth*, Parl. Papers 1895, XL, qq. 37, 826.
20. Bull, *Land, Politics & Nationalism*, pp. 37–8.
21. J. S. Donnelly, Jr., 'Landlords and Tenants', in Vaughan, *New History of Ireland V*, p. 344.
22. Bew, *Land and the National Question*, p. 9.
23. Vaughan, *Landlords and Tenants*, pp. 21–6. A 'clearance' is defined as the simultaneous ejection of over 40 families. B. Solow, *The Land Question and the Irish Economy, 1870–1903* (Cambridge: Mass., 1971), pp. 54–7; Donnelly, 'Landlords and Tenants', p. 337.
24. For the eviction see I. G. Jones, 'Merioneth Politics at Mid-century' in Jones, *Explorations and Explanations: Essays in the Social History of Victorian Wales* (Llandyssul, 1981), pp. 83–164; M. Cragoe, 'The Anatomy of an Eviction Campaign: The General Election of 1868 in Wales and its Aftermath', *Rural History*, 9 (1998), 177–93; Howell, *Land and People*, p. 65.
25. *Royal Commission of Inquiry for South Wales*, Parl. Papers 1844, XVI, report, pp. 444–6.
26. D. Jenkins, *The Agricultural Community of South-West Wales at the Turn of the Twentieth Century* (Cardiff, 1971), p. 104; Howell, *Land and People*, p. 91.
27. J. Caird, *The British Land Question* (London, 1881), pp. 18–22.
28. *Royal Commission on Employment of Children, Young Persons and Women in Agriculture*, Parl. Papers 1870, XIII, report, p. 37; *Royal Commission on Land in Wales and Monmouthshire*, Parl. Papers 1870, XXXVII, qq. 885–90, for a tenant farmer who grew up on a small farm as one of 12 children, and ran his own farm with the unpaid labour of his ten children.
29. *Royal Commission of Inquiry for South Wales*, Parl. Papers 1844, XVI, report, pp. 444–6.
30. *Royal Commission on Employment of Children, Young Persons and Women in Agriculture*, report, p. 49.
31. *Royal Commission on Labour: The Agricultural Labourer in Wales*, Parl. Papers 1893–94, XXXVI, report, p. 6.
32. Bull, *Land, Politics and Nationalism*, pp. 18–19.
33. M. Cragoe, *An Anglican Aristocracy: The Moral Economy of the Landed Estate in Carmarthenshire, 1832–96* (Oxford, 1996) for a development of this argument.
34. Ibid.; Howell, *Land and People*, p. 91. Radicals criticized the landlords for their outlook: H. Richard, *Letters on the Social, Moral and Political Condition of Wales* (London, 1867), p. 107.
35. *Royal Commission on Land in Wales and Monmouthshire*, Parl. Papers 1895, XL, q. 38,024; Jenkins, *Agricultural Community*, pp. 19–33.
36. *Report of the Committee of Council on Education (England and Wales)*, Parl. Papers 1878–79, XXII, report of Revd Shadrach Pryce, p. 674, suggests commercial transactions were generally conducted in English.
37. Bull, *Land, Politics and Nationalism*, p. 17 makes a similar comment about Ireland.
38. Morgan, *Wales in British Politics*, pp. 11–22; M. Cragoe, *Culture, Politics and National Identity in Wales 1832–1886* (Oxford, 2004).

39. *Royal Commission on Labour: The Agricultural Labourer in Wales*, Parl. Papers 1893–94, XXXVI, report, p. 6.
40. *Royal Commission on Land in Wales and Monmouthshire*, Parl. Papers 1895, XL, q. 23,014.
41. Ibid., q. 33,772. Although see q. 34,663, John Lawrence, MFH of Llangibby Hounds who said farmers joined this Hunt.
42. D. J. V. Jones, *Rebecca's Children: A Study of Rural Society, Crime, and Protest* (Oxford, 1989), pp. 275–6, 325–31. The Rebecca Rioters made some demands that rents be reduced, but this agitation was largely confined to west Wales.
43. J. R. McQuiston, 'Tenant Right: Farmer Against Landlord in Victorian England 1847–1883', *Agricultural History*, 47 (1973), 101. Roberts has yet to find an authoritative modern biographer, though see G. Williams, *Samuel Roberts, Llanbrynmair* (Cardiff, 1950).
44. A Llanbrynmair Farmer [i.e. Samuel Roberts], *Letters on Improvements Addressed to Landlords and Road Commissioners* (Newtown, 1852), pp. 9–32.
45. Bew, *Land and the National Question*, p. 22; Howell, *Land and People*, p. 87. Examples of tenants leaving farms without compensation were given to the Commission of Inquiry in 1844: *Royal Commission of Inquiry for South Wales*, Parl. Papers 1844, XVI, q. 1201 (evidence of John Rees).
46. *Baner*, 23 Mehefin 1860, pp. 2–3: 'Hawliau y Tenant'.
47. Richard, *Letters*, pp. 26–7.
48. Ibid., p. 43.
49. Ibid., pp. 2, 93–100.
50. Ibid., pp. 108–9.
51. Ibid., 103–5; Jones, 'Merioneth Election', p. 91; cf. Cragoe, *Culture, Politics and National Identity*, pp. 156–7.
52. P. O'Leary, 'Religion, Nationality and Politics: Disestablishment in Ireland and Wales, 1868–1914', in J. R. Guy and W. G. Neely (eds), *Contrasts and Comparisons: Studies in Irish and Welsh Church History* (Llandysul, 1999), p. 113.
53. Ibid., pp. 92–5.
54. For the problems of assessing the justice of these claims, see Cragoe, *Culture, Politics and National Identity*, pp. 142–72.
55. *Carnarvon and Denbigh Herald*, 19 June 1869.
56. Vaughan, *Landlords and Tenants*, p. 139; D. E. Jordan, Jr., *Land and Popular Politics in Ireland: County Mayo from the Plantation to the land War* (Cambridge, 1994), p. 187.
57. *Cambria Daily Leader*, 18 November 1869.
58. The same point was made by the new Conservative daily, the *Western Mail*: 19 November 1869: editorial.
59. *Baner*, 8 Rhagfyr 1869, pp. 3–4: Llythr y Gohebydd.
60. *Llandudno Register and Herald*, 25 December 1869. Even non-political bodies like the Chambers of Agriculture were affected: see, for example, *Pall Mall Gazette*, 6 December 1871.
61. *Baner*, 10 Tachwedd 1869, p. 9, letter of Lewis Edwards and others.
62. *Baner*, 19 May 1869, pp. 3–4.
63. *Newcastle Chronicle*, 10 July 1869.
64. *Baner*, 1 Mehefin 1870, p. 11.

65. J. P. D. Dunbabin, *Rural Discontent in Nineteenth Century Britain* (New York, 1974), pp. 211–31, 282–96. The Tithe Recovery Act did not abolish the tax, as farmers hoped. By placing the burden of payment on the owner rather than the occupier, it effectively merged tithe-rent charge with rent, and thus made its payment easier to enforce: Morgan, *Wales in British Politics*, pp. 84–90.
66. Dunbabin, *Rural Discontent*, pp. 227–9.
67. Vincent, *Land Question in North Wales*, pp. 18–24.
68. Bull, *Land, Politics and Nationalism*, pp. 101–7.
69. Morgan, *Wales in British Politics*, pp. 94–8.
70. *Royal Commission on Labour: The Agricultural Labourer in Wales*, Parl. Papers 1893–94, XXXVI, q. 2719; Morgan, *Wales in British Politics*, pp. 128–9.
71. *Royal Commission on Land in Wales and Monmouthshire*, Parl. Papers 1896, XXXV, report, p. 960.
72. For the rise and fall of political nationalism in late nineteenth-century Wales, and particularly the wreck of Cymru Fydd, see Morgan, *Wales in British Politics*, pp. 125–9.
73. K. T. Hoppen, *The Mid Victorian Generation, 1846–1886* (Oxford, 1998), pp. 551–2.
74. *Baner*, 3 Awst 87. The ideas of Henry George were received in similar fashion: *Baner*, 15 Ionawr 1890, p. 3; 22 Ionwar 1890, p. 10; *Western Mail*, 17 January 1884, 18 December 1888, 27 March 1889; P. Jones-Evans, 'Edward Pan Jones – Land Reformer', *Welsh History Review*, 4 (1968), 143–59; E. Pan Jones (ed.), *Y Ddear I'r Bobl* (Bangor, 1890).
75. R. A. Jones, *The Land Question and a Land Bill, with special reference to Wales* (2nd edn, Wrexham, 1887), p. 10.
76. *Royal Commission on Land in Wales and Monmouthshire*, Parl. Papers 1895, XL, q. 37,825.
77. Ibid., q. 38764.

6

Setting the Heather on Fire: The Land Question in Scotland, 1850–1914

Ewen A. Cameron

Introduction: Scotland and land reform

The historian of the Scottish land question has to tread a careful line between emphasising distinctiveness and recognising the generic elements of the problem. Indeed, a plausible case could be made for undermining the 'Scottish' land question on the grounds of local diversity. The troubled history of the Highlands in the eighteenth and nineteenth centuries – the clearances, the famine of the 1840s, the 'Crofters War' of the 1880s – is very different from the story of high-farming efficiency which is the dominant narrative of the Lowlands over the same period. Even this binary division between Highlands and Lowlands can be broken down: the fertile conditions prevalent in the 'Black Isle', Easter Ross and Caithness had little in common with those of the west and the Hebrides where extremely harsh conditions dominated. In the Lowlands, the best farming areas of East Lothian and Fife were a world away from conditions in Aberdeenshire or the upland areas of southern Scotland. Although many of the same historical processes affected the Lowlands as the Highlands, it was the vivid nature of the land question in the latter area which captured the public imagination and the political agenda in Scotland. The domination of Scottish politics by the Liberal party also contributed to the Scottish land question. From 1832 to 1918, there was only one general election, in 1900, at which the Liberals did not win a majority of Scottish seats, and they used the land question as a key component of their appeal north of the border. This was especially the case in the 1880s and in the period after 1906 when they conscripted the Scottish land question into their struggle with the House of Lords, but even during the

Gladstone/Rosebery administration of 1892–95 a Royal Commission was established to investigate the potential for redistributing land currently used for grazing and sport. Anti-landlordism was a key feature of radical Liberalism and early Labour politics in Scotland. The editor of the *Highlander*, John Murdoch, the Crofter MP Dr. G. B. Clark and the leader of Irish nationalism in Glasgow, John Ferguson (a dedicated single taxer), were involved in the foundation of the Scottish Labour Party in 1888. This short-lived organisation merged with the ILP in 1894 but the land remained an important issue on the left in Scotland, not least in the pages of *Forward* of Glasgow, edited by Thomas Johnston. Nevertheless, as will be explored below, land reform was not restrained by national boundaries. Single Taxers or Land Nationalisers would argue that, regardless of local diversity, there were universal grievances which arose from the private ownership of land. Further, whatever one makes of the contemporary political debate – or the current historiographical one – over Britishness, one of the principal pan-United Kingdom institutions was landownership. Of the 30 greatest British landowners (defined by gross income), 18 held land in more than one of the four nations of the United Kingdom.[1]

If one adopts the position that the generic elements of the land question deserve more emphasis than national distinctiveness, there are still important justifications for examination of the land question in Scotland. The first relates to the concentration of landownership north of the border. Until the 1870s, little was known about the concentration or dispersal of landownership in Britain. An official *Return of Owners of Land* in 1876 was followed in the late 1870s and early 1880s by successive editions of John Bateman's enumeration of landed proprietors. From this evidence it was clear that Scottish land was in remarkably few hands: 1,758 landowners owned 92.8 per cent of the total area of land in estates of more than 1,000 acres (the equivalent figures in England, Wales and Ireland were 56.1 per cent, 60.8 per cent and 78.4 per cent, respectively). This excessive concentration of land did not necessarily bring great wealth to its owners. The Duke of Buccleuch, most of whose 460,000 acres were in Scotland, earned £232,000 from his land. This compares with the Duke of Westminster who earned £290,000 from less than 20,000 acres, and the Duke of Bedford who earned £225,000 from his 86,000 acres: both Westminster and Bedford, of course, had substantial holdings in London. The most striking example of this gap between acreage and income is the Duke of Sutherland who owned 1.36 million acres, most in the north of Scotland, but earned only £142,000 from them. The Duke of Hamilton, whose estates were in industrial areas rich in minerals, gained the same income from less than 160,000 acres.[2] Nevertheless, it was the size of Scottish estates which attracted opprobrium from radicals. Relatively low landed incomes did not detract from social and political control. In 1874, poverty-stricken crofters at Bernera in the west of Lewis rioted after landlord encroachment on their grazing land. At the consequent trial in the Sheriff Court it became clear that Sir James Matheson's (the proprietor of the Island of Lewis) factor, Donald Munro, held so many local public offices that he was a virtual dictator in the island.[3]

The crofters' protests of the 1880s, the feudal system of land tenure which was central to debates about urban property relations, and the highly technical legal argument about rights to the foreshore also gave a certain distinctive element to the Scottish land question.[4] Further, Scotland was an important arena for land reformers and their opponents. Wider issues were debated in Scotland partly because the industrial area around Glasgow was such an important centre for Irish migrants. This brought figures like Michael Davitt and Edward McHugh to Glasgow to speak at Irish meetings; unlike conventional Parnellite nationalists, however, they placed greater stress on social and land reform than they did on home rule.[5] The inspiration for this activity was Henry George, who was a frequent visitor to Scotland, both Highland and Lowland. George had been castigated in Scotland as a 'wild atheistical socialist', and on his tours he found evidence of the fearful state of crofting communities, and counselled them to 'struggle to amend the law if it were unjust, and if they submitted to unjust law they were as responsible as the landlord'.[6] George spoke frequently in urban Scotland, often using the language and style of a religious preacher and working through the structure of the Scottish Land Restoration League.[7] Perhaps because of his fundamental challenge to the system of private landownership, he encountered a critical reception throughout the United Kingdom, and his views stimulated debate.[8]

One of the most notable debates in which George engaged was with the Duke of Argyll.[9] George had sent a copy of *Progress and Poverty* to the Duke, who was one of the principal defenders of private landownership in the 1880s.[10] The Duke argued that the increment gained from privately owned land was not, as George argued, 'unearned', pointing to his own investments in improvements. He was particularly exercised by George's proposal to resume the ownership of land without compensating the landowner, regarding this as corrupt in its breach of commercial principles and the level of probity which a property holder had the right to expect from the state. Argyll referred to George as 'a

Preacher of Unrighteousness' and labelled his teaching as 'immoral'.[11] In his reply George denied that land was a commodity to which property rights could be attached, on the grounds that 'the exclusive ownership of land has everywhere had its beginnings in force and fraud, in selfish greed and unscrupulous cunning'.[12] If the Duke had sought to defend the system of private landownership with reference to the Highlands, then George took up the challenge:

> Test the institution of private property in land by its fruits in any country where it exists. Take Scotland. What, there, are its results? That wild beasts have supplanted human beings; that glens which once sent forth their thousand fighting men are now tenanted by a couple of gamekeepers; that there is destitution and degradation that would shame savages; that little children are stunted and starved for want of proper nourishment; that women are compelled to do the work of animals; that young girls who ought to be fitting themselves for wifehood and motherhood are held to monotonous toil in factories, while others, whose fate is sadder still, prowl the streets; that while a few Scotsmen have castles and palaces, more than a third of Scottish families live in one room each, and more than two thirds in not more than two rooms each; that thousands of acres are kept as playgrounds for strangers, while the masses have not enough of their native soil to grow a flower, are shut out even from moor and mountain, dare not take a trout from a loch or a salmon from a stream.[13]

George went on to argue that the Malthusian pressures which the Duke identified in the Highlands were the result of the misappropriation of land by the landlords and, further, that the investments made by landowners in improving their estates came from rents extorted from tenants who might have been able to carry out improvements of equal value had they not been exploited in this manner.[14]

Georgite ideas gained significant publicity in Scotland and he was listened to with great enthusiasm. However, along with the more moderate form of land nationalisation suggested by Alfred Russel Wallace, these ideas were far in advance of the views of the Liberal electorate in Scotland.[15] Wallace may have received a letter from a Dundee worker who had read George's *Progress and Poverty* and found that it 'awakened a desire for more information as to our "land laws"', but more significant was his correspondence 30 years later with a socialist bookseller in Rutherglen who felt that his work was not sufficiently well known because it was not available in sufficiently cheap editions.[16] Traditional Liberal policies promoting the extension of smallholdings and dual ownership remained more popular. At the 1910 general elections, the Liberals won 58 of the 70 Scottish seats, at a time when their vote in England was in decline, and their policy on smallholdings was at the heart of their appeal. The Scottish Land Restoration League made limited progress and although the state purchased a significant amount of land in the Highlands in the 1920s, this should not be seen as a triumph for radical land nationalisers. Rather, the legislation of 1919 which facilitated these purchases was influenced by the failure of earlier attempts to create smallholdings on privately owned land and by the fact that in the years after the First World War Scottish landowners, especially those in the Highlands, were very keen to sell land to the government. By this process, the Department of Agriculture for Scotland and its successors became owners of substantial areas of land.

The Highland land question

It was this aspect of the Scottish land question which provided the greatest visibility. In addition, a substantial historiography has grown up around this subject, the key text being James Hunter's *The Making of the Crofting Community* (1976). This presented a stark picture of unremitting conflict between landowners and tenants. Much of the subsequent debate has been devoted to adding complexity to such topics as military recruitment, the famines of the 1840s and 1850s, the land settlement operation of the post-1886 period, and comparisons with Ireland.[17]

A new class of Highland landowners emerged in the generation following the Napoleonic Wars. Although not alien in language, culture and religion as in Ireland or Wales, they were not rooted in the history or geography of the Highlands. They were, above all, attracted by the relatively low price of Highland land and they brought considerable wealth, generated beyond the Highlands, to their new domains. Although he did have some familial roots in the region, the best example was Sir James Matheson, who purchased the island of Lewis in 1842. He was a partner in Jardine Matheson, a key figure in the development of Hong Kong and had made his money in the opium trade. His family remained in Lewis, and invested huge sums of money there, until 1917, when the island was sold to another plutocrat, William Hesketh Lever, whose expenditure in Lewis was, if anything, even greater than Matheson's, although equally unrewarding. This aspect of the land and marriage markets meant that events in the Scottish Highlands did not take place in Celtic isolation, but were closely connected to the economic history of industrial regions.[18]

The theme of distinctiveness arises from the separate legal regime relating to Highland land from 1886 to 1911. The Crofters Holdings (Scotland) Act of 1886 was closely modelled on the Land Law (Ireland) Act of 1881 in that it granted security of tenure, fair rents and compensation for improvements – although not free sale – to the small tenants in most parishes of the seven most northerly counties of Scotland, from Argyll to Shetland.[19] This was the principal legislative outcome of the series of protests which have become known as the Crofters' War. Although prefigured by earlier events, not least a series of contested evictions in the famine period in the 1840s and 1850s, this began in west Ross and Skye in the early 1880s and posed considerable law and order problems for the government in an area in which local administration was extremely weak. On a number of occasions, resort was had to military support to impose law in the region. These protests were at their peak from 1882 to 1888. The Crofters Act did not deal with the principal grievance of the crofters, their demand for the redistribution of land, and thereby disappointed the half dozen or so 'crofter MPs' who were elected for Highland constituencies in 1885 and 1886.[20] It is tempting to say that the feeble nature of the 1886 provisions for bringing more land into crofting was the stimulus for the subsequent legislation on the Highland land question, but this would be simplistic. The demand for further reform was weak in the more prosperous 1890s and although it picked up again in the more difficult circumstances of the Edwardian period, economic determinism should also be resisted. The dictates of political ideology were much more important. The year 1897 saw the establishment of the Congested Districts Board (CDB) by the Conservative administration. This was modelled on an Irish body of the same name and it introduced land purchase into the debate on the Highland land question, while emphasising the importance of economic development.

Although the Irish context is important, the CDB can also be seen as part of a longer tradition of intervention by British governments with the objective of transforming the economy of the Scottish Highlands. In the eighteenth century, the political objective was to undermine the basis for Jacobitism and was part of a wider project to introduce the English language, the protestant religion and a British identity into a potentially dangerous area of the United Kingdom. The system introduced by the clearances had been undermined by the economic collapse which followed the Napoleonic Wars and fatally wounded by the famine, poverty and emigration of the period from 1846 to 1855. The Board established to relieve famine in those years looked beyond palliatives and attempted to introduce a domestic textile industry and stimulate the fishing industry. Although Conservative policy of the 1890s was not faced with political rebellion or famine conditions, its essential aim, to break an atavistic connection with the land and induce more 'rational' economic strategies in the crofting community, was similar.

The expenditure of the CDB on infrastructure, agricultural support and economic development was a modest success and – allied with extensions to the railway network in the north and west – had a positive impact on the fishing industry. However, its overall aims were not met. Its land purchase provisions were strikingly unsuccessful. Although two large estates in Skye were purchased in 1904, the crofters – in contrast to Irish small tenants – proved uninterested in the 'advantages' of ownership. Perhaps this was because Scottish land purchase was poorly funded compared to Ireland, making the 50-year loans relatively expensive compared to the 'fair rents' established by the Crofters Commission after 1886.[21] Perhaps, also, the very atavism which the Board sought to counter was too powerful. The crofters regarded the security provided by the 1886 Act as a sufficient recognition of their historical 'title' to the land, and although there was a strong desire for more land, it did not outweigh the advantages of crofting tenure, which would be left behind if ownership was embraced. Perhaps, finally, the intimate connection in Ireland between the land question and nationalist politics and the perception of the landlord class as alien in culture and religion gave the land question there more political energy.[22] Although some of the Crofter MPs and other land reformers were involved in a Scottish Home Rule Association (established in 1886), the land question in the Highlands was not intimately connected to a wider national question in Scotland. This much became clear during the years from 1906 to 1911 as the land question became a divisive and disruptive force, even within Scottish Liberalism. Although the separate legal code for Highland land tenure was eroded in 1911 when the Small Landholders (Scotland) Act extended some of the provisions of the Crofters Act to the whole of Scotland and provided some facilities for the creation of new holdings on privately owned land, the focus of the attempts at land redistribution remained in the Highlands.

The 1911 Act, badly drafted and overtaken by the outbreak of the Great War, made little impression in any part of Scotland, although the long debate over its provisions revealed more about attitudes in the

Lowlands than the Highlands, as will be shown below. The final phase of the legislative dimension of the Highland land question came with the Land Settlement (Scotland) Act of 1919. Again, its provisions covered the whole of Scotland, but the bulk of activity was in the Highlands. The new Act provided more funds than earlier legislation and effectively provided for large-scale land nationalisation. Highland landowners were keen to sell to the government and the Board of Agriculture for Scotland became the dominant landowner in some parts of the Highlands, notably in the Island of Skye where the traditional landowning families were poverty-stricken and delighted to find a ready purchaser for their land. In the Hebrides this process used virtually all the land which was available for land settlement and had an important effect on the landscape and demography of areas which had been in decline for a considerable period. The long-term results, however, were mixed as land settlement in the 1920s created a new stratum of very small holdings which did nothing for the problems of the Highland economy.[23] The 1920s were marked by continuing protest, not least land raids by ex-servicemen, and extensive emigration.[24] By the late 1920s, after public expenditure cuts, the energy behind land settlement was dissipated and in common with the industrial areas of Scotland very difficult years were endured in the 1930s. Although the period from 1880 to 1930 contained most of the principal legislative landmarks, the Highland land question remained part of political debate in Scotland, even if governments paid little attention to it before devolution in 1999.[25]

The Lowland land question

Compared to events in the Highlands this aspect of the Scottish land issue seems marginal. This is partly a function of the relatively limited historiography on the subject, the history of the rural Lowlands not having attracted the same attention as its Highland counterpart, a matter of regret for some historians.[26] Debate had taken place over highly technical aspects of land law such as Entail and Hypothec. The former was a system which had once strictly controlled the inheritance of estates and prevented the estate from being used as security for raising capital; it had, however, been steadily eroded by legislation passed in 1770, 1836 and 1848. The latter, which remained an issue into the late-Victorian period, was similar to the English law of distress, and gave the landlord priority over other creditors in the event of non-payment of rent by a tenant, the 'hypothecation' applying even to produce which had been sold to a third party. This system was alleged to have kept rents artificially high and damaged the position of commerce in rural society. Landlords argued that the security it conferred allowed them to take a risk on giving a lease to a tenant who might otherwise have been refused access to land. Whatever the merits of the system, it was reformed in 1867 and virtually abolished in 1880. The Game Laws were another cause of agrarian controversy in the mid-Victorian period. An exceptional example of the politicisation of the relationship between landlord and tenant in the Lowlands, they generated considerable debate. To their critics, this was another area in which the landlord dominated the tenant. The latter had no right to shoot hares, rabbits or birds which damaged his crops, and the landlord had no responsibility to award compensation. As the commercial prospects of game became evident to landlords, the law was applied with even greater stringency and tenants became more restive. This was evident at elections in Scottish counties from 1865 to 1880 when seats which had long been in Tory hands were lost, contributing to the emasculation of the party in Scotland.[27] Finally, a further theme of the Lowland land question is the evident tension which emerged in the Victorian period over the terms of leases. In Scotland, these were generally long, usually nineteen years, but there was intense controversy over compensation for improvements and the practice of the new lease being calculated on the value added to the property by the tenant's improvements also led to tension. Landlords felt that it was their capital which made the improvements – whether drainage, fencing, building or even fertilisation – whereas tenants countered that their time and labour were being exploited by the landlords in the form of higher rents. This was a grievance frequently referred to by Scottish farmers at the Royal Commissions of 1881 and 1896.[28] The Lowland land question, therefore, should not be kept in the shadow of its more historiographically prominent Highland relation, but neither should it be assumed that the Scottish Lowlands merely presented a variant of English conditions and practices. It can be argued that Lowland Scottish farmers, with their emphasis on stock, fared better than the subsistence crofters of the Highlands or English arable farmers during the 'agricultural depression' of the late nineteenth century.[29] Lowland farm labourers were relatively quiescent, but due to the availability of well-paid industrial employment they were in a strong bargaining position and resisted state intervention to regulate their wages until 1917. This resistance was helped by the organisation of the Scottish Farm Servants' Union in 1912.[30]

The differences between the land question in the Lowlands and the Highlands were demonstrated between 1906 and 1911 when the Liberal government attempted to push its Small Landholders (Scotland) Bill through parliament. This Bill, eventually passed in 1911 after the reduction in the power of the House of Lords, extended the dual ownership provisions of the Crofters Act to the rest of Scotland. A new Board of Agriculture for Scotland was given power to compel landowners to create new holdings on their estates.[31] These provisions were divisive, within the Liberal party as well as between the Highlands and Lowlands. Perhaps the overwhelming distinction was that while the Highland debate was conducted in the realms of history and memory, the Lowland discussion was dominated by the more prosaic themes of agriculture and commerce. Lowland opinion, Liberal and Conservative, farming and landowning, was virtually unanimous that whatever the grievances of the Highland crofters were, there was no rational case for extending the tenurial regime of 1886 to the Lowlands, where most improvements were owned by the proprietor and the vast majority of land was held on long leases. To do so would be to risk undermining the supreme efficiency of Lowland agriculture. Some went further and argued that to create smallholdings in the Lowlands would damage the agricultural economy because large farms were more technically advanced and cost-effective. To threaten their break-up for smallholdings was to introduce an unwanted form of insecurity and undermine the willingness of landowners to invest in improvements.[32] Indeed, many opponents of Liberal legislation argued that to isolate the Scottish land question was not especially helpful. Arthur Balfour, whose home was at Whittinghame in East Lothian, made this point. 'Anyone with even the most superficial acquaintance with the facts of the case', Balfour declared, 'knows that the difference between Berwickshire and Northumberland is incomparably less than the difference in farming between Berwickshire and the crofting counties of Scotland.'[33]

Whilst debate about Scottish home rule in the Victorian and Edwardian period emphasised the need for devolved Scottish administration, the opposite was argued in some quarters when faced with the prospect of a Board of Agriculture for Scotland to oversee the new regime introduced by the Liberal government in 1911.

> Whatever may be done with the efforts to create small holdings, or to amend and extend the sphere of the Crofter Acts, we are on no account to have foisted upon us a Department (sic) of Agriculture for Scotland which is simply to be a section of the activities of Dover House. Scottish agriculture is an integral part of the mighty industry of British agriculture, and must be dealt with as such.[34]

In the event the Small Landholders (Scotland) Act had little impact in either Highland or Lowland Scotland, being poorly drafted and underfunded, but the long debate over its provisions, lasting from 1906 to 1911, revealed the complexity of the Scottish land question. It also stimulated landowners to organise for the defence of their interest, with the Scottish Land and Property Federation being formed in 1906.[35]

The urban land question

In some ways this is the most distinctive aspect of the Scottish land question, there being fewer parallels between Scottish and English cities than between English and Lowland Scottish farming. The legal system contributed to the production of a landscape of tenements common to towns large and small across Scotland.[36] Feudal tenure gave the seller of land no right of reversion, as in the English leasehold system, but an interest was retained through a perpetual feudal duty paid by the purchaser. The combination of highly priced land and the demands of feudal duties meant that profits for builders and landlords lay in maximising the number of households in each building.[37] Although the character of Scottish towns and cities cannot be explained deterministically by the legal framework – demography played a part – the 'impersonal forces of markets in land and capital' predominated.[38] One element of social engineering, and also a response to mounting squalor, was slum clearance, comparable in some ways with rural evictions. Beginning in the late 1860s in Edinburgh and Glasgow, town councils sought to use their powers and the resources of ratepayers to demolish the worst urban 'slums', and replace them with new streets and better quality housing.[39] In conception these schemes provided alternative accommodation for the cleared population, but in implementation the economics were insurmountable. Put bluntly, there was no profit in building houses which could be afforded by the population cleared from the slums. In Edinburgh's first major slum clearance scheme – which ran from the mid-1860s to the late 1880s – around 2,700 houses were demolished, 340 new ones were built and Chambers Street, 80 feet wide and replete with public buildings, was constructed. It is perhaps inappropriate to judge the work of the Edinburgh Improvement Trust in these terms, however, for its primary objective had not been the amelioration of working-class conditions through housing improvements, as critics like Rev. James Begg had lamented, but the improvement of the environment of the city and protection against 'disease and vice'.[40]

City improvement schemes were not immune from the vagaries of the economic cycle, as was evident in Glasgow during the depression induced by the failure of the City of Glasgow Bank in 1878. Difficulties in the disposing of land during this period, as well as criticism that the objective was 'social and not merely stone-and-lime improvement', induced the Glasgow Trust to construct nearly 1,200 houses, some with rents as low as £4, by the turn of the century. In contrast to Edinburgh, the Glasgow Improvement Trust oversaw the construction of houses for over 18,000 people, a third of the population that had been affected by the demolitions, although it is far from clear that those cleared from the inner city found accommodation in these new houses.[41] The most significant result of these schemes was the cautious appearance of the municipalities as landlords of rented properties: around 1 per cent of Scottish families were so accommodated on the eve of the Great War, a figure which would become much greater after 1918.[42] This development, however, was an accidental by-product and it had little impact on housing conditions. The principal reason for this was the expense of house-building and the impact it would have on the rate of local taxation. To spend a large sum of money on housing the working class risked alienating middle-class ratepayers who could, and did, take revenge at the ballot box, as Lords Provost of Glasgow discovered in 1866 and 1902.[43]

The pressures created by the urban land question in Scotland came to the surface during the Great War. A series of rent strikes originated from the cessation of house-building at the outbreak of the conflict and the influx of workers into areas like Govan and Partick where good wages could be earned. This pushed up rents and caused difficulties for those not earning inflated wages and the families of servicemen. The structure of the Scottish urban housing market also contributed to the combustible situation. Tenants could be readily 'evicted' and were subject to the attentions of 'factors' who managed portfolios of tenement properties on a commission basis for 'landlords'.[44] This area of property relations was subject to the same emotive language as the processes of dislocation in rural Scotland. Labour was deeply interested in the housing question and the rent strikes were part of an ongoing campaign which stretched back to the Edwardian period. The wartime housing 'famine' and its consequences allowed Labour to move onto this territory, important in their displacement of the Liberals as the dominant progressive force in Scottish politics. More than anyone, John Wheatley captured this ground for the ILP and, fittingly, as Minister for Health in the Labour government of 1924 he was responsible for a vital piece of legislation which accelerated house-building.[45] The escalation of the dispute encouraged the government, by an Act of 1915, to restrict rent increases for the duration of the war.[46] The government was clear that the imperatives of munitions production justified such an unusual level of market intervention. Rent restriction proved difficult to withdraw in the post-war period, however, especially when economic conditions were not propitious. This was a problem for governments in the 1920s, when the scale of house-building did not accelerate as the electorate had been led to expect in 1918. The 1915 Act did nothing to alter fundamental housing problems: conditions remained dreadful, landlords and factors powerful, tenants insecure and houses in short supply.[47] The advance of the state into housing provision and slum clearance in the inter-war period had some improving effect, but the standard of Scottish housing remained a pressing problem for governments in the period after the Second World War.

One context for the land question which does not fit neatly into an urban/rural dichotomy was that of mining communities. These were often situated on the fringes of urban settlements or even in semi-rural conditions, where the direct authority of landlords and gamekeepers fuelled a tradition of anti-landlordism. The collective memory of miners was also relevant: The tradition of the independent collier could be sustained by the possession of a smallholding, as had been common in parts of Lanarkshire, in the heartland of Scottish industrialisation, as late as the mid-nineteenth century. The most striking element of the miners' conception of the land question was the injustice of mineral royalties. These payments to proprietors under whom land miners toiled were especially high in the West of Scotland. A miners' leader, referring to the Duke of Hamilton, encapsulated the issue at a mass meeting near Motherwell in 1882:

> This honourable gentleman – (laughter) – had 12,000 miners working under the soil owned by him, and received on average 1s per ton from the produce of each miner . . . and if his Grace could not live on that, how in the name of providence could the miner . . . live on a paltry 3s 9d or 4s per day?

This issue became important in the labour movement in Scotland which conducted much of its early activity in mining communities. Outsiders such as the Land Restoration League and Michael Davitt raised the question among the miners, but activists from within these communities, not least Keir Hardie, also drew attention to it in their rhetoric.[48]

Conclusion

The point about the miners returns us to the origins of our discussion: the distinctiveness or otherwise of the Scottish land question. The complaints of mining communities had an interesting Scottish element given the extensive estates of landowners like the Duke of Hamilton or the Duke of Buccleuch, but they were by no means unique to Scotland. Along with the grievances of the crofters and the shocking housing conditions in urban Scotland, partly consequent upon feudal property law, the mineral royalties issue gave Scotland a particular prominence in the rhetoric of land reformers like Davitt or George. For these individuals, however, the problems in Scotland were an example, perhaps egregious in some respects, of the wider difficulties arising from unfettered private landownership. Hence, this chapter has sought to emphasise the need to view the Scottish land question in as wide a context as possible and not merely to stress an essential Scottish experience. Further, despite the prominence of the Highland land question in the historiography, it is important not to assume that this was the totality of the Scottish land question. Images of the Highlands had a prominent place in Scottish national identity in the nineteenth century and the chronology of Highland history – involving eviction, famine and protest – increases the visibility of the region. Nevertheless, there were important contexts of the Scottish land question in the overcrowded urban areas and even in the rural Lowlands of Scotland – a part of the country renowned for the efficiency of its farming and the quality of its arable and livestock products, although not yet well recognised in Scottish historiography or popular memory.

Notes

1. D. Cannadine, *The Decline and Fall of the British Aristocracy* (New Haven, 1990), pp. 710–11.
2. Ibid., pp. 9, 54–5, 710–11. For a detailed discussion of Sutherland, see A. M. Tindley, 'The Sutherland Estate, *c.* 1860–1914: Aristocratic Decline, Estate Management and Land Reform' (PhD thesis, Edinburgh, 2006).
3. J. S. Grant, *A Shilling for your Scowl: The History of a Scottish Legal Mafia* (Stornoway, 1992); *Report of the So-Called Bernera Rioters at Stornoway, on the 17th and 18th of July 1874* (n. p., 1874).
4. The dispute over foreshore rights is discussed in J. MacAskill, '"The Most Arbitrary, Scandalous Act of Tyranny": The Crown, Private Proprietors and

the Ownership of the Scottish Foreshore in the Nineteenth Century', *Scottish Historical Review*, 85 (2006), 277–304.

5. A. Newby, 'Edward McHugh, the National Land League of Great Britain and the "Crofters' War", 1879–1882', *Scottish Historical Review*, 82 (2003), 74–91; idem, '"Scotia Major and Scotia Minor": Ireland and the Birth of the Scottish Land Agitation, 1878–82', *Irish Economic and Social History*, 31 (2004), 23–40.
6. *Oban Times*, 1 March 1884, p. 4 and 10 January 1885, p. 4.
7. *'Thy Kingdom Come': A Sermon by Henry George in the City Hall Glasgow* (Glasgow, 1889); *The 'Single Tax' Faith: An Address by Henry George in the Temperance Institute Bridgeton* (Glasgow, 1889).
8. Even the radical Liberal Joseph Chamberlain felt that his theories were 'wild' and his methods 'unjust' (J. Chamberlain, 'Labourers' and artisans' dwellings', *Fortnightly Review*, 34 (1883), 761–76, at 761–2).
9. Duke of Argyll, 'The Prophet of San Francisco', *Nineteenth Century*, 15 (1884), 537–58; H. George, 'The "Reduction to Iniquity"', *Nineteenth Century*, 16 (1884), 134–55.
10. H. C. G. Matthew, 'Campbell, George Douglas, Eighth Duke of Argyll in the Peerage of Scotland, and First Duke of Argyll in the Peerage of the United Kingdom (1823–1900)', *Oxford Dictionary of National Biography* (Oxford, 2004); K. M. Mulhern, 'The Intellectual Duke: George Douglas Campbell, Eighth Duke of Argyll, 1823–1900' (PhD thesis, Edinburgh, 2006), pp. 190–232, esp. 221–3.
11. Argyll, 'Prophet', 546–8, 553–7.
12. George, '"Reduction to Iniquity"', 139.
13. Ibid., 146.
14. Ibid., 150–1. The question of landlord improvements was a point on which other Scottish critics of George focused. John Rae, from Wick in Caithness, also argued that landlord profit was not 'unearned', but the result of investment. He pointed to the example of the Duke of Sutherland's attempts to reclaim land, a project in which he lavished a considerable part of his vast wealth. This was perhaps an unfortunate example, since that investment yielded no 'increment', unearned or otherwise. See J. Rae, *Contemporary Socialism* (London, 1884), p. 474; A. Tindley, '"The Iron Duke": Land Reclamation and Public Relations in Sutherland, 1868–95', *Historical Research*, 82 (2009), 303–19.
15. J. R. Frame, 'America and the Scottish Left: The Impact of American Ideas on the Scottish Labour Movement from the American Civil War to World War One' (PhD thesis, Aberdeen, 1998), pp. 77–118.
16. British Library, Add. Mss 46440, f. 52 James Hogg to Wallace, 26 October 1882; f. 260–1 P. Walsh to Wallace, 18 May 1911.
17. J. Hunter, *The Making of the Crofting Community* (Edinburgh, 1976); A. Mackillop, *'More Fruitful than the Soil': Army, Empire and the Scottish Highlands, 1715–1815* (East Linton, 2000); T. M. Devine, *The Great Highland Famine: Hunger, Emigration and the Scottish Highlands in the Nineteenth Century* (Edinburgh, 1988); E. A. Cameron, *Land for the People? The British Government and the Scottish Highlands, c. 1880–1925* (East Linton, 1996); A. Newby, *Ireland, Radicalism and the Scottish Highlands, 1870–1912* (Edinburgh, 2007); A. W. MacColl, *Land, Faith and the Crofting Community: Christianity and Social Criticism in the Highlands of Scotland, 1843–93* (Edinburgh, 2006).

18. W. D. Rubinstein, 'New Men of Wealth and the Purchase of Land in Nineteenth Century Britain', *Past and Present*, 92 (1981), 132–3, 136; T. M. Devine, 'The Emergence of a New Elite in the Western Highlands and Islands, 1800–60', in T. M. Devine (ed.), *Improvement and Enlightenment* (Edinburgh, 1989), pp. 108–42.
19. Cameron, *Land for the People?* pp. 16–39.
20. I. M. M. MacPhail, *The Crofters' War* (Stornoway, 1989); Hunter, *Crofting Community*, chs 8–10.
21. A. M. McCleery, 'The Role of the Highland Development Agency: With Particular Reference to the Work of the Congested Districts Board, 1897–1912' (PhD thesis, Glasgow, 1984), pp. 252–414; Cameron, *Land for the People?*, pp. 83–123.
22. E. A. Cameron, 'Communication or Separation? Reactions to Irish Land Agitation and Legislation in the Highlands of Scotland, *c.* 1870–1910', *English Historical Review*, 120 (2005), 633–66.
23. L. Leneman, *Fit for Heroes? Land Settlement in Scotland after World War One* (Aberdeen, 1989); Hunter, *Crofting Community*, ch. 11; Cameron, *Land for the People?*, pp. 145–204.
24. I. J. M. Robertson, 'Governing the Highlands: The Place of Popular Protest in the Highlands of Scotland after 1918', *Rural History*, 8 (1997), 109–24.
25. E. A. Cameron, '"Unfinished Business": The Land Question and the Scottish Parliament', *Contemporary British History*, 15 (2001), 83–114.
26. R. H. Campbell, 'Too Much on the Highlands: A Plea for Change', *Scottish Economic and Social History*, 14 (1994), 58–75.
27. I. G. C. Hutchison, *A Political History of Scotland, 1832–1924: Parties, Elections and Issues* (Edinburgh, 1986), pp. 104–9.
28. R. H. Campbell, *Owners and Occupiers: Changes in Rural Society in South-West Scotland before 1914* (Aberdeen, 1991), pp. 122–8.
29. T. M. Devine, 'Scottish Farm Labour in the Era of Agricultural Depression, 1875–1900', in T. M. Devine (ed.), *Farm Servants and Labour in Lowland Scotland* (Edinburgh, 1984), pp. 243–55.
30. R. Anthony, *Herds and Hinds: Farm Labour in Lowland Scotland, 1900–1939* (East Linton, 1997); J. H. Smith, *Joe Duncan, the Scottish Farm Servants and British Agriculture* (Edinburgh, 1973).
31. For an overview, see Cameron, *Land For the People?* pp. 124–43.
32. See the speech by Harry Hope (Conservative, Bute), from a famous East Lothian farming family, *Hansard*, 5th ser., 26 (2 June 1911), cols 1367–71; *Scottish Farmer*, 3 September 1910, p. 777.
33. *Hansard*, 4th ser., 171 (19 March 1907), col. 704.
34. *Scottish Farmer*, 26 November 1910, p. 1047; Dover House was the London headquarters of the Scottish Office.
35. Its records are in the National Archives of Scotland, GD325.
36. M. Daunton, 'Urban Britain', in T. R. Gourvish and A. O'Day (eds), *Later Victorian Britain* (Basingstoke, 1988), pp. 58–60.
37. R. Rodger, 'Speculative Builders and the Structure of the Scottish Building Industry', *Business History*, 21 (1979), 226–46.
38. M. Daunton, 'Public Place and Private Space: The Victorian City and the Working-Class Household', in D. Fraser and A. Sutcliffe (eds), *The Pursuit of Urban History* (Edinburgh, 1983), p. 214; R. Rodger, 'The Invisible Hand:

Market Forces, Housing and the Urban Form in Victorian cities', in Fraser and Sutcliffe, *Pursuit of Urban History*, pp. 190–211.

39. Daunton, 'Urban Britain', p. 54.
40. P. J. Smith, 'Planning as Environmental Improvement: Slum Clearance in Victorian Edinburgh', in A. Sutcliffe (ed.), *The Rise of Modern Urban Planning* (London, 1980), p. 123; P. J. Smith, 'The Rehousing/Relocation Issue in an Early Slum-Clearance Scheme: Edinburgh, 1865–1885', *Urban Studies*, 26 (1989), 109.
41. W. H. Fraser and I. Maver, 'Tackling the Problems', in W. H. Fraser and I. Maver (eds), *Glasgow, Volume II: 1830–1912* (Manchester, 1996), p. 421; C. M. Allan, 'The Genesis of British Urban Redevelopment with Special Reference to Glasgow', *Economic History Review*, 18 (1965), 598–613.
42. R. Rodger, 'The Victorian Building Industry and the Housing of the Scottish Working Class', in M. Doughty (ed.), *Building the Industrial City* (Leicester, 1986), p. 183.
43. J. J. Smyth, *Labour in Glasgow, 1896–1936: Socialism, Suffrage, Sectarianism* (East Linton, 2000), pp. 51–3, 66.
44. N. J. Morgan and M. J. Daunton, 'Landlords in Glasgow: A Study of 1900', *Business History*, 25 (1983), 264–86.
45. I. S. Wood, *John Wheatley* (Manchester, 1988), pp. 54–7.
46. J. Melling, *Rent Strikes: Peoples' Struggle for Housing in West Scotland, 1890–1916* (Edinburgh, 1983), p. 77.
47. J. Melling, 'Clydeside Housing and the Evolution of State Rent Control, 1900–39', in J. Melling (ed.), *Housing, Social Policy and the State* (London, 1980), pp. 151–60.
48. A. Campbell, *The Scottish Miners, 1874–1939, Volume Two: Trade Unions and Politics* (Aldershot, 2000), pp. 82–6, at 86.

7
Irish Land and British Politics

Philip Bull

Introduction: the Irish land question

Land was a pervasive issue in British politics through much of the nineteenth and into the twentieth century. The resonances from it were still sufficiently present for Harold Wilson in one of his 1974 election campaigns to use the 'Land for the People' slogan of the 1906 general election as a metaphor for his policy on North Sea oil. Likewise in Ireland, land was a major issue for most of the nineteenth century, and continued to have powerful political repercussions right through to relatively late in the twentieth century. The land as an issue often seemed to provide a filament that linked together the politics of the four countries of the United Kingdom, but the differences lying beneath the surface in each country (and indeed regionally within each) were often significant in economic, political, and social terms. There was, however, in the three countries that constituted the island of Great Britain a sufficient commonality surrounding the land question to enable a broad political identification across those national boundaries, and in particular with the ideologies and structures of Liberal politics as they developed from the middle of the nineteenth century to the Great War. In the island of Ireland the story is a different one, and complicated by the propensity of many contemporaries (particularly British politicians) to understand it misleadingly in terms that fitted the central British political discourse and the equally significant inclination of Irish contemporaries to misunderstand how their concerns were being mutated to suit that central arena. In this chapter, an analysis is presented of the commonalities of land between Ireland and the rest of the British Isles and of what distinguished the Irish case from the wider discourses. In part, this is a study in differing perceptions and how they related to the discourses of two distinct polities held together in unified political structures.

There are several fundamental aspects of the Irish case, connected but also distinct, which form a basis upon which such an analysis can be developed. One of these was the immediacy of the sense of conquest and dispossession in Ireland. Related to this was a strong perception of illegitimacy attaching to the dominant and officially sanctioned land settlement prevailing in Ireland. There were also significant cultural differences in Gaelic (including Scottish) traditions of land holding from the Anglo-Norman system that had become naturalised and more generally accepted within England. At a different level, the political system under which Ireland was governed throughout the nineteenth century had never gained general acceptance nor been effectively legitimated in the popular consciousness. Moreover, whereas in England a class basis largely existed for rural landed relationships, in Ireland this was early eclipsed by social and political constructions that transcended major class divisions. This in turn was sanctioned (even sanctified) through a religious demography in which membership of the dominant religious group generally coincided with those sections of the population for whom the formal landed system was most unacceptable. While in England adhesion to the Church of England may have been weakened by a range of religious (and even irreligious) dissent, there was no ecclesiastical structure of the power of Irish Catholicism to provide an alternative hegemonic legitimation to that of the landed Anglican ascendancy.

In the late eighteenth century, landed relationships in Ireland were already distinctly different from those in England, and becoming rapidly more so. As industrialisation developed in Britain and economic ideologies changed, agriculture was brought more into line with the emerging capitalist practices, facilitated by the rapid expansion of demand for labour in the new urban conurbations and a corresponding reduction of population pressure in the agrarian economy. In Ireland, with the partial exception of the north east corner of the country, this was not happening. A pre-modern economy and demography persisted, with very high levels of poor rural peasantry and with a wide diversity of land tenure practices. There were two major historical and social factors that compounded this difference. A powerful legacy of dispossession denied to the landed elite the legitimacy generally enjoyed by their English equivalents. The most recent wave of landlords had been imposed upon the countryside little more than a century earlier, and longer established ones often no more than two centuries before. In these circumstances popular memory and contemporary attitudes converged to deny such elites the acceptance that in England made possible their leadership of radical changes in agriculture and social organisation. Superimposed on this was religious difference of a kind that further undermined any capacity for landlord intervention in agrarian life. The bulk of the population adhered, as they had always done, to the ancient Catholic religion of Ireland, whilst the landlord class were overwhelmingly Anglican. Thus, whatever sanction religion gave to social organisation and everyday life attached largely to the Catholic peasantry and tenantry, thereby strengthening their traditions and practices against the order that landlords might wish to impose.

This state of affairs necessarily affected the behaviour of the ruling class, which was forced into a defensive posture relative to the society over which it formally presided. Having to recognise both their own importation and the lack of cultural or religious continuity with the bulk of the population, they had to choose between conflict and accommodation – if the former, they were bound to be the loser, while the latter offered a basis for co-existence and compromise. Within the context of pre-capitalist systems this was, in some respects, no more than a variant of the paternalist assumptions of the landlord system, and it provided a relative if uneven stability assisted by the exceptional agricultural prosperity which accompanied the Napoleonic Wars. The secret to landlord success, and even survival, was to minimise the level of 'interference' with the farmers who 'rented' their land, to collect rents while ensuring that their levels were kept as low as possible, and to respect local custom on land usage, especially insofar as that involved an assumption of proprietorship by the tenant.

This was all to change. Irish landlordism, different as it had to be in the way it operated, was never insulated from the culture and assumptions of the English landlord system from which it derived, and as that culture changed, so attitudes amongst Irish landlords began to alter in subtle ways. In particular, the model emerging in the second half of the eighteenth century amongst progressive English landlords following the path of Thomas Coke of Holkham Hall in Norfolk began to influence some Irish landlords.[1] The concept of a landlord actively intervening in the management of an estate, and in particular in the organisation of farms within it and of the agricultural methods used, became attractive to a few more advanced Irish landlords who had kept abreast of developments in the sister island. A notable example was Lord George Hill of Gweedore in county Donegal. Conscientiously setting out to modernise his estate on the model of English landlord reformers, including addressing the problem of over-population by humane and responsible measures, Hill managed to antagonise his tenants, his efforts at improvement characterised as 'improving them off their land'.[2] A prominent Liberal landlord referred in 1846 to a tenant-farmer view of improvement as 'inseparable from dispossession'.[3] The wife of another constructive landlord was struck by the lack of appreciation for their efforts, complaining that 'we were to them only the receivers of a much grudged rent'.[4] Here we have the elements of two distinct cultures of agrarian society.

We have evidence from a number of sources relating how the tenant farmers saw their relationship with the landlords, including what we can deduce from those who began to advocate their cause. There are two striking examples of such advocacy dating from the 1830s and continuing for several decades after that. The individuals involved represented two distinct traditions, but their ideas were variants on the same theme. Both men were landlords, but influenced more by their respective local cultures and agrarian environments than by the Anglo-Norman model of land use. William Conner asserted the principle of 'a valuation and a perpetuity', an attempt at accommodation between customary practice and the imported landlord concept. For him the tenant belief that his occupancy was a permanent one was to be handled within the framework of landlordism by fixing rents on the basis of a valuation rather than the market place, and giving tenants occupancy in perpetuity subject to the payment of the rent thus determined.[5] The other tenant farmer advocate, William Sharman Crawford, was an Ulster landlord and an MP, who used his parliamentary position over more than two decades to introduce bills in an attempt to put into legal form the practice of tenant right, defined in his case as 'Ulster Custom'.[6] This was the practice by which an outgoing tenant received a payment, often a very substantial one, from his incoming successor. While in Ulster this was a highly formalised practice, it also existed – as we shall see – extensively elsewhere in the country. While various interpretations could – and were – put upon this custom, it is perhaps most appropriate to see it as payment for a proprietary interest, and therefore as recognition of the tenant's claim to a permanency. In that sense, although their language was different, Sharman Crawford and Conner were articulating the same tenant understanding of their relationship to the land.

It is, however, from another major source that we get our most comprehensive understanding of the views of all those connected with the land in Ireland. In the early 1840s, the government established a Royal Commission – the Devon Commission – to enquire into the law and practice of land occupation in Ireland and the minutes of evidence given before it provide extensive and diversified information on attitudes and practices associated with land issues.[7] What emerges from that enquiry is the extent to which the perceptions of the occupying tenants of agricultural land in Ireland differed from official understandings of the English-based legal formulations. In particular, the custom of tenant right – thought in the public arena to be a specifically Ulster practice applying to Presbyterian tenant farmers – was in practice commonplace throughout Ireland. Whereas in Ulster it was accorded public recognition, elsewhere in the predominantly Catholic areas of Ireland it occurred unofficially, sometimes with the covert acceptance of the landlord but often without his knowledge. The mode of enforcement was community opinion, making it unacceptable for an incoming tenant to refuse to make the customary payment to the outgoing one. Thus – as George Campbell was later to put it – there were effectively two different systems of law and practice operating in relation to land tenure in Ireland, the one sanctioned by long-established custom, the other introduced as part of the series of conquests and confiscations by English authority.[8] But in all this the latter had failed to extinguish the customary practices, thus giving them a continuing legitimacy.

This was the essence of the 'Irish land question' that was to dominate Ireland's relationship with British government for the next half century – two systems of law, two conceptions of land occupancy, and, usually, a failure on either side either to recognise or to acknowledge the fundamental cleavage which this created. In the past this had not been a major cause of conflict, the two systems co-existing uneasily but without major eruption into the public or political arena. What changed this was an external force that challenged in a new way the accommodation on which the old order had been based. This new force was ideological, had changed the whole nature of the British economy and society, and was now to have a profound, but much more negative impact, on Ireland.

The impact of political economy

The economic revolution that had transformed the political economy of Great Britain had already begun to cause concern to some Irish commentators even before the Great Famine. Notably, Isaac Butt, then a strong Conservative supporter of the Protestant establishment, had during the 1830s and early 1840s developed a strong critique of the misgovernment of Ireland by the British, a large part of his argument being based on the inappropriateness of the new philosophy of political economy to Irish circumstances. Particularly preoccupied by the issue of land, and despite his general support for the ascendancy, his sympathies lay with the tenants, whom he saw as the victims of an ideology that rejected their customary belief in their connection to the land.[9] The experience of the Famine had a paradoxical effect. For much informed Irish opinion, including Butt himself, it established beyond question the inappropriateness of applying British economic ideas to Ireland. Butt was later to write that 'It is marvellous how these discoveries of the true principles of political economy are always made out at exactly the right time for British and at the wrong time for Irish interests.'[10] In reply to those who insisted that political economy taught that the price of land should be regulated by supply and demand, Butt replied that, if applied 'to the letting of land in Ireland, it would tell us that which, as a general rule, and applied to the great mass of the population, is contrary to fact, and would therefore be untrue... Land is not an article of which the supply can be apportioned to the demand.'[11] Believing that such a philosophy would involve 'the extermination of the people', Butt also drew on support from other political economists, including J. S. Mill, to assert 'that land divided into small farms in which the cultivators have a property, yields the most comfort to the largest number of human beings'.[12] For British official and ruling class opinion, however, these views were anathema. To them, it was the lack of what they saw as modern political economy that had allowed population to exceed the capacity of its economy, thus causing the Famine. This view was not universal in British intellectual opinion, and in particular Mill argued that acceptance of local custom was essential to an effective political economy and that 'the actual cultivators should be enabled to become in Ireland what they will become in America – proprietors of the soil which they cultivate'.[13] But the major cleavage between Irish and British views largely defined the Irish land question as it emerged in political discourse after the Famine.

The aspiration of Irish tenants was for a compromise between their most basic beliefs about their permanency on the land and the reality of a landlord system based on a different concept of ownership. Conner's 'valuation and a perpetuity' was perhaps the most durable formulation for this, but it failed to feature in the ensuing political discourse. In part, this was because of his conflict with Daniel O'Connell and the Repeal movement over this very issue. O'Connell's call for leases for tenants, reflecting his essential commitment to the *laissez faire* concept of political economy, showed a failure to comprehend the nature of the tenant position and helped to confuse the issue of tenants' rights within the political arena.[14] It was Sharman Crawford who was able to attract political attention to the issue, but at a long-term cost. In introducing bills to the House of Commons to put in legislative form the custom of tenant right (or Ulster Custom), he was attempting to make more secure the practice which was so important to Ulster tenants, although probably in ignorance of the scale of the practice elsewhere in the country. But his basic premise, that a tenant had the right to sell his interest in his land, was so far removed from British conceptions of property that it was a major challenge to find the language with which to pursue his case. In attempting to communicate effectively in a British parliamentary context, Crawford chose to distinguish between British and Irish practice by focusing on the liability of Irish tenants to pay for the improvements carried out on their farms. British legislators, ignorant as they were of the preference of Irish tenants for making their own improvements rather than have landlords 'interfere' on their farms, found this alien to their conceptions of landlord responsibility. Crawford had diluted, for parliamentary consumption, a concept of tenant proprietary right to a claim for compensation in the hope, vainly as it turned out, that this might provide a more respectable capitalist argument. The bills he introduced became identified in those terms, thus reshaping the Irish tenant claim for more than two decades.

Ten bills for compensation for improvements were introduced in parliament between 1835 and 1858, all of them unsuccessful. By the latter part of that period the transition from a more comprehensive meaning of tenant right to merely compensation for improvements had been completed, with William Shee (Sharman Crawford's parliamentary colleague) defining the demand as 'the Irish Tenants right to enjoy, or be compensated for, on eviction, those permanent and durable improvements, without which a remunerative cultivation of the soil is impossible, and which, in Ireland, are always or almost always, provided at the tenant's expense'.[15] While by the end of that period Shee (who had taken over the issue following Crawford's death) was securing more parliamentary sympathy for the cause, it was emerging in a way totally unacceptable to his constituency in Ireland. It was argued by British parliamentarians sympathetic to protecting tenants against the loss of the value of their improvements that any legislation should provide for prior approval by landlords of the improvements before a case for compensation could be made and that payment should directly correspond to the cost of those improvements. This, however, was not how tenants saw the issue, as for them the sale of their interest bore no relationship to actual expenditure on improvements, and so the whole compensation for improvements campaign ended up in a cul-de-sac.

Thus can be discerned the steadily entrenching political difficulty over Irish land tenure. While Irish tenant farmers adhered assiduously to a customary practice that epitomised for them their proprietary interest in their farms, British legislators were unable to be swayed from an uncompromising commitment to a concept of property that allowed for no compromise of the rights of an absolute owner. In this they believed they were defending both property rights and proper principles of a capitalist economy. Mill had another perspective, acknowledging that the Anglo-Norman system was not the only one that was compatible with capitalist principles and that the important condition for a capitalist economy was not a particular form of ownership but clarity about where it resided. Or as he put it, with emphasis upon the sense of stability from the cultivator's point of view, there is 'a virtue in "for ever" beyond the longest term of years: a tenure for a limited period, however long, is sure to be regarded as something of inferior consideration and dignity, and inspires less of ardour to obtain it and of attachment to it when obtained'.[16]

This view did not, however, find favour amongst the decision-makers, who remained unwilling to countenance two different cultures of land tenure within the United Kingdom. The failure to find an accommodation between two rival conceptions of ownership had, as we will see, far reaching consequences and ones that were antipathetic to the development of economically viable practices in the Irish countryside.

The impact of Gladstone

Recognition of the very different culture of land tenure existing in Ireland was hard for British opinion, but not always impossible. The Devon Commission in the 1840s had recommended recognition of the right to compensation for improvements, but this was not legislated. This was the first of a number of occasions on which decisive action might have substantially settled the issue. Mill also acknowledged the compatibility of native practice with proper economic principles.[17] It was, however, not until the late 1860s that such a perspective found expression at a political level, although ultimately to limited effect. William Ewart Gladstone, on taking office in late 1868, embarked on a course that was to transform his attitudes to the land problem in Ireland. In addition to his own characteristic and assiduous commitment to doing his research on a topic, he sent to Ireland to report back to him George Campbell, a Scotsman with extensive experience as an administrator in India. With his consciousness of cultural difference and his detailed experience of very different land tenure systems, Crawford was able to get quickly to the crux of the problem in Ireland. In a report later published, he wrote that it was a case of '... two sets of laws—the English laws, and the laws or customs of the country, which, enforced in a different way, are as active and effective.'[18] He considered that the 'cardinal mistake' in the past had been the failure to recognise the validity of these Irish customs and practices, a view in part supported by the Lord Chancellor of the time who 'traced the need for legislation to the failure of the courts in Ireland to adapt English law to Irish custom and circumstances.'[19] Later George Errington pithily captured the nature of the problem, declaring that the concept of the landlord's absolute property right as encapsulated in English law had been 'roughly grafted on the native customs at an early period, [and] has always worked in direct antagonism to them', concluding that 'Either of these systems might have thriven alone; in combination, fire and water would not have been more incompatible'.[20]

Gladstone followed the implications of these ideas to the point where one of his colleagues described him as 'possessed by this idea of restitution'.[21] Another colleague referred to a concept of 'Tribal Right'.[22] These were disparaging references to the direction of Gladstone's mind in discussing with his colleagues the form of the bill that was to become the 1870 Land Act. What these comments reveal is that Gladstone had arrived at a position from which resolution of Irish land problems entered the realm of possible solution: that is, the differing perspectives of tenure rights in Ireland were inextricably related to dispossession, and more specifically to the failure of authority to extinguish earlier rights embodied in continuing practices. From this he was able to understand the commitment to the tenant right practice, and to realise that meeting the expectations of Irish farmers meant including in legislation something that went beyond compensation for improvements and applied more generally than just to those tenants who enjoyed more formally the tenant right custom.

'The idea of restitution' towards which Gladstone had been drawn led him into attempting to incorporate into the proposed land bill provision for the practice known as Ulster Custom to be given the force of law for all tenant farmers in Ireland. Short of declaring that Irish tenant farmers were co-owners of their land, this seemed as far as it was possible to go. But this was too much for those of his colleagues for whom, as for their Tory opponents, it involved a violation of the rights of property. Gladstone did succeed in including a provision that any tenants who could establish that they had enjoyed a practice similar to Ulster Custom would be covered by the legislation, and remarkably was also able to insert a clause stipulating that any tenant evicted by his landlord would be entitled to compensation for such disturbance. Moreover, in sensing that the resolution of the Irish problem lay along the path of 'restitution' of older rights Gladstone had glimpsed the way forward, even though political necessity had prevented him realising this fully in legislation. The British state had come a long way. From attempting in 1860, through Deasy's Act, to decree that the relationship of landlord and tenant in Ireland shall be 'founded on the express or implied Contract of the Parties, and not upon Tenure or Service', parliament had now in effect legislated the opposite and set up a principle of property in agricultural land in Ireland distinctly different from that in Britain.

In that short decade, however, much else had changed as well. Frustrated at the failure of attempts to recognise their claims, either through the gentlemanly parliamentary tactics of a Sharman Crawford or the more organised agitations of tenant leagues, tenant farmers had vented their anger in less orthodox ways. In particular, the rise of the Fenian movement during the 1860s had enabled tenant farmers to contribute to the more generalised sense of threat which faced the British state in Ireland, and to which Gladstone's initiatives were in part a response. By ensuring election results sympathetic to Fenianism in areas predominantly agrarian, farmers – largely uninterested in the political and revolutionary objectives of Fenians – contributed to a realisation that their issue was central to the continuing stability of British rule. In that sense the breakthrough represented by the 1870 Land Act whetted the appetites of tenant farmers for more robust methods in pursuit of their goals.

The land question, Irish nationalism and the 1881 Land Act

In the 1870 Land Act, Isaac Butt had discerned 'a struggle to escape from principles by which the framers of the Bill believed themselves bound, but which, in favour of the Irish tenant, they made every effort to evade. I fear the result has been only an elaborate failure to do the justice which it was so elaborately attempted to work out'.[23] Two clear messages emerged from this important legislation: one was that the objectives of Irish tenants had not been adequately met; the other was that the British state was able to be swayed by pressure into creating those precedents which it had long been argued it could not. To this had been added a further new dimension that was to change the very nature of the relationship between Ireland and British government. The flirtation with Fenianism, together with the failure to reform other grievances felt by the Irish, especially in relation to issues affecting Catholics, had generated a new sense that it was the very system of government that created the problems evident in Irish society. Increasingly the land issue became intermingled with the demand for some form of self-government for Ireland, feeding in powerfully to Isaac Butt's new home rule movement from 1870 onwards. By 1879, this fusion had taken irreversible form in the Land League, which openly merged the land and home rule movements under the leadership of Charles Stewart Parnell. Thus, whereas debate and persuasion had marked the attempts at land reform in Ireland through the 1840s and 1850s, and in the case of Gladstone an intellectual understanding of the problem had evolved, from the 1860s onwards, the nexus had been clearly drawn between agitational or revolutionary pressure and concessions from British government. Gladstone's relating in 1868 of his 'mission to pacify Ireland' to the preceding Fenian troubles was itself an unintended acknowledgement of that nexus. By the late 1870s, it was widely accepted in Ireland, increasingly even by moderate, middle-class Catholics, that the level of agitation and unrest was the measure of the British capacity to address Irish issues.

In the 1840s and 1850s, it had seemed that to get legal status for the Ulster Custom, or more generally the tenant right practice, would be sufficient acknowledgement of the traditional rights of Irish farmers, but Gladstone's 1870 Land Act demonstrated that this was no longer the case. While effectively this legislation gave to all tenant farmers the protection and rights embodied in the custom, in practice this was inadequate to secure what they believed to be their relationship to the land. Indeed, parallel to the campaign for compensation for improvements, it had become increasingly common since the Famine for the tenant demand to be couched in terms of what had come to be known as the 'Three F's' – Fair Rents, Fixity of Tenure, and Freedom to Sell. The third of these alone had been provided for in the 1870 Act, but experience quickly showed that in the absence of the other two it was possible for landlords to undermine or circumvent the objectives of the Act. The 'Three F's' in effect replicated what William Conner had called 'a valuation and a perpetuity', and they very quickly became the objective of Irish land reformers once the imperfections of the 1870 Act had been demonstrated. Five years of Tory government, massive agitation and unrest in Ireland through the Land League, Gladstone's return to office, and the recommendations of a new Royal Commission under Lord Bessborough resulted in 1881 in a new Land Act that effectively implemented the 'Three F's'. Under this legislation tribunals were established to determine fair rents, and so long as these were paid the tenants enjoyed security of tenure. The right to sell their interest in their farms, embodied in the 1870 Act, was continued. In effect, Irish tenant farmers had secured the substance of all that had ever been sought, and a new concept of property had entered into the British legal system in a form that was now defined as 'dual ownership'.

Three factors now combined to thwart any notion that, no matter how much it met Irish demands, the 1881 Act would not be allowed to stand as a permanent settlement of the land issue in Ireland. The first of these was a consequence of the traumatic social, political, and economic cleavage that had been demonstrated, if not indeed created, between the landlord class and their tenant farmers through the agitational experience of the Land League and which had raised more directly the notion that landlordism could be abolished altogether. Already in the platform of the Land League was a declaration that the ultimate objective was peasant proprietorship, a country of small farmers owning their own land with undivided responsibility for it. The second factor was that landlords themselves found the circumstance they were in after the 1881 Act very unattractive. They had lost even the notional sense that they were the sole owners of their land, and their revenue from the land was to be determined by tribunals. Although the tribunals were of a judicial nature and impartial, in practice, tenants had the initiative, were better organised, and were more critical to the securing of peace. As a result, landlords became increasingly disenchanted with their loss of power and what they saw as an unfair diminution in their incomes. The third factor was the Conservative party, which found highly unpalatable the existence within the United Kingdom of a property settlement that divided ownership between two parties, with the relationship between them governed by legislation. Thus, the victory of the tenants in achieving their preferred outcome had paved the way towards a different eventual outcome on Irish land.

Irish land and the Conservative party

In the year before the passage of the 1870 Land Act, Gladstone had enacted his first major Irish reform with the disestablishment of the Church of Ireland. Ancillary to that legislation were provisions to disinvest the Church of its agricultural lands, and for this purpose a scheme was devised to enable the Church's tenants to purchase their farms. This provided an important model for future schemes and in particular helped shape what were known as the Bright Clauses of the 1870

Land Act. Liberal governments, however, were more disposed to consolidating the system of dual ownership as a means of securing peace in the Irish countryside than to embark on large-scale schemes of land purchase, particularly as these were postulated on the basis of financial facilitation by government antipathetic to Gladstonian conceptions of fiscal restraint. Perhaps more importantly there was little political motive for Liberal governments to facilitate land purchase given that they saw the landlords as being the major beneficiaries of such government subsidies – a class from which they expected little electoral or other support. Indeed, any sense that Liberals owed anything to landlordism was finally erased by the secession of most of the remaining Whig elements of the party with the home rule crisis of 1886. From then on, during the Conservative–Liberal Unionist governments of 1886–92 and 1895–1905, purchase by tenants of their farms from their landlords became the preferred strategy.

Two forces combined to propel Conservative governments down the path of land purchase. Irish landlords, desperate to escape from what they saw as an increasingly unrewarding and weakened position, were pressing the party to which they were allied into helping them escape their ownership. Perhaps more important was an ideological consideration. Conservatives generally found abhorrent the system of dual ownership that had been the consequence of Gladstone's reforms, compromising in their view a fundamental principle of property ownership. Land purchase they saw as a path back to a system of individual ownership. To reinstate the landlords, no doubt theoretically their preferred option, they saw as impossible, but what they could do was to consolidate the creation of a new class of sole owners. In doing so they were belatedly, and for many of them essentially by default, falling in with Mill's original position that a peasant proprietorship was perfectly compatible both with political economy and proper principles of property ownership. For some Conservatives, however, this had become a matter of principle earlier. Two prominent Conservatives – Sir Stafford Northcote and the Irishman Edward Gibson (later Lord Ashbourne) – had begun as early as 1880 to explore possible Conservative responses to the concept of a peasant proprietary in Ireland in discussions that largely defined the later direction of Conservative policy.[24] The first significant and effective measure for land purchase was passed through parliament in 1885, initiated by Ashbourne himself, Lord Chancellor of Ireland during the short Tory administration in the second half of that year. The Ashbourne Act was enormously successful, so much so that the available funding could not meet the demand, and helped both to consolidate landlord commitment to the concept of purchase and to allay some of the tenant apprehensions about such a change.

The Ashbourne Act was not followed up successfully by subsequent Tory governments. These ministries, dominated by the 'Hotel Cecil' and in particular on Irish matters by Lord Salisbury and his nephews Arthur and Gerald Balfour, were affected by two considerations which undermined the effectiveness of their policies on Irish land. The first of these was a truculent attitude towards the Irish, encapsulated in Salisbury's remark that they should 'take a licking' before getting the benefits of reform.[25] And it was precisely this that Arthur Balfour as Irish Chief Secretary proceeded to attempt by aggressive, if not brutalising, responses to the new 'Plan of Campaign' agitation, earning himself the sobriquet 'Bloody Balfour'. This was certainly counter-productive in terms of creating the degree of co-operation between tenants and landlords that might have given some prospect of successful land purchase schemes. The second reason related to Arthur Balfour's propensity to be too clever by half, and to add sophisticated complexities to his legislative initiatives. Responsible either for amending acts or substantive acts on land purchase in Ireland in 1887, 1888, 1889, and 1891, none of his schemes attracted enough interest from tenants to push forward the progress of purchase. L. P. Curtis has suggested that the reason for this was that 'The tenants... preferred the Ashbourne Act simply because they could understand it'.[26] It took another Chief Secretary, even though again a nephew of Lord Salisbury, to carry through land purchase to its next stage and effectively its culmination in the creation of a peasant proprietary. George Wyndham, after an initial failed attempt, threw the task of finding an acceptable solution for both sides over to a conference representative of Irish landlords and tenants. This conference, which met in December 1902 and January 1903, evolved a scheme that with little change was drafted into what became the Wyndham Land Act of 1903. It is a matter for reflection that Lord Ashbourne was an Irishman and that the other, and final, successful measure for land purchase was devised by Irishmen, and that the Englishmen responsible for the intervening attempts had failed to understand sufficiently what would engage with the aspirations of Irish tenants.

Many tenants were initially reluctant to embark on land purchase schemes, in large part because they could not see a sufficiently tangible benefit to balance the greater degree of responsibility that would fall on their shoulders as owners. Observation of successful schemes was therefore very important in familiarising tenants with what was involved and the benefits that might accrue. The Church measure of 1869 was a start in this regard, but the Ashbourne Act much more so. Another development, in part attributable to Arthur Balfour, also helped. The Congested Districts Board, set up in 1891, successfully carried through a number of purchases of estates for resale to tenants in areas of over-population after a reorganisation to improve farm viability. But tenants were hard headed in protecting their economic interests, as of course were landlords. The challenge for any purchase scheme was to find the price at which the tenant was prepared to buy and that at which the landlord was willing to sell. Failing to bridge this gap was the weakness that plagued purchase between 1886 and 1903. It was the willingness of the government to contribute substantially to meeting that gap by treasury advances, and also the existence of bonuses to encourage landlords to settle more quickly with their tenants, that enabled the 1903 Act largely to complete the process of land purchase and bring about the end of landlordism in Ireland. This supposedly ought also to have marked the end of what had long been called the Irish land question, but the matter was not as simple as that.

Land and the Irish nation

The issue of land tenure in Ireland would perhaps have been more easily resolved at an earlier time and with many fewer complications had there been more of a willingness to accept, with Mill, that differing systems could operate within a political entity without necessarily conflicting with what were then considered to be the proper principles of political economy. The consequences of the long struggle over the land, however, were far reaching and had implications well beyond those immediately associated with the issue itself.

There was but one land issue, and that in itself was remarkable in the circumstances. Tenant farmers in Ireland, particularly in the post-Famine era, ranged from very prosperous farmers in the rich and fertile regions in the east of the country, through the so-called 'strong farmers' of the midland and other regions, to poverty-stricken peasants eking out a fragile existence on rocky, infertile land in the west and other over-populated areas of the country. As had happened in England through the revolution in agriculture from the late eighteenth century onwards, the more prosperous farmers had undergone a transformation in their cultural and social as well as their economic circumstances, moving much closer in their way of life to that of their landlords. Thus, in Ireland as in England, such farmers were building grander houses for themselves, while their wives and daughters had replaced menial farm work with charitable, cultural, and other outside activities, and their sons were being educated to new levels to enable them to enter the professions. But in Ireland there was another layer to this: such farmers and their families were generally staunch supporters of the Catholic Church, to which they had contributed significantly over the years in enabling it to build churches, establish convents and schools, and assume a role appropriate to the largest religious denomination in the country. Moreover, to that Church the landlord class and the ascendancy class more generally did not subscribe. This meant that, in terms of the social pyramid of increasingly the greatest importance to the bulk of the population, these farmers were at the pinnacle. This compounded the growing sense of resentment at the limitations on the control of their land, making them ardent in their commitment to their tenant right, well disposed to the idea of absolute ownership in their own hands, but very canny as to the terms on which they were willing to purchase.

What common interest did such farmers and entrepreneurs have with marginal peasant cultivators in the impoverished areas of the country? The effect of the long struggle to obtain recognition of deeply held rights of tenure had gradually cemented an alliance that transcended what would normally have been cleavages based on fundamentally divergent economic interests. What held this very diverse cross-section of the population together on the land issue was another issue for which it became largely a metaphor – that of Irish nationality. From the Land League of the early 1880s onwards, political organisation and strategies so intertwined both issues that it became impossible to distinguish them from each other in political terms, and this facilitated a process by which unity was achieved across the nation regardless of economic status and indeed of the rural/urban divide, excluding by and large only the ascendancy class. In effect, but not entirely so, the principal excluded category became one that could be defined in religious terms – if you were Catholic, you were more than likely caught up in the political mobilisation around the land/national issues, and if you were Protestant, you were probably excluded and hostile to it. Out of this new hegemony, prosperous farmers reinforced by a prosperous urban Catholic middle class, were forged the political tools through which land reform was achieved.

Land thus helped to define nationality in new terms. As the old ascendancy, the symbol of patriotism in the eighteenth century, became identified with the forces of anti-nationality, possession of land became the Holy Grail that opened up for ordinary people a sense of identity.

While the returns in status and prosperity brought by land reforms were very substantial for more prosperous farmers, the rhetoric associated with the metaphoric nexus of land and nationality held out continuing hope of greater status and opportunity for the landed poor and the landless. Any tangible prospect of such advance did not long survive national independence, but the aspiration for it continued to bedevil the processes of modernisation in Ireland for many years, and perhaps helped to create what one Irish historian has called a 'begrudger' mentality.[27] The role of land in the evolution of forms of nationalism can be discerned in the political development of Isaac Butt. A staunch defender of the old ascendancy before the Famine he was cast in the mould of the Protestant patriots, believing that the interests of Ireland required the leadership of an elite able to defend its interests in the British world. His fundamental commitment to an Irish polity, however, was evident at the time to two very different nationalist opponents, Daniel O'Connell and John Mitchell, the former declaring with prescience that 'we will have him struggling with us yet'[28] and the latter that he had 'never advocated the Union upon Imperialist principles or because he thinks it useful to Great Britain'.[29] For Butt himself, the proof of the pudding was in the eating. As Joseph Spence has pointed out, a decade after Butt had in the *Dublin University Magazine* 'begun pointing out Ireland's grievances, none of them had been redressed'.[30] The Famine was the *coup de grace* to Butt's early approach. His trajectory from then on was to establish that Irish nationality required above all that Ireland be treated in its own terms, and that structures be evolved that worked for Ireland – including structures that meant political autonomy should these be proved necessary. For Butt, land was a critical continuity for him, running through his testing of the Union and his definition and modifying of Irish nationality. It continued to perform similar functions for those after him. While it is possible that the settlement brought about by the Wyndham Act might have severed the nexus between land and nationality, opening up a distinctive new sense of identity based on a society of small farmers, the link between the two could not be so easily severed. Land continued to divide, even if it did so increasingly within the Catholic/farmer hegemony rather than between it and the old ascendancy.[31]

On the land, the unity across classes was for limited purposes only. For the poorer peasants, land purchase was never a viable option and their objectives were often more revolutionary in both social and political terms, but also looking to land redistribution as their way forward. This was usually highly divisive, and directed not only against landlordism but also others in the community who held large tracts of lands, especially the holders of grazing lands who were usually themselves part of the Catholic/nationalist community. This was to be a major problem in Irish politics, leading to the early twentieth-century creation of the Dudley Commission, the last major British enquiry into the Irish land question. This Commission, and the renewed agitation for redistribution of land parallel to it, revealed that the culture of land agitation could disproportionately affect political developments after the substantive economic issue had been resolved. For those who were land deprived, it had been their muscle through aggressive agitations that had secured the legislative reforms sought by their more prosperous counterparts, but for the latter, if any redistribution of land was to take place, then they, as more efficient farmers, should be the ones to acquire it. This issue was finally settled, not by British government nor by those Irish nationalists who had presided over these conflicts, but by the revolutionary Dáil Éireann which issued a decree in 1920 against claimants for land redistribution, describing their actions as a 'stirring up of strife amongst our fellow countrymen'.[32]

The long struggle over the land had heightened expectations about the right to land in a country where its availability was limited and population pressed heavily on resources. The identification of the issue with the very essence of national identity had entrenched a culture that was ultimately antipathetic to what had become an essential attribute of modern agriculture, namely the consolidation of farms to create more viable enterprises. Much of this legacy derived from a failure to resolve the conflict between traditional rights and a modern economy. This was not unique to Ireland, and had its parallels for example in the conflict generated in parts of England by enclosure. But the mechanisms for resolution in Ireland did not exist – or rather the political institutions were too alien from native custom to be able to resolve, or even repress effectively, the older beliefs and customs.

Notes

1. For the changes happening in English landlordism see, for example, F. M. L. Thompson, *English Landed Society in the Nineteenth Century* (London, 1963); J. D. Chambers and G. E. Mingay, *The Agricultural Revolution, 1750–1880*, (London, 1966); J. Beckett, *The Aristocracy in England 1660–1914* (Oxford, 1986).
2. E. E. Evans, *Facts from Gweedore, Compiled from the Notes of Lord George Hill* (Belfast, 1971), pp. v–vi.

3. E. Batt, *The Moncks and Charleville House: A Wicklow Family in the Nineteenth Century* (Dublin, 1979), p. 233.
4. D. Thomson and M. McGusty (eds), *The Irish Journals of Elizabeth Smith, 1840–1850* (Oxford, 1980), p. 6.
5. W. Conner, *Two Letters to the Editor of the Times on the Rackrent Oppression of Ireland, its Source, its Evils and its Remedy* (Dublin, 1846).
6. W. Shee, *Papers, Letters and Speeches in the House of Commons on the Irish Land Question, with a Summary of its Parliamentary History, from the General Election of 1852 to the Close of the Session of 1863* (London, 1863).
7. *Report and Minutes of Evidence from Her Majesty's Commissioners of Enquiry into the State of the Law and Practice in respect to the Occupation of Land in Ireland* [Devon Commission], Parl. Papers 1845, XIX–XXIII.
8. G. Campbell, *The Irish Land* (London, 1869), pp. 6–7.
9. For Butt's more developed views on the land see his *The Irish People and the Irish Land: A letter to Lord Lifford, with comments on the Publications of Lord Dufferin and Lord Rosse* (Dublin, 1867).
10. I. Butt, *The Irish Deep Sea Fisheries: A Speech Delivered at a Meeting of the Home Government Association of Ireland on Tuesday, the 17th of October, 1871* (Dublin, 1874), p. 17.
11. I. Butt, *Land Tenure in Ireland: A Plea for the Celtic Race* (Dublin, 1866), p. 57.
12. Ibid., p. 64.
13. J. S. Mill, *The Principles of Political Economy* (3rd edn, London, 1852), i, p. 401.
14. K. B. Nowlan, *The Politics of Repeal: A Study in the Relations between Great Britain and Ireland, 1841–50* (London, 1965), p. 146.
15. Shee, *Papers, Letters and Speeches*, p. viii.
16. Mill, *Principles*, i, p. 401.
17. Ibid., pp. 403–6.
18. Campbell, *Irish Land*, pp. 6–7.
19. E. D. Steele, *Irish Land and British Politics: Tenant Right and Nationality, 1865–1870* (Cambridge, 1974), p. 309.
20. G. Errington, *The Irish Land Question: A letter to the Rt Hon. H.C.E Childers, M.P.* (Dublin, 1880), p. 5.
21. Robert Lowe, quoted in Steele, *Irish Land*, p. 254.
22. Duke of Argyll, quoted ibid., p. 287.
23. Quoted in R. D. C. Black, *Economic Thought and the Irish Question, 1817–1870* (Cambridge, 1960), p. 70.
24. Northcote to Gibson, 18 December 1880; Gibson to Northcote, 21 December 1880, House of Lords Record Office, Ashbourne Papers, B71/9-10.
25. L. P. Curtis, *Coercion and Conciliation in Ireland, 1880–92: A study in Conservative Unionism* (Princeton, 1963), p. 169.
26. Ibid., p. 354.
27. J. J. Lee, *Ireland 1912–1985: Politics and Society* (Cambridge, 1989), p. 646.
28. Quoted in D. Thornley, *Isaac Butt and Home Rule* (London, 1964), p. 16.
29. Quoted in T. de Vere White, *The Road of Excess* (Dublin, 1946), p. 99.
30. J. Spence, 'The Philosophy of Irish Toryism, 1833–52: A Study of Reactions to Liberal Reformism in Ireland in the Generation between the First Reform Act and the Famine, with Especial Reference to Expressions of National Feeling among the Protestant Ascendancy' (PhD thesis, London, 1991), p. 51.

31. For a fuller exploration of the longer term political significance of the Wyndham Land Act see P. Bull, *Land, Politics and Nationalism: A Study of the Irish Land Question* (Dublin, 1996), pp. 157–75, and Bull, 'The Significance of the Nationalist Response to the Irish Land Act of 1903', *Irish Historical Studies*, 28 (1993), 283–305.
32. Quoted in M. A. G. Ó Tuathaigh, 'The Land Question, Politics and Irish Society, 1922–1960', *Irish Studies*, 2 (1982), 170–1.

8
Richard Cobden, J. E. Thorold Rogers and Henry George

Antony Taylor

Introduction

Land and its ownership were at the heart of radical and reform politics throughout the nineteenth and early twentieth centuries. At crucial periods in the late nineteenth century, the land issue convulsed popular opinion. During these years, 'Land Quacks' as the Earl of Derby described them, incited a frenzied debate about the future of the great estates.[1] Despite wide agreement about the significance of the land campaign for both opponents and defenders of the aristocratic landed monopoly, the intellectual origins of the campaign remain obscure. In a series of visits to Britain after 1881, Henry George discovered a receptive audience for his rhetoric of imposing a Single Tax on land values. Central to the Georgeite land campaign of the 1880s was a pre-existing radical constituency, whose ideas were shaped by exposure to the memory of Richard Cobden. The contribution made by Cobden to the land question warrants re-examination. The Cobdenite inheritance provided an intellectual coherence and a credibility missing from more visceral sentiments about the dispossession of the people from the land. In the years between 1864 and Henry George's visits, the land question was reframed to incorporate these Cobdenite nostrums. During this period, radicalism established a pedigree for the land reform platform, in which key allies conferred status and respectability on the movement. The main figure in this process was the Oxford University economist and radical activist, James Edwin Thorold Rogers. This chapter rescues the career of Rogers from obscurity. It examines Cobden as a land reformer and analyses Rogers's posthumous annexation of his reputation for the land campaign. Thereafter it considers the significance of Rogers as an economic historian and his importance for George's land reform platform.

James Edwin Thorold Rogers straddled the world of middle-class reformism and popular plebeian radicalism. His historical writings, which sought to impose a coherent history on the agitation for land reform, played a crucial role in preparing the ground for Georgeite ideas. George, as the chapter will demonstrate, greatly admired Rogers's work and urged it upon his followers. The militant land reform groups inspired by Rogers duly found a home in Georgeite campaigns against corrupt aristocrats, imperial bureaucrats, land monopolists and in pursuit of the Single Tax. A consideration of these continuities lends substance to the argument that Rogers was a unique figure, bridging the radical worlds of the mid and late nineteenth century. Furthermore, it helps modify existing interpretations of the position of Henry George within the history of pre-labourist radicalism on the eve of the Great War.

J. E. Thorold Rogers and the Cobdenite heritage

Relatively little has been written about Rogers.[2] To contemporaries, however, he was well known. From 1862, he held the Drummond Professorship of Political Economy at Oxford. His political interests spanned land and franchise reform to encompass the rights of Dissenters and Cobdenite international arbitration. During the 1860s, he was one of a trio of advanced liberals within academia who made the transition to the popular platform. In company with Goldwin Smith and Henry Fawcett, he displayed a high level of dedication to the radical political agitations of the later nineteenth century and helped provide a new direction for the popular reform campaign of 1864–67.[3] Alongside his academic interests, he pursued an active career as a member of the Reform League, taking up the position of President of the Oxford Branch of the League in 1866–67; in May 1866, he was present at the Hyde Park riots and in London appeared on radical platforms alongside veteran agitators like Ernest Jones and The O'Donoghue to promote the message of manhood suffrage.[4] According to his own account, he was 'the first person of some position' to chair meetings of Joseph Arch's Agricultural Labourers' Union in the 1870s.[5] Within the world of Oxford, however, he was something of an outsider, never quite evolving into the figure of a 'public moralist' described by Stefan Collini.[6] His unabashed radicalism placed a gulf between himself and his colleagues. As Christopher Harvie has argued, figures like Rogers straddled mutually incompatible worlds.[7] His outspokenness and visible platform presence brought him into collision with the High Church traditions of the university. In 1868, he was voted out of the Drummond Chair after a vitriolic campaign to exclude him that included the circulation of his radical speeches around 'hunting fields and public and private dining tables'.[8] At the same time, the university helped shape his politics. In keeping with the Oxford High Church tradition, his early intellectual development was influenced by the Tractarian movement. For a while he contemplated entering the Church of England, and took up a post as voluntary assistant curate at Headington near Oxford. His earliest campaigns were in support of the Clerical Disabilities Act of 1871, which lifted the barrier to clergymen electioneering or standing for parliament.[9] By the late 1860s, he had moved to a position of support for Nonconformity. He became an advocate of the abolition of the university test to exclude Dissenters, and spoke in support of the disestablishment of the Church of Ireland in the general election of 1868.[10] Whilst garnering a number of significant accolades from the wider academic community, Rogers's relationship with Oxford continued to be problematic until his death in 1890.

Rogers, however, was best-known as an acolyte of Richard Cobden. Indeed his strongest legacy to the reform movements of the end of the nineteenth century was the degree to which he merged and intertwined the traditions of middle-class Cobdenism with popular plebeian radicalism. Rogers began his political career as an ardent free trader, gaining his undergraduate degree in 1846, the year of the repeal of the Corn Laws. His ties with Cobden were both political and familial. Alongside T. Fisher Unwin and Francis Hirst, he was one of the tight circle of in-laws of the Cobden family who were fiercely protective of their mentor's posthumous reputation. Cobden's eldest sister was his sister-in-law, and Cobden's father had at one stage been a tenant of Rogers's father, George Vining Rogers. This was politics as both clan and connexion. Rogers gave an elegy to Cobden's memory at West Lavington Church two days after Cobden's funeral in 1865 that was published in pamphlet form and became a popular tribute to the lost leader. In it Rogers drew Christ-like comparisons with the departed Cobden, lamenting that at Easter time

> Two days ago, the greatest and wisest men in England gathered in this church and churchyard in order to render the last offices of loving homage to the most single-hearted and generous statesman who has ever lived in the history of mankind. The burial of other men has been solemnized with greater pomp and more numerous attendance, has been marshalled by authority and accompanied by all the circumstances which art could invent in order to shew honour to departed

> eminence. But on this occasion as never before, the great concourse of mourners was gathered out of the deep wish felt to do reverence to a man whose memory will live as long as the world shall endure.[11]

Subsequently Rogers became the chief custodian of the Cobdenite heritage. In his role as disciple, the idea for the foundation of the Cobden Club in 1867 for the pursuit of free trade is usually attributed to him.[12] Until his death in 1890, he exerted himself strenuously to ensure that the memory of Cobdenism remained before the public, to the extent that many of our surviving images of Cobden are mediated through the collection of speeches and documents he collated with John Bright to commemorate his hero.[13]

For Rogers, opposition to privilege and narrow aristocratic landholding was at the heart of the Cobdenite programme. Cobden's attitudes towards aristocracy, privilege and the land issue harmonized well with Rogers's own ideas and experiences at Oxford. As a curate at Headington, Rogers had seen the sufferings of the rural poor at first hand. His experience at Oxford cemented many of the attitudes he had arrived at during that time. Rogers's views on the Oxford Colleges were a natural progression from his ideas on landed wealth. Rogers depicted the colleges as places of aristocratic and royal endowments where feckless sons of the great landed houses squandered their education and spent their time in boisterous and unruly pranks. His earliest writings took issue with the college system and caused some of the tensions that surrounded his career in the university. The overprivileged colleges, 'the gifts of private munificence' he saw as a 'really public wrong'; he advocated instead the dismantling of the college system and the admission of Dissenters.[14] Elsewhere, beneath many of the public and political issues of the nineteenth century, he saw the dead hand of aristocracy at work, orchestrating the conservative, anti-reform agenda. In discussions about a contribution to the volume *Essays on Reform* in 1867 at the time of the agitation for the Second Reform Bill, he proposed an article on 'Bribery', reflecting his concerns about aristocratic influences in rotten and closed boroughs. The article never materialized.[15] Visiting Ireland in 1869, he observed the workings of the great estates of the Anglo-Irish aristocracy at first hand. His verdict on absentee aristocratic dynasties was swingeing. It was 'a scandal which disgraces the government of the greatest nation upon earth and hinders the perfect union of the two races which must have a common destiny and ought to live in common amity'. For him, 'the effect of transmitting rents to an absentee proprietor is exactly the same as paying a tribute. No one doubts that a country which pays a tribute is much the worse off'.[16] In foreign affairs he detected the same malign aristocratic influences. His repeated insistence on non-intervention, international arbitration and 'national' militias rather than standing armies was innately Cobdenite. Rogers also followed Cobden in his analysis of empire, fearing that it propagated privileged hereditary land-holding at home, replenished by overseas investments.[17]

Cobden's dislike of the aristocracy, which he saw as a declining and monopolistic 'hidalgo' class, led him towards land reform. Yet, while often seen as a prototypical land reformer, he was, at best, lukewarm on the subject.[18] He found the implications of a movement devoted solely to land reform troubling. Whilst realizing the importance of breaking up the landed monopoly, and alluding to this subject frequently in the 1840s and 1850s, Cobden was above all a pragmatist. He was cautious about the consequences of a land campaign that might unleash the forces of radicalism and popular politics. Equally he feared that inertia on this subject might encourage an outpouring of popular resentment with serious consequences for property and landowners. He wrote in a series of articles in the *Morning Star* of the transfer of the allegiance of the agricultural labourers 'from the castle to the "Union" ' and suggested: 'Is there no danger that, like their rooks, they may learn to look the scarecrow in the face, and that some Romsey Hampden may find a voice and exclaim "Let um come! Who be afeared?" '[19] His solution was the adoption of a model that he first encountered during his visits to France to cement the 1859 Anglo-French Trade Treaty: the encouragement of a small peasant proprietorship. He hoped that the establishment of Freehold Land Societies would foster the creation of voters in the shires who might act as a counterweight to the regional power of aristocratic magnates, help undermine landed influence and circumvent territorial noble interests. To this end he actively encouraged the formation of Freehold Land Societies in the years after 1849. Cobden remained less committed, however, to other more direct action against landownership. He made little effort to support the regular motions put before the House by Locke King for a Real Estate Intestacy Bill. This measure advocated the end of primogeniture for intestate estates where, in the absence of a will on the death of the proprietor, landed estates simply reverted to the oldest son as dictated by the law of primogeniture. Locke King's bills suggested instead that estates should be divided amongst all surviving children on the European model.[20]

Cobden's role as a totem of the land movement can largely be attributed to Rogers. At Rochdale in 1864, Cobden gave his last speech before his death the following year. Posthumously the occasion became invested with great sentiment and gravitas. George Jacob Holyoake, who was there, recalled that it was 'the longest speech of his life to the largest audience he had ever met in one room':

> I was that night more conscious than ever before of his [Cobden's] wonderful self-possession in speaking. He held up, as it were in the air, a chief sentence as he spoke it, and supplied, before he left it, the qualification he saw it needed, or the amplification he saw it required, so that malignity could not pervert it, nor ignorance misunderstand it.[21]

A sunset glow of sentiment and pathos illuminated this moment. Cobden never spoke publicly again. The speech is often seen as a homily in favour of land reform, and is sometimes depicted as the beginning of the land reform campaign of the 1860s and 1870s. For the land reform MP for Salford, Arthur Arnold, it expressed Cobden's belief that 'success would attend a properly conducted effort to establish free trade in land'.[22] The words that if he had still been a young man 'I would take Adam Smith in hand, and I would have a League for free trade in land just as we had a League for free trade in corn' were much reported and became emblematic of the apparently more radical direction taken by Cobden in his later years.[23] Cobden's reference to this subject, however, was tantalizingly vague and proffered no strategies that might be pursued to drive such a programme through a legislature composed largely of landowners. His comments were a relatively minor part of a much longer series of reflections on contemporary foreign affairs. The main body of the speech was preoccupied with the closing stages of the American Civil War, the Schleswig-Holstein Question and a digression into the lack of geographical understanding revealed by university graduates. The section on land reform occupied barely 13 lines in the *Manchester Examiner and Times*'s report of proceedings.[24]

At the time, the oration was seen mainly as a contribution to debates on education. The concerns Cobden expressed about graduates' knowledge of geography in the speech were widely debated by educational reformers.[25] It was Rogers who converted the speech into a rallying cry against the aristocracy and the excessive over-concentration of landed wealth and power in relatively few hands. Rogers was present at the speech, and was alluded to by Cobden (and cheered by the audience) during the course of it. Thereafter Rogers's influence is discernible in the popular exaltation accorded to the oration as a declaration of war on the great estate owners. Retrospectively, even those who had been present viewed it in these terms.[26] It was recalled, in the presence of Rogers, at the foundation meeting of the Land Tenure Reform Association on the Strand to promote 'the free transfer of land' in 1869.[27] The most visible rewriting of the speech occurred, however, in Rogers's analysis of the Cobdenite platform in his influential *Cobden and Modern Political Opinion* (1873). Here Rogers elevated the lines in the speech relating to land reform, and the name of the man behind them. Beginning his chapter on the land with them, he commented: 'These references might be multiplied, for Cobden was never weary of advocating a thorough and searching reform of the Land System in the United Kingdom'.[28]

The Cobden familiar to land reformers was henceforth an advocate of land reform first and a free trader second. The most common image of him was as a 'sturdy yeoman' whose own lineage bore the scars of dispossession and displacement for his Sussex farming family at the hands of the enclosers.[29] In this guise, his posthumous presence was of some significance at land reform meetings into the late nineteenth and early twentieth centuries. There is an element of wishful thinking in the words of some of Cobden's admirers about his land-reforming zeal. For Charles Trevelyan, speaking to a Glasgow audience in 1906, 'Cobden never intended to stop at free trade and neither do I'.[30] His pronouncements on land reform were frequently quoted and the Rochdale speech, or variations on it, remained central to land reform endeavours. In 1896, the Durham Miners launched their pioneer Georgeite Yellow Van Committee with references back to Cobden, asserting that 'Cobden foreshadowed this, the land agitation of which the yellow van movement is a part'. Quoting his wisdom on land reform, they took the Anti-Corn Law League as their inspiration: 'The successful labour of the Anti-Corn Law League with which the names of Richard Cobden and John Bright will ever be inseparably associated, shew clearly that the people can be aroused to attack land monopoly if only they are properly organised'.[31]

The agitations around plebeian land hunger traditionally had a somewhat incendiary quality. The land reform campaign always struggled to escape from its associations with gutter politics. In 1907, an exchange in the Commons between the land reformer Sir Henry Campbell-Bannerman and the Tory Sir Alexander Acland Hood typifyed these tensions. 'The Prime Minister proceeded to read extracts from a speech made by Sir Alexander Acland Hood with regard to the new Army scheme and quoted the Chief Whip's statement that "the Radicals generally denounced the landowning class as idlers, land-robbers and despoilers of the poor." "Where has the Tory whip been to hear this violent language?" asked the Prime Minister "What obscure public house has he been spending his time in?" '[32] An aura of unrespectability hung about the land reform platform, which the Cobden connection was intended to counter. Rogers successfully expanded the boundaries of Cobdenism as high politics to allow for the inclusion of the underground tradition of popular revolt on the land issue that Cobden himself had always feared. By re-branding Cobdenism as a movement primarily about the land and its ownership, Rogers left the movement open to appropriation by a more plebeian class of land militants and ultimately Henry George. Incorporating the unrespectable world of land millenarians, extremists and popular politicians in turn radicalized Cobdenism, giving it the appearance of a dangerous ultra-radical crusade. *Reynolds's Newspaper* expressed this tension in the popular appeal of Cobden at the time of his death. Portraying him as 'a man who refused to be muzzled', and with his speech on the land question in mind, it asserted: 'Mr Cobden and his fellow labourers gave utterance to sentiments and threats which were at least as seditious and revolutionary in their tendency as anything spoken or written by the numerous Chartists, on which a trembling royalty and oligarchic usurpation wreaked their utmost malignity'.[33] In radical journals of the 1880s and 1890s, orthodox Cobdenism rubbed shoulders with amateur ballads of dispossession and internal exile (often of dubious quality) like the 'Song of the Land Reformer':

> The land for the people, the land for the state,
> 'Tis the birthright of freedom, their heritage great,
> The title deeds old, as the first days of time,
> Tell of family noble, of Founder divine.
> The land for the people, the land for the state,
> 'Tis dishonour to tell they've ever been separate,
> While the wild birds of heaven, their high pastures claim,
> 'Tis disgrace, earth's true landlords all landless remain.[34]

Land reform and British history

In advance of the ideas of Henry George, many of Rogers's own commentaries on the aristocracy demonstrated a slippage between the respectable and unrespectable sides of the land reform platform. On occasion, he crossed the line. Rogers's more fiery utterances were taken up with enthusiasm by the radical and even socialist press. The Social Democratic Federation organ *Justice* eagerly quoted a statement of his on landlords from the 1880s that: 'The action of these has clearly been the cause of agricultural distress, of the beggars, of the peasants and the extra pauperisation of the towns, as dirt is the cause of disease, and extravagance of ruin'.[35] Campaigns like the Cobdenite campaign against entail and primogeniture in the 1860s were suffused with an anger and resentment that boosted their appeal to extremists in the land reform camp. Their rhetoric drew on the traditional radical themes of debt and debauchery amongst the scions of landed aristocratic houses that were a marked feature of the popular platform.[36] A series of letters edited by Rogers on this subject in 1864 inveighed against the damage done by the practice of favouring eldest sons with the inheritance of estates, to the detriment of younger brothers forced to find their own way or to marry well. Under the title of the 'Moral Aspect of Primogeniture', it featured a titillating account by an abandoned woman, courted by the younger son of a noble family, but then rejected in order that her *beau* might make a more suitable marriage alliance in order to support himself: 'But he grew weary of his life... He only cared for pleasure, and he sank deep and deep down into debt... He wanted to be free of me – he had a chance of marrying well, ranging himself, and getting a post under the government. I stood not in his way. I set him free.'[37] Much of this was in the vein of moral condemnation of aristocratic life-styles which Cobden and other critics of aristocracy often articulated and which became central to the radical liberal tradition and the Georgeite platform.[38] Rogers's perspective harmonized with Joseph Chamberlain's later comments on the continuing moral and social degradation of the great aristocratic houses, when in his speeches of the 1880s he quoted Francis Bacon, that 'they were like potatoes, the best part was underground'.[39] Around these issues of debauchery and the land, the respectable land reform journals and the readers of more fiery radical newspapers like *Reynolds's Newspaper* found they were able to unite.

Perhaps the most significant contribution made by Rogers to the land question was in his role as a historian. In the 1880s, he was one of a group of younger historians breaking away from traditional narrative histories, accounts of high politics and entrenched 'drum and trumpet' approaches. In this, he was inspired by the work of Stubbs and Maitland who set out to discover the wellsprings of English constitutional thought and to define the role of the Freeborn Englishman within it.[40] He is often seen as a pioneer of the new discipline of economic

Figure 8.1 Popular hostility to aristocratic landowners in a cartoon by 'Cynicus' (Martin Anderson), 1893.
Source: Image taken from original in possession of the author of Chapter 4 (A. Taylor).

history. His own intention was to provide a more popular account of a 'people's history' that tied in firmly with his own social gospel. His work on prices, wages and the English economy from the Middle Ages was unashamedly focussed around plebeian concerns. In it, he declared that 'History, which crowds its canvas with these great names, tells us nothing of the people. But they who take note of the pittance which the peasant or artisan earned, and of the cost at which he spent his wages on his needful food, can interpret the hardships of his lot, the poverty of his life, the barrenness of his labour, the growing hopelessness of his condition.'[41] Rogers's work explored such neglected concerns and provided a new approach that rapidly became the orthodoxy for liberal and later Left historians in the twentieth century.[42] In his influential work, *Six Centuries of Work and Wages,* first published in 1884, Rogers argued that the pay and conditions of English rural smallholders and urban workers had reached their zenith in the sixteenth century. Consolidating their position in the wake of the Black Death, this was a golden age for the agrarian small proprietor in which English rural society flourished. Thereafter the dissolution of the monasteries, enclosures, more intensive farming methods and more expensive food had forced wages down and increased the pressures on rural smallholders. By the eighteenth century they were an endangered social group, declining in wealth and status, and forced into day labour for subsistence wages. This argument with its emphasis on rent, prices and wages established the essential ingredients for the historical understanding of English rural life up until the Hammonds and beyond.[43] No one had investigated the decline of rural smallholding with such close attention to detail before, and across such a wide variety of sources and contexts. Rogers was in no doubt that the fate of the small rural proprietor class arose from malign intent: 'I contend that from 1563 to 1824, a conspiracy concocted by the law and carried out by parties interested in its success, was entered into, to cheat the English workman of his wages, to tie him to the soil, to deprive him of hope, and to degrade him into irremediable poverty'.[44] The approach taken by Rogers grew out of liberal narratives of political progress and reform. In his work, the people struggled against the corrupt and oligarchic landed dynasties that exercised an influence disproportionate to their political talents, and whose presence disfigured the political history of Great Britain by manipulating parliament, throne and altar to their own ends. Anticipating Henry George, Rogers contrasted English peasant pluck and virtue, with aristocratic vice, venality and vulgarity. Rogers's verdict on the landed aristocracy was a swingeing one. In his final pages, he described them as 'by turns turbulent, servile and greedy, and now probably the most unnecessary, as a body, that any civilised society exhibits and endures'.[45] Rogers was the first in a long line. Drawing on his work, a later slew of liberal 'people's histories' from the 1890s onwards focussed on the political obstacles to reform posed by the great territorial dynasties.[46]

The re-interpretation of past wrongs offered by Rogers in his works re-energized the land reform movement. Addressing the Duke of Argyll's description of the land reform cause as 'that loud and almost incoherent cry',[47] he clothed the movement in a series of historiographical justifications that provided a unified political narrative for the agitation. From the 1870s, in a number of major volumes which became required reading for land militants, he provided the historical underpinning for the anti-aristocratic and land reform platform. Traditionally, the origins of the land question were located in the dispossession of Anglo-Saxon England after the Norman Conquest. This interpretation, which had roots in the seventeenth and eighteenth centuries and was central to the imagination of the constitutional reform agenda, had a long lineage. For many radicals, the Norman Yoke provided an ancestral sense of grievance. The feelings it inspired were both fervent and sentimental. Rogers, however, re-examined this picture and removed the accretions of folk memory and wilful misinterpretation that surrounded it. He was sceptical about the historical validity of 'Norman Yokery'. In this, he followed Cobden who had no time for vague ancestral memories of dispossession from the land. In his book, *The British Citizen*, Rogers dismissed the Norman Yoke altogether. He argued that the Norman Conquest had little detrimental impact on the long-standing village customs that safeguarded the status and position of the peasantry. Pointing out that William the Conqueror claimed to be an heir to the Saxon kingdoms, he remarked: 'Beyond securing his own authority and rewarding his successors, William had no wish to change the constitution of the country, least of all to interfere with the local customs and self-government of the villages. The inhabitants of these places exchanged a Saxon overlord for a Norman overlord and very likely did not find the latter more oppressive than the former had been'.[48] Rogers concentrated instead on the 'New Conquest' period following the Reformation, when, in a world of spiralling rents, falling wages and collapsing prices for agricultural yield, agrarian innovation stagnated.[49] For him, this marked the true collapse of the British peasantry, its death knell sounded by rural unrest and the collapse of Ket's rebellion in Norfolk in 1549. In this summation, his ideas meshed with the emphasis of the Whig tradition on literate independent small-holders, who embraced reform and challenged Stuart and parliamentary despotism.[50]

Elsewhere in his work, Rogers linked the themes of land and parliamentary reform with reassessments of the careers of traditional heroes of British radicalism and Whiggery. His published lectures on the careers of Wiklif, John Wilkes, Laud and Horne Tooke were expressive of the broader currents of popular politics within which he located his reform ideas.[51] Informed by a deep sense of history, Rogers was alert to potential alternative lines of development that might have been followed by the British state from the sixteenth century onwards and which were refracted through the historical experience of Britain's near neighbours. The Netherlands was the country that most clearly came to mind for Rogers, as both inspiration and model for the British state. The source of many of Britain's constitutional liberties after the Glorious Revolution of 1688, it embodied the classic Enlightenment virtue of tolerance for religious difference and proved an innovator in farming methods and land reclamation. For Rogers's purposes, its chief importance was that it achieved this without recourse to monopolistic, large aristocratic landownership on the British model.[52] Following Rogers, land reformers became keen to explore the models and precedents used by kindred Anglo-Celtic communities in Europe and beyond with the aim of modifying Britain's own proscriptive land laws.[53] Overall, Rogers's re-interpretation of British history gave the campaign for land reform greater weight and academic rigour, as well as possible models for alternative development. It now had a convincing story to tell. Rogers's work rescued it from a situation in which it was unsure of its history, its aims and its direction.

From J. E. Thorold Rogers to Henry George

Rogers's *Six Centuries of Work and Wages* appeared in 1884 during the climactic debates surrounding the Third Reform Bill. In many ways it captured the tempo of the parliamentary reform campaign and went through 11 subsequent editions by 1912.[54] The book was much quoted during the controversy surrounding the passage of the Reform Act, which the House of Lords attempted to stall or to prevent entirely. His own writings on the subject show he was a strong unicameralist, who believed in the complete abolition of the upper chamber on the 1649 model.[55] Even before the publication of *Six Centuries of Work and Wages* and his other major writings, his ideas on the aristocracy had been well received by reformers. They had already achieved a wide currency in the 1870s, when George Howell recommended his ideas on land.[56] At times of tension with the Lords the sale and circulation of them peaked. During the controversy provoked by the Upper House's rejection of Lloyd George's 1909 Budget, the *Labour Leader* recommended the publication of a cheap edition of his *The Economic Interpretation of History* – 'a work which every student ought to possess'.[57] His book on Holland was also well received, providing ammunition against landowners from its publication in the late 1880s. Rogers's work found a readership across the political and social divide, in keeping with his own emphasis on a new school of history that stressed the economic and social reasons for the decline of the English peasantry, rather than a mere folklore of dispossession.[58] It even circulated in the white settler colonies, where colonial land reformers found an echo of the English land question in the clash between large expatriate proprietors and migrant small-holders, sometimes escaping from the very situations described by Rogers in his books. For Rogers, there were possibilities that the settler colonies in particular might proffer models and strategies for an effective escape from land monopoly.[59]

Writing with the benefit of hindsight, the land reformer Frederick Verinder captured the complexities and eccentricities of the land reform project of the 1880s and 1890s in his reminiscences:

> Herbert Spencer wanted to 'restore the land' to the heirs, executors and assigns of the pre-historic cave-dwellers. I think Charles Bradlaugh only went back to the Ancient Britons. A little old lady in rusty black, who looked as if she had walked out of a Dickens novel, asked me to 'restore' to her a great estate in Suffolk by finding the one birth, marriage or vaccination certificate which was, as usual in such cases, the only proof missing. A man from Stepney wrote in similar vein.[60]

Rogers himself was wary of movements like Georgeism which inhabited this ambiguous terrain. Georgeism, with its talk of the sequestration of land and emphasis on the non-compensation of landowners, seemed the fulfilment of his prophecy that: 'As long as landowners cling to anti-social experiments, such as primogeniture, [which] the power of strict settlement, and the conveyance of land by secret deeds unquestionably are, so long will those who would advocate the maintenance of private property in land be disabled from defending what is legitimate, and must leave the field to those who assail the institution itself'.[61] Yet, despite his hostility to the platform politics of Henry George, which he believed set 'class against class', Rogers's ideas provided a gateway to the circulation of George's *Progress and Poverty* in Britain.[62] Rogers's books acted as a central strut in an otherwise diffuse and incoherent movement. Regardless of the differences in strategies and tactics advocated by land reformers, by the 1880s, they were the heirs to a common legacy and historical understanding which had been pioneered in Rogers's writings. His scholarship provided the gravitas and rigour required by critics of existing patterns of landownership. It appealed particularly to followers of George, whose movement was rooted in an autodidactical tradition of scholarship and private study, but who were disadvantaged by the relatively humble circumstances of their leader and the unsophisticated (albeit accessible) nature of his writings. The movement drew consolation from its vision of George, 'the ex-compositor' as 'a man of the people, a Rousseau without Rousseau's vices, expressing his thought with the simplicity of Cobden and Bastiat', but needed a more methodical and considered text to support their views.[63] Rogers's work fulfilled this task admirably. George himself was a great admirer of Rogers. He wrote to the Birmingham land reformer Thomas F. Walker from New York in 1884: 'I have been reading Thorold Rogers's *Work and Wages* with much interest. It is worth your reading, and will give you many effective points. It is still, it seems to me, the most effective book against the aristocracy of England that has been written for many a day'.[64] Subsequently, Rogers provided the motto for the movement as recorded by Henry George Jr. in *The Menace of Privilege*: 'Every permanent improvement of the soil, every railway and road, every betterment of the general condition of society, every facility given for production, every stimulus applied to consumption raises rent. The landowner sleeps, but thrives. He alone, amongst all the recipients in the distribution of products, owes everything to the labour of others, (and) contributes nothing of his own'.[65] For members of the Georgeite English Land Restoration League, reading Rogers was an initiation into the secret lore and rituals of the movement. It rapidly became part of an accepted canon. A ditty in the *Single Tax* journal recorded of Harry S. Murray, a dedicated Highlands land campaigner who had offered his motor car to the movement in 1899:

> He's great in George and Mill and Smith,
> He's great in Thorold Rogers' study,
> He's great in spirit and in form,
> He'd face the Tories in a body.[66]

For most Georgeites, reliance on the works of Rogers proved that they were simply Cobdenites after all. It showed that their platform was the culmination of Cobden's exhortation to campaign on the land issue in Rochdale before his death. George proudly followed in Cobden's footsteps during his tour of Britain in 1884.[67] At St. James's Hall in London, he declared that 'the horrible agrarian revolutionary doctrine of his – as they heard it called – what was it? Why simply the carrying out of the

Figure 8.2 Henry George's proposals for land reform alarm the shade of William the Conqueror: *The Owl*, 19 March 1884.
Source: Reproduced by permission of Birmingham Libraries and Archives.

principles of Richard Cobden, simply the carrying out of the principles of free trade'.[68] In his *Protection or Free Trade*, he returned to the subject of the Cobdenite legacy and the matter of Cobden's 1864 speech, summarizing its importance for a later generation of land reformers: 'Richard Cobden saw that the agitation of the tariff question must ultimately pass into the agitation of the land question, and from what I have heard of him I am inclined to think that were he in life and vigour today, he would be leading in the movement for the restoration to the British people of their natural rights in their native land'.[69]

Conclusion

In his study of the mid nineteenth-century university Liberals, Christopher Harvie regards them as having left little lasting legacy, and failing in their efforts to create an alliance between platform-based agitations and a politics of philosophical and intellectual liberal humanism.[70] Rogers must be regarded as an exception to this judgement. He remained a significant figure until his death in 1890; thereafter his works continued to feature in discussions of the land into the 1940s and beyond.[71] Moreover, it was not simply as an 'arch-Cobdenite' that he was remembered. Rogers expanded the boundaries of Cobdenism, and radicalized its key elements. The body language and posture of Rogers's platform was an extreme one, drawing on an excessive use of language that had a long provenance within radicalism, but which he twinned successfully with a more cerebral Cobdenism. Through the memory of Cobden he moved the land campaign beyond a fervent but ill-thought out anti-Normanism, a politics of sentiment rather than anything else, to a practical and plausible provenance for the land issue. Indeed, it may not be hyperbole to attribute the revival of the land agitation in the 1880s to his influence. Most important of all, Rogers bequeathed to the land agitation an academic pedigree that was taken up and refined by a new generation of Georgeites after his death. This vision of British history which 'historicized' the agrarian past provided a half-way house for radicals who wished to discern the decline of the peasant producing class in the advent of capitalism.[72] Rogers converted Cobdenism into a creed that believed in rural trades unionism, and a new vision of the colonies that saw some benefits in empire. As David Martin has demonstrated, the land reform movement was a promiscuous tradition.[73] Traditionally, land reformers were unsure of the movement's history, its aims and its *raison d'etre*. Invested with an academic pedigree the movement gained in strength and numbers until the eve of the Great War. Under Rogers's influence, Cobdenite doctrines of land reform were renovated, resurfacing within radical liberalism, Georgeism and socialism.

Notes

1. See H. J. Perkin, 'Land Reform and Class Conflict in Victorian Britain', in J. Butt and I. F. Clarke (eds), *The Victorians and Social Protest* (Newton Abbot, 1973), p. 178.
2. The only significant treatments of Rogers's career remain J. C. Ward, *British Economists and the Empire* (London, 1983), pp. 51–70 and A. Kadish, *Historians, Economics and Economic History* (London, 1989), ch. 1.

3. For Fawcett, see L. Goldman (ed.), *The Blind Victorian: Henry Fawcett and Victorian Liberalism* (Cambridge, 1989), pp. 1–38.
4. In February 1867, Rogers proposed a motion for manhood suffrage at a demonstration at the Agricultural Hall, Islington: *The Bee-Hive*, 16 February 1867, p. 5. For a sketch of his radical career, see ibid., 10 April 1875, pp. 1–2.
5. J. E. Thorold Rogers, *Six Centuries of Work and Wages* (London, 1884; 1903 edn), p. 513.
6. Rogers receives only one mention as an academic liberal campaigner for his role in the Eastern Question agitation in S. Collini, *Public Moralists: Political Thought and Intellectual Life in Britain* (Oxford, 1991), pp. 231–2.
7. C. Harvie, *The Lights of Liberalism: University Liberals and the Challenge of Democracy, 1860–1886* (London, 1976), pp. 135–6.
8. Kadish, *Historians*, p. 22.
9. See J. E. Thorold Rogers, 'The Exclusion of the Clergy from Seats in the House of Commons', *Fraser's Magazine*, 75 (1867), 769–78.
10. For Rogers's campaign against the Church of Ireland, see his speech at St. James's Hall, *The Bee-Hive*, 17 July 1869, p. 6.
11. J. E. Thorold Rogers, *A Sermon Preached at West Lavington Church on Sunday, April 9 1865* (Oxford, 1865), p. 9.
12. A. Howe, *Free Trade and Liberal England, 1846–1946* (Oxford, 1997), p. 117; *Rochdale Observer*, 30 March 1890, p. 3.
13. See J. Bright and J. E. Thorold Rogers (eds), *Speeches by Richard Cobden* (London, 1870).
14. J. E. Thorold Rogers, *Education in Oxford: Its Methods, its Aims and its Rewards* (Oxford, 1861), pp. 192–3.
15. Harvie, *Lights*, pp. 129–33; G. C. Brodrick et al., *Essays on Reform* (London, 1867).
16. J. E. Thorold Rogers, *The Irish Land Question: A Letter Written in September 1869 to the Late Sir John Gray M.P.* (Oxford, 1881), pp. 17–18.
17. J. E. Thorold Rogers, 'British Finance: Its Present and Future', *Contemporary Review*, 34 (1879), 281–303.
18. F. M. L. Thompson, 'Cobden, Free Trade in Land and the Road to the Abbey National' in A. Howe and S. Morgan (eds), *Re-thinking Nineteenth Century Liberalism: Richard Cobden Bicentenary Essays* (Aldershot, 2007), pp. 68–79.
19. *Mr Cobden on the Land Question* (London, 1873), pp. 13–14.
20. For Locke King's bills 'for the better settling the Real Estates of Intestates', regularly brought before parliament from 1854, see *Newcastle Weekly Chronicle*, 9 June 1866, p. 4; *National Reformer*, 7 March 1869, p. 145; G. C. Brodrick, 'The Law and Custom of Primogeniture', in J. W. Probyn (ed.), *Systems of Land Tenure in Various Countries* (London, 1881), pp. 156, 165.
21. G. J. Holyoake, *Bygones Worth Remembering* (2 vols, London, 1905), i, pp. 159–60.
22. A. Arnold, 'Free Trade in Land', *Contemporary Review*, 20 (1872), 880.
23. W. Hinde, *Richard Cobden: A Victorian Outsider* (New Haven, 1987), p. 323; D. Read, *Cobden and Bright: A Victorian Political Partnership* (London, 1967), p. 189.
24. *Manchester Examiner and Times*, 24 November 1864, p. 4; *Rochdale Observer*, 26 November 1864, p. 6. For the text of the speech, see J. Bright and J. E. Thorold Rogers (eds), *Speeches on Questions of Public Policy by Richard Cobden*

MP (London, 1880), pp. 478–96; J. Morley (ed.), *The Life of Richard Cobden* (London, 1896 edn), ii, p. 215.
25. See, for example, *Manchester Examiner and Times*, 4 April 1865, p. 6.
26. See the comments of T. B. Potter, President of the Cobden Club, in *Reynolds's Newspaper*, 16 April 1865, p. 3.
27. *The Bee-Hive*, 1 September 1869, pp. 1, 5. For the origins of the Land Tenure Reform Association, see D. Martin, *John Stuart Mill and the Land Question* (Hull, 1981), pp. 39–41, 42–3.
28. J. E. Thorold Rogers, *Cobden and Modern Political Opinion: Essays on Certain Political Topics* (London, 1873), pp. 73–5. For a review of the book emphasizing the significance of Cobden's speech for Rogers, see *Manchester Examiner and Times*, 30 January 1874, p. 7. Rogers referred to the speech repeatedly throughout his writings: see J. E. Thorold Rogers, 'Socialism and Land', in J. Samuelson (ed.), *Socialism, Labour and Capital* (London, 1890), p. 59.
29. Howe, *Free Trade*, p. 146. By the 1900s, Cobden had been appropriated by the Labourist tradition, and in the labour press was rubbing shoulders with icons of yeoman and peasant rebellion like Jack Cade and Wat Tyler: see *Labour Leader*, 29 April 1910, p. 7.
30. Quoted in A. J. A. Morris, *C. P. Trevelyan, 1870–1958: Portrait of a Radical* (Belfast, 1977), p. 55.
31. *Land and Labour*, 1 November 1896, pp. 86–7. References to Cobden proliferated in this journal; see ibid., 1 January 1891, p. 7; 1 August 1895, p. 71. For Cobdenite memories amongst the Durham miners, see *Newcastle Morning Chronicle*, 4 April 1909, pp. 1–2, and for Keir Hardie's admiration of Cobden, see 'In Cobden Country', *Labour Leader*, 2 July 1909, p. 417.
32. *The Tribune*, 22 April 1907, pp. 2–3.
33. *Reynolds's Newspaper*, 9 April 1865, p. 1. A. Howe notes the appeal of Cobden and the popular manifestations of his name in pub signs, the naming of streets and even a bridge; see Howe, *Free Trade*, pp. 142–6.
34. *The Radical*, 12 February 1880, p. 7.
35. *Justice*, 31 January 1885, p. 5.
36. See A. Taylor, *'Lords of Misrule': Hostility to Aristocracy in Late Nineteenth and Early Twentieth Century Britain* (London, 2004), ch. 1.
37. *Letters of J. E. Thorold Rogers and Mr Henry Tupper on the History and Working of the Laws of Primogeniture and Entail* (Manchester, 1864), pp. 25–8.
38. *Labour Leader*, 5 November 1909, p. 717. There is praise for Rogers's arguments and research in *The Worker*, 28 May 1904, p. 12.
39. Quoted in H. Macpherson (ed.), *Peers or People: A Record of Wrong* (Dundee, n.d.), p. 39.
40. Kadish, *Historians*, pp. 13–16. For Stubbs and Maitland see J. Vernon, 'Narrating the Constitution: The Discourse of "the Real" and the Fantasies of Nineteenth-Century Constitutional History', in Vernon (ed.), *Re-reading the Constitution: New Narratives in the Political History of England's Long Nineteenth Century* (Cambridge, 1996), pp. 204–29.
41. Rogers, *Six Centuries*, pp. 431–2; idem, *The Economic Interpretation of History* (London, 1888); idem, 'The History of Rent in England', *Contemporary Review*, 37 (1880), 672–90.
42. Ruskin History Workshop Students Collective, 'Worker-Historians in the 1920s', in R. Samuel (ed.), *People's History and Socialist Theory* (History

Workshop, 1981), pp. 17–20; R. Samuel, 'British Marxist Historians, 1880–1980', *New Left Review*, 1 (1980), esp. 38–41.

43. Rogers's reassessment accorded with re-examinations of patterns of landownership in Ireland; see C. Dewey, 'Celtic Agrarian Legislation and the Celtic Revival: Historicist Implications of Gladstone's Irish and Scottish Land Acts, 1870–1886', *Past and Present*, 64 (1974), 30–70. For the Hammonds, who drew on these new findings about the land, see S. Weaver, *The Hammonds: A Marriage in History* (Stanford, 1997), pp. 97–108.
44. Rogers, *Six Centuries*, p. 398.
45. Ibid., pp. 385, 573–4.
46. See, for example, W. G. Wilkins, *The Penny History of the Poor People of England: The Rise and Progress of Poverty in England from the Norman Conquest to Modern Times* (London, 1911), pp. 5–6.
47. Duke of Argyll, 'Land Reformers', *Contemporary Review*, 48 (1885), 470.
48. J. E. Thorold Rogers, *The British Citizen: His Rights and Privileges* (London, 1885), pp. 31–2.
49. Christopher Hill, on somewhat slender evidence, includes Rogers amongst those who preached a traditional 'Norman Yoke' perspective: C. Hill, *Puritanism and Revolution: Studies in Interpretation of the English Revolution of the Seventeenth Century* (London, 1968 edn), p. 122.
50. T. E. Cliffe Leslie, 'The Land System of the Country: A Reason for the Reform of Parliament', *Fraser's Magazine*, 75 (1867), 145. For historical and economic interest in the small proprietor, see C. Dewey, 'The Rehabilitation of the Peasant Proprietor in Nineteenth Century Economic Thought', *History of Political Economy*, 6 (1974), 17–47.
51. J. E. Thorold Rogers, *Historical Gleanings, Second Series. A Series of Sketches: Wiklif, Laud, Wilkes and Horne Tooke* (London, 1870), esp. pp. 180–5.
52. Idem, *Holland* (London, 1888), pp. x–xi.
53. See, for example, *The Labour Party and the Agricultural Problem with Reports of Visits to Ireland and Denmark* (London, 1913), pp. 3–6.
54. *Labour Leader*, 26 September 1912, p. 688.
55. J. E. Thorold Rogers, *The House of Lords* (London, n.d.), pp. 257–70; idem, *A Complete Collection of the Protests of the Lords* (London, 1875), i, pp. v–lxviii.
56. G. Howell, *Notes on Books and Reading Re-printed from the Bee-Hive* (London, 1875), p. 30.
57. *Labour Leader*, 12 March 1909, p. 163.
58. See, for example, discussion of Roger's work in the anarchist *Freedom*, 1 March 1896, p. 71, in 'How I became A Socialist', *The Scout: A Monthly Journal for Socialists*, 1 February 1896, in J. Keir Hardie, *From Serfdom to Socialism* (London, 1907), pp. 40–1, 48; and in P. Kropotkin, *The State: Its Historic Role* (London, 1899; 1969 edn), p. 47.
59. For the circulation of *Six Centuries of Work and Wages* in the Australian colonies, see B. Scates, *A New Australia: Citizenship, Radicalism and the First Republic* (Cambridge, 1997), p. 51; for Rogers's view of the land issue in the Australian colonies, see J. E. Thorold Rogers, 'The Colonial Question', in *Cobden Club Essays: Second Series, 1871–2* (London, 1872), pp. 399–455.
60. F. Verinder, 'Some Recollections of Henry George and the Early Days of the Movement', *Single Tax*, 1 January 1922, pp. 215–16.

61. J. E. Thorold Rogers, 'Contemporary Socialism', *Contemporary Review*, 97 (1885), 59.
62. Rogers, *Six Centuries*, pp. 531–2.
63. See *Single Tax*, 1 January 1925, p. 1.
64. George to Thomas Walker, 13 June 1884, Henry George Papers, Correspondence, 1854–1939, Microfilm Letters, Reel 3, January 1883–December 1884, New York Public Library [NYPL].
65. Henry George, Jr., *The Menace of Privilege: A Study in the Dangers to the Republic from the Existence of a Favoured Class* (New York, 1905), p. 21.
66. *Single Tax*, 1 September 1899, p. 57.
67. James Russell to Henry George, 3 March 1884, Henry George Papers, Correspondence, 1854–1939, Microfilm Letters, Reel 3, January 1883–December 1884, NYPL.
68. *Bolton Guardian*, 29 January 1884, p. 9.
69. H. George, *Protection or Free Trade: An Examination of the Tariff Question with Especial Regard to the Interests of Labour* (New York, 1992 [1886]), p. 324.
70. Harvie, *Lights of Liberalism*, pp. 129–33.
71. *Land and Labour*, 1 July 1893, p. 3, 1 May 1893, p. 34, 1 December 1895, p. 100; F. A. Ridley, *The Revolutionary Tradition in England* (London, 1948), p. 47.
72. See P. Ward, *Red Flag and Union Jack: Englishness, Patriotism and the British Left, 1881–1924* (Woodridge, 1998), pp. 24–5.
73. Martin, *John Stuart Mill*, pp. 25–43.

9
London and the Land Question, *c.* 1880–1914

Roland Quinault

Introduction: the neglect of the London land question

Victorian and Edwardian Britain was the most urbanized country in the world in the late nineteenth and early twentieth centuries, and there was a distinctly urban aspect to the land question in that period. Yet historians have paid relatively little attention to the urban land question. In the 1950s and early 1960s, Jim Dyos pioneered the scholarly study of Victorian urban history, but he paid little attention to urban politics and none to the land question.[1] In 1961, David Reeder, another pioneer, published an article on the politics of urban leaseholds, but he did not follow it up with any more general study of the urban land question.[2] In 1976, Roy Douglas published a good general history of the land question from the late Victorian period, but he concentrated mainly on rural rather than urban aspects of the land reform movement.[3] In his *Property and Politics* (1981), Avner Offer examined the urban land issue in the context of legal and economic ideas and developments.[4] In 1983, David Englander, Martin Daunton and Philip Waller all published useful books considering various aspects of the urban land question.[5] Since then, however, there have been few further studies of the topic, partly because the focus of much Victorian urban history has shifted from economic and political topics to social and cultural ones.

The relative neglect of the urban land question is particularly marked with respect to London; most of the studies mentioned above concentrated on the major provincial cities rather than on the metropolis. That is strange because London was the largest and richest city in the world in the period and the land on which it stood was enormously valuable. The total rent-roll for London was over £37,000,000 in 1889 and by 1900, it was greater than all the agricultural rent for England and Wales.[6] In

1903, it was estimated that the value of all land in the county of London was £500,000,000 and that it was increasing at the rate of £10,000,000 a year.[7] Thus London was a classic example of the rapid increase in land values that prompted the American reformer, Henry George, to advocate a single tax on land values, as he famously did in his 1879 bestseller *Progress and Poverty*. But the land reform movement in London developed independently of Georgeite influence. Moreover, as Ian Packer has pointed out, many aspects of the national campaign for urban land reform originated in London.[8] Packer attributed the prominence of London in the reform campaign to its unique combination of high-profile great landowners, short leases, high rates and overcrowding.[9] He did not explain, however, why land reformers were slow to focus their attention on London before the 1890s and why land reform never became a burning issue in the capital. He also paid little attention to the structure of landownership and occupancy in the metropolitan area.

One reason why the land reformers were slow to focus their attention on London was because issues relating to land in the metropolis were not linked up with the national question as they were in Ireland, Wales or Scotland. Another reason was that there was a lack of data about landholdings in London. The 1873 *Return of Landowners* – the only one of its kind since the Domesday Book – excluded London, although it contained by far the most valuable land per acre in the United Kingdom.[10] John Bateman, who used the 1873 return to compile a list of the great landowners of Britain and Ireland, noted that the rent-roll of many families 'would look more imposing by far were London included in the return'.[11] Around the turn of the century, however, that omission was gradually made good by both private and municipal research. By 1915, about 90 per cent of landholdings in the county of London had been mapped and that evidence was collated, much later, by the historians Ralph Hyde and Peter Lindert.[12] Thus we now have a fairly accurate picture of metropolitan landownership in the early twentieth century. That gives us a firm factual basis from which to assess the peculiar nature of the land question in London.

London's landlords

Victorian and Edwardian London was predominantly a city of tenants and sub-tenants, for the vast majority of its residents lived in rented or leased properties. Most residential properties in London were built and let on 99-year leases with shorter periods for commercial properties. The leasehold system was economically convenient because it spread risk and reward. In the County of London, shortly before the First World War, only about 3 per cent of all households were made up of freehold owner-occupiers and 71 per cent of the population lived in sub-let apartments.[13] The capital's landlords ranged from millionaire dukes with prime estates in central London to prosperous leaseholders and humble shareholders in building societies.[14] Most of the 38,200 ground landlords, however, owned only one or two properties. The level of rents charged ranged enormously – from £42 an acre in Plumstead, on the outer edge of south-east London, to over £4,000 an acre in the best part of the West End and over £6,000 an acre in the City.[15]

The biggest London landowners were public bodies, notably the Crown with over 5,000 acres worth in excess of £2.3 million in annual rental. That was closely matched by the aggregate total for local government bodies including parish vestries, the City Corporation and the London County Council (LCC). The largest commercial landowners were the dozen or so railway companies, which collectively owned nearly 3,000 acres, while over 1,000 acres belonged to the dock and canal companies. Insurance companies were less important landlords than they later became, but the Prudential held property worth £68,000 per annum. Schools, colleges and educational charities collectively owned over 2,200 acres. Dulwich College, in south London, had much the biggest estate, followed by Eton, Harrow and several Oxford and Cambridge colleges. The Church of England, as represented by the Church Commissioners and Anglican charities, owned 1,600 acres worth nearly £700,000. The City livery companies also owned valuable estates, as did hospitals, such as St Thomas's. The combined total of the charitable and public estates was very considerable and it led Sidney Webb to observe that much of London was already 'municipalised' or 'nationalised', although he considered that their proceeds were often 'woefully misapplied'.[16]

The top fifty private landlords in London collectively owned about 9,000 acres – less than half the total for public bodies and companies. Nevertheless, they were mainly concentrated in the wealthy districts that stretched from Chelsea across the West End to Hampstead. Most of those estates belonged to long-established aristocratic or gentry families, including three dukes, two marquises and several earls and barons. At the top of the landlord tree was the Duke of Westminster who owned the 475-acre Grosvenor estate, which had an assessed annual rental value of £423,000.[17] The estate included the exclusive residential districts of Mayfair and Belgravia, along with the more socially mixed areas of Pimlico and Victoria. Annual rents from the Mayfair estate rose from about £80,000 in 1869 to £135,000 in 1891, while the income from lease renewals rose from £108,000 in 1845–64 to £650,000 in 1874–99.[18]

The second wealthiest private landlord was the Duke of Bedford. The ninth duke, who died in 1891, added over a million pounds to his capital when the leases on his Bloomsbury estates were renewed.[19] The annual rental of his 250-acre London estate jumped from £102,000 in 1880 to £339,000 in 1892.[20] Third in the pecking order was Viscount Portman with a 226-acre estate in Marylebone, which comprised over 1,750 properties. In 1888, most of the 99-year leases expired and the value of the estate rose by £1,250,000 and the annual revenue to £218,000.[21] In 1899, Lord Portman sold the land on which Marylebone station was built for £260,000.[22] Earl Cadogan also saw the value of his 211-acre Chelsea estate rise enormously when the leases fell in and by the 1890s, he had a rental income of £180,000.[23]

Some of the wealth that the great aristocratic landlords accrued from their London estates was transferred to their rural estates. The Duke of Bedford, for example, subsidized his loss-making Thorney estate, in the Fens, with the profits from what he described as 'a few lodging-houses in Bloomsbury'.[24] The depressed state of agriculture in the later Victorian period ensured that many rural estates were a financial liability. Consequently, wealthy London landlords acquired rural estates, not for their agricultural value, but because they were ideal for rearing and shooting game birds. The sandy and flinty brecklands on the Norfolk and Suffolk border were too poor to cultivate, but they were ideal for pheasant and partridge rearing. Consequently, they attracted several London landlords, including Earl Cadogan, who bought the Culford Hall estate in Suffolk, which he expanded into an 11,000-acre shooting property.[25] The radical land reformer, R. L. Outhwaite, complained that pheasants had replaced the local people in Breckland merely to satisfy the social aspirations of plutocrats.[26] But the creation of big shooting estates in the district actually increased the demand for local labour.[27]

Very wealthy London landlords also acquired vast deer forests in the far north of Scotland. In 1848, the Marquis of Westminster rented much of western Sutherland – a vast tract of wilderness, which was later bought by his grandson, the second Duke of Westminster. Another leading London landlord, the Duke of Portland, acquired 100,000 acres around Langwell and Braemore in Caithness, which was famous for its red deer. Thus wealth from London properties helped both to alleviate and to foment the land question in other parts of Britain.

The great aristocratic landlords of London were never able to exercise the same political influence over their urban tenants as they did over their rural tenantry. Whereas most farms were let on annual tenancies, urban properties were generally held on long leases and often sub-let. The Marquis of Northampton's Clerkenwell estate, for example, was divided up into 600 tenements, which were leased to house farmers, who sub-let them to poor families who were unaware who was the ground landlord.[28] Even in the more affluent parts of London there was very little social or political contact between the large landlords and their tenants. Consequently, few landlords or their representatives contested parliamentary or local government constituencies where their London estates were located. One exception was the Hon. R. W. Grosvenor who, in 1865, was elected an MP for the borough of Westminster – where his family was the leading ground landlord. He obtained, however, only a handful more votes than the radical Liberal candidate John Stuart Mill, and in 1868, he received fewer votes than the Conservative candidate, the newsagent W. H. Smith. Later in the century, Earl Cadogan – a Tory Cabinet minister who owned much of Chelsea – did not allow his sons to stand for the parliamentary borough of Chelsea for fear of upsetting his tenants.[29]

The politics of leases and rates

The rapid rise in rental income and lease renewal premiums for London landlords in the late Victorian period gave the impression that metropolitan property was a goldmine from which quick and easy profits could be made. But nearly all the large London estates had been acquired two or three centuries earlier when they were still largely green fields beyond the built-up area. Their initial development required careful planning and large capital outlay and thereafter they required constant care and further investment. On the Grosvenor estate in the later Victorian period, for example, a third of the income from lease renewals was spent on improvements, which helped to preserve the exclusive character of the estate.[30]

Rebuilding costs, however, fell on the leaseholders and they had to conform to guidelines set down by the freeholders. One critic complained that the lessees on the Grosvenor estate in Mayfair had to rebuild in a style laid down by 'the dictatorial architectural caprices of a millionaire Duke'. The conduct of the Duke of Westminster was defended by his estate surveyor, Eustace Balfour, who was a brother of Arthur Balfour and a nephew of Lord Salisbury. The latter suggested that the Grosvenor estate should publish the number of properties it owned 'to disabuse the public mind as to the Dukes of Bedford and Westminster owning practically the whole of the area within the County of London'. Salisbury's suggestion was not, however, taken up by the board of the Grosvenor estate – presumably because it would have drawn public attention to the extent and value of its holdings.[31]

The rising cost of lease renewals in the late-Victorian period led to the formation, in 1883, of the Leasehold Enfranchisement Association. In 1884, Henry Broadhurst, a radical Liberal MP and former stonemason, introduced a leasehold enfranchisement Bill – the first of several abortive proposals in the period. The measure would have allowed some residential leaseholders to buy the freeholds of their properties from their ground landlords. That would have benefited middle-class occupiers at the expense of their ground landlords, many of whom were Whigs, who still supported William Gladstone's Liberal government. Thus leasehold enfranchisement was a divisive issue for the Liberal party and it was exploited as such by the rising Tory star, Lord Randolph Churchill. He attacked the 'bloated' London estates of the Whig dukes and argued that the multiplication of freeholds was essentially conservative and would improve sanitation, which had been neglected by the large estates.[32] Churchill drew up his own Bill for leasehold enfranchisement in urban sanitary districts.[33] There was, however, no support for leasehold enfranchisement from the Conservative leader, Lord Salisbury. He owned 20 valuable acres around St Martin's Lane in the central West End and he generally defended the interests of the ground landlords.

The secession of most of the Whig London landlords from the Liberal party in 1886 increased the pressure for leasehold enfranchisement and a select committee was established to consider the issue. Yet the London system of 99-year leases was not common in other urban areas apart from Liverpool and south Wales and thus the proposed reform had little nationwide appeal.[34] Leasehold enfranchisement, moreover, would be of no benefit to the working classes, the great majority of whom rented their homes – usually from leaseholders. In 1891, Asquith, a rising figure in the Liberal party, opposed leasehold enfranchisement on the grounds that a large body of small landowners would be less amenable to public opinion than a small body of large landowners.[35] Many Liberals believed that the best way to address the urban land problem was not by leasehold enfranchisement, but by reforming local taxation.

One of the main criticisms of London landlords was that they did not contribute to the rates that paid for much of local government expenditure.[36] In 1864, Gladstone had pointed out that the cost of metropolitan improvements – such as the Thames Embankment – fell on 'temporary and fugitive occupiers' and not on the ground landlords who benefited most from those improvements.[37] He voiced the same complaint in 1887, by which time the abolition of the dues on coal and wine imported into London had placed an even greater financial burden on London ratepayers.[38] In the same year, the London Municipal Reform League and the English Land Restoration League formed a united committee, chaired by Lord Hobhouse, for the taxation of ground rents. They wanted to levy a 'betterment' rate on ground landlords whose properties benefited from municipal improvements, such as street widening and slum clearance.[39] Their proposals were endorsed by some Progressive members of the new LCC and a number of Liberal candidates for London seats at the 1892 general election.[40] Their stance had some appeal because the Liberals won 13 more seats in London than they had won at the last general election in 1886.

A leading Liberal, Sir George Trevelyan, who leased a house in Belgravia from the Grosvenor estate, complained that the duke of Westminster had benefited from the provision of schools that were funded by his rate-paying tenants.[41] But the duke's agent pointed out that no school on the estate was a charge upon the rates. He claimed that he had constantly to advise the duke 'against his great tendency to over-generosity' and cited the provision of artisan dwellings at low rents, open gardens and a free public library.[42] *The Times*, commenting on the dispute, noted that lessees also benefited from increased property values and Sidney Webb conceded that much unearned increment went to the leaseholder, the house-farmer and other middlemen.[43] In 1894, the Liberal government passed an Equalisation of Rates Act for London. The Act provided for a limited subsidy for the poorer parts of London, such as the East End, funded by the richer parts: the West End and the affluent suburbs.[44] This measure was not particularly popular in the metropolis, however, and the Liberals lost all but eight of their London seats at the 1895 general election.

Although the Liberal Progressives kept control of the LCC, their high spending policies pushed up rates and prompted renewed calls for a reform of local government taxation in London. For example, a Fabian tract advocated the replacement of rates by a 10 per cent death duty on London property, which would fund the combined expenses of the London School Board and the LCC.[45] The expenses of the LCC rose even more sharply when it took over the Board schools in 1903. At the same time, there was also a steep rise in local rates, particularly in the poorer areas of London, such as the East End. That was occasioned by a rapid increase in local authority expenditure on social housing, roads, tramways, gas, water and electricity. The level of capital expenditure on such projects declined after 1903, but local authorities were left with large debts at a time when the economy was faltering.[46]

Most London tenants were not directly affected by the rise in rates because although they were technically ratepayers – and entitled to vote as such – in practice they did not personally pay rates. It was estimated that landlords paid the rates for over half of all the houses in London and for 80 per cent of those in some working-class districts.[47] Although landlords tried to recoup the cost of the rates through rent, the level of rent was mainly determined, not by the level of rates, but by the supply and demand for housing.

At the 1906 general election, there was a large swing to the Liberals in London, who won the majority of the metropolitan seats, including virtually all those in working-class constituencies. Even Chelsea returned a Liberal MP, despite the fact that working-class homes on the Cadogan estate had been largely replaced by middle-class mansion blocks.[48] The new Liberal Prime Minister, Sir Henry Campbell-Bannerman, was sympathetic to land reform and he advocated a rate on ground values as a way of strengthening the hand of the municipalities.[49] He appointed John Burns – a working-class MP for Battersea – as the new President of the Local Government Board. Burns had originally supported Henry George's proposal for a single land tax, but once in office he soon rejected the idea of a land valuation survey for England. In 1907, moreover, the Progressives lost control of the LCC to the Municipal Reformers. The result reflected widespread dissatisfaction with the recent rate rises.

Lloyd George and the London land question

In 1909, the land question was re-ignited by the Chancellor of the Exchequer, David Lloyd George. He had long regarded urban landlords as parasites that grew rich on unearned increment created by the labour of others. Consequently, he wanted to rate land separately from the improvements on it and give tax relief for the latter.[50] His 1909 Budget included a minimal charge on ground rents, a 20 per cent tax on land sales above valuation, a 10 per cent lease reversion duty and a general valuation of all land holdings. Those proposals prompted the House of Lords to reject the Budget in an unprecedented fashion and thus brought the land question to the forefront of public attention.

Lloyd George directed his rhetorical fire mainly on the dukes, who were all Unionists and who included the two wealthiest private London landlords. In a speech at Limehouse, he criticized the Duke of Westminster for demanding £4,000 in ground rent – a ten-fold increase – and a fine of £50,000 for a new 63-year lease from Gorringe's, the drapers, in the Buckingham Palace Road.[51] Yet, that demand was not excessive by current standards: the ground rent paid by Selfridge's department store was £10,000 a year. Over the 50 years that Frederick Gorringe had leased his premises he had done very well out of the nobility, gentry and affluent professionals who were resident tenants on the Grosvenor estate.[52] Furthermore, some astute commercial lessees made monkeys out of their landlords. Peter Jones, in Sloane Square, secured a 999-year lease from the Cadogan estate for which its current owners – the John Lewis partnership – pay just £6,000 a year![53]

By the late Edwardian period, many London landlords were rather less well-off than they had been. The death duties introduced in 1894 by Gladstone's Chancellor, Sir William Harcourt, were beginning to bite and the death of the first Duke of Westminster in 1899 led to duties of £600,000, which were paid by the sale of some marginal properties on the Grosvenor estate. The value of prime residential properties in the West End had also declined – by as much as a half in the case of large houses in Grosvenor Square. That reflected the new practice of staying at hotels during the London Season rather than renting a town house.[54] The rental market gradually improved, but the Great War accelerated the fashion for a less pretentious London lifestyle.

In the years before the First World War, the Liberal radicals, led by Lloyd George, launched a two-pronged land reform campaign: rural and urban. In 1912, Lloyd George devoted most of his time to the rural land question, but in 1913, he switched his main focus to the big cities and London in particular. There he could rely on support from an active Liberal pressure group: the 'Town Tenants' League'. The league had been set up in 1906 by W. H. Dickinson, the Liberal MP for St Pancras North, to represent shopkeepers and small businessmen, especially those with short leases, which were common in London. The main driving force behind the league was B. B. Evans, a Kilburn draper and progressive LCC councillor, who supplied examples of shopkeepers' grievances to Lloyd George on condition that this activity remained confidential.[55] Lloyd George responded by promising tenants both continuity of tenure and compensation for improvements.[56]

In November 1913, Lloyd George, in a speech at Holloway, in north London, went further and endorsed leasehold reform. His new stance lacked Cabinet approval, but it worried the Conservative leadership, who responded in kind. Walter Long – in a speech at the same venue in Holloway – promised tenants compensation for improvements, extended leases and an independent land court.[57] Lloyd George then went further and pledged the government to site rating in a speech at Glasgow. In his 1914 Budget, Lloyd George announced that there would be a rate on land values with a partial de-rating for improvements. He thus offered the prospect of some relief for hard-pressed London ratepayers. In 1913, the rate burden per person in London was more than twice that in the rest of England and Wales.[58] That was mainly because the capital received less financial support from the Exchequer and had higher service costs than the rest of the country.

Lloyd George's urban land reform campaign had a limited impact in London, but it prompted one great London landlord to reduce his holdings. In 1913, the eleventh Duke of Bedford sold his Covent Garden estate for over two million pounds, much of his properties in Bloomsbury for £300,000 and the freehold of the Hotel Russell for £45,000. His agent, Rowland Prothero, later stated that Covent Garden was sold because 'it was detached and from its nature might be a dangerous property for an individual to hold'.[59] The duke had been criticized for making large profits from Covent Garden, which had a reputation for dirt because of the market and for immorality because of the theatres and other places of entertainment. The duke's sell-off was not, however, imitated by other large London landowners before the war.

As part of the Liberal Land Campaign, a Land Enquiry Commission had been established in 1912 to produce separate reports on rural and urban land tenure conditions. Both the members of the commission and most of those who gave evidence to it were committed Liberals. In April 1914, the Land Enquiry Committee report on urban land was published. It proposed new powers for local authorities, particularly in regard to housing and site value rating.[60] The report received relatively little notice, however, and Lloyd George was informed that London was 'unmoved' by his proposals.[61] A land valuation Bill was prepared but it was unpopular with many wealthy Liberals and soon dropped. Not long afterwards, the outbreak of the First World War pushed Lloyd George's land reform proposals off the political agenda and also sowed division amongst the leading land reformers.[62] Consequently, Ian Packer has claimed that Lloyd George's Land Campaign did not so much fail as fail to happen.[63] What is certain is that it had been clear for decades that there was only limited and fitful support for urban land reform in London. Why was that the case?

As we have seen, Londoners showed little deference towards their wealthy private landlords who were widely regarded as parasitical and greedy. A land reformer wrote of the great aristocratic landlords in 1873:

'they exist; and that is their service. It was the service of most of their ancestors'.[64] Yet the critics of the large landlords were also often motivated by self-interest and even by snobbery. In E. M. Forster's 1910 novel, *Howards End*, the wife of a wealthy businessman denounces London landlords for replacing terrace houses with flats and thus lowering the tone of the neighbourhood. A more important complaint by middle-class residents was the rising cost of ground rents and especially of lease renewals. In some cases, however, the expiry of leases benefited the poor because ramshackle dwellings were then renovated and entrusted to more responsible tenants. The Ecclesiastical Commissioners, for example, entrusted over 5,000 of their poorer properties to Octavia Hill. In 1913, the Secretary of the Land Nationalisation Society noted that great estates were generally better managed than small ones and he concluded that fragmented ownership was a key cause of slums.[65] Many of the great estates, moreover, were owned by charitable trusts.

There were other reasons why there was limited opposition to the landlord interest in London. The largest group of landowners in the metropolis were public bodies, which provided services to the wider community. They ranged from hospitals, asylums and schools, to railway and canal companies and included the Crown – whose revenue went to the Exchequer. Thus the attacks on the great private landlords were directed at a group that collectively owned only a small part of London, albeit a very valuable one. The vast majority of private landlords, moreover, were not very wealthy people, but shopkeepers and other members of the lower middle classes, who owned one or two properties from which they drew rental income. That provided them with some security against business failure and also a pension in old age. Those minor landlords played a crucial role in the commercial life of London and were often prominent in local government, but they have left little imprint on history and consequently have been overlooked by historians.

Conclusion

The urban land reform campaign was a failure before the First World War and during the inter-war period it died as a major political movement. Yet it left a legacy that had a long-term influence on the pattern of landownership in Britain. Over the course of the later twentieth-century owner occupation, rather than tenancy, became the preponderant form of land tenure in urban Britain. That process was assisted by the 1967 Leasehold Enfranchisement Act, which belatedly implemented a measure that London reformers had hoped to enact in the 1880s. The act effected a big change in parts of suburban London, where estates – such as that of Dulwich College – were largely sold to their resident leaseholders. Yet the most valuable private estates in central London were exempted from the 1967 Act and they continue to exist today. Those estates are now generally about a third of their former size, but they still belong to the same old families and remain immensely valuable. The Grosvenor estate is now worth more than that of the Crown, which is followed in value by the Cadogan, Portman and former Portland estates. Only the Bedford estate has dropped significantly down the table and in 2001, there were only two newcomers in the list of the top ten landlords: Paul Raymond and Mark Pears.[66] Thus the wealthiest London landlords have survived the creation of a 'property-owning democracy'. Consequently, continuity, as well as change, has characterized the pattern of land tenure in London over the last century. In the twenty-first century, however, the prohibitive cost of private housing, the limited supply of mortgages and a chronic lack of social housing may yet revive the urban land question.

Notes

1. See, for example, H. J. Dyos, *Victorian Suburb: A Study of the Growth of Camberwell* (Leicester, 1961).
2. D. A. Reeder, 'The Politics of Urban Leaseholds in Late Victorian Britain', *International Review of Social History*, 6 (1962), 413–30.
3. R. Douglas, *Land, People and Politics: A History of the Land Question in the United Kingdom 1879–1952* (London, 1976).
4. A. Offer, *Property and Politics 1870–1914* (Cambridge, 1981).
5. D. Englander, *Landlord and Tenant in Victorian Britain 1838–1918* (Oxford, 1983); M. J. Daunton, *House and Home in the Victorian City: Working Class Housing 1850–1914* (London, 1983); P. J. Waller, *Town, City and Nation: England 1850–1914* (Oxford, 1983).
6. S. Webb, *Fabian Tracts Number 8: Facts for Londoners* (London, 1889), p. 8; Offer, *Property and Politics*, p. 254.
7. B. B. Gilbert, *David Lloyd George: The Architect of Change 1863–1912* (London, 1987), p. 269, citing Lloyd George's speech at Newcastle, 4 April 1903.
8. I. Packer, *Lloyd George, Liberalism and the Land: The Land Issue and Party Politics in England 1906–1914* (London, 2001), pp. 28–30.
9. Ibid., p. 65.
10. *Return of Owners of Land in England and Wales, Exclusive of the Metropolis* (London, 1875).
11. J. Bateman, *The Great Landowners of Great Britain and Ireland* (London, 1883), p. xvii.
12. R. Hyde, 'Mapping London's landlords: The Ground Plan of London 1892–1915', *Guildhall Studies in London History*, 1 (1973), 28–34; P. H. Lincert, *Who*

Owned Victorian England?, Working Paper Series No. 2, Agricultural History Center, University of California, Davis, California (1983).
13. Daunton, *House and Home*, p. 274: Table 11.1.
14. Webb, *Facts*, p. 8.
15. Lindert, *Who Owned Victorian England*, Appendix: Table B2.
16. Webb *Facts*, p. 9.
17. Lindert, *Who Owned Victorian England*, Appendix: Table B1.
18. F. H. W. Sheppard (ed.), *Survey of London, Volume 39: The Grosvenor Estate in Mayfair, Part I General History* (London, 1977), pp. 47–8.
19. John, Duke of Bedford, *A Silver-Plated Spoon* (London, 1959), pp. 116–17.
20. D. Spring, Intoduction to J. Bateman, *The Great Landowners of Great Britain and Ireland* (Leicester, 1971), p. 19; Lindert, *Who Owned Victorian England*, Appendix: Table B1.
21. H. A. Doubleday, Geoffrey H. White and Lord Howard de Walden (eds), *The Complete Peerage* (London, 1945), x, p. 602; J. Hyder, *The Case for Land Nationalisation* (London, 1913), p. 129.
22. Hyder, *Land Nationalisation*, p. 112.
23. Hon. Sir E. Cadogan, *Before the Deluge, Memories and Reflections 1880–1914* (London, 1961), pp. 3–4.
24. Hyder, *Land Nationalisation*, p. 146.
25. Cadogan, *Before the Deluge*, pp. 34, 101.
26. R. L. Outhwaite, *Peer or Peasant* (n.p., n.d.), pp. 36–7.
27. *The Victoria County History of Suffolk* (London, 1907), ii, p. 364.
28. H. Broadhurst and R. T. Reid, *Leasehold Enfranchisement* (London, 1885), pp. 43–53.
29. Cadogan, *Before the Deluge*, p. 145.
30. Sheppard, *Grosvenor Estate*, pp. 48–63.
31. Ibid., pp. 63–5.
32. R. Quinault, 'Lord Randolph Churchill and Tory Democracy, 1880–1885', *Historical Journal*, 22 (1979), 147–9.
33. Broadhurst and Reid, *Leasehold Enfranchisement*, pp. 129–38, Appendix II: Churchill's draft Bill.
34. Packer, *Lloyd George, Liberalism and the Land*, pp. 30, 108.
35. Waller, *Town, City and Nation*, p. 260.
36. J. A. Yelling, 'Land, Property and Planning', in M. Daunton (ed.), *The Cambridge Urban History of Britain Vol. III 1840–1950* (Cambridge, 2000), p. 479.
37. *Hansard*, 3rd ser., 176 (1 July 1864), cols. 660–1.
38. *Times*, 30 July 1887, p. 11: Gladstone's speech at Memorial Hall, Farringdon Road, London, 29 July 1887.
39. S. Webb, *A Plea for the Taxation of Ground Rents* (London, 1887), pp. 5–13.
40. Douglas, *Land, People and Politics*, pp. 113, 115, 118.
41. *Times*, 6 February 1892, p. 15.
42. *Times*, 9 February 1892, p. 7; 12 February 1892, p. 15: letters from H. T. Boodle.
43. *Times*, 17 February 1892, p. 9; Webb, *Facts*, p. 9.
44. See also J. Davis, *Reforming London: The London Government Problem 1855–1900* (Oxford, 1988), pp. 168–75.

45. *Fabian Tract Number 30, The Fabian Municipal Programme Number 1, The Unearned Increment.*
46. Offer, *Property and Politics*, pp. 224–6.
47. J. Davis, 'The Progressive Council, 1889–1907', in A. Saint (ed.), *Politics and the People of London: The London County Council 1889–1965* (London, 1989), p. 43.
48. H. Pelling, *Social Geography of British Elections, 1885–1910* (London, 1967), p. 31.
49. Campbell-Bannerman's speech at the Albert Hall, 21 December 1905, quoted in Douglas, *Land, People and Politics*, p. 135.
50. B. B. Gilbert, 'David Lloyd George: The Reform of British Landholding and the Budget of 1914', *Historical Journal*, 21 (1978), 124.
51. *Times*, 31 July 1909, p. 9.
52. Cf. Hyder, *Land Nationalisation*, pp. 144–5.
53. *Evening Standard*, 27 March 2005, p. 39.
54. Sheppard, *Grosvenor Estate*, pp. 67–8.
55. Packer, *Lloyd George, Liberalism and the Land*, pp. 108–9.
56. *Times*, 31 October 1913, p. 9.
57. *Times*, 1 December 1913, p. 64, 19 January 1914, p. 9; Offer, *Property and Politics*, p. 390.
58. *The Daily News Year Book, 1913* (Brighton, 1972 edn), pp. 213–20.
59. Lord Ernle [R. E. Prothero], *Whippingham to Westminster* (London, 1938), p. 214.
60. For a detailed account of the Urban Land Report see Packer, *Lloyd George, Liberalism and the Land*, pp. 95–114.
61. B. B. Gilbert, *David Lloyd George: Organizer of Victory 1912–1916* (London, 1992), p. 85.
62. R. Douglas, 'God Gave the Land to the People', in A. J. A. Morris (ed.), *Edwardian Radicalism 1900–1914* (London, 1974), p. 159.
63. Packer, *Lloyd George, Liberalism and the Land*, pp. 141, 155.
64. J. Macdonnell, *The Land Question* (London, 1873), p. 84.
65. Hyder, *Land Nationalisation*, p. 321.
66. K. Cahill, *Who Owns Britain* (Edinburgh, 2001), p. 162.

10
The Edwardian Land Question

Paul Readman

Introduction

Historians of late nineteenth- and early twentieth-century Britain have paid much attention to the cultural significance of contemporary interest in land, landscape and the rural. Since the publication of Martin Wiener's seminal *English Culture and the Decline of the Industrial Spirit* (Cambridge, 1981), many scholars have argued that national identity found powerful expression through a ruralised Englishness. The repositories of this Englishness included the poetry and prose of writers like P. H. Ditchfield, Alfred Austin and Thomas Hardy, landscape preservation (the National Trust being founded in 1894), the folk song revival and pastoral trends in photography and pictorial art.[1] In these years, Krishan Kumar has remarked, 'the essential England was rural'.[2] Now, it may be that the Wiener-inspired model of Englishness exaggerates the reactionary character of ruralist concerns: interest in the culture of the countryside and even the distant rural past was in no way confined to conservatives, as recent studies of the early preservationist movement have shown.[3] That said, there is little reason to doubt that land and nation were closely connected in the popular imagination, albeit in different ways.

Yet, if cultural historians have devoted considerable attention to exploring the inter-relationship between land and nation in England, the same is not true of political historians. This neglect is especially surprising given the now well-understood synergies between nationalism and the politics of land in the Irish, Welsh and Scottish contexts.[4] Scholarly attempts to view the English land question through the prism of the nation have been conspicuous by their absence. As has been often remarked, the existence of English nationalism is routinely denied, and this might be one reason why historians have shied away from the question. But it is at best a partial explanation, as scholars of English politics have not eschewed engagement with themes touching on patriotism or national identity in other contexts: patriotic and nationalistic languages were an inescapable feature of political life in Victorian and Edwardian England, finding expression in debates on imperialism, free trade, education policy and a host of other matters.[5]

Focusing on the period between the 1890s and 1914, this chapter argues that Englishness played an important part in the politics of the English land question. For Liberals and Conservatives, land politics involved debate about the physique and national character of the people, the Englishman's liberties and freedoms and the preservation of national stability at a time of growing social tension, among other things. In the context of widespread alarm about rural depopulation and its supposedly harmful effects on national character and racial efficiency, legislation to preserve a sturdy class of rural-dwellers on the land appeared to be a national imperative. This perspective was prominent in Liberal party thinking, informing initiatives like the 1907 Smallholdings Act and Lloyd George's Land Campaign of 1912–14. But it also played a part in the Unionists' policymaking, not least with regard to their growing interest in peasant proprietorship as a remedy for national ills.

Conservatives, Unionists and the land question

The aristocracy and gentry retained a strong presence in the Conservative party until the First World War. In 1885, 45.8 per cent of Conservative MPs were drawn from landed families; 20 years later, the equivalent figure was 40.1 per cent.[6] At least in terms of the social composition of the rank-and-file, not much seemed to have changed; but statistics can deceive. As E. H. H. Green has shown, in ideological and policy terms the Conservatives underwent a tectonic shift in these years, transforming themselves from the party of landed property to the party of property in general.[7] What Lord Salisbury once called 'pure squire Conservatism'[8] was replaced by a more democratic variant, one that acknowledged the effects of mass enfranchisement on the character of the political nation. The party's response to the land question was central to this ideological realignment. Influenced by patriotic considerations, this response shifted from a late Victorian championing of the old rural order, seen by its defenders as distinctively English, to an Edwardian advocacy of land reform as a means of bolstering the social stability, health and moral fibre of a nation menaced by the twin perils of socialism and rural decay.

'Pure squire Conservatism' died fairly hard. Its ideal was the socially harmonious village community where all knew their place but none was in dire want, thanks to the enlightened stewardship of the landlord. Exemplars of such benevolent landlordism could readily be found within the late Victorian Tory peerage. Individuals such as Lords Wantage and Tollemache practised *noblesse oblige*, providing decent housing for their labourers and granting them allotments on good terms.[9] Such actions, of course, were not solely motivated by humanitarian considerations. They aimed to preserve traditional rural society, with its rigid tripartite division between landlords, farmers and labourers. Far from seeking to transform farm workers into smallholders, as in radical plans, the agenda here was 'to save the old English labourer from extinction' by giving him an allotment to supplement (but not replace) the wages he received from the farmer.[10]

In the 1880s and 1890s, efforts were made to institutionalise 'pure squire Conservatism' and give it political force. Faced by the radical Liberal agitation for 'three acres and a cow', the fifth earl of Onslow established the Land and Glebe Owners' Association for the Voluntary Extension of the Allotments System in 1886. This organisation advocated the discretionary provision of allotments in order to head off demands for compulsory legislation, foster class harmony and ensure a supply of good farm workers; it did not seek to give labourers the opportunity of becoming self-sufficient cultivators themselves.[11] A further attempt to institutionalize traditional agrarian Conservatism was made by the 12th earl of Winchilsea, who founded the National Agricultural Union (NAU) in 1893. Convinced that 'the peers ... are ... the natural leaders of the agricultural interest', he conceived the NAU as an elite-led pressure group, though one whose membership was open to all those who lived by the land.[12] Winchilsea was actuated by a patriotic desire to inculcate class unity by encouraging farmers and labourers to rally behind their landlords and 'stand together as Englishman for the cause of Old England' in defence of both the 'national industry' – agriculture – and the traditional social order with which it was associated.[13]

Both Onslow's Association and Winchilsea's Union rejected radical plans for the legislative creation of small cultivators by the state. This was in line with traditional Conservative party policy, which had typically operated on the assumption that, in the words of the historian J. A. Froude, the existing land system of England was a product of 'economic laws as absolute as the law of gravity'.[14] It was upon this assumption that Conservatives fell back in the mid-1880s, when faced with Liberal proposals for smallholdings legislation. Such proposals, they railed, amounted to an 'economically mischievous' attempt at the 'artificial' creation of a now largely vanished class, in defiance of the *telos* of national economic development.[15] Worse still, Conservatives claimed, the Liberals sought to replace the historic English land system with an alien and undesirable French one, thereby adding further patriotic insult to economic injury. Tory politicians and commentators portrayed the peasant proprietors of France (and other continental countries) as suffering 'wretched' lives of 'dirt, penury, and slavery'. Inhabiting squalid mud-floored cottages, they were overworked and impoverished, subsisting on a 'meagre' diet of tomatoes, lentils, salad and other such stuff which 'our people would refuse to endure'.[16]

The idea of a distinctively 'English' system of great estates and large farms worked by wage labour, and associated with national greatness, persisted in Conservative political discourse until 1914. Speaking in 1899, Walter Long told a meeting of the Central Chambers of Agriculture that

> The land system, associated as it had been so long with the national history of the country, had done more than any other institution of the country to build up the national character and to make the British people what they were (cheers); and the nation which was so justly proud of the deeds of her sons in other parts of the world owed more to the land system than to any other possession for the production of those sons.[17]

Doubtless Long's words were music to the ears of this particular audience; yet by the time they were spoken, the trend of Unionist opinion was beginning to move away from this position, and that of pure squire Conservatism more generally. Onslow's Association had failed to prevent legislative action. In 1887, faced with mounting demands for reform, not least from its Liberal Unionist allies, Salisbury's government passed an act giving local authorities the power to buy or rent land, even compulsorily, for letting in allotment plots of one acre. This was followed by a smallholdings act in 1892, which gave County Councils the ability to purchase plots of land each of up to 50 acres in extent for sale to individuals as smallholdings. Avowedly 'experimental' and in the end ineffective, it was arguably more of a bid for labourer votes at the upcoming general election than anything else.[18] But it did represent a turning of the ideological tide, as did the demise of Winchilsea's NAU by the end of the decade.

There were several reasons for the change in Conservative attitudes. First, mounting evidence of the economic viability of *petite culture* helped disarm the objection that the legislative creation of smallholders was economic madness. In the context of agricultural depression, which hit large arable farms the hardest, there developed growing enthusiasm for low-acreage, intensive farming of the sort practised with considerable success in the Low Countries and Denmark.[19] But considerations of economic practicality were more enabling factors than anything else; for Conservatives, the crucial issues were the threats to national well-being that the rise of socialism and rural decay seemed to present.

Fear of socialism was no new thing, but by the 1900s, it had assumed far greater prominence than previously on the right. The growth of trades unionism and the emergence of the Labour party were important here, but perhaps more so was the belief that Liberals were succumbing to 'collectivist' ideas. In no sphere of policy did this seem more evident than that of the land question. Liberal plans to create a large class of small farmers who neither owned the soil they worked nor rented it from landlords, but instead held it on state or local authority tenancies – plans which found expression in the 1907 Smallholdings Act – appeared to presage land nationalisation. The increasing popularity of land value taxation among Liberal ranks helped confirm this impression.[20] In this context, many Unionists saw the defence of property rights as an urgent priority. Given the democratisation of the political nation effected by the Third Reform Act, the creation of peasant or 'yeoman' proprietors emerged as a usefully populist means by which Conservatives could present themselves as patriotic upholders of the nation's institutional and social cohesion.

The argument was simple: property ownership conduced to political Conservatism; hence small proprietors would resist 'revolutionary' ideas and so it was of national benefit that their number be increased. The merit of this argument had been acknowledged by Tories for some time, with Salisbury having declared, as early as 1892, that 'a small proprietary constitutes the strongest bulwark against revolutionary change, and affords the strongest support for the Conservative feeling and institutions of the country'.[21] Although privately convinced of the Tory proclivities of 'primitive Hodge', Salisbury's words were little more than rhetoric, designed to promote the 1892 Smallholdings Act which he rightly felt was of negligible use, except perhaps as a vote-winner. But by the 1900s, the 'bulwark' argument had moved out of the sphere of rhetorical politicking and into the realm of practical policymaking.

This change is nicely illustrated by the trajectory of Onslow's views on the legislative creation of peasant proprietors, which between the 1880s and the 1900s shifted from a position of principled hostility to one of principled support. As chairman of the 1905–06 Departmental Committee on Smallholdings, he arrived at the opinion that giving wage-earning labourers allotments to tend in their spare time was not enough (allotment numbers had, after all, expanded dramatically in the 1880s and 1890s). They needed the opportunity of becoming independent cultivators of the soil and if the voluntary action of landlords proved insufficient, then compulsory legislation was justified.[22] 'Can anyone doubt', he asked party leaders in an internal memorandum of 23 March 1907, 'that if the wisdom of the early Victorian era had so arranged that the owners and occupiers of the soil had been largely but gradually multiplied, the Conservative instincts of the nation would have been increased, property would now be more secure, the position of every landowner, small or great would have been strengthened?'.[23]

Support for land reform as a means of bolstering private property became still more prominent in Unionist discourse in the context of the 1909 Budget and the constitutional crisis it provoked. In the eyes of many on the right, Lloyd George's land tax and valuation proposals, associated as they were with the cry of 'peers versus people', appeared to point directly towards land nationalisation, 'class war' and the destabilisation of state institutions, the defence of which had long been central to Conservative patriotism. Yet the Tory response to this challenge was not primarily characterised by a reactionary defence of the old order. It is true that elements of the old argument remained present in Tory discourse. But even many 'Diehard' opponents of the People's Budget – both in the Commons and the Lords – supported quite radical schemes of land reform, among them Charles Bathurst, Lord Selborne, Lord Milner, Henry Page Croft and Austen Chamberlain. All of these figures endorsed smallholdings legislation in conjunction with Tariff Reform; some – like Bathurst – were closely connected to the Unionist Social Reform Committee (USRC), an important exponent of radical agrarian measures between 1911 and 1914.[24] Even E. G. Pretyman's anti-Budget 'Land Union' recognised that state action in defence of property rights was justified, being officially committed 'to actively support the creation of small ownerships'.[25]

As demonstrated *a fortiori* by the Diehards, support for peasant proprietorship was well entrenched in Edwardian Conservatism, being seen as a means of combating what Lord Lansdowne in his reply to Lloyd George's famous Limehouse speech called the 'expropriation' and 'robbery' of Liberal policies.[26] By 1909, this support extended to leadership level. During a speech at Birmingham in September of that year, Arthur Balfour made official his party's commitment to the legislative creation of small owners: 'nothing', he declared, 'can be more desirable and important'.[27] This declaration was duly taken on board by the rank and file. At the general election of January 1910, four-fifths of Unionist candidates for English county constituencies mentioned what many termed 'the land policy of Mr Balfour' in their election addresses.[28]

This commitment to peasant proprietorship persisted until World War One, with Lord Milner's 1912–14 Committee on land policy concluding that more peasant proprietors were required 'if the present social order is to endure'.[29] Land reform bills were even introduced by Unionist peers (the Earl of Dunmore's Small Ownership and Land Bank Bill, for example, passed its second reading in May 1911). One such peer was Lord Selborne, a prominent 'Diehard', who in a private memorandum of July 1912 emphasised the Tories' patriotic rationale. 'The Unionist Party is resolved to do its utmost to increase the number of occupying and cultivating owners of the soil', he explained, 'because it believes that the greater the number the owners of the soil, the greater the strength of the Nation and the greater the stability of the National Institutions'.[30] That same summer, Lansdowne – as Unionist leader in the Lords – gave public expression to these private sentiments in a series of speeches, in which he acknowledged that the old land system was in decline and thus needed supplementing with a system based on small ownership. This policy was endorsed by the new Conservative leader Andrew Bonar Law and it was to be re-articulated the following year, as the party grappled with the new challenge posed by Lloyd George's Land Campaign.[31]

But the 'bulwark' argument did not represent the totality of the Unionist case for reform. The idea that peasant proprietorship offered a solution to the decay of the English countryside was also important, particularly on the radical wing of the party. The late nineteenth-century agricultural depression had contributed to these perceptions of rural decay, but the evidence of large-scale rural depopulation was crucial. In 1861, approximately 45 per cent of people had lived in rural districts; by 1911, the figure was 22 per cent.[32] The depopulation of the countryside fuelled anxiety about the health and moral fibre of Englishmen, as thousands left their village homes for the city slums. This anxiety increased due to the Boer War, which not only revealed the physical unhealthiness of the national stock (many volunteers for service being rejected as unfit), but also demonstrated how town-bred Tommies had difficulty overcoming the resistance of the armed farmers of the Transvaal and Orange Free State. With increasing competition from other great powers after 1900 and the growth of the movement for 'national efficiency', land reform emerged as a way of bolstering the health and character of the English race.

Against this background, the arguments of radical Unionists like Jesse Collings and Gilbert Parker proved influential. In his important tract *The Land for the People* (London, 1908), Parker – later chairman of the 1910 Unionist Small Ownership Committee – presented the national deterioration caused by 'loss of rural population' as no startling revelation, but 'a common truth'. His assertion that 'under present conditions we are declining, losing in wealth, in men, in national character, in personal physique' reflected the views of many in his party, and it was one with which Balfour – who supplied the preface to Parker's pamphlet – was apparently sympathetic.[33]

Indeed, following Balfour's public commitment to small ownership, much was heard from Conservatives about the benefits peasant proprietorship would have for the English character, and these benefits were often expressed using a language of race. At the general election of January 1910, this language formed part of candidates' appeals. In his address to the voters of North Cumberland, Claude Lowther affirmed that one of the 'blessings' of small ownership was that 'it would arrest the decay of the race by attracting people to the land'.[34] Sometimes, such claims were linked to defensive considerations. In South East Essex, J. R. B. Newman told voters that he hoped for 'a generous Imperial subsidy to aid what is a truly Imperial object – the Extension of our Small Holdings and Allotments Acts – enabling us as in days gone by to rely on a country-bred and sturdy race should the hour of England's necessity come by sea or land'.[35]

Continued Unionist commitment to land reform into the years of the Land Campaign saw continued concern for the Englishman's health and character. As Lansdowne declared in a speech at Matlock in 1913, 'We believe that ownership is better for the man, that nothing will make him so independent or so self-reliant, will give him such an interest in his farm, and such a sense of citizenship as the complete ownership of a few acres of land'.[36] The proposal of the USRC for agricultural wage boards, set out in *A Unionist Agricultural Policy* (London, 1913), operated on the assumption that the rural population was the physical 'backbone' of the nation. Arthur Steel-Maitland and others associated with the USRC suggested that better wages for agricultural labourers would help preserve a healthy rural population and hence 'the physique of the nation'.[37] Laissez-faire in the matter of agricultural wages, the USRC argued, 'has produced results inimical to the race'.[38]

As is clear from the Wage Boards proposal, Unionist thinking on the land question towards the end of the Edwardian period was moving in quite radical directions. And it was radical not only in the sense that it proposed a level of state intervention hitherto ruled inadmissible by Conservatives, but also because it implied – with its focus on the character of the ordinary Englishman – a democratic conception of the nation's worth. In Conservative discourse, the indices of national strength were changing, becoming more oriented towards the common man; increasingly *defined*, indeed, by the common man and his condition.

In making this new departure, the Edwardian Unionist party had in fact adopted much of the analysis of Collings, who for years had campaigned for land reform to restore the vanished class of 'yeomen' that enclosure had destroyed.[39] (Balfour seemed aware of this: In his Birmingham speech of September 1909, he described his policy as that of the 'old Radicals'.)[40] When put forward by the then radical Liberal Collings in the 1880s, this argument had infuriated landed opinion on both sides of the House, but times had changed. In his *Land Problems and National Welfare* (London, 1911), the Lincolnshire landlord and USRC member Christopher Turnor made clear that the existing system of landholding was productive of national evils, and called for reform to encourage small ownership. In doing so, he drew on a radical vision of English history, one clearly derived from that of Collings, to whom he paid tribute.[41] For Turnor as for Collings, enclosure not only damaged the 'national welfare' by divorcing the people from the soil; it 'was of itself an unrighteous [policy], for it was the robbery of the poor legalized by Acts of Parliament', and as 'Parliament has taken away the land; it must now reverse the process'.[42] Hugh Aronson's *Our Village Homes* (London, 1913) offered a similar perspective.[43]

Not all Unionists accepted this historical analysis. But by the 1900s, mainstream Conservative opinion accepted that in a country where property had historically been seen as a key determinant of citizenship, the concentration of landownership in the hands of a few was a national danger. As one prominent Tory commentator claimed in an 1909 article for the *Nineteenth Century*:

> A democratic form of government and a feudal land system are incompatible... Ten thousand families could hold the bulk of the land when they held in their hands all political power, but they can

> no longer do so when political power is in the hands of 7,000,000 voters, the vast majority of whom are landless. We cannot afford to delay the reform of our land system any longer.... Property owners are the natural defenders of the state and its institutions. This historic fabric of Great Britain rests on a dangerously narrow basis – a basis which sufficed in the past, but which suffices no longer. The enemy is at the gates.... The political enfranchisement of our people should be followed by their economic enfranchisement. Property owners are conservative. A thorough reform of our land system will be the most democratic, and at the same time the most conservative measure of modern times.[44]

These words reflected a refurbishment of Tory ideology. Conservatives now thought that the constitution could best be protected not by the defence of aristocratic property alone, but by the defence of property in general.[45] Hence their espousal of small ownerships, a policy focused on the common people rather than the elite, and therefore deemed appropriate to a rapidly democratising nation.

Liberals, land reform and Englishness

Unionists were right to identify land policy as a key feature of *fin-de-siècle* Liberalism. In all, over two-thirds of candidates for English seats mentioned land reform in their addresses at the 1906 general election.[46] This electoral emphasis was maintained throughout the period before 1914, with 67 per cent of Liberal candidates for English county constituencies referring to land policies in their election addresses at the general election of January 1910, for example.[47] For Liberals, the basic problem with the English land system was 'landlordism': too much real property was concentrated in too few hands. Notoriously, the 1876 *Return of the Owners of Land* had revealed that over one-quarter of England and Wales was owned by around 700 people.[48] From this it was inferred that ordinary people found it very difficult to gain any stake in the soil of their native country, their independence as individuals being circumscribed by enervating dependence on rural squires and urban *rentiers*. Some idea of the effects of a monopolistic land system, as imagined by Liberals, is given in F. Carruther Gould's cartoon of 'The Tony Village', dating from the mid-1890s (Figure 10.1).

Late Victorian and Edwardian Liberals proposed a range of remedies for this state of affairs. Initially, reformers argued that the solution was to remove the 'feudal' encumbrances that tied up landed property in

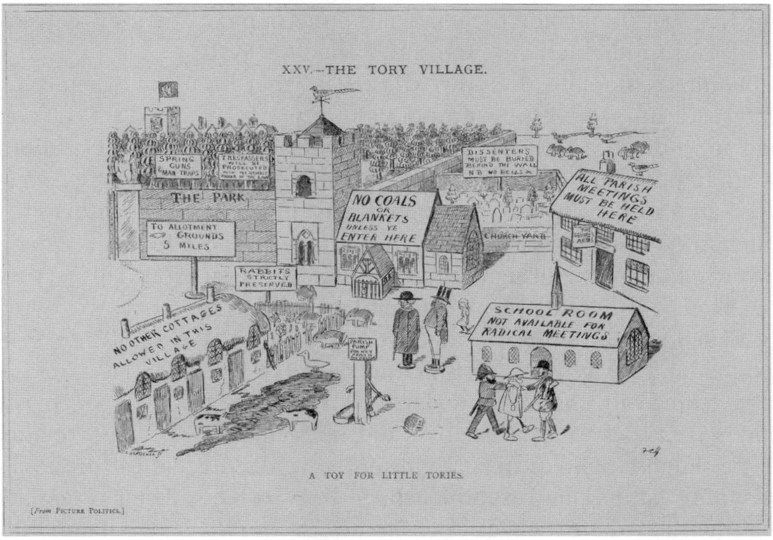

Figure 10.1 F. C. Gould, *The Tory Village: A Toy for Little Tories*, from F. C. Gould, *Cartoons of the Campaign* (London, 1895).
Source: Reproduced by permission of Cambridge University Library.

a small number of hands. By abolishing primogeniture and strict settlement, and by simplifying the complicated process of land transfer, it was felt that a system based on small proprietors would emerge to supplant that of the closed Tory village. Promoted by Liberals like Joseph Kay, G. C. Brodrick and Arthur Arnold, the agitation for 'free trade in land' climaxed in the later 1870s and 1880s, but tailed off rapidly thereafter.[49] By the time of the Third Reform Act, the preferred solution of many was legislation to enable local authorities to acquire land for allotments. Possession of an allotment would give the labourer a stake in the soil and open up the prospect of ultimately becoming a self-sufficient farmer. However, the Allotment Acts of 1887 and 1890 (along with an increase in the voluntary supply of allotments from landlords) largely met the demand, and Liberals looked to other measures. Some hoped that parish councils would revive civic life in the countryside by breaking the stifling dependence of the inhabitants on landlord goodwill, thus inculcating in 'the villager . . . a real sense of what belongs to the citizenship of a free country'.[50] But the passage of the Local Government Act of 1894 proved not to be the looked-for 'rural Magna Charta' and Liberal enthusiasm for land reform fell into abeyance for some years, not least because of the party's internal divisions in the years between Gladstone's retirement and the end of the Boer War.

Reunited after the divisions caused by that war, the Liberals put forward a number of new proposals directed at landlordism. Liberals had long deplored the stringent conditions of tenure that landlords often imposed on farmers, regarding them as restrictive of personal freedom and a disincentive to investment in the land. To protect tenant farmers' interest in the soil they cultivated, Campbell-Bannerman's government passed an Agricultural Holdings Act in 1906. This was followed, in 1907, with the Smallholdings and Allotments Act, which enabled local authorities and centrally appointed commissioners to acquire land for letting as small farms. By 1914, over 200,000 acres had been rented out under its provisions.[51] Yet, while the 1906–07 legislation was far from insignificant, it did not achieve any transformation of the English land system. This spurred on more radical proposals, including land value taxation, which over half of Liberal candidates had mentioned in their election addresses in 1906.[52] The land value of a piece of land was deemed to be its base value aside from that accruing from improvements made to it by its user; according to the land taxers, land values rightfully belonged to the community – hence they ought to be subject to public taxation. This argument informed Lloyd George's 'People's Budget' of 1909. Lloyd George had been sympathetic to land value taxation for some time, and the Land Clauses of the Budget were designed to lay the foundations for its eventual introduction. Soon after the Budget, and before the controversy it had generated had abated, Liberal agrarian policy culminated in the Land Campaign, which set out a wide range of reforms. These included an agricultural minimum wage, further land tenure reform, increased provision for the compulsory purchase of land for public purposes, leasehold enfranchisement and the institution of land value taxation as the basis of local rating.

This great surge of reformist activity on the land question between 1906 and 1914 was directed at what Lloyd George frequently described as the 'feudal' land system of modern Britain. As such, it was consonant with the long-running Liberal campaign against privilege and in favour of individual freedom that the party had inherited from the Gladstonian period. Thanks in large part to the work of Ian Packer, this much is well known.[53] What is far less well known, however, is the patriotic dimension to this campaign.

As for many of their Unionist counterparts, rural depopulation was a crucial stimulus to the patriotic sentiment of Liberal land reformers. In their analysis, the monopolistic land system was inimical to that personal liberty so prized by Britons. Unable to gain access to an allotment or smallholding, forced to work for meagre wages and denied decent accommodation, the countryman's life lacked any real independence. Because of this, so it was claimed, the English national character was deteriorating. As George Harwood, MP for Bolton, told a Liberal conference after the 1906 landslide, lack of access to land meant that the 'national qualities' of the Swiss, German and French exceeded those of the English, who were 'a nation of helots, and stood in a position of slavery'.[54] This was not merely seen as shamefully incongruous with Britain's self-image as 'the island home of liberty', it was charged with further demoralising effects. Much contemporary opinion held that liberty begat moral virtue: freedom and the chance of an independent career would inspire hard work, frugality, temperance and so on. The trouble was, in Liberal eyes, that the land system denied a man access to land and hence a self-sufficient livelihood, meaning that he had little incentive to develop virtuous habits. The introduction to the Land Campaign's rural *Report* made precisely this point, quoting Arthur Young's early nineteenth-century observations on the morally destructive effects of the land monopoly.[55] For Liberals, therefore, measures granting access to land and a good cottage, decent wages and secure tenure – as those proposed by the Land Campaign sought to do – were means whereby the ordinary labourer would be able to make a career on the land as an independent, upright and truly freeborn Englishman.

But Liberal land reform did not just aim to bolster the English national character, it also aimed to address concerns about the physical efficiency of the English race. Liberals claimed landlordism had driven people off the land and into overcrowded and unsanitary slums, so causing 'race deterioration' or 'degeneration'.[56] As Lloyd George put it in one of his Land Campaign speeches, a 'haemorrhage' was 'bleeding the country', depriving the nation of 'a large, strong, robust population' of rural inhabitants, which among other things, made the best fighting men.[57] One moral drawn from this was that measures like smallholdings, land tenure reform and a minimum wage for agricultural labourers were required, so as to encourage people to remain on the land and help create what the Liberal President of the Allotments and Smallholdings Association, Sir Walter Foster, called 'a stronger and sturdier race'.[58] But there was a further moral here too, one that pointed to the need for urban as well as rural land reform. According to Liberals, the racially degenerative effects of city slums were largely a consequence of *urban* landlordism. A particular cause of complaint was the speculative withholding of vacant land that might otherwise be used for housing, so forcing prices up at the cost of the nation's health and strength. Land value taxation was promoted as a means of discouraging such speculation, increasing the supply of building plots and therefore bringing down the levels of overcrowding. Lloyd George was especially keen on this line of argument:

> The greatest asset of a country is a virile and contented population.... Every good farmer knows that if he is to produce the best class of cattle and of horses on his holding he must look after their feeding, their shelter, and, in the case of horses, their training. Why should men and women have less thought and attention given to them than cattle? Statesmanship is, after all, farming on a great scale. Mr. Rowntree points out in his great work that one result of our present system of wages and housing is that 50 per cent of the recruits that come up for service in the Army are rejected as unfit because of their physical inferiority. You apply that throughout every walk of our national life, and you see what an enormous loss is entailed by the nation by its neglect to attend to questions which affect the physical and mental vitality and efficiency of the race.[59]

As illustrated by the language of Lloyd George, Liberal land policy was informed by a real desire to improve the physical character of the race; indeed, this racial agenda was probably more pronounced in Liberal than in Unionist thinking. It was presented in patriotic terms, and certainly casts doubt on the claim that the Conservatives had a monopoly on the language of patriotism at this time.[60] But it also shows that Edwardian Liberal ideas of national character were influenced by a fuzzy, unsystematic biological determinism, a conviction that the physique of the race had a significant effect on the destinies of the nation. This is an important point, and serves as a corrective to standard readings of Edwardian Liberalism as dominated by an enlightened progressivism.

Beneath this concern with race, health and national character was a more general patriotic vision. A particular perspective on the English national past informed the land reform proposals of Edwardian Liberals. Much of the language they used to promote measures like smallholdings drew on a romantic idea of rural England before the late eighteenth- and early nineteenth-century enclosure movement, one that had wide purchase on contemporary culture, being reflected in the then-wildly-popular art of Helen Allingham, for example.[61] But Liberal arguments were also connected to interpretations put forward in the historical literature of the time, such as that of Gilbert Slater and

J. L. and Barbara Hammond, which described the pre-enclosure past in favourable terms and enclosure as causing great hardship to the poor.[62] Liberals were quick to mobilise these claims behind the cause of reform, making extensive use of quotations from Slater and the Hammonds in their propaganda, with the former even being enlisted to write a 20-page 'Historical outline of land ownership in England' for publication in the Land Campaign's official report.[63] Supported by such sources, Liberals presented the pre-enclosure past as a prosperous and peopled Merrie England, where even the humble enjoyed access to the soil. Common land played a crucial part here. It had been the commons that provided the ordinary Englishman – the much-vaunted 'yeoman' farmer – with an independent way of life, free from the drudgery of wage-slavery and the tyranny of the squire. But with enclosure, Liberals from Lord Carrington to radical land nationalisers contended, this way of life had been brutally extinguished, and although they did not seek any literal return to past conditions, they insisted that some sort of restitution was necessary on the grounds of natural justice and national need. As President of the Board of Agriculture, Carrington described the 1907 Smallholdings Act as a 'remedy' for enclosure's effects.[64] In this interpretation, land reform was a means of restoring to the nation what Campbell-Bannerman termed 'something of the England of yore'.[65]

The reading of Edwardian Liberal land reform offered here stands in contrast to Conservative allegations that the Liberals had embraced a novel and dangerous socialistic doctrine – one based on the 'confiscation' of private property. However, it is misleading to take contemporary criticism of Liberal land policies at face value, as some scholars have perhaps come close to doing.[66] It is true that Liberals sought to impose limits on the rights of property in land, not least by introducing compulsory legislation like that contemplated by the Land Campaign. But this aim drew upon and developed already-existing traditions of Liberal-radical thought. The idea, for example, that private land use was limited by considerations of public interest had a long pedigree in Liberal political discourse and was supported by jurisprudential precepts, which laid down that in the final analysis all land in England belonged to the state, whose prerogative was to ensure that it was used in the best interests of the nation as a whole.[67] This perspective exerted a powerful influence on Liberal demands that interference in the current system of landholding was justified on the grounds that this system did not conduce to the national welfare. Drawing on older radical ideas, advocates of land tenure reform, for instance, argued that indebted landowners hobbled by strict settlements were unable to sell or develop their estates, while tenant farmers were reluctant to make improvements to the land they cultivated due to fear of being turned out without compensation. Similarly, Liberal supporters of land value taxation and land nationalisation based their claims on the idea that the selfish interest of landlords – who might put 'the pheasant ahead of the peasant' – ought not to trump that of the nation, for whom unfettered access to land was the constant nurse of English character, health and happiness.[68] Patriotism, not confiscatory collectivism, informed that conviction of radical Liberal land reformers that an Englishman did not in fact have 'the right to do as he liked with his own'.

Such a perspective on the ideological content of the language of Edwardian land politics sheds considerable light on the character of early twentieth-century Liberalism. Much has been made of the idea that Liberal thought and policy was transformed by the ideology of 'The New Liberalism'. In this interpretation, the increasingly dominant radical section of the party fell under the influence of thinkers like J. A. Hobson and L. T. Hobhouse, and in large part abandoned laissez-faire principles for social democracy. The agrarian policies and measures promoted by Liberals have been seen as part of this shift to the left.[69]

It is certainly true that legislation such as the 1907 Smallholdings Act or that proposed by Lloyd George's Land Campaign was incompatible with laissez-faire principles, but these principles were never as important to Liberal government or doctrine as is sometimes made out.[70] As Jonathan Parry has shown, nineteenth-century Liberalism was founded on an agenda that aimed at class reconciliation.[71] The Irish and Scottish land legislation passed by Liberal governments in the 1870s and 1880s, which ran counter to laissez-faire, was informed by this agenda. So too were the proposals for the reform of the English land system put forward by Liberals from the time of the 1906 Landslide onwards. Presented as a project of national integration and renewal, Liberal policy on the English land question was a patriotic endeavour consonant with the time-honoured aims of Liberal reform. Even in the 1900s, it was little influenced by the 'New Liberal' collectivism identified as so important by historians.

Conclusion

The demonstrable contemporary importance of the *fin-de-siècle* land question is in large part due to the interconnection between the politics of land and the politics of patriotism. This was true not just in the Celtic heartlands, but in England too. Both main parties drew on patriotic rationales for their land policies and presented them in patriotic terms. For the Conservatives, protecting the nation from confiscatory and socialistic ideas was a prime concern, and informed their proposals for legislation to widen the basis of property ownership. Anxieties about the degradation of the nation's health and character also motivated Conservative reformism, but they had more of a purchase on Liberal minds. Much of the land legislation proposed and enacted by the Liberal governments of 1905–14 was designed to combat the supposedly degenerative effects of landlordism on national life. Smallholdings, land tenure reform and the taxation of land values would give the countryman an independent life on the land, check rural–urban migration and alleviate slum overcrowding in the towns.

Taken together, then, Conservative and Liberal responses to the land question were directed towards differing projects of national renewal. In the context of the concerns thrown up by rural depopulation, agricultural depression, urban overcrowding, the rise of socialism, military setbacks in South Africa, international competition and so on, land reform offered a means of revitalising the nation. Even mainstream Conservative opinion came to take this perspective, for circumstances were no longer conducive to complacent acceptance of the status quo. Moreover, in the years after the Third Reform Act and particularly after 1900, the existing land system appeared anachronistically – and dangerously – undemocratic. In denying ordinary Englishmen access to the soil of their own country it not only threatened the decay of national health and character, but also appeared antithetical to contemporary constitutional arrangements, which through the widened franchise allowed the same ordinary Englishmen much-improved access to the political nation.

Notes

1. See, for example, A. Helmreich, *The English Garden and National Identity* (Cambridge, 2002); D. P. Corbett, et al. (eds), *The Geographies of Englishness: Landscape and the National Past 1880–1940* (New Haven, 2002); J. Taylor, *A Dream of England: Landscape, Photography and the Tourist's Imagination* (Manchester, 1995); G. Boyes, *The Imagined Village: Culture, Ideology and the English Folk Revival* (Manchester, 1993); D. Gervais, *Literary Englands: Versions of 'Englishness' in Modern Writing* (Cambridge, 1993); A. Howkins, 'The Discovery of Rural England', in R. Colls and P. Dodd (eds), *Englishness: Politics and Culture 1880–1920* (London, 1986).
2. K. Kumar, *The Making of British National Identity* (Cambridge, 2003), p. 211.
3. P. Readman, 'Landscape Preservation, "Advertising Disfigurement", and English National Identity, *c.* 1890–1914', *Rural History*, 12 (2001), 61–83; idem, 'Preserving the English Landscape', *Cultural and Social History*, 5 (2008), 197–218.

4. See, for example, P. Bull, *Land, Politics and Nationalism* (Dublin, 1996); M. Cragoe, *Culture, Politics, and National Identity in Wales, 1832–1886* (Oxford, 2004); E. A. Cameron, *Land for the People? The British People and the Scottish Highlands, c. 1880–1925* (East Linton, 1996).
5. See, for example, H. Cunningham, 'The Conservative Party and Patriotism', in Colls and Dodd, *Englishness*, pp. 283–307; P. Readman, 'The Liberal Party and Patriotism in Early Twentieth Century Britain', *Twentieth Century British History*, 12 (2001), 269–302.
6. J. P. Cornford, 'The Parliamentary Foundations of the Hotel Cecil', in R. Robson (ed.), *Ideas and Institutions of Victorian Britain* (London, 1967), p. 310.
7. E. H. H. Green, *The Crisis of Conservatism: The Politics, Economics and Ideology of the British Conservative Party, 1880–1914* (London, 1995).
8. A. Roberts, *Salisbury: Victorian Titan* (London, 1999), pp. 499–500.
9. M. A. Havinden, *Estate Villages: A Study of the Berkshire Villages of Ardington and Lockinge* (London, 1966), pp. 88–9; F. Impey, 'Lord Tollemache, the Labourer's Lord', *New Review*, 9 (September 1893), 299–313.
10. 'Lord Tollemache's Cottage Farms', *Chambers's Journal*, 5th ser., 2 (1885), 770–1.
11. Earl of Onslow, *Landlords and Allotments* (London, 1886).
12. *Cable*, 26 August 1893, p. 360. For more on Winchilsea and the NAU, see P. Readman, 'Conservatives and the Politics of Land: Lord Winchilsea's National Agricultural Union, 1893–1900', *English Historical Review*, 121 (2006), 25–69.
13. *Cable*, 21 December 1895, p. 390.
14. J. A. Froude, 'On the Uses of a Landed Gentry', in *Short Studies on Great Subjects*, ed. D. Ogg (London, 1963 [1887–83]), pp. 255–77.
15. P. Greg, 'The New Radicals', *National Review*, 5 (April 1885), 166; H. Chaplin, *Hansard*, 3rd ser., 282 (20 July 1883), col. 110; R. E. Prothero, *The Pioneers and Progress of British Farming* (London, 1888), pp. 128, 137–40.
16. F. P. Verney, 'Peasant Properties in France', *National Review*, 10 (December 1887), 551; F. M. de Borring, 'The Peasant Proprietor of the South', *National Review*, 6 (November 1885), 348–50; [H. Reeve], 'Plain Truths and Popular Fallacies', *Edinburgh Review*, 162 (October 1885), 578; H. S. Constable, *Letters to County Newspapers on Radicalism and Socialism* (London 1886), esp. pp. 1–9, 145–67, at 160.
17. *Times*, 6 December 1899, p. 11.
18. J. R. Fisher, 'Public Opinion and Agriculture 1875–1900' (PhD thesis, Hull, 1972), pp. 780–1.
19. See, for example, H. Rider Haggard, *Rural England* (London, 1906); idem., *Rural Denmark and its Lessons* (London, 1911); J. Collings, *Land Reform* (London, 1906).
20. At the 1906 general election, 45 members of the English League for the Taxation of Land Values were returned to the Commons as Liberal MPs: *Land Values*, February 1906, p. 176.
21. *Times*, 3 February 1892, p. 6.
22. *Departmental Committee on Small Holdings*, Parl. Papers 1906, LV, report.
23. *History of the Onslow Family by the 5th Earl of Onslow*, typescript MS, 9 vols. V, p. 1325 (Surrey History Centre G173/1/5).

24. Green, *Crisis*, pp. 290–4, 297. For the activities of the USRC more generally, see J. Ridley, 'The Unionist Social Reform Committee, 1911–14: Wets before the Deluge', *Historical Journal*, 30 (1987), 391–413.
25. 'The Land Union' (LU leaflet no. 22), Coll. LU leaflets, British Library: 8139.ee. 46.
26. *Times*, 9 August 1909, p. 8.
27. *Times*, 23 September 1909, p. 7.
28. Calculated from 234 addresses in *British Political Party General Election Addresses* (Brighton, 1984–85), 28 microfilm reels, pt. 1, 1892–1922, reel 5, 1910.
29. I. Packer, 'The Conservatives and the Ideology of Landownership, 1910–1914', in M. Francis and I. Zweiniger-Bargielowska (eds), *The Conservatives and British society, 1880–1990* (Cardiff, 1996), p. 47.
30. G. Boyce (ed.), *The Crisis of British Unionism: Lord Selborne's Domestic Political Papers, 1885–1922* (London, 1987), pp. 85–6.
31. *Times*, 31 July 1912, pp. 7–8.
32. J. Saville, *Rural Depopulation in England and Wales 1851–1951* (London, 1957), p. 61.
33. Parker, *Land for the People*, pp. 32, 34.
34. *Election Addresses*, reel 5, January 1910.
35. Ibid.
36. *Times*, 23 June 1913, p. 4.
37. *Unionist Agricultural Policy*, p. 5.
38. Ibid., p. 11.
39. Collings, *Land Reform*.
40. *Times*, 23 September 1909, p. 7.
41. Turnor, *Land Problems*, pp. 116–19.
42. Ibid. pp. 16, 234–5.
43. Aronson, *Village Homes*, esp. preface, v–vi and 111–12.
44. J. E. Barker, 'The Land, the Landlords and the People', *Nineteenth Century*, 66 (October 1909), 550–1, 566.
45. Green, *Crisis*.
46. A. K. Russell, *Liberal Landslide: The General Election of 1906* (Newton Abbot, 1973), p. 65.
47. Figure calculated on the basis of 221 addresses in *Election Addresses*, reels 4 and 5: 1910.
48. J. Bateman, *The Great Landowners of Great Britain and Ireland* (5th edn, Leicester, 1971).
49. G. C. Brodrick, *The Reform of the English Land System* (London, 1883); J. Kay, *Free Trade in Land* (2nd edn, London, 1879); A. Arnold, *Free Land* (London, 1880); E. Spring, 'Landowners, Lawyers, and Land Law Reform in Nineteenth-Century England', *American Journal of Legal History*, 21 (1977), 56–7.
50. Sir W. Harcourt: *Land and People*, 1 December 1891, p. 93.
51. C. S. Orwin and W. F. Darke, *Back to the Land* (London, 1935), pp. 22–3, 28.
52. Russell, *Liberal Landslide*, p. 65.
53. I. Packer, *Lloyd George, Liberalism and the Land: The Land Issue and Party Politics in England, 1906–1914* (Woodbridge, 2001).

54. Land Law Reform Association, *Nineteenth Annual meeting* (London, 1906), p. 9.
55. 'Go to an ale-house kitchen of an old enclosed country, and there you will see the origin of poverty and poor rates. For whom are they to be sober? For whom are they to save? Such are their questions. For the Parish? If I am diligent, shall I have leave to build a cottage? If I am sober, shall I have land for a cow? If I am frugal, shall I have half an acre of potatoes? You offer no motives; you have nothing but a parish officer and a workhouse! Bring me another pot!': *The Land: The Report of the Land Enquiry Committee* (3rd edn, London, 1913), i, p. xxvi.
56. For example, F. A. Channing, *Memories of Midland Politics, 1885–1910* (London, 1918), p. 362; Sir H. Campbell-Bannerman, *Times*, 22 April 1907, p. 18.
57. *Times*, 13 October 1913, p. 13 and 22 October 1913, p. 9.
58. *Hansard*, 4th ser., 175 (13 June 1907), col. 1626.
59. *Times*, 18 October 1910, p. 7.
60. Cf. H. Cunningham, 'The Language of Patriotism, 1750–1914', *History Workshop Journal*, 12 (1981), 8–33.
61. See, for example, H. Allingham and S. Dick, *The Cottage Homes of England* (London, 1909); M. B. Huish and H. Allingham, *Happy England* (London, 1903); H. M. Cundall, *Birket Foster* (London, 1986 [1906]), esp. pp. 132–3; P. Readman, 'The Role of Land and Landscape in English Cultural and Politic Debate, *c.* 1880–1914' (PhD thesis, Cambridge, 2002), pp. 25–6, 185–90.
62. G. Slater, *The English Peasantry and the Enclosure of Common Fields* (London, 1907); J. L. and B. Hammond, *The Village Labourer* (London, 1911); W. Hasbach, *A History of the English Agricultural Labourer* (London, 1908).
63. *The Land*, i, pp. lxi–lxxxiii.
64. Carrington, preface to C. Grant, *The Small Holdings and Allotment Handbook* (Bristol, 1908), pp. vi–vii.
65. Liberal Publication Department, *The case for Dissolution: A Speech Delivered by the Right Hon. Sir H. Campbell-Bannerman* (London, 1905), p. 12.
66. For example, M. Fforde, *Conservatism and Collectivism, 1886–1914* (Edinburgh, 1990), esp. pp. 49–51.
67. P. Readman, *Land and Nation* in England: Patriotism National Identity, and the Politics of Land, 1880–1914 (Woodbridge, 2008), pp. 112–34.
68. Ibid., pp. 129–30.
69. Fforde, *Conservatism*, 49. For Fforde's view that Liberal politics generally were more and more driven by collectivist ideology, see ibid., pp. 19–23, 44–54, 103–11.
70. E. F. Biagini (ed.), *Citizenship and Community* (Cambridge, 1996).
71. A theme pursued in his *Rise and Fall of Liberal Government in Victorian Britain* (New Haven, 1993).

11

Unemployment, Taxation and Housing: The Urban Land Question in Late Nineteenth- and Early Twentieth-Century Britain

Ian Packer

Introduction

Nineteenth-century British radicals had a long-standing interest in land reform as a means of attacking the dominant social and political role of great landowners. But it was not until the 1880s that a number of factors coincided to bring 'the land' to the very centre of British politics. These included the prolonged agricultural depression and the protests it produced within rural society, the extension of the franchise to the working class in the counties in 1884–85 and the defection of most Liberal landowners to the Unionist alliance in 1886.[1] All these developments gave the Liberal party an incentive to promote rural land reform, both to attack their landed enemies and to gain the votes of the newly enfranchised agricultural labourers. The 1894 Local Government Act, which empowered parish councils to acquire land for allotments, and the 1907 Smallholdings Act were important parts of the programmes of the 1892–95 and 1905–15 Liberal governments.[2] But as rural land reform made an appearance on the national political stage, it brought into the limelight a number of arguments which were already gaining ground in local government and which suggested land reform could present a solution to some pressing problems of urban life. This was an attractive option to many Liberals, who were only too eager to blame landowners for all society's ills; and while large landowners were obviously less prominent in complex and economically diverse urban societies than in the countryside, there were enough high-profile examples to make them plausible targets for radical enmity.[3]

Road to Utopia, penal colony or irrelevance? Land colonies and the unemployed

The demand that land should be made available to the poor had a very long pedigree in British working-class radicalism. Ultimately it drew on the concept that land was not a form of property like any other – it belonged to all the people. This was justified on a wide variety of grounds, including the idea that land was necessary to existence, that it belonged to God rather than private owners and that it had been owned by the people in the past and had been stolen from them, either at the imposition of the 'Norman Yoke' in 1066 or the enclosures of common land from Tudor times onwards. The followers of Thomas Spence in the 1810s and 1820s, the Owenites in the 1830s and 1840s and the Chartists all had schemes to return the people to the land and so eradicate poverty and inequality.[4] As society became more urbanised these plans were increasingly propounded as a solution to urban difficulties and especially to unemployment. If there were too many people for the work available in the towns, it seemed an attractive solution to set them up as cultivators on the land that really belonged to the people anyway; there would always be a ready market for agricultural produce, however much the demand for industrial goods fluctuated, and it was more feasible to turn people into smallholders than to organise them into factories or workshops.

These practical concerns meshed with a deep-seated antipathy to industrial production and urban conditions; one that saw life on the land as a return to a lost idyll of independence and self-sufficiency.[5] This ideal was part of the reason why so many British people saw emigration to the 'virgin territories' of North America and Australasia as so attractive. Internal colonisation represented an attempt to create these free societies within Britain. The powerful attraction of this ideal of yeoman independence ensured that land settlement retained its place in radical thought and emerged particularly strongly in times of high unemployment. It was championed by the Land and Labour League in the 1860s and by prominent radicals like Charles Bradlaugh and Henry Labouchere in the 1880s. It also formed an important part of the programme proposed by early socialists.[6] By the 1890s, the idea had gained a further boost from agricultural depression and rural depopulation. Keir Hardie urged the Commons to provide 'home colonies on the idle lands about which we have heard so much discussion'.[7]

Hardie's speech was also indicative of how the radical nostrum of land settlement had developed in the later nineteenth century. For many, the ideal was no longer to plant individual cultivators on the soil but groups or colonies of families working together in co-operation, holding their land in common or, more probably, as tenants of the community. This reflected current thinking about the need for agricultural co-operation to boost efficiency in the face of foreign imports. But it also emerged from the role that radicals and socialists were increasingly playing on local authorities, including poor law boards of guardians, once their franchise was opened up in 1894. Some activists attempted to re-activate ancient Poor Law statutes which allowed local boards of guardians to acquire publicly owned land for the unemployed. This idea appealed particularly to those confronted by mass unemployment in the East End of London, including both Keir Hardie, MP for West Ham and Canon Samuel Barnett, founder of the Toynbee Hall settlement. Metropolitan boards of guardians seriously investigated the feasibility of this scheme in the 1890s. The future Labour leader, George Lansbury, who was elected as a socialist member of Poplar board of guardians in 1894, soon emerged as the key figure in these initiatives.[8]

Though the Local Government Board (LGB) blocked Lansbury's plans to buy a farm in Essex in 1895, he renewed his efforts in 1903. This time he was able to circumvent the Board with the help of Joseph Fels, an American businessman, who had re-located to England and was an enthusiastic follower of Henry George.[9] Fels bought an estate at Laindon in Essex in 1904 and turned it over to the Poplar guardians. In 1905 the Unemployed Workmen Act set up a Central Unemployed Body (CUB) in London, made up of representatives from local distress committees and charged with co-ordinating relief to the unemployed in the capital. Lansbury was a key member of the CUB and Fels indicated in 1905 that he would present the committee with another Essex estate, at Hollesley Bay, which he had bought in 1904. Thus, when the new Liberal government came into office in December 1905 the ideal of settling the unemployed on the land was closer to realisation than ever before and seemed poised to make the transition from local to national politics.

However, this high-point was not reached by the enthusiasm of radicals and socialists alone. The 1880s had also witnessed the beginnings of interest in land colonies from a very different direction. The unemployment of that decade provoked some detailed social analysis and the promotion of new solutions that claimed to be based on 'scientific' study of the problem by civil servants, economists, ministers of religion and social investigators. Overwhelmingly, they did not reject land colonies, but they did radically re-envision their nature. Instead of a way of reforming society, they were seen as a means of removing 'surplus' labour from urban areas and subjecting the labourers to some form of re-training to make them more employable, including in agricultural pursuits. This idea appealed to the eminent economist, Alfred Marshall, and in 1889 Charles Booth, in his survey of London, proposed this should be the fate of the entire 'Class B' of very poor inhabitants of the capital – about 340,000 people.[10] His namesake, William Booth, head of the Salvation Army, opened a farm colony at Hadleigh in Essex in 1891 to train the urban unemployed in skills to equip them for emigration to North America.[11] This stimulated a good deal of interest among those who saw labour colonies as a possible means of subjecting the unemployed, or at least the 'unworthy' of them, to compulsory discipline and re-education. A number of government committees looked into this possibility, especially in connection with the Vagrancy Acts, and the idea of 'penal' labour colonies gained widespread support in some business and charitable circles.[12]

There were, therefore, two very different views of the purpose of land colonies by 1905. Both helped push the issue forward and the advocates of labour colonies could look to the future with confidence. Unemployment was an important political issue in the years leading up to the 1906 general election and land colonies seemed to offer a solution. However, instead of becoming part of government policy, the land colonies movement ground to a halt. This reversal of fortune was exemplified in the fate of the CUB's estate at Hollesley Bay.[13] The LGB blocked Lansbury's plan to turn it into a permanent colony of smallholders and a frustrated Lansbury resigned from the committee overseeing its administration in February 1907. The LGB insisted that Hollesley Bay remain a source of temporary relief work for some London unemployed, turned down Joseph Fels's offer of a further colony of smallholders at Maylands in Essex and instructed any experiments in land colonies by other councils to follow LGB guidelines. These events killed off Lansbury's hopes of using Hollesley Bay as the gateway to a socialist commonwealth.[14] But they also stymied plans for a network of penal colonies to remove and retrain the unemployed. All that was left was an adjunct to existing schemes of public works to relieve unemployment.

This decision was ultimately the responsibility of John Burns, Liberal President of the LGB. He was deeply sceptical about the whole land colonies idea, a view that may well have been influenced by his strong dislike of Lansbury.[15] By 1907 he was convinced Hollesley Bay was 'a costly piece of political bribery' by Lansbury.[16] But Burns's decisions were not just personal and he faced no political backlash when he effectively halted the land colonies experiments. This was because the closer these experiments came to reality, the clearer it became that they faced powerful opposition. This was crystallised by the LGB's enquiries into the London Poor Law in 1906, which accused a range of guardians, including those of Lansbury's authority in Poplar, of incompetence, wastefulness and corruption.[17] Included in this denunciation was a damning indictment of Poplar's land colony at Laindon as hugely expensive, poorly run and totally unable to help its unemployed members find work. This was undoubtedly crucial in turning opinion in the CUB against further development of Hollesley Bay.[18] But it also revealed some of the problems with the base of support for land colonies.

One essential issue was that while men like Hardie and Lansbury saw land colonies as a way of transforming rural and ultimately urban society, they had promoted them and justified them as a solution to unemployment. By 1905–06, land colonies formed part of a much wider debate about how to deal with the unemployed, rather than an assault on landownership. This drained away some of their wider political appeal by distancing them from other aspects of the land issue. Without this more broadly based support, the whole concept of land colonies was vulnerable to detailed criticism on the grounds of its ineffectiveness in dealing with unemployment. The LGB enquiry of 1906, for instance, pointed up the vast expense involved in existing land colonies and the colonies' poor record in actually converting the unemployed into smallholders.[19] The advocates of 'penal' labour colonies were not in a position to repel these attacks. The taint of extravagance was scarcely one they could relish and it compounded longstanding worries about whether it would be legal to detain people in labour colonies and the complaint from farmers regarding unfair competition from state-supported produce. Without further expansion, the effectiveness of land colonies could only be judged by their ability to reduce unemployment and what research there was revealed they usually only offered the unemployed another opportunity of short-term casual work.[20]

In a wider context, the demise of land colonies schemes was part of the move away from all state-supported relief works in 1905–14.[21] The Unemployed Workmen Act of 1905, which gave land colonies their brief opportunity, also demonstrated that state-sponsored work schemes could not solve the political issue posed by the unemployed in economic downturns. It was no longer sufficient to try and help some workmen through hard times with these sorts of initiatives. The Tories were claiming they could end unemployment altogether with tariff reform and Labour was pressing for a massive increase in the state's responsibilities by guaranteeing employment as a 'right'.[22] Faced with these sorts of challenges, the leading figures in the Liberal government decided new approaches were needed that could be claimed to yield short-term, tangible results, rather than necessitating the restructuring of the whole of rural England. Lloyd George and Churchill turned to labour exchanges and unemployment insurance in 1908–09 as policies that could help the unemployed cope with periods out of work and smooth their re-entry into employment, rather than attempting the huge task of draining an overfilled urban labour market. Though this did not end all support for 'the land' as a solution to urban unemployment, it marked a decisive move away from the idea that land reform would play a major role in tackling the problem.[23]

Land taxation: from Henry George to Lloyd George

The other central aspect of the urban land question that many radicals hoped would become government policy after 1905 was land taxation. It, too, had started to become prominent as an issue in the 1880s and had been closely linked to London's problems. Metropolitan radicals were increasingly exercised by the issue of London's rising rates bills and outraged that the capital's ground landlords, who – as Roland Quinault's contribution to this collection demonstrates, included some prominent aristocrats – did not contribute to local taxation while the price of their properties soared.[24] But while it was London Liberals who started to raise the issue in the Commons in the late 1880s and early 1890s, land taxation steadily spread out into the rest of the party. The idea was relentlessly proselytised by the followers of Henry George, the American author of *Progress and Poverty*, who claimed that poverty was the fault of great landowners and could be cured by replacing all taxes with a tax on land, fixed at its rental value, thus rendering its ownership literally worthless.[25] While this doctrine was probably not very well understood, let alone accepted, by most Liberals, George was admired for the vigour of his anti-landlord polemics and gained a small but very active following, who believed he had found the key to society's well-being.[26] After the 1906 election, there were probably six or seven Georgeite enthusiasts on the Liberal benches in the Commons, including the indefatigable Josiah Wedgwood.[27]

But even more importantly, land taxation was taken up by many Liberals active in urban local government, because it seemed to offer a solution to some pressing political issues. In the late 1890s, Liberals and socialists on the newly created London County Council and the recently expanded Glasgow Council, in particular, began to press for the power to levy local land taxes.[28] Firstly, it could be argued that a local tax on land (or 'site value rating' as it came to be called) in addition to, or in place of, the existing rating system, could promote more house building. It would do this by forcing more land onto the market, by rating potential building plots at their selling price rather than their current use value.[29] As site value rating was only paid on land values, it would also remove the anomaly that when houses were put up on land, its rate burden automatically increased. These arguments seemed particularly attractive at the end of the 1890s and start of the 1900s when house building was in a prolonged slump and shortages of working-class housing were obvious in some cities. But site value rating could also be presented as the solution to the problem of rising rates, which worried many urban Liberals. Rates were the only direct tax that most working-class people paid and rate rises tended to be highest in the poorest areas because they had the greatest social problems, but the lowest property values. Liberals were reluctant to tackle this problem by increasing central grants to local authorities, because they believed if tenants had to pay less in rates, then landlords would benefit by raising tenants' rents.[30] Rating the capital value of land, rather than its use value, might provide a new stream of revenue for hard-pressed local authorities and at the same time penalise landlords. It is no wonder that many urban Liberals found the idea attractive.

Support for site value rating soon spilled out of local government and into national politics. In 1904 and 1905, bills on the subject even passed the Commons because some urban Tories did not wish to be seen to be opposed to the idea.[31] At the 1906 election, 52 per cent of Liberal candidates mentioned land taxation in their election addresses and Henry Campbell-Bannerman, the party leader, publicly endorsed site value rating.[32] Burns at the LGB was once again the man responsible for turning a scheme devised by Liberals in local government into national legislation. But while he had been implacably opposed to land colonies, he was on record as publicly supporting site value rating.[33] Moreover, he was regularly reminded of the significance of the issue by both Campbell-Bannerman and his successor, H. H. Asquith.[34] The cabinet even drafted in the attorney-general, Sir William Robson, to help Burns produce a bill.[35] But no bill appeared, despite hopeful pronouncements from the government. Burns was defeated by the complexity of the problems he faced and especially the need to devise a scheme to reform the valuation system for land in such a way that land and buildings were valued separately – necessary in order to draw up any plan for site value rating.[36] By late 1908, there was increasing frustration among the ranks of committed land taxers in the Liberal party. But they could not find a way round Burns's inaction on the subject. Site value rating was far too abstruse a subject for the cabinet to think of replacing or overruling Burns on the subject. Even if there had been a more effective head of the LGB, it was impossible to imagine that a Liberal Bill on site value rating would pass the House of Lords or that sufficient public fury could be aroused on such a complex issue in order to force the Lords to give way.

Thus, while support for site value rating was much more widespread within Liberalism than backing for land colonies, after 3 years of Liberal government it had little more chance of success. This gloomy outlook was transformed by David Lloyd George, the new Chancellor of the Exchequer appointed in April 1908. He was faced with an immediate crisis when preparing for the next Budget in 1909.[37] Spending commitments on social reforms and the Navy meant that a huge rise in expenditure could only be covered by a raft of tax increases. From the 1890s, the Liberals had been moving towards increases in direct taxes on the very wealthiest as the only equitable way to pay for rising expenditure.[38] But no Liberal chancellor had expected to be faced with the scale of rises in income tax and death duties necessary in 1909. Lloyd George needed a strategy to distract attention from the way in which his tax rises would hurt some prominent Liberal supporters and leave the government open to the charge of harming the economy by destroying the capital needed for investment. He was also looking for a way to reinvigorate the government's appeal in the face of a long string of by-election defeats.[39] The answer he came up with was to supplement the key tax rises in the 1909 Budget with a range of new taxes that would assault the Liberals' traditional enemies. This involved a full-frontal attack on the brewers and distillers with drastic increases in taxes on spirits and liquor licenses. But the Budget's most controversial proposal was a series of new taxes on land, which were designed to assault the great landowners of Britain and the House of Lords that had so infuriatingly blocked major Liberal legislation in 1906–08.[40]

This strategy totally transformed the role of land taxation in British politics. Before 1909, it was essentially a scheme to reform the way in which local rates were calculated. While many Liberals were favourable, it could scarcely be described as a front-rank issue. Lloyd George transferred it to the national arena and made it the central topic of debate in 1909 by using his land taxes as the springboard for a series of oratorical assaults on landownership. The Conservatives responded with a furious attack on the proposed land taxes and held them up in the Commons for 22 days of acrimonious debate in the summer of 1909.[41]

The outcome of this extraordinary transformation of land taxation was paradoxical. Not only did it become much better known, it was widely assumed in political circles in 1909–10 to be, on balance, a vote-winner for the Liberals. The government's performance in by-elections picked up after the introduction of the Budget and the Unionists' analysis of the 1910 general election results led them to conclude that land taxation was popular, at least in big urban centres.[42]

However, the triumph of land taxation in 1909–10 proved a heavily qualified success. Once the Lords rejected the Budget in November 1909, Lloyd George's taxes lost their political centrality and were replaced by the battle over the power of the peers in the constitution. It was the House of Lords, not land taxation, that dominated political debate in 1909–11.[43] Moreover, the attempt to collect the three land duties, once the Budget finally passed in 1910, was fraught with difficulty.[44] A new national land valuation required every owner of a piece of land, however small, to fill in a series of baffling forms. The process was not complete by 1914 and was estimated to have cost over two million pounds. The land duties were so complex that they ran into a barrage of legal actions and interminable court proceedings. By 1914, all three duties were either totally or partially suspended while these issues were being resolved and the sum collected from the duties was only just over £600,000. Land taxation had dismally failed to offer a great new source of revenue, despite its supporters' claims. Moreover, it had not produced a boom in house building. The years after the Budget actually coincided with a slowdown in house construction which Unionists gleefully attributed to the new land taxes. There may well have been some truth in these claims, if only because builders feared their profits would be taxed under the new duties.[45]

In fact, 1909 proved the high point for Edwardian land taxation. The travails of the Budget duties did not mean that the Liberals lost interest in taxing the land, but the importance of this approach was substantially reduced. When Lloyd George set up an enquiry into all aspects of the land issue in 1912, the urban half of the enquiry considered the question of national land taxation and site value rating in detail, making use of preliminary figures from the new land valuation, helpfully provided by the Inland Revenue.[46] They concluded that a new, simpler, national land tax would be impossible to implement, as it might lead to 'very grave depression in the property market, and violent changes in the value of land' and put unsustainable burdens on agricultural land.[47] At the local level, the enquiry believed site value rating would contribute little to local authority revenue. The only way to relieve the pressure on local rates was to extend the scope of central government grants to local authorities by at least five million pounds.[48] The enquiry suggested a modest scheme of site value rating (starting with 1*d*. of existing rates) should accompany the grants as a way of ensuring landlords did not benefit from these increased grants. Rather more dubiously, it hoped site value rating might still encourage more house building. Thus, while site value rating retained a place in Liberal thinking, the land enquiry in effect downgraded it to a supporting role in the new scheme for increased central grants to local authorities.

These ruminations unexpectedly sprang to prominence because of changes to Lloyd George's budgetary plans.[49] In January 1914, it became clear that further immediate increases in naval expenditure were inevitable and the 1914 Budget would have to contain significant tax rises for the first time since 1909. The chancellor was unwilling to produce a Budget whose only proposals would annoy Liberals worried about more money being spent on armaments and which contained no good news on the domestic front. Having cast around for the most likely scheme to hand, he decided to make use of the deliberations of his land enquiry and announced that the new taxes would also pay for 11 million pounds in increased grants to local authorities in 1915–16 and provisional extra grants for December 1914 to March 1915. In the future, local authorities could levy some combination of existing rates and site value rates, but they would only be able to lower existing rates, thus hopefully ensuring landlords could not benefit from any reductions in local taxes. This elaborate plan was halted by the outbreak of World War One, but its scheme for provisional grants in 1914–15 had already been abandoned because of the government's inability to push the requisite legislation through parliament in time. These hurried additions to the 1914 Budget and their subsequent partial withdrawal provoked a good deal of criticism and some considerable embarrassment for Lloyd George. But they were not a signal that he wished to return land taxation to the centre of political debate. No new national land taxes were considered in the financial crisis of 1914 and site value rating was merely an adjunct to the plan to increase central grants to local authorities. Above all, the Budget of 1914 was not accompanied by the extravagant anti-landlord rhetoric of 1909. It was presented as a vehicle of social reform and relief to hard-pressed ratepayers, rather than a means of assaulting the landed elite.[50] The significance of land taxation as an issue was clearly in retreat by 1914 and the government's plans for land reform had started to take a very different direction and to focus on housing reform.

The new Liberalism: housing and town planning

The final aspect of urban land reform to make its appearance in Edwardian politics was a series of issues connected to the development of housing and town planning. It was necessarily rather harder to blame great landowners for problems connected to housing in large towns than in the countryside. Most towns of any size and cities had complex patterns of landownership.[51] Even where there were large urban estates, their owners were removed from any direct connection with the nature of urban housing because they usually leased out their land to builders, who then constructed houses which they sold on to further purchasers, with the obligation to pay an annual sum (the ground rent) to the landowner. These houses were then rented out, and to most urban-dwellers, 'the landlord' was a small businessman who owned the house they rented, not a great aristocrat. Since the 1880s, though, there had been grumbles from those mainly middle-class people who had bought houses built on land leased on a short-hold basis. After 99 years, the land reverted to the original landowner's descendents and he could charge a fee for renewing the lease and push up the ground rent. The Leasehold Enfranchisement Association was founded in 1884 to campaign for ground landlords to be forced to sell their land to the owners of the buildings constructed on it whenever the lease fell due. But this was very much a minority concern, as most towns and cities were built on the freehold or a long leasehold (999 years) system, though it continued to trouble politics in some towns, like Southport, down to 1914.[52]

However, while the standard of working-class housing generally continued to rise in the second half of the nineteenth century, increasing criticism was voiced by the end of the century about the persistence of slum areas and the poor quality of most working-class houses, especially the high density of houses per acre. Solutions to these problems were suggested by a number of individuals and groups who gradually coalesced into what became the movement for town planning.[53] The best known was undoubtedly Ebenezer Howard and the 'Garden City' he inspired at Letchworth, but this was only one example of a much broader movement. The key idea behind town planning was to argue that when new suburban areas were developed, the estates should be laid out in accordance with an overall plan, which would provide for a lower density of houses per acre and suitable amenities and break away from the traditional grid-like pattern for working-class houses. Land would be cheaper in the suburbs than in inner-city developments and this would allow the new housing to be built at a cost that would make it affordable for working people to rent. But if land values rose as an area was developed, this would push the new housing out of reach of working-class families. The solution the town planners developed was to suggest that local authorities should be able to buy up land and offer it for development, so ensuring it was provided at a reasonable price.[54]

This idea connected the town planning movement firmly to the urban land issue, because it made the success of its ideas dependent on the ability of local authorities to acquire huge swathes of land on the outskirts of towns at relatively low cost. This would involve giving local councils new powers of compulsory purchase and reforming the methods of calculating the price paid and would scarcely be welcome to landowners. But without these powers, it was landowners who stood in the way of the town planners' ideas, either because they could refuse to sell land, or else charge prices that made low cost housing development impossible. This link between town planning and land reform was evident from the very start of the movement. Some of the key personnel in the early days of town planning, for instance, were also prominent in the Land Nationalisation Society (LNS). Indeed, F. W. Steere, the first secretary of the Garden City Association was the also the secretary of the LNS.[55] In turn, all these projects were closely associated with Liberal reformers. Some of the earliest examples of how the new planned developments might look were provided by Liberal industrialists: W. H. Lever, George Cadbury and Joseph Rowntree all built new estates on these lines, in part to house workers at new factory sites.[56] The New Liberal thinkers, like C. F. G. Masterman, who were grouped around *The Speaker* (soon to become the *Nation*) enthusiastically promoted town planning as an agenda for the next Liberal government, and Campbell-Bannerman gave the idea a very generalised endorsement in his pre-election oration at the Albert Hall on 21 December 1905.[57]

This help was crucial because town planning enthusiasts needed new national legislation to allow local authorities to operate their schemes. They lobbied the Liberal government persistently through the National Housing Reform Council, a body set up in 1900 by William Thompson, a Liberal alderman on Richmond Council in Surrey and Henry Aldridge, from the LNS.[58] Their first success was when Burns finally agreed to a town planning section to his 1909 Housing Act. Burns was sceptical about the town planners, describing the inhabitants of Letchworth as 'A picturesque array of cranks', but he needed to provide some more substance to his otherwise exiguous bill and including some town planning provisions was one way to do this.[59] The 1909 Act was still very limited, though. It allowed councils to plan new estates, rather than whole areas, and only after a very cumbersome process. Most importantly, it did not give councils effective powers to purchase land before it was developed. By 1914, however, 74 local authorities had drawn up 105 schemes (though only two had actually been approved by the LGB), so town planning had at last entered the realms of practical politics.

After the 1909 Act, the next great opportunity for the town planning movement arrived in 1912 with Lloyd George's land enquiry. The enquiry's urban half needed to develop a programme that would provide the kind of popular electoral appeal the chancellor was seeking. It clearly regarded land taxation as unable to fulfil this role again, despite its success in 1909. The alternative the enquiry turned to was the unfinished programme of the town planning movement. The core of the enquiry's urban report, published in April 1914, was a proposal to give all local authorities a duty to ensure there was adequate housing within their area.[60] They would be required to draw up plans for suburban development and empowered to compulsorily purchase land for new building, which would then be leased to private developers or public utility societies (an early form of housing association). They would also be given powers to develop transport links. Ultimately, local authorities would benefit from rising land values, but in the short term, the LGB would be able to compel them to act. The result would be a flood of affordable but high quality housing for working-class occupiers. The influence of the town planning movement was obvious in these proposals. The staff of the urban enquiry had interviewed various luminaries of the movement and the urban report quoted from their publications freely.[61] But the crucial conduit for the town planners' views was undoubtedly Seebohm Rowntree, the most influential figure on the enquiry and the author of the chapter on housing. He was already familiar with town planning from his involvement in his father's planned estate at New Earswick, outside York, and was scarcely likely to be hostile to these views.

The urban report proposed that housing should, in effect, become the cornerstone of the Liberals' appeal at the next election. But it still insisted that this huge programme of social reform was actually part of the urban land issue. The connection was the necessity to acquire land for development cheaply – a subject upon which the urban report dwelt at length. The enquiry could still argue that it was the landlord who stood in the way of progress and it was essential to tackle the role of landowners in the economy in order to achieve social reform. This huge programme took some time for the urban enquiry to put together, though, and it was not ready when Lloyd George launched his Land Campaign in October 1913. The campaign, therefore, focused largely on rural issues.[62] But the Liberal leadership had begun to approve the main elements in the urban campaign in the spring and summer of 1914.[63] Only the outbreak of World War One prevented the Liberal government from presenting the urban enquiry's proposals to the country at the next election. By 1914, it had clearly taken the place of land taxation at the centre of the urban land issue.

The First World War was not just a hiatus in this aspect of urban land reform. Effectively, it killed it stone dead. There was very little house building between 1914 and 1918, resulting in drastic housing shortages when the war ended.[64] Faced with the prospect of no homes for the heroes returning from the trenches, the Coalition government embarked on a huge (if much criticised and only partially successful) programme of state-subsidised council housing. Political controversy about housing for the rest of the inter-war period focused on how many council houses should be built and how they should be subsidised. The role of landowners was irrelevant to this controversy, if only because so many landowners took advantage of rising land prices after the First World War to sell up, as the contributions in this volume from F. M. L. Thompson and John Beckett and Michael Turner discuss. Landowners could no longer plausibly be presented as the great obstacle to cheap housing.[65] Moreover, the pre-war ideas of the town planners had relied on private builders and public utility societies continuing to build most of the new houses that working people could afford to rent. But after 1918, this was unrealistic as there was little scope for an economic return on this housing. The retention of wartime rent controls, stricter housing regulations, spiralling costs and the attractiveness of other investments combined to convince builders and potential investors that there was little point in building for the working-class market. There was no possibility of reviving the combination of anti-landlordism and housing reform that had seemed so attractive to Liberals in 1914.

Conclusion

The urban land issue may have attracted less attention than its rural counterpart, but in the Edwardian era, it briefly flared into prominence. Undoubtedly, this was partly because hostility to landowners was such an important feature of Liberalism in this period. But it also represented an attempt to use land reform in ways that were directly relevant to what was, by the late nineteenth century, an overwhelmingly urban society and to knit 'the land' together with social reform. In the early 1900s, plans to employ the land issue to tackle problems connected to unemployment, local taxation and housing were all pushing their way up from local government and into national politics. Some of these ideas were deeply rooted in radical politics, while others represented new approaches. But all saw land reform and hostility to great landowners as central to the achievement of important programmes of social reform, rather than irrelevant survivals from nineteenth-century radicalism. All looked to the Edwardian Liberal governments to translate these ideas into legislation. But the fates of these movements were very different. By 1914, land colonies for the unemployed had been marginalised and land taxation, while still an important subject of controversy, was in retreat from the central role it had played in the 1909 Budget. Housing reform, though, seemed on the verge of becoming a crucial item in the Liberal government's programme, only to be halted by the outbreak of war. After 1914, the political landscape was very different and there was to be no way back for the urban land issue. But that does not mean that its post-war irrelevance should be read back into the prewar period. In 1914, the urban land issue was still an important part of British politics.

Notes

1. For the 1880s as the 'Troubled Decade' for landowners, see D. Cannadine, *The Decline and Fall of the British Aristocracy* (New Haven, 1990), esp. pp. 25–31.
2. I. Packer, *Lloyd George, Liberalism and the Land: The Land Issue and Party Politics in England, 1906–14* (Woodbridge, 2001), pp. 21–6, 38–48.
3. There are a number of examples of conflicts between the owners of great estates in towns and local councils (though these tended to die down after the 1880s): see D. Cannadine, *Lords and Landlords: The Aristocracy and the Towns, 1774–1967* (Leicester, 1980), pp. 49–59 on, for instance, the Duke of Norfolk in Sheffield and Lord Derby in Bury.
4. M. Chase, *The People's Farm: English Radical Agrarianism, 1775–1840* (Oxford, 1988); A. Hadfield, *The Chartist Land Company* (Newton Abbot, 1970).
5. E. Biagini, *Liberty, Retrenchment and Reform: Popular Liberalism in the Age of Gladstone, 1860–1880* (Cambridge, 1992), pp. 50–60, 84–93, 184–91.
6. See, for instance, D. Campbell, *The Unemployed Problem – the Socialist Solution* (London, 1892).
7. *Hansard*, 4th ser., 8 (7 February 1893), col. 730.
8. J. Harris, *Unemployment and Politics: A Study in English Social Policy, 1886–1914* (Oxford, 1972), pp. 135–44; J. Shepherd, *George Lansbury: At the Heart of Old Labour* (Oxford, 2002), pp. 60–4.
9. M. Fels, *Joseph Fels: His Life Work* (New York, 1916), pp. 41, 50–4.

10. A. Marshall, 'The Housing of the London Poor', *Contemporary Review*, 45 (1884), 224–31; C. Booth, *Life and Labour of the People of London* (London, 1889), i, pp. 165–8.
11. Harris, *Unemployment*, pp. 124–35, 141–2.
12. *Departmental Committee on Vagrancy* (1906), Cd. 2852; R. Johnston, ' "Charity that Heals": The Scottish Labour Colony Association and Attitudes to the Able-bodied Unemployed in Glasgow, 1890–1914', *Scottish Historical Review*, 77 (1998), 77–95.
13. Harris, *Unemployment*, pp. 191–9.
14. G. Lansbury, *My Life* (London, 1928), pp. 145–9.
15. British Library, Add MS 46324, Burns diary, 18 Apr. and 5 June 1906.
16. British Library, Add MS 46325, Burns diary, 4 April 1907.
17. *Report to the President of the Local Government Board on the Poplar Union* (1906), Cd. 3240.
18. British Library, Add MS 46299, fos 128–32, R. Wakefield to Burns, 11 November 1906.
19. Harris, *Unemployment*, pp. 132–4, 194–5.
20. See for instance Beveridge's article in the *Morning Post*, 31 May 1906, quoted in J. Harris, *William Beveridge: A Biography* (Oxford, 1977), p. 124.
21. E. P. Hennock, *British Social Reform and German Precedents: The Case of Social Insurance, 1880–1914* (Oxford, 1987), pp. 152–67.
22. N. Blewett, *The Peers, the Parties and the People: The British General Elections of 1910* (London, 1972), pp. 50–1 for the crisis facing the government over unemployment policy in 1908.
23. Some land colonies continued to exist into the inter-war period: see Johnston, ' "Charity that Heals" '. But even the Labour party were very cautious about land reform as a solution to unemployment after 1918: Bodleian Lib., MS dep. c. 164, Addison papers, 'Office conference on agricultural policy', 5 June 1930.
24. Packer, *Lloyd George, Liberalism and the Land*, pp. 28–9; A. Windscheffel, *Popular Conservatism in Imperial London, 1868–1906* (Woodbridge, 2007), pp. 143–5.
25. H. George, *Progress and Poverty* (London, 1908 edn), pp. 286–90.
26. A. Taylor, *Lords of Misrule: Hostility to Aristocracy in Late Nineteenth- and Early Twentieth-Century Britain* (Basingstoke, 2004), pp. 45–72.
27. C. A. Barker, *Henry George* (New York, 1955), pp. 378–416; J. Wedgwood, *Memoirs of a Fighting Life* (London, 1940), p. 67.
28. A. Offer, *Property and Politics, 1870–1914* (Cambridge, 1981), pp. 229–31; J. Smyth, *Labour in Glasgow, 1896–1936: Socialism, Suffrage, Sectarianism* (East Linton, 2000), pp. 42–5.
29. See, for instance, C. P. Trevelyan: *Hansard*, 4th ser., 103 (19 February 1902), col. 480.
30. National Archives, Inland Revenue MS 73/2, J. Wedgwood, 'Memorandum on the Taxation of Land Values' [1909].
31. *Hansard*, 4th ser., 131 (11 March 1904), cols 911–16 and 145 (14 April 1905), cols 263–8.
32. A. K. Russell, *Liberal Landslide: The General Election of 1906* (Newton Abbot, 1973), p. 65; *Times*, 29 November, 1905, p. 6.
33. *Liberal Magazine*, 11 (1903), 114.

34. Robinson Library, University of Newcastle, C. P. Trevelyan papers, MS Ex. 21, Trevelyan to M. K. Trevelyan, 18 December 1906; British Library, Add MS 46282, Asquith to Burns, 16 April 1908.
35. Bodleian Library, Harcourt papers 576, W. Robson, 'Valuation Bill', September 1908.
36. National Archives, Cabinet papers, 37/95/122, J. Burns, 'Valuation Bill', 10 October 1908.
37. B. Murray, *The People's Budget 1909/10* (Oxford, 1980), pp. 117–47.
38. H. V. Emy, *Liberals, Radicals and Social Politics, 1892–1914* (Cambridge, 1973), pp. 191–3 on Sir William Harcourt's 1894 Budget.
39. Blewett, *Peers*, pp. 46–51.
40. I. Packer, 'Economic Strategies and the New Liberalism', *Journal of Liberal History*, 54 (2007), 14–21; G. C. Peden, *The Treasury and British Public Policy 1906–1959* (Oxford, 2000), pp. 30–72.
41. Murray, *People's Budget*, pp. 209–35.
42. Blewett, *Peers*, p. 73; British Library, Add MS 49736, fos 63–5, Balfour papers, A. Chamberlain to Balfour, 29 January 1910.
43. Blewett, *Peers*, pp. 315–29.
44. Offer, *Property and Politics*, pp. 363–9; B. Short, *Land and Society in Edwardian Britain* (Cambridge, 1997), pp. 38–89.
45. *The Land: The Report of the Land Enquiry Committee* (London, 1914), ii, pp. 82–3.
46. House of Lords Record Office, Lloyd George papers, C/6/6/3, Sir M. Nathan to Lloyd George, 22 November 1913.
47. *The Land*, ii, pp. 634–6.
48. Ibid., pp. 591–609, 628.
49. I. Packer, 'The Liberal Cave and the 1914 Budget', *English Historical Review*, 111 (1996), 620–35.
50. Lloyd George at Ipswich, *Times*, 23 May 1914, p. 9.
51. *The Land*, ii, pp. 348–52.
52. D. Reeder, 'The Politics of Urban Leaseholds in Late Victorian England', *International Review of Social History*, 6 (1961), 413–30; J. Liddle, 'Estate Management and Land Reform Politics: The Hesketh and Scarisbrick families and the Making of Southport, 1842 to 1914' in D. Cannadine (ed.), *Patricians, Power and Politics in Nineteenth-century Towns* (Leicester, 1982), pp. 133–74.
53. A. Sutcliffe, *Towards the Planned City: Germany, Britain, the United States and France, 1780–1914* (Oxford, 1981); D. Hardy, *From Garden Cities to New Towns: Campaigning for Town and Country Planning, 1899–1946* (London, 1991).
54. L. Chiozza Money, *Riches and Poverty*, 6th ed. (London, 1908), pp. 203–4.
55. Hardy, *Garden Cities to New Towns*, p. 19.
56. W. Creese, *The Search for Environment: The Garden City* (New Haven, 1966), pp. 110–203.
57. *The Speaker*, 7 January 1905, pp. 349–50; *Times*, 22 December 1905, p 7.
58. Sutcliffe, *Towards the Planned City*, p. 61.
59. British Library, Add MS 46324, Burns diary, 11 October 1906; W. Ashworth, *The Genesis of Modern British Town Planning* (London, 1954), pp. 167–91.
60. *The Land*, ii, pp. 148–57, 289–94.

61. Lloyd George papers, C/2/1/29, R. Buxton to Lloyd George, 14 September 1912; *The Land*, ii, pp. 153–4; A. Briggs, *Social Thought and Social Action: A Study of the Work of Seebohm Rowntree* (London, 1961), pp. 95–9.
62. Lloyd George papers, C/2/4/6, R. Reiss to Lloyd George, 4 February 1914 for concern within the enquiry at the delay to the urban proposals.
63. Lloyd George papers, C/1/1/18, E. Montagu to Lloyd George, 12 June 1914.
64. S. Merrett, *State Housing in Britain* (London, 1979), pp. 33–60.
65. Cannadine, *Lords and Landlords*, pp. 420–1 on the urban situation in particular.

12
Land Reform and the English Land Market, 1880–1925

John Beckett and Michael Turner

Introduction

On 31 December 1921, the *Estates Gazette* reflected on 4 years of hectic trading in the land market since the end of the Great War. It noted that one (unnamed) London firm of agents had sold 1,776,727 acres across the United Kingdom over that time. The *Gazette* speculated that if this was representative of trading in more general terms 'one quarter of England must have changed hands in four years'.[1] If so, it was nothing short of revolutionary. This was turnover on a scale unknown since the sixteenth century Dissolution of the Monasteries or even the Norman Conquest. But was this really the case? Was the country close to a revolution in landownership in the years immediately after 1918 and, if not, why should a sober journal such as the *Estates Gazette* be indulging in such flights of fancy? Historians have generally accepted the conclusions drawn by the *Estates Gazette*, if only because they chimed with similar claims, many of which appeared in such reputable places as the editorial columns of *The Times*.[2]

Testing these claims against the available evidence for movement in the market is far from straightforward. In an earlier contribution to this debate, we suggested that the scale of land sales in 1919 and 1920 represented a blip in longer term trends, largely resulting from the absence of activity during the war years.[3] Our data were derived from material generated in the Estate Exchange and published by the Royal Institute of Chartered Surveyors, but this is not necessarily conclusive.[4] This chapter suggests that whatever the reality of the sales of land in the 4 years after the First World War was, the claims made by the *Estates Gazette* at the end of 1921 were indicative of a more deep-seated and ongoing discussion about the land market with which it is hard for us to empathise today. As far as the *Estates Gazette* could see, the simple fact was that the much-discussed and long-heralded need for land reform was seemingly being achieved without the state intervention that had hitherto seemed necessary. By placing the claims and counter claims of these years into the longer term context of the land market and the debate about ownership, what follows demonstrates that the movement in the market in 1918–21 was interpreted by contemporaries in a way which suited the protagonists in the debate but exaggerated its importance.

The impact of agricultural depression and land reform, *c.* 1880–1914

The land question had been on the political agenda since the mid-nineteenth century, and it is not our intention to reiterate the various strands of debate.[5] Rather, this chapter seeks to disentangle the debate about land from the realities of the land market, and in particular to ask why the *Estates Gazette* should have been so concerned in 1921 about the potential revolution in landownership and what this implied for social, economic, and political leadership within the state. It is known that landowners had been pessimistic about the land market from about 1880, and that their pessimism was based on a perception of the impact of the long-run agricultural depression on the market. This perception coincided with broader, politically motivated discussions about the iniquities of a land market in which a privileged few owned most of the land, and the great majority had no permanent stake whatsoever. The findings of the *Return of Owners of Land 1872–73* published in 1876 were reinforced by the reworking of the key figures undertaken by John Bateman, and published in 1881 and 1883.[6] Although originally designed to provide evidence of the *spread* of ownership, the findings of the *Return* were made to demonstrate that this was a myth and that property ownership was in fact heavily concentrated. The *Return* provided further fuel to the simmering fire of the land reform movement.[7]

Unfortunately for landowners, Bateman's figures appeared in print just at the point where they really were struggling with the cold winds of agricultural depression. They perceived, rightly as it transpired, that agriculture, having been made to survive by its own devices after the Repeal of the Corn Laws, was being neglected by a government interested only in the profits of industrialisation and invisible earnings, and that as owners and farmers they were left to face the realities of the Great Agricultural Depression during the 1880s and 1890s alone. The knock-on effects reverberated through landed society in terms of falling rent-rolls and declining land values, and were highlighted by the 1890s *Royal Commission on the Agricultural Depression*.[8] Add into this mixture the encumbered estates legislation and the introduction of death duties, not to mention renewed attention to both the concentration of land ownership and its absentee nature during the land wars in Ireland and to a lesser extent in Wales, and the political significance of property in these years is apparent. In 1897, the 11th Duke of Bedford published his book *A Great Agricultural Estate*, which included dire warnings about 'the broken, bankrupt condition of landlords'.[9] It began to look as if the agricultural depression would precipitate the dismantling of the great estate system lock, stock and barrel. Rowland Prothero (later Lord Ernle), wrote that between 1883 and 1890 'landlords and tenants ... stood on the verge of ruin'.[10]

Inevitably, many landowners were forced to bring land to the market, as Table 12.1 shows. While a market in agricultural land always exists, the table suggests some abnormality in the late 1890s, explicable in terms of the effects of 20 years of more or less unremitting depression, which were compounded by the introduction of death duties. By 1891, the Liberals were committed to levies on mining royalties, to death duties, and to taxation of land values and ground rents. Only death duties made it onto the statute book, in 1894. Even at the moderate level of 8 per cent they raised numerous hackles among the landowning community and were frequently cited as the cause of landlord poverty.[11]

Plenty of individual examples can be found of landowners responding to the combination of depression and death duties. In the late 1880s and early 1890s, the Duke of Newcastle and Lords Carlisle, Hardwicke, Ripon, Southampton, and Tollemache all disposed of property. Between 1868 and 1895, Lord Carrington sold land for a total of £238,669; in 1895, the break-up began of Lord Hill's 16,554-acre Hawkestone estate in Shropshire, and in the same county, the 4,000-acre Condover estate was auctioned the following year. Between 1898 and 1901, the Duke of Beaufort sold his 26,000 Monmouthshire acres, which included eight castles and Tintern Abbey. Also during the 1890s, major owners in Cardiganshire parted with 50,000 acres, and between 1894 and 1897 Lord Ancaster sold the Gwydir estate in north Wales. Others tried to sell but failed to find a purchaser, among them the Duke of Leeds, and Lords Rodney, Wilton, Cholmondeley, Westmorland, and Saye and Sele.[12] Some, unable or unwilling to sell, went bankrupt. Most of the 6,000 acres belonging to Lord Beaumont in the West Riding were sold in 1888–89, and the 3,600 acres owned by the Buckworths of Cockley Cley

Table 12.1 Land sales in England, 1896–1922 (in £s)

Year	London Mart And Winchester House (£)	Country (£)	Private treaty Sales (£)	Grand total (£)
1896	4,476,801	3,972,190	2,105,272	10,554,263
1897	5,257,723	5,598,238	1,349,863	12,205,824
1898	6,674,428	5,372,429	1,316,013	13,362,870
1899	6,290,314	4,385,576	1,677,980	12,353,870
1900	4,934,769	2,757,101	1,310,655	9,002,525
1901	5,553,098	3,109,581	1,408,542	10,071,221
1902	5,748,221	2,705,403	1,561,896	10,015,520
1903	5,767,007	2,654,751	1,676,061	10,097,819
1904	4,896,879	1,990,212	650,316	7,537,407
1905	4,781,674	2,271,806	1,365,139	8,418,619
1906	4,335,294	2,100,690	1,552,372	7,988,356
1907	3,343,592	1,708,705	512,365	5,564,662
1908	2,733,491	1,829,562	1,056,965	5,620,018
1909	2,782,192	2,230,583	1,331,450	6,344,225
1910	2,279,727	2,547,317	867,084	5,694,128
1911	2,623,646	4,508,730	1,265,418	8,397,794
1912	2,554,302	4,698,263	1,836,978	9,089,543
1913	2,345,937	4,039,511	2,188,663	8,574,111
1914	1,866,631	3,462,110	1,357,020	6,685,761
1915	803,670	1,824,343	942,711	3,570,724
1916	928,859	2,946,455	1,232,203	5,107,517
1917	1,546,005	5,546,125	1,435,296	8,527,426
1918	2,299,376	7,148,014	1,935,208	11,382,598
1919	6,250,837	9,233,867	6,057,430	21,542,134
1920	5,655,062	7,580,898	5,039,879	18,275,839
1921	3,029,800	3,378,314	4,450,832	10,858,946
1922	3,041,772	3,322,396	4,072,535	10,436,703

Source: *Year Books* of auction sales (London, Estate Exchange, 1914–22).

in Norfolk went on the market in 1900 – in both cases, in connection with bankruptcy.[13]

Many more examples could be quoted, hardly surprisingly in the light of the figures in Table 12.1, but for contemporaries the issue was less about individual examples of hardship and rather more about the significance of these sales for the redistribution of land. The potential Liberal reforms, of which only death duties were introduced, were on hold while the Conservatives were in power from 1895, but the Liberal landslide in the 1906 general election bought land reform firmly back onto the political agenda. Lloyd George had been actively involved in the Welsh Land Movement of the late 1880s, and few landowners could have been surprised when, as Chancellor of the Exchequer, he turned towards the land as a potential source for funding the new Liberal government's expensive legislative programme. What he proposed in 1909, in what came to be called the 'People's Budget', was relatively modest – a tax on vacant land, ground rents and mining royalties, a Reversion Duty on the termination of a lease, a tax on capital gains, and an increase in estate duties. Coming as they did on top of the years of agricultural difficulty and the growing impact of death duties – as more and more families experienced them at first hand – these proposals appeared to the landed classes in a rather different light and helped to provoke the constitutional crisis of 1909–11, which magnified their real significance.[14] Lloyd George used his unique rhetorical style to confront the seemingly reactionary activities of a House of Lords dominated by the landed interest.[15] His Liberal Land Campaign was both an attempt to build on the 'People's Budget' and to steal some ground from Labour. His strategy was widely believed to have helped to revive the government's fortunes in these years. For historians, it led through the Finance Act of 1910 to the associated and voluminous land valuation enterprise which still awaits a project to unlock its secrets on a national land ownership canvas.[16]

In the wake of the constitutional crisis, the Liberal government set up a Land Inquiry in 1912 to consider the whole land question. This led to a report on rural issues in 1913 and another on urban issues in 1914. The cabinet accepted the findings of the rural inquiry in October 1913 and the party subsequently mounted a Land Campaign which was still in progress when the First World War broke out. The major policy plank was not specifically about the land market; indeed, its main proposal was that a Ministry of Land should be established, along with a judicial commission empowered to secure the development of rural England. This development project was to include the building of cottages, improvement of agriculture, development of smallholdings, granting of greater security of tenure and fair rents to farmers, and the setting up of wages boards to secure a living wage for the labourer.[17] These were policies the landowners were always likely to resist, but their party of choice, the Conservatives, found the proposals hard to combat. The party set up no fewer than three committees to examine land policy over the period 1912–14.[18]

For its part, the Labour party also set up a policy-making committee on the land question in 1912, specifically to meet the Liberal threat in those areas and constituencies in which Labour expected to grow.

Indeed several by-elections were fought that year during which an existing Lib–Lab electoral pact collapsed precisely over the issue of land reform.[19] The rise of the Labour party had, as one of its banner headlines, the question of land and public ownership, and while land nationalisation was not a uniting feature of Labour party politics, both the Labour and Liberal parties saw the land question as an important political ground on which to do battle with the Conservatives. This added more weight to Liberal land politics.

The Liberal Land Campaign was so successful that Lloyd George was expecting the party to fight the election due in 1915 on the land question.[20] For him, it was a relatively easy way to attract the industrial classes to Liberalism on a popular, anti-aristocratic ticket. In the event, Lloyd George's plans for a radical attack on the landlords, as well as the anticipated election, came to nothing because of the war.[21] Instead, the deepening crisis of food supply encouraged Lloyd George to appoint Rowland Prothero (Lord Ernle) as President of the Board of Agriculture to initiate interventionist policies, leading to the famous plough up campaign.[22]

In the years before the First World War, the worries about Lloyd George's intentions were widespread. *The Times* carried several editorials in 1912 on the land question, partly reflecting a fear that the volume of sales was on the increase.[23] But it was also a fear that land was being lost to the social group with which it had so long been connected. The *Estates Gazette* carried an editorial on 24 February 1912 entitled 'The Breaking-up of Estates', in which it discussed the need for state aid to help tenants purchase their farms since many were being offered this opportunity.[24] A government committee of 1912–13 took note of cases where owners were selling their land without much reference to the wishes of their tenants, simply citing the burdens of ownership and the complications of death duties.[25]

Contemporary opinion held that the effect of the agricultural depression on ownership was felt most strongly just prior to the First World War. During one week in June 1910, 72,622 acres were offered from 36 separate English counties, and in the same week a year later, the figure was 98,300 acres. In 1912, one firm claimed that during a 4-month period it had 'put through the market land to the value of no less than 1¼ millions Sterling'.[26] Well over 100,000 acres changed hands in both 1910 and 1911, and even more during the two following years. In 1912, 19 aristocrats were seeking purchasers for substantial tracts of territory, among them the heavily indebted Lords Londesborough and Winchilsea. By the time the First World War broke out, something in the region of 800,000 acres of English land had changed hands for £20 million.[27] Almost every major landowner in Wales sold some land between 1910 and 1914.[28]

Despite land being brought to the market, a great deal remained in the hands of its original owners, partly because few estates disappeared altogether. No one could be quite sure whether the landlords were going under, or simply complaining because after centuries of protection they were finally being exposed to the realities of market forces. The 1881 Settled Land Act had made it easier to break entails, and in so doing had reduced their capacity to keep land out of the market. George Lambert and Francis Channing, in dissenting from the final report of the *Royal Commission* on the agricultural depression claimed that the landowners' losses had been greatly exaggerated.[29] In these circumstances, we have to pick our way between the landlord-inspired propaganda, the reality of changes in the pattern of ownership between the 1870s and 1914, and the extent to which these coloured the debate about land reform.

The post-war land market

The preoccupations of the Great War diverted attention away from the Liberal attack on land and the land question, but in the last year of the war, and certainly after the Armistice, the question came back into play. Many families simply picked up in 1918 where they had left off in 1914. Lord Londesborough returned to the market in 1918 to sell parts of his Willerby estate which had not attracted a buyer in 1912.[30] When the third Baron Wenlock of Escrick Park near York died in 1912, his daughter moved into one of the family's other houses at Skipwith and started to sell off farms to tenants. The shrinkage of the Escrick estate continued after the war. Eventually the original house was converted into flats in 1935 and then in 1948 it was let to Queen Margaret's School, which still holds it.[31]

Also, as before the war, landowners often sold outliers rather than the main estate. During 1917, Lord Pembroke sold his detached estate in North Wiltshire and Sir Francis Astley-Corbett, whose seat and main estate was in Lincolnshire, sold his Everleigh property in Wiltshire of 4,500 acres. The purchaser immediately sold all the outlying farms, totalling 3,000 acres.[32] There were plenty of other examples. Stowe, in Buckinghamshire, was sold in 1921 by Lady Kinloss after her son and heir, Richard Morgan-Grenville, fell in the war. As *The Times* commented gloomily, 'the trustees simply yield to the economic conditions . . . the fate of Stowe is the fate of half the great places'.[33] The introduction of super tax in Austen Chamberlain's 1919 Budget, combined with a rise in death duties, seemed like a further assault on the group. The 1919 Finance Act, which applied to deaths after 31 July 1919, replaced an estate duty of 12 per cent with one of 20 per cent. This was a spectacular increase over the quarter of a century since death duties were introduced, and the raised levels of duty were held by landowners to have forced them into the market. The Willoughbys, Lords Middleton, faced two sets of death duties in 1922 and 1924. They brought most of their Nottinghamshire estates to the market in 1925, including the Elizabethan prodigy house Wollaton Hall in which they no longer lived. They might blame death duties, but they also had mortgage debts to repay, and these sales enabled them to consolidate their property in Warwickshire. They remain significant landowners today.[34]

When estates such as Stowe, Stoke Rochford, and Wollaton came into the market, there were grounds for wondering whether traditional landed society was being fatally undermined – for arguing, in other words, that the land question posed for so many years prior to 1914 was now being answered simply by market forces.[35] The first suggestion that the land market might have assumed revolutionary proportions after the war came in 1919. In March of that year, the *Estates Gazette* told its readers that a 'revolution in landowning' was taking place as more and more estates came on to the market. Two months later an advertisement announced 'England changing hands', and by the end of 1919, the market reports were full of the phrase 'England is changing hands'.[36] This was the *annus mirabilis* of the property market. One firm had announced three quarters of a million acres for sale during the year, and within a few weeks in the summer more than two million acres were advertised for sale in *The Times*, and probably well over one million had actually been sold during the year.[37] Such was the frenzy that on 30 and 31 December 1919 *The Times* devoted two major articles to what it saw as the extraordinary activity in the land market.[38]

The temptation to emphasise the significance of what was happening, to interpret the figures in the worst possible light, and to suggest that doom and gloom was everywhere, was hardly one the press could overlook, as in the following extract from *The Times* in 1920. Beneath the headline 'Changing Hands. A Note of Resignation', the newspaper claimed:

> We all know it now... 'England is changing hands'.... Will a profiteer buy it? Will it be turned into a school or institution? Has the mansion house electric light and modern drainage? For the most part

> the sacrifices are made in silence. 'The privileged classes', to use the old name, take it all for granted.... The sons perhaps are lying in far-away graves; the daughters, secretly mourning some one dearer than a brother, have taken up some definite work away from home, seeking thus to still their aching hearts, and the old people, knowing there is no son or near relative left to keep up the old traditions, or so crippled by necessary taxation, that they know 'the boy' will never be able to carry on when they are gone, take the irrevocable step; the obliging agent appears, deferential, sympathetic, yet businesslike.[39]

We have given examples which have demonstrated one of the truisms of the post-war land market: much of the land put up for sale was coming from long-established aristocratic owners. Of the 902 separate sales entries in the *Estates Gazette*'s Annual Reviews for 1918–21, 211 give details of the sellers. The *Estates Gazette* betrayed its concern over the 'End of the Old Order' by giving much prominence to the landed members of that selling market. The most frequent seller was the Duke of Rutland, named in five separate transactions, one in 1918 and the others in 1920. Where the acreage he sold was listed it amounted to three sales at 28,500 acres, which yielded over £878,000, and a further two sales which raised £607,000 of which over £100,000 included town properties as well as land, though our capacity for separating the bricks and buildings from the land is compromised by the absence of detail. The Duke of Leeds, the Duke of Sutherland, and the Countess of Warwick sold three properties apiece, the Dukes of Bedford, Marlborough, and Northumberland two apiece, the Earl of Pembroke three, and the Marquesses of Abergavenny, Anglesey, and Northampton, and the Earls of Dysart and Yarborough two each. Lord Gerard disposed of large parts of his Eastwell Park Estate in Kent in three separate sales. Table 12.2 gives the list in the form of a hierarchy to demonstrate that there was little doubt that a significant number of large and influential members of the traditional landed aristocracy were disposing of significant acreages. The prominence of aristocrats points to the headline value they offered to the press.

What this kind of language did not pick up was perhaps the most significant change in the post-war market: the purchase of estates not by other landowners but by tenants. Owner occupation increased from about 11 per cent of the cultivated acreage of England and Wales in 1914 (including home farms occupied by larger landowners) to 36 per cent by 1927, an increase from 2.9 million to 9.2 million acres, with roughly one quarter of the cultivated area changing from being tenant land to being owned by farmers.[40]

Table 12.2 Hierarchy of buyers and sellers of land in England, 1918–21

	Numbers	Numbers less double counting	Acres	Selling price £
a. The sellers				
Crown	1	1	3,250	65,675
Duchy of Cornwall	1	1	5	?
Dukes & Duchesses	27	16	77,953	2,789,164
Marquesses	12	10	18,182	757,271
Earls & Countesses	28	23	54,747	1,362,276
Viscounts	6	5	3,103	118,198
Lords & Ladies	73	65	148,248	3,754,101
Knights	26	21	33,399	1,012,231
Family estates	16	12	26,508	1,734,609
Institutional estates	7	6	9,591	336,102
Armed services	14	14	29,888	762,780
Total	211	174	404,872	12,692,506
Total (where both acres & sale price are known)	117	103	302,145	9,030,386
b. The buyers				
Foreign crown	1	1	150	30,000
Earls & countesses	1	1	?	40,000
Lords & Ladies	5	5	4,685	17,215
Knights	7	7	12,206	195,000
Family estates	2	2	1,290	80,000
Institutional estates	7	7	15,761	150,000
Armed services	1	1	2,270	100,000
Total	24	24	36,362	612,215
Total (where both acres & sale price are known)	7	7	20,204	542,215

Source: Estates Gazette, 1918–21.

This broad scenario was first established by the compilers of the *Agricultural Output of England and Wales* in 1927. This was more or less a census of production, which took as its base the year 1925. It estimated that 'over 25 per cent of holdings in the country, comprising a fairly similar percentage of the total acreage of crops and grass' was 'owned by their occupiers'. This state of affairs was significantly different from the position before the war, and 'very largely due to the purchase of holdings by their occupiers at a time when many large estates were changing hands and had been broken up'.[41]

While the *Estates Gazette* and the 1925 report focussed tightly on the post-war years, S.G. Sturmey's research suggested that governments were concerned the land market was already too volatile before 1914. In particular, there was some concern that tenant farmers might somehow lose their entitlement to their farms if landowners were forced by whatever circumstances to sell up.[42] The necessary, if unwanted, remedy was for tenants to borrow on mortgages, and buy their 'own' farms 'in order to protect themselves from unknown owners who might not be as easy-going as long-established county families'.[43] Admittedly, tenants were often given little real choice if they were offered first refusal by a landowner about to put the property on the market, although their enthusiasm for such a change in status was doubtless tempered by the removal in 1921 of corn bounties. In the 1920s and 1930s, this change in government policy was to bring significant financial pressure to bear on many owner occupiers, and it also filtered down the agricultural ladder to impact on the wages of agricultural labourers.[44] In the meantime, the sale of small properties to individual farmers was not the kind of headline news likely to stir editorial writers on the *Estates Gazette*.[45]

Assessment

What we have proposed so far is that from around 1880 the gathering debate about land reform coincided with economic trends which forced landowners to part with estates, but that the trend in the land market (Table 12.1) does not support the idea of a particular crisis in 1918. In turn, that leads us to ask whether the fears expressed by landowners before 1914, and by commentators after 1918, were exaggerations which led to a misunderstanding of the reality of the land market in these years and, if so, what explains the misunderstanding? By setting this claim into the longer context of the land market between about 1880 and 1925, we show in what follows that the facts about the market, which were available to any reader of the *Year Book of Auction Sales*, were less crucial to contemporary debate than the wider context of land reform more generally. Because many of the sales were by great landowners normally renowned for their landed stability, the issue was political as much as it was economic. The sales took place against a background of debate about the land question, which raised contemporary perceptions of what was, or was thought to be happening. We turn now to examine how contemporary perceptions, fuelled by some aberrant statistics, created an atmosphere of crisis which only partially reflected the contemporary reality.

After 1918, the land question remained or, at least, the *Estates Gazette* assumed it remained, a political issue which came back on to the political agenda with the ending of the war. Not surprisingly, the volume of land sales slowed rapidly during the war, as the market largely disappeared. But with the Armistice, those who were interested in these matters clearly expected the debate to be taken up where it had left off in 1914. When a respectable journal such as the *Estates Gazette* could resort to counting land transactions and extrapolating from a single example into a major crisis in the market, it was clear that something was significantly amiss. It may have been that a renewed interest in the land market immediately after the war reflected a pre-war position in which editors still expected the land to be a political issue once the country had recovered from the horrors of war. To that extent they would have seen great significance in the quantity of land brought to the market immediately after the Armistice.

Nor could there be any doubt that something remarkable was happening. The number of acres put on the market between 1918 and 1921 clearly implied that many owners were selling. Table 12.1 demonstrates where the post-war trends sit within the wider land market, but what these figures also show is that these years were an aberration. This was partly because the market had been artificially constrained by wartime conditions, and partly because sales took place in these years for financial reasons, because of loss of heirs in the war, and also because there was a substantial increase in the taxation of current income in the Budgets of 1919 and 1920. Though the market did not come to a complete standstill after 1921, it is evident that this marked a post-war peak. Land continued to come onto the market up to 1925, but according to Sturmey, 'After 1925, land sales practically ceased'.[46]

Estates continued to come onto the market through the inter-war years, and for many years thereafter, but these sales did not raise the same hackles and in part this was because the politics of the land question had also faded away. Before the war, the land question was a real political issue, but it failed to reignite subsequently. In part, of course, this was because it was associated with the Liberals (in power 1905–14) who, despite continuing to lead the coalition until 1922, did not return to power in their own right.

The abolition of landlordism remained part of Liberal policy in 1922, 1924, and 1926 and they even conducted a survey in 1924–25 as part of a policy review. It became a land policy which was a 'last ditch for a Liberal Party whose best, perhaps even its only, hope lay in a deadlock between the two larger parties which would give the Liberals the balance of power'.[47] In their 1924–25 survey, they revisited the ideas of 1913, with the intention of having a new land inquiry to look again at the position of agriculture and to bring in ideas from abroad. As a result, the party came to favour Virtual Freehold, which was interpreted by some members as land nationalisation. But Lloyd George's voice and presence, which was largely responsible for the political power of the pre-war campaign, had been silenced by the 1920s.[48]

The political hegemony of the Conservatives after 1918 meant that the issue really did not resurface. In land reform questions, the mantle fell to the Labour party, which brought forward a number of ideas in the inter-war years.[49] In the longer run, these led to the development of policies based on control of land use rather than on nationalisation, and by 1943, the party had decided against adopting land nationalisation as a policy.[50] This was partly in response to a recognition that a silent revolution was taking place. Whatever the extent of sales, no one could ignore the all too obvious evidence of estate sales, country house demolitions, and the acquisition of farms by tenants with overtones of the re-creation of the idealised yeoman farmer. In turn, this also resulted in a long-term reduction of the power of the old aristocracy, undermined by declining rent and land values, and hastened by a rent freeze in wartime.

The old aristocracy often felt, rightly or wrongly, so pessimistic about the future that they could see little point in hanging on to their estates or, for that matter, the lifestyle that they had sustained. Pressures persuading landowners to sell included the cost of running estates (partly as a result of rising labour costs), and the anticipated prospects for non-landed investments (equities and bonds) at least until the 1929 Wall Street crash. The Royal Commission on Oxford and Cambridge universities in 1922 reflected on the relative merits of land and securities. It concluded that 'during the last two and a half years there has been an exceptional combination of unusually high prices for agricultural land with unusual facilities for the investment of money in sound and long-dated securities at remunerative rates of interest'.[51] All this pointed in the direction of the land reformers' programme being achieved by stealth during the inter-war years. Nor could the land reformers do anything other than approve of measures which hit the aristocracy in other directions, such as the increase in death duties and the abolition of primogeniture in 1925 through the Law of Property Act. Such reforms undermined the landowners and made landowning itself less attractive.[52] In the words of the Marquess of Northampton, 'landowning on a large scale is now generally felt to be a monopoly and is consequently felt to be unpopular'.[53] Of course, some landowners still thought it worthwhile extending their acres, and there were plenty of newcomers with wealth to invest who were looking for something rather more substantial than a tenant farm.[54]

The time-honoured traditions and positional advantages enjoyed by the landed interest were under pressure. Where the impact was on their financial position, land sales ensued, and also the closing and demolition of houses. By the time Evelyn Waugh wrote *Brideshead Revisited*, he believed the end of the old order was in sight, despite the best efforts of the National Trust from about 1933 to save some of the better examples of English country houses. Financial pressures were accompanied by cultural considerations, namely a loss of faith in landownership and the lifestyle that accompanied it, such that land sales were not the social disaster they might once have been. In this sense, the propaganda of the radicals stretching back to the decades before the war had created an atmosphere in which it was difficult to retain confidence in the old landed society.

The 'revolutionary' proportions of the land market in the immediate aftermath of the First World War were a myth. A great deal of land did change hands, but as we showed in Table 12.1, this was little more than a statistical aberration caused by the problems of selling land in wartime, and it was all part of a long-term trend. But to contemporary observers, the position certainly looked worse than it probably was. They remembered a pre-war situation in which landowners had been complaining of the need to part with land to make ends meet, and had at the same time been under what they considered to be the very real threat posed by Lloyd George and his land reform campaign. Although by 1918 the electoral map was quite different from 1914, with Lloyd George at the head of a coalition seeking to re-establish the peacetime role of the state, there was no immediate reason for the press to expect the issue of land reform to go away.

As it was, the issue itself seemed less relevant when the greater owners were being undone by market forces, but in any case it passed into insignificance when the Conservatives returned to power, the Liberals entered what turned out to be political oblivion, and the Labour party adopted land policies which did not lead to the nationalisation sought by some of their number. Placed in this context, the problems of landowners after the war seemed politically very significant. In the longer term, the land reform campaign faded away, and the changes to the pattern of ownership so feared before 1914 took place quietly. They witnessed a major transfer not within the landed community but from the landowning aristocracy to the tenant farmers. The revolution took place without anyone really noticing, and certainly not the press for whom tenant farmers made nothing like the headlines of a duke, an earl, a viscount, or even a maharajah.

Notes

1. *Estates Gazette*, 31 December 1921, p. 909.
2. F. M. L. Thompson, *English Landed Society in the Nineteenth Century* (London, 1963), p. 332; A. Howkins, *The Death of Rural England: A Social History of the Countryside since 1900* (London, 2003), p. 36; P. E. Dewey, *War and Progress: Britain 1914–1945* (London, 1997), p. 160.
3. J. Beckett and M. Turner, 'End of the Old Older? F. M. L. Thompson, the Land Question, and the Burden of Ownership in England, *c.* 1880–*c.* 1925', *Agricultural History Review*, 55 (2007), 265–84.
4. F. M. L. Thompson, 'The Land Market, 1880–1925: A Reappraisal Reappraised', *Agricultural History Review*, 55 (2007), 289–300.
5. R. Douglas, *Land, People and Politics: A History of the Land Question in the United Kingdom, 1878–1952* (London, 1976).
6. J. Bateman, *The Great Landowners of Great Britain and Ireland* (London, 1883).
7. J. V. Beckett, 'Agricultural Landownership and Estate Management', in E. J. T. Collins (ed.), *The Cambridge Agrarian History of England and Wales, vol. VII: 1850–1914* (Cambridge, 2000), pp. 701–6.
8. On falling rent rolls, see M. E. Turner, J. V. Beckett and B. Afton, *Agricultural Rent in England 1690–1914* (Cambridge, 1997), esp. pp. 245–52. On the Royal Commission, see Royal Commission on Agriculture, *First Report of Her Majesty's Commissioners Appointed to Inquire into the Subject of Agricultural Depression: Minutes of Evidence with Appendices*, Parl. Papers 1894, XVI, Parts I–III; Idem, *Second Report of Her Majesty's Commissioners Appointed to Inquire into the Subject of Agricultural Depression, Minutes of Evidence*, Parl. Papers 1896, XVI; Idem, *Final Report of Her Majesty's Commissioners Appointed to Inquire into the Subject of Agricultural Depression, Appendix*, Parl. Papers, 1897, XV.
9. Duke of Bedford, *A Great Agricultural Estate* (London, 1897), p. 69.
10. Lord Ernle, *English Farming Past and Present* (6th edn, London, 1961), p. 383.
11. M. J. Daunton, 'The Political Economy of Death Duties: Harcourt's Budget of 1894', in N. Harte and R. Quinault (eds), *Land and Society in Britain, 1700–1914* (Manchester, 1996), pp. 137–71; M. Daunton, *Trusting Leviathan: The Politics of Taxation in Britain, 1799–1914* (Cambridge, 2001), especially chapter 8 with his conclusion that 'perhaps the dukes did, after all, have reason to be depressed' about the incidence of death duties (p. 255).
12. Thompson, *English Landed Society*, p. 320; A. Adonis, 'Aristocracy, Agriculture and Liberalism: The Politics, Finances and Estates of the Third Lord Carrington', *Historical Journal*, 31 (1988), 882; *Victoria County History of Shropshire*, vol. IV (London, 1989), p. 250; J. Davies, 'The End of the Great Estates and the Rise of Freehold Farming in Wales', *Welsh History Review*, 7 (1974), 189.

13. H. A. Clemenson, *English Country Houses and Landed Estates* (London, 1982), p. 103.
14. Douglas, *Land, People and Politics*, p. 144; P. Mandler, *The Fall and Rise of the Stately Home* (New Haven, 1997), pp. 160–76.
15. D. Lloyd George, *The Rural Land Problem: What it is* (London, 1913); B. B. Gilbert, 'David Lloyd George: The Reform of British Landholding and the Budget of 1914', *Historical Journal*, 21 (1978), 117–41, which sets out Lloyd George's position on land; I. Packer, *Lloyd George, Liberalism and the Land: The Land Issue and Party Politics in England, 1906–14* (Woodbridge, 2001).
16. B. Short, *Land and Society in Edwardian Britain* (Cambridge, 1997).
17. *The Land: The Report of the Land Enquiry Commission* (3rd edn, London, 1913); Birmingham University Library, Charles Masterman Papers, 34/1/3i.
18. I. Packer, 'The Conservatives and the Ideology of Landownership, 1910–1914', in M. Francis and I. Zweiniger-Bargielowska (eds), *The Conservatives and British Society, 1880–1980* (Cardiff, 1996), pp. 44–7.
19. See M. Tichelar, 'Socialists, Labour and the Land: The Response of the Labour Party to the Land Campaign of Lloyd George before the First World War', *Twentieth Century British History*, 8 (1997), 127–44, esp. 137–9.
20. Ibid., 129.
21. Douglas, *Land, People and Politics*, pp. 158–67; A. Offer, *Property and Politics, 1870–1914* (Cambridge, 1981), pp. 371–83.
22. A. Howkins, *Reshaping Rural England: A Social History 1850–1925* (London, 1991), p. 265.
23. *Times*, 7 October 1912, p. 9 ('The Liberals and the Land') and 17 October 1912, p. 7 ('The Secret Land Inquiry').
24. *Estates Gazette*, 24 February 1912, pp. 300–1.
25. *Report of the Departmental Committee Appointed to Inquire into the Position of Tenant Farmers on the Occasion of any Change in the Ownership of their Holdings*, Parl. Papers 1912–13, XLVII. See also E. H. Whetham, *The Agrarian History of England and Wales, vol. VIII: 1914–39* (Cambridge, 1978), p. 52.
26. H. Durant, 'The Development of Landownership, 1873–1925, with special reference to Bedfordshire', *Sociological Review*, 28 (1936), 94, quoting from Jesse Collings, *The Colonization of Rural England* (London, 1914), i, p. 259.
27. Thompson, *English Landed Society*, p. 322.
28. Davies, 'End of the Great Estates', 189–91.
29. Royal Commission on Agriculture, *Final Report*, Parl. Papers 1897, XV, Report by Mr. George Lambert, pp. 204–24, esp. pp. 206–9, Report by Mr. F. A. Channing, pp. 225–370, esp. pp. 230–1. See also F. A. Channing, *The Truth about the Agricultural Depression* (London, 1897), p. 294.
30. H. J. Habakkuk, *Marriage, Debt, and the Estates System: English Landownership, 1650–1950* (Oxford, 1994), p. 684.
31. Hull University Library Archives DDFA, Papers of the Forbes Adam/Thompson/Lawley family (Barons Wenlock) of Escrick near York, especially DDFA3/9/35; DDFA[6]/12/1-9; DDFA5/11/303; DDFA5/14; DDFA5/13/1086–9.
32. Thompson, *English Landed Society*, p. 329, citing *Estates Gazette*, 6 January, 14 April, 16 June, 30 June and 18 August 1917.

33. J. V. Beckett, *The Rise and Fall of the Grenvilles: Dukes of Buckingham and Chandos, 1710–1921* (Manchester, 1994), p. 283.
34. Idem, 'Contesting the Urban Fringe: Nottingham City Council, Wollaton Hall and Broxtowe Hall, 1924–37', *Transactions of the Thoroton Society*, 108 (2004), 159–71.
35. Idem, *Rise and Fall of the Grenvilles*, pp. 282–3. In the years following his marriage in 1907, Christopher Hatton Turnor rationalised the management of his estate centred on Stoke Rochford Hall, ending with the sale in 1917 of the 6,000 acres of the Wragby part of the estate: J. Martin, 'Turnor, Christopher Hatton (1873–1940)', *Oxford Dictionary of National Biography* (Oxford, 2004).
36. *Estates Gazette*, 3 January 1920, 'Review of the Year 1919', p. 12; Thompson, *English Landed Society*, p. 330.
37. Precise details from *Times*, 31 December 1919, p. 4, but final speculation attributed to the authors.
38. *Times*, 30 December 1919, p. 19 ('The Estate Market, A Remarkable Year, Unprecedented Turnover'), and 31 December 1919, p. 4 ('The Estate Market... Keen Public Interest').
39. *Times*, 19 May 1920, p. 19.
40. *Report of the Departmental Committee Appointed to Inquire into the Position of Tenant Farmers on the Occasion of any Change in the Ownership of their Holdings*, Parl. Papers 1912–13, XLVII; S. G. Sturmey, 'Owner Farming in England and Wales, 1900–50', in W. E. Minchinton (ed.), *Essays in Agrarian History* (Newton Abbot, 1968), ii, p. 295. See also Whetham, *Agrarian History*, p. 52; Thompson, 'Land Market'.
41. Ministry of Agriculture and Fisheries, *The Agricultural Output of England and Wales, 1925*, Parl. Papers 1927, XXV, Cd. 2815, p. 96.
42. Sturmey, 'Owner Farming in England and Wales', pp. 281–306, esp. p. 288.
43. Whetham, *Agrarian History*, p. 52.
44. C. V. J. Griffiths, *Labour and the Countryside: The Politics of Rural Britain 1918–1939* (Oxford, 2007), pp. 188, 235.
45. D. K. Britton, 'The Sale Value of Farm Land between the Wars', *Farm Economist*, 6 (1949), 126, 129; Howkins, *Death of Rural England*, p. 36; A. Offer, 'Farm Tenure and Land Values in England, *c.* 1750–*c.* 1950', *Economic History Review*, 44 (1991), 1–20.
46. Sturmey, 'Owner Farming in England and Wales', p. 296.
47. For which see M. Dawson, 'The Liberal Land Policy, 1924–29', *Twentieth Century British History*, 2 (1991), 272–90, esp. 273.
48. Royal Commission on Oxford and Cambridge Universities, *Report*, Parl. Papers 1922, X; Birmingham University Library, Charles Masterman Papers, box 34.
49. On this, see Chapter 13, below.
50. On the debates in the Labour party about land and land nationalisation see Griffiths, *Labour and the Countryside*, esp. pp. 230–2; and for a continuation of the story into the 1940s see K. Manton, 'The Labour Party and the Land Question, 1919–51', *Historical Research*, 79 (2006), 247–69.
51. Royal Commission on Oxford and Cambridge Universities, *Report*, Parl. Papers 1922, X.

52. Law of Property Act 1922, 12 & 13 George V, *c*. 16; Law of Property (Amendment) Act 1924, 15 & 16 George V, *c*. 5; Law of Property Act 1925, 15 & 16 George V, *c*. 20.
53. Thompson, *English Landed Society*, p. 334.
54. Thompson, 'The Land Market', 293–7.

13

Socialism and the Land Question: Public Ownership and Control in Labour Party Policy, 1918–1950s

Clare Griffiths

Introduction

> If today Keir Hardie were to come into the Conference room and ask what were the Labour Party debating and he was told the principle of land nationalisation and that the year was 1953 and we had had six years of a Labour Government, he would have said: 'I should have thought you would have got rid of that subject long ago' (Stanley Orme, delegate from Altrincham and Sale constituency Labour party, speaking at the Labour party conference, 1953).

The shade of Keir Hardie acted as the conscience of the British Left, summoned up when old socialist shibboleths seemed in danger of being abandoned in favour of reformism. By the early 1950s, however, the Labour party had acquired another set of sacred reference points to cling to: a newer definition of what Labour stood for, based on what it had done, rather than what its founding fathers believed in. The achievements of Labour's first majority administration (1945–51) in nationalisation and welfare provision addressed some of the Labour movement's most enduring concerns. Such unprecedented peacetime intervention in the economy, and the establishment of a new ambitious 'welfare state' centred on the National Health Service, came to be identified as embodying the purposes and principles of the Labour party: the achievement of its defining historical commitments. Yet, when the delegate from Altrincham and Sale dragged Keir Hardie's name into a debate on the party programme at the 1953 party conference, it was a reminder that some of the oldest radical causes remained as unfinished business. One notable absence from the agenda of the Attlee governments was the old socialist commitment to the public ownership of land.

Land nationalisation was one of the great lost causes. As part of a mainstream political programme, it survived long enough to be included in the text of the Labour party's manifesto at the 1945 general election, though only as a goal for the longer term, not as an immediate priority. At this most auspicious moment for launching sweeping political and economic change, the public ownership of land occupied a somewhat apologetic place alongside the list of industries and services regarded as ripe for socialisation.[1] Yet it had once been common for socialists in Britain to talk about land nationalisation as a vital element in a reconfiguration of the national economy and for the achievement of greater social equality and opportunity. A *Clarion* pamphlet at the end of the nineteenth century described the abolition of land monopoly as the most pressing part of the socialist agenda, claiming that, without 'thoroughgoing methods of land socialisation', any other reforms could only be superficial.[2]

There has been relatively little scholarly discussion of socialism and land nationalisation, or indeed of socialism and the land question more generally. Links between 'green politics' and the political left during the late nineteenth and early twentieth centuries have been explored in a number of books about 'back to the land' experiments and ideas of the 'simple life',[3] while Martin Wiener highlighted examples of a romantic attachment to left-wing ideas of back to the land as variations on his theme of a dominant cultural mood and the 'decline of the industrial spirit'.[4] However, most histories of the modern Labour party make little reference to land as a significant political issue, in either its rural or its urban dimensions: land rarely even makes it into the index. Recent articles by Michael Tichelar[5] and Kevin Manton[6] lament a general neglect of the subject and seek to remedy it by offering surveys of some of the answers which Labour politicians were offering to the land question in the first half of the twentieth century. Labour history still tends to be written as though land was never a significant topic for socialists in Britain, and as though its place within the Labour party programme was essentially irrelevant in the broader narrative of the party's development.

Labour and land value taxation

Far from being alien to Labour politics, the land question was a central feature of the political landscape in which the Labour interest emerged at the end of the nineteenth century. Attlee commented that the agitation for land reform and the ideas of Henry George 'were instrumental in creating a receptivity to Socialist ideas in many minds.'[7] Yet, looked at another way, the excitement surrounding the project of land value taxation actually made it difficult for the Labour party to develop a distinctive 'socialist' policy in this area. In the years before the First World War, and again in the mid-1920s, Labour found itself competing with the radicalism of the Liberal land campaigns, and the fact that several of the leading figures in developing a land policy for Labour were themselves recent defectors from the Liberal party made the task of establishing a separate platform all the more challenging. One of the leading proponents of Henry George's ideas was Josiah Wedgwood, a former Liberal MP who joined the Labour party in 1919. He had already written a pamphlet on the Single Tax for the ILP (Independent Labour Party),[8] and his efforts to define a land policy for the Labour party continued to prioritise the introduction of land value taxation. For Wedgwood, the land question was about abolishing landlordism, and he suspected that nationalisation would only result in the replacement of private landlords by a new landlord in the form of the state.[9] He warned that state ownership would 'enslave' the whole population and encourage large-scale cultivation and industrial farming.[10] Land value taxation, by contrast, could complement a programme of land settlement promoting smallholdings, giving economic independence to the agricultural worker and offering a platform on which to appeal to the rural electorate.[11]

Others in the Labour party were far less convinced about the political or practical virtues of promoting a new peasantry. The general secretary of the National Union of Agricultural Workers, R. B. Walker, disputed Wedgwood's diagnosis of 'land hunger' amongst farmworkers and was sceptical about the economic viability of smallholdings.[12] Moreover, many within the party were suspicious that land value taxation was a distraction from more socialist objectives and would merely perpetuate the private ownership of land. The Labour party established an advisory committee in 1923 'to consider and report upon what system of land ownership, taxation, and rating would secure to the community the maximum benefits from the land', but its membership was deeply divided over the competing routes of land value taxation and land nationalisation. When Wedgwood produced a pamphlet summarising the committee's recommendations, he placed the main emphasis on a tax on site values at 1d. in the £ and local land rates based on land values: measures which promised to bring land into full use and reduce the anti-social practice of leaving plots idle, thereby addressing problems of unemployment, the loss of population through emigration and urban overcrowding. However, he also had to acknowledge other proposals from the committee with which he had far less sympathy: a gradual progress towards nationalisation, to be funded on the proceeds of land value taxation.[13]

As the party met in conference for the first time under a Labour government in 1924, a resolution which it passed in support of land value taxation was described as 'one of the resolutions that had been before practically every one of the twenty-four conferences that had been held.'[14] One of the keenest supporters of the policy within Labour was Philip Snowden, who claimed that if the 1924 government had survived to introduce a second Budget, its most significant feature would have been 'a proposal for a drastic Taxation of Land Values.'[15] Expectations remained high when Labour returned to office in 1929, and Labour and Liberal MPs petitioned Snowden as Chancellor to include the measure in his Budget, though it was not until 1931 that he introduced a valuation scheme, as a prelude to levying the tax, hailing this as 'a landmark on the road of social and economic progress'.[16] In fact, the valuation was abandoned after the fall of the Labour government, and the legislation itself was repealed in 1934.[17]

Land value taxation remained part of Labour's programme, despite arguments that it undermined the party's commitment to the more socialist objective of nationalisation. 'There might be something respectable in talking about taxing it', observed J. E. Williams from the Amalgamated Engineers' Union, but the only thing which would satisfy the workers would be to take the land back.[18] However, over time, wranglings about the relative merits of land value taxation and land nationalisation began to be resolved into distinct policies for urban and rural land. In 1928, land policy was summarised in these terms: 'the policy of the Labour Party in regard to Agricultural Land is, definitely and solely, Nationalisation. The policy with regard to urban land – an entirely different problem, is, for the present, the Taxation of Land Values.'[19] The fact that land policy was often identified as coterminous with agricultural policy and that Labour cited public ownership as a fundamental condition for the development of a socialist agriculture tended to distract attention from this continuing interest in land value taxation as a policy.

The elision between land and rural policy was a common and longstanding problem in political discussion. 'There is some confusion in people's minds as to what is meant by the term "land" which is so frequently used by Socialists', an ILP pamphlet had commented in 1901. 'It means not merely the soil, but clay, rock, coal, iron, copper, water, and every other material of which the earth is composed.'[20] Socialists attacked the deleterious effects of private landlordism for housing and the mining industry, making it clear that the land question had urban as well as rural dimensions, and in listing the problems resulting from the private ownership of land at the party conference in 1919, a representative of the Miners' Federation found plenty of things to include: 'it hampers industry, checks production, crowds the towns by depopulating the countryside, obstructs the provision of good housing, lowers the standard of public health both physical and moral....'[21] Nonetheless, when Labour politicians referred to 'land', they often meant agriculture, and the development of land policy was closely linked to the party's attempts to develop a rural political programme and to attract a rural following. In a heated discussion on the subject of land at the 1926 party conference, one agricultural trade unionist emphasised his 15 years of experience of farm work as a good qualification to comment: 'They had a lot of people getting up to speak at the Conference whose knowledge of the land question was confined to a flower box on the window sill.'[22]

Land nationalisation and the Labour party

As the Labour party made efforts to draw up an agricultural policy, the desirability of land nationalisation was taken as a given. 'The ultimate aim of public ownership' was acknowledged in the party's earliest discussions about agriculture, even whilst the proposals focused entirely on practical, reformist measures concerned with working conditions, the provision of smallholdings, access to credit and the state of rural housing.[23] According to Labour's 1926 agricultural programme, a change in the system of land tenure was fundamental to the future progress of agriculture, and the need for public ownership was too great to admit a piecemeal acquisition of land as an option.[24] National ownership and control of the land were also treated as central to the party's next major statement on agricultural policy – *The Land and the National Planning of Agriculture* – in 1932. The most obviously socialist of Labour's declarations on the subject, this document said relatively little about how and when agricultural land would become public property, but gave greater emphasis to the mechanisms for public control over the use of land. A plethora of commissions and corporations and committees would ensure that land was farmed to its full potential, in some cases through direct public farming on land owned by the nation. A mixed economy was prescribed for the immediate future, envisaging the survival of a substantial amount of traditional tenant farming, though with the significant substitution of the state as landlord, replacing a moribund private landlord system.[25]

Private landlords were blamed for the economic failings of contemporary agriculture, but they were also held responsible for the persistence of outmoded social hierarchies in the countryside. 'All the power of tyranny, all the power of feudalism will disappear on the day the land passes into national ownership', promised George Dallas, agricultural trade unionist and one of the leading figures in the development of Labour's agricultural policy in the 1920s and 1930s.[26] The belief that public ownership of land would produce a freer and more equal society accounted for much of its early appeal on the left. Land nationalisation, no less than land value taxation, had been a missionary cause in the late nineteenth and early twentieth centuries, promoted through impassioned manifestos, speaker meetings, societies and the famous touring vans to take the message to the people. Alfred Russel Wallace addressed his book *Land Nationalisation* (1892) to 'The Working Men of England', claiming the policy as a reform which would tackle the chief cause of poverty, destroy the 'evil' of landlordism and introduce a more productive 'occupying ownership' on land whose real ownership would be vested in the state.[27] The Land Nationalisation Society, with numbers of Labour and socialist figures amongst its lists of vice-presidents, stressed the importance of public ownership in practical terms – to revive agriculture, address problems of poverty and poor housing, and even to safeguard historical monuments and encourage popular access to the countryside. But for many socialists, the system of land ownership had not merely failed in practice: it was also fundamentally and morally wrong. It was common in socialist discussions of the land question to talk about the theft of the land from the people, indicting the present-day landowning class as the descendents of 'land-grabbers', who had 'seized control of Parliament... to legalise their thefts.'[28] James Bruce Glasier devoted a section of his book on 'the meaning of socialism' to the topic of land, approaching the land question in terms of 'The Great Disinheritance', and arguing that landlordism and capitalism were 'different forms of the same evil power': only public ownership and control could re-establish 'social justice and equality'.[29] When taken to its extreme, the emphasis on an historical dispossession treated landlords as owners of stolen property, with the implication that the land should be seized by the community as an act of restitution.[30] Some land nationalisers were more temperate in their language, and one of the best known of them all, Joseph Hyder, secretary of the Land Nationalisation Society, believed that 'Private property in land is a mistake, not a crime.'[31] Nevertheless, the language of theft remained very common, with the implication that land nationalisation would 'enable the nation to re-acquire its lost rights of ownership.'[32]

One problem with this analysis was that land had often changed hands so many times since the original 'theft' that its current owners could scarcely be regarded as anything other than innocent parties. In modern Britain, ordinary individuals and even social organisations, like trade unions and co-operative societies, owned land, and ideas about a righteous confiscation were criticised as irrational and potentially destabilising.[33] Even so, outbursts by the Labour party's rank and file often treated the subject as one with clear moral imperatives. A delegate at the 1934 party conference reminded fellow members that the Labour party had been 'very largely pioneered by men who believe that the land of the country belongs to the people of the country', adding: 'and we are going to have it without having to pay for it.'[34] As party leader in the late 1930s, Clement Attlee took the trouble to muster arguments against land nationalisation by confiscation: that it was arbitrary, penalising some forms of property ownership but not others, and that it was 'stupid to arouse unnecessary antagonism.'[35]

The cost of compensation was one daunting element in attempts to turn land nationalisation from a political daydream to a practical policy proposal. In their study of land nationalisation in 1921, Emil Davies and Dorothy Evans estimated the cost at £4,000 million.[36] It is perhaps understandable that a pragmatic approach to the land question was to be found amongst Labour's leadership from an early stage. 'I know the true ideal is that of nationalisation and public ownership', Ben Turner acknowledged, as chairman of the party conference in 1912. 'Alas, the people take much educating and convincing on the subject, but we must have a land policy that will ease the situation until the ideal of nationalisation has been accomplished.'[37] Again and again, even those professing to pledge themselves to the policy offered reasons why land nationalisation would not be an immediate priority for any new socialist government. Writing before the 1929 general election, G. D. H. Cole explained that, although a 'crucial reform', land 'socialisation' would have to wait its turn behind more pressing subjects such as mining and unemployment.[38] Yet, in 1931, a Labour government did make a modest attempt to pursue the ambition of taking agricultural land into public ownership, and even to float the notion of direct farming by the state. The 1931 Agricultural Land (Utilisation) Act was much reduced from its original scope by the time the legislation reached the statute books, but it still allowed the Minister of Agriculture to take over land which was not being farmed properly, to ensure that local authorities made provision for smallholdings to meet local demand and to set up demonstration farms to encourage agricultural improvement and the exploitation of modern scientific and technological development. It was celebrated by the Labour party as the 'greatest land reform measure of modern times'.[39] But the parliamentary response to Labour's proposals for the establishment of a state-owned land corporation and experiments with large-scale cultivation had given the party a taste of the challenge which would face any more far-reaching proposals. One Labour MP commented that they had encountered so much opposition to nationalising a little bit of the land that 'I don't know what will happen if we try to nationalise the lot.'[40]

In reaffirming a commitment to socialism after the collapse of the second Labour government in 1931, J. R. Clynes declared that 'when we reach the stage of there being a conscious dominant Labour and Socialist majority one of its first tasks must be to give to the people of our country the land which they truly call their own but is the private possession of a few.'[41] Calls for land nationalisation grew more strident and were accompanied by a clearer articulation of the economic justification for public ownership. A Fabian conference in April 1932 came to general agreement that an enabling Bill should be introduced at the earliest possible moment, 'nationalising land "in principle" and that all questions of compensation should be left over till afterwards.'[42] Christopher Addison, former Minister of Agriculture and one-time Liberal, also argued that, while the move to new forms of land management and use would have to be gradual, there was no reason why the transfer of ownership should not take place 'promptly', on 'an appointed day'.[43]

Whilst much of the detail of how to implement a programme of land nationalisation remained unclear, there were also plenty of concerns about how the electorate would respond. As part of a rural campaign in 1933, the Labour party urged voters to concentrate on the benefits which national ownership could bring, putting aside their prejudices and not being put off by what things were called.[44] The dangerous word in this case was clearly 'nationalisation', and it is striking how little the term was used in outlining a policy of land nationalisation to the rural electorate. In their study of farmers and politics in the period after 1945, Peter Self and Herbert Storing discussed Labour's vulnerability to concerns about offending the farming vote, noting that, 'The old socialist panacea of land nationalization had also to be shelved, for nobody supposed that farmers liked it.'[45] However, in the 1920s and 1930s, Labour still chose to keep the principle of land nationalisation at the centre of its agricultural programme, dressing it up in ways intended to make it more appealing. Labour promoted its agricultural policy with leaflets entitled 'Labour demands the land for the people' and 'Why we must get the land'. 'Public', or more often, 'national ownership' were the preferred terms, whilst the emphasis was always placed on the outcomes which would follow once the nation was the farmer's landlord, 'so that the producers of our food may get the help towards good farming which private landlords no longer give'.[46]

Agriculture and planning: new versions of the land question

The articulation of the land question had been very closely connected with anti-landlordism, but after the First World War it was the economic fortunes of agriculture as a sector, rather than the problematic influence of landlords, which became the more pressing issue. The pattern of rural landownership was changing, and the growth of owner occupancy provided a different set of arguments in favour of land reform. The wave of land sales between 1919 and the mid-1920s produced a generation of farming families who acquired substantial mortgages along with their changed status.[47] Anxieties arose about the ability of such farmers to invest properly in their land and to modernise their farming practice to meet the challenges of falling crop prices and competition from imports, whilst the fragmentation of land ownership following the breakup of large estates also threatened to make any scientific approach to land management far more difficult.[48] Owner-occupation provided a challenge for Labour's land policy. For some politicians, like Wedgwood, it was a positive social development, to be encouraged and welcomed. Others viewed it as an obstacle, creating a new constituency of private owners opposed to the project of land nationalisation and compromising the possibilities of developing a more modern and efficient agricultural sector. Yet, the family farm remained a powerful ideal, amidst concerns that agriculture was fundamentally different from other industries and could not be planned entirely according to scientific principles and economies of scale. The acknowledgement of a role for such farms became a way of softening and limiting the policy of public ownership. In the 1950s, John Mackie, himself a farmer, argued in a Fabian pamphlet on land nationalisation that, 'It would be better, because of the pride of ownership, to leave owner-occupied farms in the hands of their present owners until they gave them up or they became vacant for any other reason. There is no reason why the continuity of a farming family should be broken because of the sale of the farm to the State.'[49]

Party literature presented national ownership as the key to restoring agricultural prosperity and turning farming into a public service, but Labour politicians were careful to distinguish between ownership and the process of farming itself. As Noel Buxton, Labour's first minister of agriculture, commented, 'Public ownership of land is intended to socialise the land and not to socialise farming.'[50] Nationalisation would not necessarily mean a change in how the land was farmed, though the assumption was that public ownership would encourage the development of more efficient forms of farming, and that all kinds of agriculture would be improved by the enhanced investment and equipment which would be on offer by freeing up over-burdened owner-occupiers and replacing disinterested private landlords with the greater diligence and resources of the state. Nationalisation was even held out as a condition for greater economic support for farming: only by taking possession of the land could the state justify public expenditure which would otherwise find its way into private landlords' pockets.[51] All this left open the question of how far this new land ownership would lead to a new socialist agriculture. The argument seemed to be resolving into two strands, one of which aimed at public ownership of land as an inherently socialist objective that might yet be compatible with the continuation of an essentially capitalist form of agriculture, whilst the other looked at public ownership in terms of its practical outcomes and the way in which it would enhance control over and investment in the land. Public ownership would not in itself deliver socialism. Even in the supposed utopia of the USSR, one Fabian visitor observed that 'Russia has the land but a cunning peasant will be working it for many a day to come.'[52]

The presentation of land nationalisation as a 'functional' solution,[53] justified as a logical response to the problems of the agricultural industry, served to reinforce the idea of public ownership of land as a specifically rural policy. It was no coincidence that the Labour party's Land Nationalisation Committee, which began meeting in May 1932, shared most of its membership with the party's Agricultural Policy Committee. But when the New Fabian Research Bureau set up its own committee to look into land nationalisation in 1933, its efforts to recruit 'experts' showed that the issue was not being narrowly equated with agricultural policy: desirable profiles for members included a representative of a corporate real estate department, someone knowledgeable in county council work and a town planner.[54] The growing interest in planning had encouraged a return to thinking about the broader ramifications of the land question. Labour warned that the continuance of private land ownership threatened not only the prospect of an efficient agricultural industry but also 'to hamper town planning and housing' and 'to deprive the people of their rightful heritage of natural beauty and of national parks.'[55] Land nationalisation was given a role in debates about landscape preservation and access: Christopher Addison suggested that 'there are no other means whereby our national treasures in landscape, mountain, or coastland scenery may be safeguarded from the spoliations of the developer as well as obtained for proper public enjoyment and use.'[56]

The 1934 Labour party programme argued that the only way to ensure 'effective and bold action' was to bring about the 'unified ownership of the land', both rural and urban, and the 1937 *Immediate Programme* listed land as the second element in a series of four 'vital measures of reconstruction': 'The land should belong to the people, and national planning requires that the use of land shall be controlled in the public interest'.[57] That juxtaposition of the policies of ownership and control pointed to ambiguities in Labour's apparent commitment to nationalisation, and a tendency to emphasise the possibilities of a gradual, opportunistic expansion of the amount of land in public ownership gave some socialists cause for concern.[58] Nonetheless, on the eve of the Second World War, the Labour party appeared to be offering land nationalisation as a policy which was both necessary and achievable. 'I believe the case for National ownership of Agricultural land is unanswerable', commented Christopher Addison in 1939. 'I believe also that the methods that have been propounded for its acquisition are fair in themselves and can be applied without difficulty.'[59]

The 1940s and beyond

The manifesto on which the Labour party fought the 1945 general election was, in all its essentials, the programme which it had agreed before the war. However, the experience of war had shaped a new context which gave added weight to many of the party's established arguments about land. This was particularly the case with regard to Labour's agricultural policy. The War Agricultural Executive Committees across the country offered an embodiment of many of Labour's ideas about the control of agricultural production, the oversight of farmers' enterprise and the imposition of penalties for those whose farming did not meet the needs of the public interest. Whilst the disciplinary role of the 'War Ags' was unpopular and invidious, greater financial rewards for the farming population, dramatic achievements in domestic food production and the reinvigoration of a once 'derelict' countryside spoke well for the possibilities under a system of control, and Labour was eager to point out the similarities between this system and its own pre-war proposals.

One of the implicit conditional in the treatment of farmers during the war was that the tenure of land was assumptions on its full and proper use in the public interest. The ultimate sanction for bad farming was dispossession, and some saw this as a potential starting point for a wider nationalisation. Edwin Gooch, president of the National Union of Agricultural Workers, proposed a resolution at the 1943 Labour party conference that 'all land requisitioned by the County Committees should be retained after the war, and should be the first step in a new plan of national ownership and administration of agricultural land.'[60] Others recognised that the disciplinary regime in farming might offer its own route towards a form of socialist agriculture, even while most land remained in private hands. As the editor of a collection of Fabian essays outlining a practical socialist programme for agriculture in the post-war period, F. W. Bateson argued that any policy of general land nationalisation could only be carried out against the public mood and 'in the teeth of the opposition of the great majority of British farmers'. Public opinion, as Bateson interpreted it, had not yet reached the point of finding it intolerable that individuals should have a private share of a natural resource, though it was outraged at the misuse of land. He concluded that an 'English' solution could be found in a compromise between public control and private ownership. Landowners would retain their rights to enjoy, exploit and benefit financially from their property, but could not claim exclusive rights of access to their land or do whatever they chose with it.[61]

What is perhaps most notable about the waning of land nationalisation as an element in the Labour party's programme in the 1940s is that general interest in the subject had never been as great as it was during the Second World War. Within wartime debates about land use, the principle of state ownership of land was not necessarily bound within a nexus of socialist policies. There had long been an element of technocratic support for the policy: the agricultural economist C. S. Orwin, who claimed to have 'no politics where the land is concerned',[62] made a case for it in the 1920s, proposing state acquisition of agricultural land on the grounds that the old system of land management had broken down.[63] In the 1940s, Orwin was still promoting the idea that state ownership could improve the standard of farming, allowing a shift towards larger, more rational units of cultivation, and enabling the proper use of machinery and scientific management. A report which he oversaw on 'Country Planning', published in 1944, emphasised the illogicality of contemporary land holdings, illustrated by drawing a line across six miles of farmland which crossed 27 boundaries and encountered 23 different owners, and concluded that 'there is a conflict between maximum farm efficiency and private interests in property which cannot be ignored.'[64]

The focus on domestic food production during the Second World War and in the immediate post-war years might have been expected to give added impetus to such schemes of land reform which promised to unlock greater agricultural efficiency. But the stimulus for more radical engagement with the land question came mainly within the context of debates on planning and concerns about the potential for private interests to obstruct the necessary post-war rebuilding. During the war, a socialist commitment to the public ownership of land was expressed far more forcibly by Common Wealth than by the Labour party, fitting easily within the former's populist attack on vested interests. In its list of 24 questions designed to help voters make up their minds about which party was for them, the second question asked readers to consider whether 'The only way to stop private landowners from obstructing good town and country planning is common ownership of the land?'[65] The expected answer was, of course, 'yes'. Common ownership, in Common Wealth's prescription, would allow the country to build what it wanted where it wanted, adopting the principle that 'property has no absolute rights, and that the needs of human beings must come first.'[66] The importance of establishing the precedence of the common good over private landed interests was not limited to one point on the political spectrum, however. A 1943 Fabian Society pamphlet on land was able to cite a seemingly unlikely supporter of the case for nationalisation: Lord Astor who, as lord mayor of Plymouth, expressed the view that 'public ownership of land in a city is vital to its replanning.'[67] Indeed, emphasis on the limitations of private property in land was very common in debates on reconstruction. In his Penguin Special volume, *Christianity and Social Order*, the Archbishop of Canterbury, William Temple, laid stress on the obligations of stewardship and trusteeship: 'Land not beneficially used should involve liability to fine, or, in extreme cases, to forfeiture.' He supported the idea of public ownership for urban land, though preferred a solution of owner-occupancy in the countryside.[68] Even if it stopped short of endorsing national ownership as the solution to the land problem in an era of reconstruction, the Uthwatt report of 1942 had also been forthright in talking about the 'subordination to the public good of the personal interests and wishes of the landowners', dismissing a 'purely individualistic approach to land ownership' as 'no longer completely tenable'.[69]

Within the Labour party, an emphasis on the importance of land reform as a way to ease the implementation of plans for reconstruction had become a more common refrain than older themes about social justice and weakening the entrenched power of a landed class. The notion of land nationalisation as a route to achieving greater equality and a wider distribution of wealth had been re-interpreted during the 1920s and 1930s until public ownership was envisaged for the most part as a tool for positive intervention by the state: to invest in and support agriculture, to enable a fuller use of productive land, to control development and even to promote landscape conservation and allow greater public access. Land nationalisation was offered as a pragmatic answer, not just to problems of agricultural development and farm management, but to the urban and suburban challenges of post-war rebuilding. Reviewing the complexities of agreeing compensation and dealing with development rights as laid out in the Uthwatt report, Lewis Silkin, a future Labour minister of town and country planning, argued in 1943 that 'The only satisfactory solution is nationalisation of all land in urban areas.'[70] This conclusion would have come as a surprise to those who had engaged with the subtle shifts in Labour's land policy before the Second World War, when nationalisation had emerged as a policy applying solely to agricultural land. The debate was now about urban development. A National Executive Committee resolution on housing and town planning at the 1943 party conference noted that 'the only means of securing courageous, imaginative, and efficient planning is by the public ownership of land'.[71]

Land nationalisation was given as a commitment in Labour's 1945 general election manifesto, *Let Us Face the Future*, though only 14 per cent of Labour candidates at the election included it in their election addresses.[72] The national statement was in itself somewhat half-hearted. When zealots in the late 1940s complained about the failure of a Labour government to go ahead with a programme of land nationalisation, the party leadership pointed them back to the small print in the manifesto promises of 1945: that 'Labour believes in land nationalisation and will work towards it....'[73] Herbert Morrison had defended this position at the party conference in May 1945, responding to the concerns of delegates who feared that the power of the landlords would act as a break on many of Labour's plans:

> I gather that the point of criticism is that we have not, in this section of the document, made an affirmation in favour of the complete,

> nation-wide nationalisation of the land during the first five years of a Labour Government. It is a fact that we do not propose to do it.... We stand for it in the Party programme; we affirm its desirability, and in time we will do it.[74]

Morrison's argument was about practicalities and priorities. As he saw it, the only urgency was to acquire tracts of agricultural land which were being farmed inefficiently – and there were already powers in place to do this. Otherwise, the time-consuming effort of conducting the valuation of the nation's land would distract from more pressing business, whilst the costs of compensation could not be justified alongside the pressing claims on public spending, for welfare, housing and education. Labour's message to rural voters in the 1940s retained an insistence on the value of land nationalisation, whilst observing that there were more important things which needed to be tackled first.[75]

As the emphasis seemed to shift from a principled commitment to national ownership of the land towards a more instrumental approach, focusing on the acquisition of particular pieces of property to meet specific needs, it began to look as though the Labour party had forgotten that land nationalisation had supposedly been postponed rather than cancelled. The party's manifestos for the general elections of 1950 and 1951 omitted to make any general commitment to the policy: the closest they came was in the 1950 document, in the observation that 'public ownership will be used as the means of bringing into sound cultivation good food-producing land not fully used'.[76] However, interest in the subject of land nationalisation was reignited at the 1953 party conference in Margate, when delegates were invited to discuss the draft policy document 'Challenge to Britain', presented as a radical statement outlining 'drastic Socialist measures' necessary to 'win the peace', and including provisions which promised 'More from our land'. State-sponsored schemes to extend cultivation on marginal land echoed some of the ambitions of the plough-up campaigns during the war, accompanied by a renewed commitment to use public ownership as a means to encourage more productive farming.[77]

There followed one of the most extensive conference discussions of land policy since the 1930s, with a series of amending resolutions, one of which, tabled by the Lanark constituency Labour party, called explicitly for a renewed commitment to land nationalisation: 'We reaffirm acceptance of the principle of land nationalisation and that the Party will place a plan for carrying this out before the electorate at the next General Election.'[78] The Lanark resolution was defeated by 4,367,000 votes to 1,794,000. But that still meant that over a quarter of the votes cast in the conference hall in the early 1950s were in favour of restating a principled commitment to land nationalisation, in the face of pragmatic warnings about unsettling public confidence, imperilling agricultural productivity in the short-term, and condemning a future Labour government to unnecessary and draining financial burdens. Edwin Gooch, who had spoken up a decade earlier in favour of keeping confiscated lands as the basis of an estate in national ownership, now chose to rebuke zealous proponents of nationalisation for their misplaced priorities: 'Land nationalisation in itself would not produce an additional ounce of food.'[79]

Conclusion

The 1953 debate was not quite the last to be heard of the policy of land nationalisation. In a speech in February 1960, Hugh Gaitskell offered a rather surprising concession to the old cause, in the context of thinking about effective control over the planning process: 'It's absurd to think that we can overcome the present crisis in town and country planning without more public enterprise – we may even have to go back to some of our old ideas about the ownership of urban land.'[80] Later still, in Labour's 1983 manifesto-cum-'suicide note', the party restated an old commitment to free up opportunities for young people to break into farming, promising to encourage this through the workings of a new 'Rural Land Authority', controlling the land already in public ownership and also beginning 'to extend public ownership to tenanted land'.[81] But no one could claim that land nationalisation had a realistic place on a mainstream political agenda in the second half of the twentieth century. Is it too much to assume that it had ever been a practical policy commitment?

The goal of national ownership of land was a fundamental tenet for many on the British left before the Second World War. By the 1930s, the policy was bolstered by technocratic justifications, but for most people, it remained more an ethical than an economic question. Perhaps this is why it tended to be treated with a degree of vagueness which made it such a difficult subject for political action. In any far-reaching socialist programme, land was a central issue. Private ownership of land affected housing provision, access to land for agriculture or other forms of economic activity, social relationships between landlords and tenants, disparities of wealth across the population, the scope for planned development to meet the needs of the community and even opportunities for public leisure. Yet the financial challenge of transferring land to public ownership, and the electoral challenge of promoting a policy guaranteed to cause alarm amongst large sections of the general public, kept land nationalisation as a statement of political faith rather than a practical element in Labour's programme. To ask the question of when Labour abandoned a commitment to land nationalisation may be to overestimate its status as a realistic policy at any point. For many years, the Labour party had compromised on advocating greater social control and direction over the use of land, pending an opportunity to nationalise it. It asserted the right of the community to 'resume' its ownership of a common resource, whilst always scheduling a general nationalisation in an unspecified future. There was too much potential economic disruption and administrative complexity, too much electoral risk and too many vested interests to confront. No matter what ingenious devices were proposed, with valuations based on taxation figures and compensation provided through bonds which would replace rent receipts with interest payments, the financial consequences of a general nationalisation on an appointed day were too great to contemplate. Labour had in fact ended up by settling on precisely the outcome which socialists had identified and criticised in Liberal proposals before the First World War: to address the land question by means of state control rather than public ownership.

Notes

1. See M. Chase, '"Nothing Less than a Revolution"?', in J. Fyrth (ed.), *Labour's High Noon: The Government and the Economy 1945–51* (London, 1993), pp. 87–90.
2. L. Hall, *Land, Labour and Liberty or the ABC of Reform*, Clarion pamphlet no. 30 (London, 1899), pp. 12–13.
3. F. MacCarthy, *The Simple Life: C. R. Ashbee in the Cotswolds* (Berkeley and Los Angeles, 1981); J. Marsh, *Back to the Land: The Pastoral Impulse in England, from 1880 to 1914* (London, 1982); P. C. Gould, *Early Green Politics: Back to Nature, Back to the Land, and Socialism in Britain 1880–1900* (Brighton, 1988).
4. M. J. Wiener, *English Culture and the Decline of the Industrial Spirit, 1850–1980* (Cambridge, 1981), pp. 118–26.
5. M. Tichelar, 'Socialists, Labour and the Land: The Response of the Labour Party to the Land Campaign of Lloyd George before the First World War', *Twentieth Century British History*, 8 (1997), 127–44; idem, 'The Labour Party and Land Reform in the Inter-War Period', *Rural History*, 13 (2002), 85–101; idem, 'The Conflict over Property Rights during the Second World War: The Labour Party's Abandonment of Land Nationalisation', *Twentieth Century British History*, 14 (2003), 165–88; idem, 'The Labour Party, Agricultural Policy and the Retreat from Rural Land Nationalisation during the Second World War', *Agricultural History Review*, 51 (2003), 209–25; idem, 'The Scott

Report and the Labour Party: The Protection of the Countryside during the Second World War', *Rural History*, 15 (2004), 167–87.
6. K. Manton, 'The Labour Party and the Land Question, 1919–1951', *Historical Research*, 79 (2006), 247–69.
7. C. R. Attlee, *The Labour Party in Perspective* (London, 1937), p. 29.
8. J. C. Wedgwood, *Henry George for Socialists* (London, 1908).
9. See comments in *Report of the 26th Annual Conference of the Labour Party* [hereafter, *Conference*] (London, 1926), pp. 218–19.
10. J. and E. Wedgwood, *The Road to Freedom and What Lies Beyond* (London, 1913), pp. 67–9.
11. See J. C. Wedgwood, *Labour and the Farm Worker* (London, 1925).
12. Foreword to ibid.
13. J. C. Wedgwood, *The Land Question – Taxation and the Farm Worker* (London, 1925).
14. *24th Conference* (London, 1924), p. 174.
15. *25th Conference* (London, 1925), p. 269.
16. *Hansard*, Commons, 251 (27 April 1931), col. 1411.
17. R. Douglas, *Land, People and Politics: A History of the Land Question in the United Kingdom, 1878–1952* (London, 1976), pp. 206–8.
18. *23rd Conference* (London, 1923), p. 215.
19. E. F. Wise, speaking at 1928 party conference: *28th Conference* (London, 1928), p. 233.
20. Independent Labour Party, *Land and Machinery* (London, 1901).
21. *19th Conference* (London, 1919), p. 170.
22. *26th Conference* (London, 1926), p. 228.
23. See *The Labour Party and the Agricultural Problem* (London, 1914), Labour's first major statement on agricultural policy.
24. Labour Party, *Labour's Policy on Agriculture* (London, 1926), p. 5.
25. Labour Party, *The Land and the National Planning of Agriculture* (London, 1932).
26. *28th Conference* (London, 1928), p. 251.
27. A. R. Wallace, *Land Nationalisation: Its Necessity and its Aims* (5th edn, London, 1909), pp. v, 30, 192–3.
28. T. Higdon, writing in *Land Worker* (the journal of the National Union of Agricultural Workers), April 1921.
29. J. B. Glasier, *The Meaning of Socialism* (Manchester, 1919), p. 24.
30. For a fuller discussion of the theme of dispossession, see C. V. J. Griffiths, *Labour and the Countryside: The Politics of Rural Britain 1918–1939* (Oxford, 2007), ch. 1.
31. J. Hyder, *The Case for Land Nationalisation* (London, 1914), p. 341.
32. Wording of ILP resolution at the Labour Party conference in 1914: *14th Conference* (London, 1914), p. 118.
33. A. E. Davies and D. Evans, *Land Nationalisation: The Key to Social Reform* (London, 1921), p. 61.
34. H. Eastwood, Bolton Labour Party, in *34th Conference* (London, 1934), p. 160.
35. Attlee, *Labour Party*, pp. 182–4.
36. Davies and Evans, *Land Nationalisation*, p. 69.
37. *12th Conference* (London, 1912), p. 65.
38. G. D. H. Cole, *The Next Ten Years* (London, 1929), p. 268.

39. Labour Party, *Two Years of Labour Rule* (London, 1931).
40. J. H. Alpass, *Hansard*, Commons, 255 (24 July 1931), cols 1855–8.
41. *31st Conference* (London, 1931), p. 176.
42. British Library of Political and Economic Science, London School of Economics [hereafter BLPES], Fabian papers, J2/142-9, 'Notes on Easton Lodge Week-End', 16–17 April 1932.
43. C. Addison, et al., *Problems of a Socialist Government* (London, 1933), p. 239.
44. *From One Countryman to Another*, Labour Party/*Daily Herald* leaflet (1933).
45. P. Self and H. J. Storing, *The State and the Farmer* (London, 1971), p. 200.
46. *Britain's People need much more fresh food/Britain's Land could grow much more fresh food*, Labour Party leaflet (1938).
47. A. Howkins, *The Death of Rural England: A Social History of the Countryside since 1900* (London, 2003), pp. 36–40.
48. See comments in Political and Economic Planning Report, 'Agriculture: An Industry', 12 July 1933, part 4, p. 6 (copy at BLPES, Fabian Society papers, J22/3).
49. J. Mackie and H. Walston, *Land Nationalisation, For and Against*, Fabian Tract 312 (London, 1958), p. 8.
50. Bodleian Library, Addison papers, 126/160.2, memorandum on land tenure and organisation, Advisory Committee on Agricultural and Rural Problems, June 1925.
51. H. Harben, *Labour and the Land: An Agricultural Policy* (London, 1921), p. 12.
52. J. Morgan, 'Agriculture', in M. Cole (ed.), *Twelve Studies in Soviet Russia* (London, 1933), p. 121.
53. Harry Walston later used the notion of a 'functional nationalisation' in Mackie and Walston, *Land Nationalisation*, pp. 18–19.
54. BLPES, Fabian papers, J22/2/1-2, memorandum by Margaret Cole, 9 November 1933.
55. Labour Party, *A Nation Without Poverty* (London, 1935), p. 6.
56. C. Addison, *A Policy for British Agriculture* (London, 1939), p. 85.
57. Labour Party, *For Socialism and Peace* (London, 1934), p. 24; Labour Party, *Labour's Immediate Programme* (London, 1937), p. 4.
58. See, for example, comments by G. R. Mitchison in BLPES, Fabian papers, J32/2, memorandum on 'Nationalisation of the Land', 5 September 1935.
59. C. Addison, *A Policy for British Agriculture* (London, 1939), p. 283.
60. *42nd Conference* (London, 1943), p. 200.
61. F. W. Bateson, 'The Ownership of Agricultural Land', in Bateson (ed.), *Towards a Socialist Agriculture: Studies by a Group of Fabians* (London, 1946), pp. 173–5.
62. Foreword to Bateson, *Towards a Socialist Agriculture*, p. v.
63. C. S. Orwin and W. R. Peel, *The Tenure of Agricultural Land* (2nd edn, Cambridge, 1926), p. viii.
64. Agricultural Economics Research Institute, Oxford, *Country Planning: A Study of Rural Problems* (London, 1944), p. 84.
65. *Which Way Shall I vote?*, Common Wealth leaflet G.E./3 (London, 1945).
66. *The Way to Prosperity: Capitalism or Socialism?*, Common Wealth leaflet G.E./9 (London, 1945).

67. L. Silkin, *The Nation's Land: The Case for Nationalisation* (London, 1943), p. 21.
68. W. Temple, *Christianity and Social Order* (Harmondsworth, 1942), pp. 117–18.
69. Report of the Expert Committee on Compensation and Betterment, Cmd. 6386 (September 1942), pp. 11–12.
70. Silkin, *The Nation's Land*, p. 21.
71. *42nd Conference* (London, 1943), pp. 202–4.
72. R. B. McCallum and A. Readman, *The British General Election of 1945* (London, 1947), p. 100.
73. Labour Party, *Let Us Face the Future* (London, 1945).
74. *44th Conference* (London, 1945), p. 133.
75. See, for example, C. McCall, *Village Life and the Labour Party Today* (London, 1947), p. 7.
76. I. Dale (ed.), *Labour Party General Election Manifestos 1900–1997* (London, 2000), pp. 61–78. The deployment of public ownership as a disciplinary measure against bad farming was by then a recognised feature of governmental powers, enforced under wartime defence regulations and re-stated through Labour's 1947 Agriculture Act. By the time of the repeal of the legislation in 1958, around 3,000 farmers had lost their farms as a result of powers granted to county agricultural executive committees during the war and in the post-war period: see B. Short, 'The Dispossession of Farmers in England and Wales during and after the Second World War', in B. Short, C. Watkins and J. Martin (eds), *The Front Line of Freedom: British Farming in the Second World War* (Exeter, 2007), p. 166.
77. *52nd Conference* (London, 1953), p. 71.
78. Ibid., p. 139.
79. Ibid., p. 146.
80. Quoted in K. Coates, *Common Ownership: Clause IV and the Labour Party* (Nottingham, 1995), p. 40.
81. I. Dale (ed.), *Labour Party General Election Manifestos 1900–1997* (London, 2000), p. 257.

14

Epilogue: The Strange Death of the English Land Question

F. M. L. Thompson

There has never been any doubt in the minds of historians – least of all among those contributing to this volume – that the land question was an important, even a burning, issue in late Victorian Britain, and was building up an impressive head of steam on the eve of the First World War. So impressive, indeed, that there seems little doubt that from the sometimes tumultuous progress of the red vans and the yellow vans down the country lanes in the 1890s, through to the enthusiastic response to the Liberal Land Campaign in 1913–14, land reform in one shape or another was a genuinely popular cause, something more than the pet cry of a clique of radical politicians and intellectuals. This surge of popular demand for land reform, although reflected in the large group of committed land reformers sitting on the Liberal benches after 1906 and in the somewhat less wholehearted commitment of the Asquith government, had not resulted in any decisive settlement of the land question. Thus in 1914, there was still much unfinished business on the land reform agenda, as indeed the Liberal Land Campaign indicated; moreover, its proposals were regarded by land-taxers and land-nationalizers as merely a first instalment of a lasting settlement of the land question. Then on 4 August, controversy and agitation were suspended, and were never resumed. The effect was instantaneous: 'The Land Campaign' of *The Times*'s leader on 5 August referred to the invasion of Belgium and the likely date for the simultaneous arrival in France of the German army and the British Expeditionary Force.[1] There was never again popular agitation, or even party political controversy, on the scale of the pre-1914 passion and vehemence. The great land question simply fizzled out, ending not with a bang but a whimper. That is the strange death that needs to be explained.[2]

The whimper was indeed heard quite loudly in Westminster from time to time after 1918, but without attracting much attention among the electorate. What seems to have happened is that the political veterans of the pre-1914 battles who survived into interwar politics had not forgotten the campaigns of their youth, but the rest of the public had moved on. Figures such as Noel Buxton, Josiah Wedgwood, Philip Snowden and of course David Lloyd George tried to keep the issues alive, but the response was not encouraging. The last time that *The Times* ran a leader under the heading of 'The Land Question', taking it as a serious matter, was on 7 October 1912, when it declared 'the Liberals must decide whether the policy of Cobden and Bright and Gladstone in regard to land is to be abandoned for that of Henry George'.[3] Naturally, the Liberals declined to decide. Lloyd George had, indeed, already put Liberals into an ideologically indefensible position, if they still held to the Cobdenite creed, as many did. Veterans might have recalled that John Stuart Mill had been drummed out of the Cobden Club in 1871 for the heresy of advocating the taxation of the future 'unearned increments'. Mill argued that these derived from the fact that 'the incomes of landowners are rising while they are sleeping, through the general prosperity produced by the labour and outlay of other people', and that therefore such increments were legitimate objects for taxation.[4] Strict followers of Cobden, on the other hand, held that any such taxation would be nothing less than confiscation. The Increment Value Duty in the 1909 Budget, although hedged with many qualifications and exemptions, embraced this confiscatory principle, to the delight of land reformers and the fury of the Tories. By 1913, Lloyd George was prepared to go much further, signalling his readiness to introduce national site value taxation – that is, an annual tax on the 'bare site' value of all land, a decisive step in the direction of Henry George's single tax. It was an undertaking which was to return to cause him trouble and humiliation in 1931.[5]

Members of the pre-1914 Liberal government who were of a Cobdenite or Gladstonian persuasion, of whom there were several, were troubled by the Georgeite tendency of taxation policy, but whatever their private misgivings, in public they paraded a united front in support of Lloyd George, hoping that by staying hitched to his bandwagon the Liberals would win the approaching 1915 general election. After the War had buried such expectations the doctrinal split in the Liberal ranks, to which *The Times* had drawn attention in 1912, grew wider, or at least more divisive, the smaller the parliamentary Liberal party became. Indeed the final rift among the few survivors of the pre-1914 Liberal cabinet, in 1931, was over a clash on land tax almost as much as over a clash of personalities.[6]

As for *The Times*, while it continued to regard the break-up of estates and the decline of the old landed aristocracy as serious social and economic issues, it treated such direct political and ideological attacks on landowners as were resumed in the interwar years as matters for gentle chiding or ridicule, not important enough to warrant refutation. Thus in 1924, when Labour had taken up the running in anti-landlord rhetoric, a cabinet minister (Stephen Walsh, Secretary for War), who promised that the Labour government would restore to the people the lands which English landowners had 'crept in at the dead of night' and stolen, was simply sent on his way by *The Times* with a lesson in the accepted historical orthodoxy that enclosures had been no more than a re-arrangement of the pieces of land already in individual ownership, and that there had been no robbery from anyone.[7] As for the shrunken Liberals, Lloyd George's 1926 Land Programme, 'the Green Book', was regarded by E. G. Pretyman, a veteran of the fight against the 1909 land taxes and chairman of the still active Land Union, 'more as a joke than anything else'.[8] In complete contrast to the first Land Campaign of 1913, Lloyd George's second Land Campaign of 1926 was a flop, and by the time of the 1929 general election had been quietly forgotten. And so, in due season, the English land question dropped out of the history books too. In the older general accounts of Britain since 1914, those of A. J. P. Taylor and C. L. Mowat for instance, at least land values taxation rated an interwar reference, but even that leaves no trace in Peter Clarke's *Land of Hope and Glory* (1996).[9]

C. F. G. Masterman, radical politician and commentator, briefly Chancellor of the Duchy of Lancaster (1914–15), was quick off the mark in providing an explanation for the death of the land question. 'Liberalism looked on saddened and amazed', he wrote in 1920,

> while the new Parliament destroyed all the results of the vigorous campaign [of 1913–14]. The Coalition dug the grave wide and deep. They flung into it the Land Taxes of Mr Lloyd George, the Land Valuation of Mr Lloyd George and the Land Policy of Mr Lloyd George. They dumped earth upon it. They stamped down the ground over the grave. They set up a stone to commemorate their victory for testimony to the passing stranger. 'Here buried for ever, lies the Land Crusade.' ... Never, it would seem, was a cause so sensationally and utterly destroyed.[10]

Before the War, Masterman had been one of Lloyd George's most ardent admirers, and was bitterly disillusioned by his betrayal of the 'Land

Crusade' when his government repealed the 1909 land valuation and land taxes in 1920. Even discounting his personal feelings, however, Masterman had identified an important political explanation of the death of the land question: Lloyd George, as head of the Coalition government, had lost credibility as a land reformer, and the divided, quarrelsome and weakened Liberals were incapable of implementing any solution to the land question, even if they could contrive to agree on one. The best that Wedgwood and other land-taxers could manage was to sing the Henry George 'Land Song' (allegedly composed by Wedgwood himself, and which had been sung at the close of public meetings of the Georgeite campaigns in the 1890s) in the House of Commons in protest at the repeal of the 1909 land valuation.[11]

More recently Ian Packer has provided a detailed account, and explanation, of the death of the land question, caused by the First World War rendering politically irrelevant and electorally ineffective the great Edwardian land reform issues.[12] With its emphasis on the disarray and decline of the Liberal party, and the emergence of pressing post-war problems of labour unrest, mass unemployment and disruption of international trade, this is a coherent explanation of the party-political dimension of the death of the land issue, while it rather ignores the wider economic, social and political implications of this casualty. Indeed it invites the question of how far land reform had ever been relevant beyond its utility as a political cry. That is to say, if land reform was sidelined by more immediately urgent problems in the 1920s, there were also several pre-war matters widely held to be pressing, notably labour unrest, unemployment, the temporarily shelved matter of tariff reform and above all Ulster, and the reason that these had not kicked land reform into the long grass was not their lack of urgency so much as the audacity of Lloyd George's rhetoric in claiming that land reform would solve all the other problems. Except, of course, Ulster. The Tory view was that the 1913 Land Campaign was simply a Liberal ploy to divert attention from Ulster. As a *Times* leader put it in November 1913, Lloyd George in a great campaigning speech at Middlesbrough 'added more items to the long list of marvels that land policy is going to produce – raise everybody's wages, increase employment, abolish slums, give everybody a good house and a bit of land, benefit farmer and shopkeeper, make the desert bloom, and fill the land with happy peasants and well-fed artisans'.[13] Similar rhetoric failed to carry conviction in the 1920s partly because there was no longer a united Liberal party which believed in it, and partly because the appeal of land reform had been whittled away by the achievement, whether directly, obliquely or by stealth, of many of the objectives of generations of land reformers.

First, however, it should be recalled that the English land question – and even more the Welsh and Scottish land questions – had historically ridden on the back of the Irish land question. It had been one of the chief fears of English landowners and their allies, and one of the great hopes of English land reformers, that measures adopted to deal with the Irish situation would sooner or later be applied to the British mainland. One reason for the Liberal party's adoption of home rule was to place Ireland in constitutional isolation and thus minimize the risk that the regrettably necessary interference with Irish property rights of measures like the three Fs, land courts and land purchase would infect the mainland, hence giving home rule a defensive rather than a radical slant. In any event, as far as British governments were concerned the Irish land question was finally solved when Ireland was cast adrift in 1922, or at least what was left of the question became a matter for the Free State. Hence in the interwar years the cause of land reform in Britain was deprived of its traditional pace-setter.

At the same time, the driving force of land reform was weakened by the partial fulfilment of many of its aims, often indirectly and inadvertently rather than through any particular reformist success. The fundamental purpose of land reform since the days of Paine, Spence, Cobden and Bright, John Stuart Mill and the Chartists – some might say since the Levellers – was to abate the power of the aristocracy, destroy the 'aristocratic monopoly' and bring about a redistribution of the land. Different groups proposed different means for achieving these ends, but it was these general aims that underpinned the popular appeal of land reform. By the early 1920s, even a short-sighted egalitarian could not have failed to notice that the power and influence of the aristocracy, and of the entire landowning class, had been greatly reduced over the previous half century. This was the result of the extension of the franchise in the Third and Fourth Reform Acts, and the hobbling of the Lords by the Parliament Act, but these political triumphs of reformers were only part of the story. Erosion of the economic power of landowners may have been under way since the end of the eighteenth century, but it had been almost imperceptible until greatly accelerated by the decline in rents and the decline in the value of agricultural land in the late nineteenth century. A decisive shift in the balance of power between landowners and tenant farmers in favour of tenants was evidenced before 1914 in the inability of landlords to raise rents despite the modest revival of agriculture, and was confirmed by the wartime rent freeze. Even more to the point the steep fall of at least one-third in the value of land in the late nineteenth century, irrespective of what happened to rent levels, led many landowners to try to sell land, either because of the squeeze on their income or because it seemed desirable to have less land and more stocks and shares in their portfolios.[14]

Having languished in the doldrums since the end of the 1870s, the land market picked up in the few years before 1914 with the emergence of reasonably strong demand from sitting tenants as well as from new men, and there was a run of estate sales. Suspended during the war, in 1919 this became a veritable flood, and between then and 1921, it was reckoned that a quarter of England changed hands. Taken literally this would imply that something like eight million acres changed hands in just 3 or 4 years, and the claim might have been a headline-grabbing exaggeration. Nevertheless, it has been established that, over a rather longer period, the proportion of agricultural land in England in the hands of owner-occupiers increased from 11 per cent in 1914 to 36 per cent in 1927, meaning that farms covering about six million acres had changed from being tenanted to being in the hands of owner-occupiers. Part of this switch in tenure may well have been the result of landowners taking farms in hand, which would not cause any change in ownership, but the contemporary view was that most of the switch was produced by tenant farmers purchasing their farms. In addition to this rise in owner-farming, there was a considerable flow of new money in these post-war years into estate buying by businessmen with swollen wartime fortunes to invest, estates which remained farmed by tenants. All in all the contemporary perception of a massive transfer of land was well-founded.[15]

Already in 1919, Edward Wood, a leading figure on the House of Commons Agriculture Committee, had noted that 'a great deal of land is every day passing through the market and changing hands. It is not an exaggeration to say that there is a silent revolution going on every day in the matter of land up and down the country.' Wood became attached to the 'silent revolution' formula, repeating it in 1925, when he was Minister of Agriculture, declaring: 'It is often said, and said with truth, that there is at this moment going on in agriculture a silent revolution as regards land ownership.'[16] The 'silence' of this 'revolution' in landownership was strictly relative, since the national press, following the lead of the property press, gave it considerable publicity in 1918–21, but it was certainly a massive transfer of land negotiated through the market and without any of the uproar, violence and expropriation of 'agrarian reform' in the Soviet Union. The sales were often held to be the effect of death duties, which had been increased to a top rate of 40 per cent in 1919; but while this was the reason for selling in some cases, market forces, self-interest and improved asset management were responsible for most of the sales.[17]

Great estates of course did not vanish any more than dukes and earls disappeared, but it was clear enough that a considerable redistribution of land was taking place without any help from land reformers' pet schemes. Moreover, the sales were converting tenant farmers into owner-occupiers; this was often a reluctant, defensive, move, for tenants feared that new landlords might raise rents, but it was nevertheless realizing in a completely unexpected way the old radical aim of reviving the yeomen farmers, except that the new commercial farmers bore little resemblance to the idealized prototype and had the disobliging habit of being conservative and protectionist in their politics. Optimists among land reformers managed to find new arguments for their policies out of these developments. As the Labour election programme of 1929 put it: 'Landlordism has ceased to be able to perform its functions and cannot be allowed to go on starving the land of capital ... The land must therefore pass under Public control.'[18] The Labour MP J. M. Kenworthy (later tenth Lord Strabolgi) followed this up at the 50th annual meeting of the Land Nationalization Society in March 1931, declaring that 'the landed aristocracy was disappearing in England, and a silent revolution was taking place only comparable to the break-up of the feudal system. The landed aristocracy did perform a function. The good landlord did put capital into the land ... There would be no re-equipment of the land so long as it remained in private hands.'[19]

A less partisan view, likely to have been shared by most of the electorate who had any view at all on the land question, would have been the precise opposite – that this silent revolution made great schemes of land reform unnecessary and redundant. The social structure of the countryside was changing and the appearance of the new class of owner-farmers was accompanied by the disappearance of some of the country houses of the gentry and aristocracy: a few became schools or hotels, more were simply abandoned by owners unable to afford the upkeep of either the fabric or the country-house lifestyle, and were demolished or left to decay. By the 1930s, it was quite plausible to conclude that major land reform was being witnessed in England without any resort to compulsory land purchase schemes or to expropriation, as in some countries, and without violence and burning of houses as in Ireland.

Equally telling evidence of the dwindling appeal of land reform was the silence which greeted the abolition of primogeniture. Although it had long been acknowledged that the law of primogeniture was of very little practical significance, since it only applied to the succession to real property on intestacy, its abolition had for equally long held great symbolic importance for the anti-aristocratic cause, as the emblem of feudalism, reaffirmed as recently as 1913 in *The Land Hunger*, the late-Cobdenite broadside on 'Life under Monopoly'.[20] Then primogeniture was swept away, along with other 'feudal' remnants such as gavelkind, copyholds and manorial courts, in the great law reform measure introduced by Lord Birkenhead in 1922 and finally enacted in 1925, a virtual revolution in the law.[21] The 1925 Law of Property Act came tolerably close to enacting the Victorian 'free trade in land' programme, but the Land Law Reform Association, which had still been holding annual meetings before 1914, was no longer around to celebrate this triumph and the only group which took much notice was the Law Society, with disgruntled solicitors complaining that their arcane knowledge was being made redundant and their income from conveyancing was being undermined.[22] The Law correspondent of *The Times* chided feminists for not even noticing that the abolition of primogeniture meant that husbands and wives were at last placed on an equal footing with regard to each other's property: 'Feminists, however, have so far shown no appreciation of Lord Birkenhead's action in this matter, being, apparently, more interested in getting votes for immature girls of 21 than in improving the relative position of their sex generally.'[23] Thus, in characteristically English fashion a kind of fudged settlement of many of the issues raised by the land question had been reached. It was no less characteristic that the rump of the land-reforming tendency found such an indecisive settlement unimpressive, and tried to press on towards a conclusive defeat of landlordism. 'Comprehensive reform of the existing Land System and taxation of land values' was in the 1922 election manifesto of the Asquith Liberals, though it was no higher than eighth in a ten-point programme, and this was echoed in the 1924 programme of the Lloyd George Liberals, which rightly claimed that 'Liberalism has a special responsibility for promoting and carrying through great policies of land reform'.[24] These promises conspicuously failed to win votes, and so in 1926, Lloyd George made the Liberals' last great effort on the land reform ticket, with the production of the 'Green Book' setting out a policy for rural land.

This was a replay of the pre-war campaign strategy, with the recruitment of an imposing commission of enquiry, this time paid for by the Lloyd George Fund but including such prominent critics of Lloyd George as F. D. Acland and Charles Masterman, which produced a substantial detailed report on rural conditions that formed the basis of policy recommendations.[25] There was, however one crucial difference in the chief thrust of the recommendations. The main appeal of the rural Land Campaign in 1913–14 had been to agricultural workers, with the promise of establishing a minimum wage and maximum length of the working week, to be administered by agricultural wages boards under central direction. This had been immensely popular with the labourers and not unpopular with farmers, who were sweetened with an undertaking that increases in wages would be paid for by rent reductions, enforced by rent tribunals. In the event Agricultural Wages Boards were established in 1917, as part of the Corn Production Act, and although abolished by the Coalition government in 1921 were reintroduced, with rather weaker powers but as it turned out more permanently, by the Labour government in 1924. This form of interference with the market mechanisms for settling wage rates was certainly no part of the aims of Cobdenite land reform. Nevertheless, the establishment of Agricultural Wages Boards not only precluded Lloyd George from resurrecting them as part of a radical land reform policy in 1926, but also marked one more partial settlement of a facet of the land question.

The consequence was that the 'Green Book' was obliged to concentrate on offering a policy intended to appeal to farmers, that of a watered down version of nationalization under which the state was to buy out the landowners and give sitting tenants a new form of 'cultivating tenure' that would provide security of tenure conditional on practising good husbandry. This at least was a novelty, of a sort. When Lloyd George had revealed a detailed preview of the new ideas in September 1925, however, they had instantly been dismissed as 'An Obsolete Policy' in a *Times* leader. Obsolete mainly on the grounds that there was nothing new in the policy: 'There is not a single idea... which those of us who are old enough do not remember in the speeches of town-bred reformers half a century ago.' Obsolete also, significantly, because rural economic and social conditions had changed, so that once justified grievances or shortcomings had vanished:

> Landowners may maintain themselves in these days by the possession of royalties or of urban estates or by the practice of a profession or business, but the agricultural landowner who lived off his rents is as extinct as the Dodo. And the alleged insecurity of the good tenant farmer... is a myth. Landowners are not evicting good tenants. They are running after them and competing with each other to secure them.[26]

The Liberal 'Brown Book', with proposals for urban land reform, was also a simple re-hash of old ideas, offering leasehold enfranchisement and site value taxation for urban land. A Land and Nation League was set up, hoping to stage a re-run of the 1913 Land Campaign, with a target of 10,000 public meetings, and a newspaper, the *Land News*, was launched. 'Staging' was the operative word, for there was a singular lack of public interest and the League's first task was to try to create a show of public concern. The Lloyd George Fund might buy a professional publicity machine, but its attempt to orchestrate a flood of letters to the national and provincial press exposing the iniquities of the leasehold system was an own goal. The League's circular to firms of surveyors and estate agents unguardedly revealed that 'we are anxious to increase public interest in these questions [of the injustice and anomalies of the leasehold system]', and explained that 'there is growing evidence in trade journals and elsewhere of a growing feeling on this matter, which only needs stimulating in order to create an effective public opinion'. Inevitably some copies of this letter were delivered into hostile hands, and the League's campaign was laughed out of court.[27]

Although *Land News* continued to appear until 1929, it had soon swung round to becoming an organ for Lloyd George's Keynesian unemployment policy, for the rural policy of the 'Green Book' had little attraction either for the new generation of owner-farmers or for the mainstream tenant farmers who were suspicious of the prospect of bureaucratic interpretation of what would constitute 'good husbandry' in the new regime of 'cultivating tenure'. Hence the vaunted new Land Campaign of 1926 was a complete flop. This exposure of the hollowness of the claim that there was still a great public demand for land reforms marked the end of the Liberals' – and Lloyd George's – attachment to the land question.

Even site value rating vanished from the party's policies until it re-appeared after 1945. That did not prevent Lloyd George getting into a damaging muddle over the land tax clauses of Snowden's 1931 Budget, which at first he welcomed as a re-enactment of his own 1909 Budget, and then a few weeks later denounced as an indefensible measure of double taxation, on the ground that property owners already paid income tax under Schedule A on their income from land. Snowden's inclusion of a new land valuation as part of the Budget's Finance Bill, because it was a necessary instrument for his new land tax, certainly followed the 1909 procedural path, but the new tax of 1d in the £ on the bare site value of all except purely agricultural land was quite different from the 1909 taxes on incremental value and undeveloped land, and also different from Lloyd George's undertaking in 1913 to impose a site value tax only to the extent that he had proposed a tax of 1/2d in the £ whereas Snowden opted for a rate of 1d in the £. Even that difference vanished when Lloyd George negotiated a compromise with Snowden, withdrawing his objection to 'double taxation' in return for a reduction in the proposed tax rate to 1/2d in the £, with further reduced rates for fully developed land.[28] These tax and valuation proposals provoked heated controversy, perhaps the last occasion on which land reform engaged impassioned support and opposition. The storm, however, was a parliamentary exclusive, fought out between a rump of Liberals and land-taxers; most Labour MPs were less than enthusiastic about the taxes, and many in the Cabinet were at most indifferent.[29] Groups of dedicated activists naturally got excited, and the English League for the Taxation of Land Values took care to expel Sir John Simon, one of its vice-presidents and member of the pre-1914 Asquith administration, as soon as he denounced the Snowden proposals.[30] This League, however, was a dwindling leftover from pre-1914 days (as was the Land Nationalisation Society, still in 1932 conducted by its original 1893 secretary, Joseph Hyder), and its members could comfortably fit into a small West End restaurant for their annual meeting. There is no sign that the public cared one way or the other about Snowden's tax, even though he promised that his land valuation would become the basis for land nationalization in the future.

Within weeks this Budget debate was overtaken by the 1931 financial crisis, the resignation of the Labour Government and the formation of the predominantly Conservative National Government under Ramsay Macdonald, and the land valuation and tax was quickly shelved. It was not perhaps forgotten by everyone, but when its repeal was quietly announced by Neville Chamberlain in 1934 only a few Labour politicians protested. The landowning Labour MP, Sir Francis Acland, denounced the repeal of the 1931 taxes as 'scandalous', but rather inadvisedly revealed the weakness of the land reformers by pointing out that he was a supporter of the 1909–10 Budget who had not changed his views: 'there were six other loyal survivors, and five renegades', he said.[31] Snowden was incensed by this act of betrayal, for while the land valuation had been suspended, ostensibly as an economy measure, the land tax had been retained as a symbolic gesture – though without the valuation it could never have been collected – which Baldwin had supported as a reward for the loyal acceptance by Labour members of the National government of many deeply repugnant measures. Venting his frustration and bitterness, Snowden rounded on Ramsay Macdonald as a lickspittle, calling him 'a serf of the Tories' who would swallow any humiliation in order to stay in office.[32]

The public scarcely noticed this spat. The land question was moribund, if not completely dead. It is possible to argue, especially with the 1931 anti-climax in mind, that the land question was simply overtaken by events, by the emergency of financial crisis and the problems of mass unemployment. On the other hand, it is clear that land reform had been losing its appeal for most of the public ever since the 1913 high water mark, and this can well be explained by the partial, and often indirect or unintended, fulfilment of many of the original purposes of land reform. Thus, when after 1945 special land taxes were once again on the political agenda, the traditional objects of attack, the landed aristocracy, were well on the way to becoming part of the national heritage, and the taxes were now aimed at a new breed of property developers. When Tories like Iain Macleod in 1965 or Timothy Raison in 1975 called for the introduction of 'a tax on the appreciation of urban building land values', even though when in office they somehow never found time to do anything about it, one can be sure that the land question had definitely not returned from the dead.[33]

Notes

1. *Times*, 5 August 1914, p. 3.
2. I. Packer, *Lloyd George, Liberalism, and the Land: The Land Issue and Party Politics, 1906–1914* (Woodbridge, 2001) devotes a concluding chapter to 'The strange death of the land issue' (pp. 178–93), which has a more purely party-political explanation than the one advanced here.
3. *Times*, 7 October 1912, p. 9.
4. Land Tenure Reform Association, *Report of the Inaugural Meeting* (1871), pp. 9–10.
5. A. Offer, *Property and Politics, 1870–1914* (Cambridge, 1981), p. 394; and see below, pp. 266–7. See also B. Gilbert, 'David Lloyd George: The Reform of British Landholding and the Budget of 1914', *Historical Journal*, 22 (1978), 117–41.
6. See below, pp. 266–8.
7. *Times*, 16 December 1924, p. 15.
8. Ibid., 23 June 1926, p. 18. For Pretyman's role in 1909–14 and the formation of the Land Union, see Offer, *Property and Politics*, pp. 366–7, 382, 398; M. Fforde, *Conservatism and Collectivism, 1886–1914* (Edinburgh, 1990), pp. 110–17.
9. A. J. P. Taylor, *English History, 1914–1945* (Oxford, 1965), p. 286; C. L. Mowat, *Britain between the Wars, 1918–1940* (London, 1955), pp. 368, 379, 419.
10. C. F. G. Masterman, *The New Liberalism* (London, 1920), pp. 163–4, quoted in K. O. Morgan, *The Age of Lloyd George* (London, 1971), pp. 208–9.

11. *Land and Liberty*, 1 August 1920, pp. 454–5, quoted in A. Taylor, *Lords of Misrule* (Basingstoke, 2004), p. 63.
12. Packer, *Lloyd George, Liberalism and the Land*, ch. 10. The earlier account by R. Douglas, *Land, People, and Politics: A History of the Land Question in the United Kingdom, 1878–1952* (London, 1976) presents a narrative of a continuous land question which never dies.
13. *Times*, 11 November 1913, p. 9.
14. F. M. L. Thompson, 'The Land Market in the Nineteenth Century', *Oxford Economic Papers*, n.s. 9 (1957), 304–8; idem, *English Landed Society in the Nineteenth Century* (London, 1963), pp. 318–25; H. J. Habakkuk, *Marriage, Debt and the Estates System; English Landownership, 1650–1950* (Oxford, 1994), ch. 8; J. V. Beckett, *The Aristocracy in England, 1660–1914* (Oxford, 1986), ch. 14.
15. S. G. Sturmey, 'Owner-Farming in England and Wales, 1900–50', *Manchester School of Economic and Social Studies*, 23 (1955), 246–68; Thompson, *English Landed Society*, pp. 332–5. The issue of the scale of these land transfers is examined in more detail in J. Beckett and M. Turner, 'End of the Old Order? F. M. L. Thompson, the Land Question, and the Burden of Ownership in England, *c.* 1880–1925', *Agricultural History Review*, 55 (2007), 269–88 and F. M. L. Thompson, 'The Land Market, 1880–1925: A Reappraisal Reappraised', ibid., 289–300.
16. *Hansard*, 5th ser., 118 (22 July 1919), col. 1198; ibid., 187 (3 Aug. 1925), col. 983. Later still, as Lord Halifax, Wood was Viceroy of India, and then Foreign Secretary at the time of Munich.
17. On this process, see, in addition to the works cited in notes 14 and 15, A. Adonis, 'Aristocracy, Agriculture and Liberalism: The Politics, Finances and Estates of the Third Lord Carrington', *Historical Journal*, 31 (1988), 871–97; P. Barnes, *Norfolk Landowners since 1880* (Norwich, 1993), ch. 4; D. Cannadine, *The Decline and Fall of the British Aristocracy* (New Haven, 1990), pp. 103–12; H. A. Clemenson, *English Country Houses and Landed Estates* (London, 1982), pp. 109–50; P. Mandler, *The Fall and Rise of the Stately Home* (New Haven, 1997), ch. 6; D. Spring, 'Land and Politics in Edwardian England', *Agricultural History*, 58 (1984), 17–42; F. M. L. Thompson, 'English Landed Society in the Twentieth Century, I: Property, Collapse and Survival', *Transactions of the Royal Historical Society*, 5th ser., 40 (1990), 1–24.
18. I. Dale (ed.), *Labour Party General Election Manifestos, 1900–1997* (London, 2000), p. 36.
19. 50th AGM and conference of the Land Nationalization Society: *Times*, 30 March 1931, p. 18.
20. *The Land Hunger: Life under Monopoly* (London, 1913), pp. 23, 200, 231.
21. *Times*, 20 May 1922, p. 17: leader on 'Law and the Land', which rightly noted that the public did not seem to realize the radical nature of Birkenhead's measure which would enable land to be transferred 'without the intolerable prolixity and complications of even our improved system of conveyancing'.
22. An annual meeting of the Land Law Reform Association was last reported in *The Times* on 18 March 1909 (p. 8) though it was still listed in the 1919 *Constitutional Yearbook for 1919* (p. 474), but not, apparently, in any further annual reference books: J. Campbell, *F. E. Smith, First Earl of Birkenhead*

(London, 1983), pp. 485–6. Strict settlements and entails were not abolished, as 'free trade in land' had desired, but were uncoupled from the fee simple ownership by ensuring that full legal ownership of all land vested in a trustee. Compulsory registration of title also had to be fudged because of solicitors' resistance: it had been introduced for the London County Council area in 1897, but provision for its gradual extension county by county was postponed for ten years in the 1925 Act, and by 1939, only Middlesex and Croydon had adopted it. Not until the 1950s was the Law Society bought off by an agreement that solicitors should be paid the same fee for conveyancing of registered and unregistered land.

23. *Times*, 7 December 1925, p. 16: 'The New Acts Explained'.
24. I. Dale (ed.), *Liberal Party General Election Manifestos, 1900–1997* (London, 2000), pp. 37–8, 45.
25. M. Dawson, 'The Liberal Land Policy, 1924–29', *Twentieth Century British History*, 2 (1991), 272–90. The pre-1914 Land Enquiry had been financed by official Liberal party funds, whose origin, however, in the sale of honours was no different from that of the 'tarnished' Lloyd George Fund of the 1920s, or indeed of that of Tory Party funds: see Lord Selborne's House of Lords Motion on Party Funds, *Times*, 24 February 1914, p. 12 ('a duke is just as indispensable to Mr George as a mother-in-law is to the editor of a comic paper... just as the fictitious proceedings attributed to dukes are the basis of Mr George's speeches, so the actual contributions of those who want to be dukes are the basis of his organization').
26. *Times*, 18 September 1925, p. 13: 'An Obsolete Policy'.
27. *Times*, 1 March 1926, pp. 14, 20.
28. *Hansard*, 5th ser., 254 (24 June 1931), cols. 537–42, Snowden proposed a graduated tax with a minimum rate of 1/8d in the £ on fully developed land.
29. P. Snowden, *An Autobiography* (London, 1934), p. 915.
30. *Times*, 5 June 1931, p. 16. Simon left the Liberal party shortly after this, and formed the National Liberal party, supporting Macdonald's National Government.
31. *Times*, 6 June 1934, p. 14.
32. *Times*, 4 July 1934, p. 14; Snowden, *Autobiography*, p. 919.
33. *Times*, 5 January 1965, p. 5 and 5 December 1975, p. 4.

Index

Note: The locators following the letter 'n' denote the note numbers.

Abergavenny, marquis of, 227
Acland, Francis (politician), 265, 267
Addison, Christopher (politician), 244, 247
Agricultural Holdings Act
  1883, 9–10, 103
  1906, 192
Agricultural Land (Utilisation) Act (1931), 243
Agricultural Output of England and Wales (1927), 228
agriculture
  attitudes of farmers and landowners, 7, 95–6
  depression, 187–8, 220–1, 261
  Ireland, 7, 129–30
  labour party, 242–3
  owner-occupation, 245
  productivity, 62
  progressive, 25–32, 96
  rent, 77
  Royal Commission (1894–97), 221, 225
  Scotland, 7, 109, 117
  tenants, 50
  Wales, 7, 93–6
Agriculture Act (1947), 256n76
Agriculture, Board of, 224
Aldridge, Henry (land reformer), 212
Alfred the Great, 43, 59–60
Alison, Archibald (writer), 29–30
Allingham, Helen (artist), 194
Allotment Act
  1887, 191
  1907, 191–2
allotments, 10, 12n29, 40, 45, 57, 75, 183–8, 191–3, 201
Allotments and Smallholding Association, 193
America, 9, 85–6, 131, 151, 202, 204
Ancaster, earl of, 3, 221
An English Autumn Afternoon (1852–55), 33
Anglesey, marquis of, 227
Anglo-French Trade Treaty (1859), 150
Anti Corn Law League (ACLL), 4, 10, 63, 66, 74–88, 152
  and Chartism, 75
Arch, Joseph (politician), 147
Argyll, Duke of, 17n22, 111–12
aristocracy
  defence of land, 111–12
  landholding, 2–3, 110–11, 169–71
  land sales, 219–33
  political outlook, 97
  power base, 4–5, 83–5, 231–2
  radical hostility towards, 38–9, 62, 66–7, 74–6, 80–3, 149–62, 174–5, 177, 201, 205, 214–15, 261
  'theft' of land, 60–1, 65, 202, 242–3, 259
Arnold, Arthur (politician), 151, 191
Aronson, Hugh (author), 189
Ashbourne, Lord, 138
Ash, Kent, 41
Ashton under Lyne, 63
Ashworth, H. (ACLL activist), 78
Asquith, H. H. (politician), 172, 257, 267
Astley-Corbett, Sir Francis (landowner), 225
Attlee, Clement (politician), 243
Austen, Jane (author), 41
Austin, Alfred (author), 181
Australia, 202
  Land question in, 165n59

Bairstow, Jonathan (police informant), 59
Baldwin, Stanley (politician), 267
Balfour, Arthur (politician), 118, 139–40, 171, 187, 188
Baner Ac Amserau Cymru, 98, 101, 102
Barham, Richard (author), 37, 48
Barnett, Canon Samuel, 203
Barrell, John (art historian), 20–1
Bateman, John, 2, 51n4, 110, 168, 220
Bateson, F. W. (author), 248
Bathurst, Charles, (politician), 186
Beal, James (auctioneer), 85
Beaufort, duke of, 221
Beaumont, Lord, 221
Beckett, John, V., 12, 14, 214
Bedford, Duke of, 2–3, 110, 170, 171–2, 176, 221, 227
Begg, Rev. James, 119
Benet, J. (politician), 44
Beresford, Kathryn, 5, 11
Bermingham, Anne (art historian), 21
Bew, Paul (historian), 94
Birmingham Political Union, 46
Black Book, John Wade's (1820), 60
Blackwood's Magazine, 5
Bonar Law, Andrew (politician), 187
Booth, Charles (social investigator), 204
Booth, William (Salvation Army), 204
Bowkett, Thomas (Chartist), 68
Boyne, viscount, 3
Bradlaugh, Charles (politician), 159, 202
Brideshead Revisited, 232
Bright, John (politician), 6, 66, 76, 82, 86, 87, 152, 261
British Yeoman and Rural Gazette, The, 43
Broadhurst, Henry (politician), 172
Broderick, G. C. (politician), 191
Brougham, Henry (politician), 84
Brown, Ford Madox (author), 33
Buccleuch, duke of, 3, 110, 122
Buckinghamshire, 225
building societies, 4, 59, 68–70, 169
Bullingdon Green, Oxford, 29, 31
Bull, Philip, 7
Burchardt, Jeremy (historian), 45
Burns, John (politician), 174, 204, 207–8
Bute, marquess of, 3
Butt, Isaac (politician), 130–1, 135, 142
Buxton, Noel (politician), 246, 258
Byng, John (diarist), 28

Cadbury, George (philanthropist), 212
Cadogan, earl, 170, 171
Cadogan estate, 174–5, 178
Caird, James (politician), 85
Cambridge, University of
  Royal Commission (1922), 231
Cameron, Ewen, A., 9
Campbell-Bannerman, Sir Henry, 152, 174, 192, 195, 207, 212
Campbell, George (author), 133
Canterbury Magazine, The, 43
Cardiganshire, 95, 221
Carlisle, Lord, 221
Carlyle, Thomas (author), 43
Carmarthenshire, 95
Carnarvonshire, 95, 97
Carrington, Lord, 195, 221
Catholic Association, 49
Catholicism, 8, 48–9, 60, 99–100, 128–30, 136, 141–3
Cawdor, earl, 96
Central Chambers of Agriculture, 184
Central Unemployed Body, 203–5
Chamberlain, Austen (politician), 186, 226
Chamberlain, Joseph (politician), 86, 87n8, 154
Chamberlain, Neville (politician), 267
Chambers, John (historian), 19
Charter, The, 69
Chartist Land Company, 6
Chartists, 3–4, 15n20, 57–70, 261
  ACLL, 75
  Land Plan, 65–70, 82
  National Convention (1839), 64
Chase, Malcolm, 3
Cholmondeley Lord, 221
Christianity and Social Order (1942), 249
Churchill, Lord Randolph (politician), 172

Churchill, Winston (politician), 206
Church of England, 38, 97, 127, 137, 147–8
  church land, 63–4, 66–7
  Disestablishment of, 99–100, 137, 139, 148
  as landowner, 65, 67, 169, 183
Clare, John (poet), 20, 22n14–15
Clarion, 238
Clark, G. B. (politician), 110
Clerical Disabilities Act (1871), 148
Clynes, J. R. (trades unionist), 244
Cobbett, William (author), 38, 39, 40, 43–4, 46–7, 48, 49, 50, 51, 63
Cobden Club, 86, 87, 258
Cobden, Richard (politician), 4–6, 10–11, 74–88, 258, 261, 265
  legacy, 146–62
Coke, Thomas (landowner), 128
Cole, G. D. H. (historian), 243
Colley, Linda (historian), 41
Collings, Jesse (politician), 11, 188, 189
Collini, Stefan (historian), 147
Combe, George (phrenologist), 89
commercial property, 168–9, 175–7
common land, 11–12, 19–34, 61, 63, 65–7, 195
Commons Preservation Society, 6, 33
Common Wealth Party, 249
Congested Districts Board (1897), 114–15
Connacht, 95
Conner, William (landowner), 129, 131
Conservative party, 43–4, 103–4, 231–2
  defence of landed property, 1, 6–7, 152–3, 185–90
  and Georgism, 11
  and Ireland, 137–43, 260
  and land question, 182–90, 232–3, 260
  and patriotism, 194
  and Scotland, 117
  and taxation, 208–9
Constable, John (artist), 20–1, 29, 41
Cooper, Thomas (Chartist), 35n20
Corbett, H., 98
Corn Production Act (1917), 265
Cosway, Sir William (landowner), 48
Cragoe, Matthew, 8, 87
Crawford, Sharman (politician), 83, 129, 131–2, 134–5
crofters, 109–22
Crofters' War (Scotland), 9, 109, 111, 114
Croft, Henry Page (politician), 186
Crome, John (artist), 23, 25–6, 30
crown lands, 64, 65, 169, 178
Curtis, L. P. (historian), 139
Cymru Fydd, 108n72

Daily News, 77, 101
Dallas, George (trades unionist), 242
Darnley, Lord, 49
Daunton, Martin (historian), 167
Davenport, Allen (Spencean), 3, 62
Davidoff, Leonore (historian), 41
Davies, Emil (author), 243
Davitt, Michael (politician), 102, 111, 121–2
Declaration of the Rights of the People (1839), 64
Delane, J. T. (editor), 86
Denmark, 185
depopulation, 11, 182, 187–8, 197, 202, 259
Derby, earl of, 146
Devon, 45
Dickens, Charles, 40
Dickinson, W. H. (politician), 175
Disraeli, Benjamin (politician), 43
Ditchfield, P. H. (writer), 181
Donegal, 129
Douglas, Roy (historian), 1
Doyle, Christopher (Chartist), 63–4
Drysdale, George (radical), 86
Duchy of Cornwall, 228
Dudley, earl of, 3
Dulwich College, 169, 178
Dunmore, earl of, 187
Durham miners, 152
Dyck, Ian (historian), 39
Dyos, Jim (historian), 167
Dysart, earl of, 227

Eastwell Park estate, Kent, 227
Economist, The, 77
Edinburgh, 119–22
Ellis, Tom (politician), 92, 102–3
emigration, 40, 85, 115–16, 202, 204, 239–40
enclosure, 11–12, 19–34, 61, 143, 156, 189, 194–5, 202
Englander, David (historian), 167
England, Ireland and America (1835), 82
English Land Restoration League, 14, 160, 173
English League for the Taxation of Land Values, 267
Englishness, 41–2
  'Freeborn Englishman', 154–8
  landscape, 19, 40–1, 181–2
  regional attributes, 47–9
  urbanization, 44
entail, law of, 3, 4, 12, 57, 66, 75–85, 90n63, 116, 154, 225n22
Errington, George (author), 134
Escrick Park estate, 225
Essays on the Nature and Principles of Taste (1791), 29–30
Essays on Reform (1867), 149
Essex, 203–4
Estates Gazette, 219–20, 224, 226–35
Eton School, 169
Evans, Dorothy (author), 243
eviction, 94–5, 99, 100–2, 113–16

Fabians, 244, 246, 248, 249
Farmers, 79, 80, 97, 102, 128–30, 131–2, 139–41, 205, 248, 263
Farmers' Alliance, 9
Fels, Joseph (businessman), 203, 204
Fenianism, 135–7
Finance Act (1919), 226
food, 4, 5, 37, 42, 51, 59, 63–4, 74, 156, 224, 245–52
Forster, E. M. (novelist), 177
Forster, William (politician), 86
Forward, 110
Foster, Sir Walter (land reformer), 193
Fox, William J., 76
France, 89–90, 184, 193
Freehold land societies, 5
free trade, 74–88
Froude, J. A. (historian), 183

Gainsborough, Lincs, 23–5
Gainsborough, Thomas (artist), 20–1
Gaitskell, Hugh (politician), 252
Game Laws, 1, 6, 9, 76–7, 80, 86, 112, 117, 121, 170
Garden City movement, 211–14
Gee, Thomas (publisher), 102
general elections
  1868, 87, 95, 100, 148, 171
  1892, 173
  1895, 173
  1906, 174, 196n20
  1910 (January), 187, 188
  1922, 264
  1945, 248, 250
  1950, 251
  1951, 251
  1983, 252
George, Henry (author), 11, 78, 111–12, 122, 146–7, 153–4, 156, 158–62, 168, 174, 203, 238–9, 258–60
  Progress and Poverty (1880), 11, 112, 159, 168, 206
  Protection or Free Trade (1886), 161
George, Henry Jr. (land reformer), 160
Georgeites, 13, 62, 112–13, 146–7, 152, 159–62, 206–11
Gerard, Lord, 227
Germany, 193
Gibson, Thomas Milner (radical), 84
Gladstone, William Ewart (politician), 7–9, 87, 100, 103, 133–6, 172–3
Glamorganshire, 93
Glasgow, 119–22, 176, 206
Glasier, James Bruce (author), 242
Gleig, Rev. G. R., 41, 45
Gooch, Edwin (trades unionist), 248, 252
Gould, F. Carruthers (cartoonist), 190–1
Green, E. H. H. (historian), 182
Greg, H. R. (ACLL activist), 78
Griffith, John, 'Y Gohebydd' (journalist), 101

Griffiths, Clare, 14
Grosvenor Estate, London, 169, 173, 175
Grosvenor, R. W. (politician), 171
Ground Game Act (1880), 9
Gwydir estate, 221

Hadleigh Farm Colony, 204
Hall, Catherine (historian), 41
Hamilton, duke of, 110–11, 121, 122
Hammond, J. L. and Barbara (historians), 11, 156, 194, 195
Hampstead Heath, 33
Hancock, Neilson (economist), 83
Harcourt, Sir William (politician), 175
Hardie, J. Keir (politician), 122, 202–3, 237
Hardwicke, Lord, 221
Hardy, Thomas (author), 181
Hargreaves, William (free trader), 86, 91n64
Harney, George Julian (Chartist), 62, 66
Harrow School, 169
Harvie, Christopher (historian), 147, 162
Harwood, George (politician), 193
Haymaking, Osney Meadow, 18
Helsinger, E. K. (historian), 39
Highlander, 110
Hill, Christopher (historian), 60
Hill, Lord George, 128
Hill, Octavia (social reformer), 177
Hill, William (Chartist), 61
Hirst, Francis (journalist), 148
History, uses of, 42, 127–8, 153–8, 189–90, 243, 259
Hobhouse, L. T. (intellectual), 196
Hobson, J. A. (intellectual), 196
Hodges, Thomas Law (politician), 49
Holland, 185
Hollesley Bay Estate, 203, 204
Holyake, George (radical), 151
Hood, Sir Alexander Acland (politician), 152–3
Hope, George (farmer), 79
Hoppen, K. T. (historian), 104
housing
  rural, 3, 41, 50, 57–8, 183–4, 193n55, 223
  urban, 13, 119–22, 173–8, 193–4, 207, 211–15, 241–2, 247, 251–2
Housing Act (1909), 213
Hovel, Mark (historian), 58
Howard, Ebenezer (journalist), 211
Howe, Anthony, 4, 164n33
Howell, David (historian), 94, 95
Howell, George (trades unionist), 158
Howitt, William (author), 5
Hunter, James (historian), 113
Hyde, Ralph (historian), 168
Hyder, Joseph (land reformer), 242–3, 267
Hypothec, 116

Iffley, Oxon, 26
Independent Labour Party (ILP), 239, 240–1
Ingolsby Legends (1836), 37
Inland Revenue, 209
Ireland, 1, 7, 15, 60, 82–3, 165n43, 168, 260–1
  Congested Districts Board (1891), 140
  Devon Commission (1845), 129–30
  Disestablishment, 137, 139–40, 148
  Dudley Commission, 143
  Encumbered Estates Act, 93
  Famine, 93–5, 130–1
  farming conditions in, 110, 126–43, 149–50, 221, 261, 263
  farming conditions in, cf. Scotland, 113–15, 127
  farming conditions in, cf. Wales, 92–105
  home rule, 138, 261
  Irish Freehold Land Society, 82
  Irish land League, 136–7
  Irish Tenant Right League, 82–3
  Land Act (1870), 7–8, 134–6, 137–8
  Land Act (1881), 8, 102, 114, 135–7
  land system in, 127
  nationalism, 110–11, 135–7, 181

Purchase of Land Act (Ashbourne Act, 1885), 9, 138–9
religion, 130, 136, 140–3
Wyndham Land Act (1903), 139, 142
Ivanhoe (1819), 43

John Bull, 5, 47
Johnston, Thomas (editor), 110
Jones, Ernest (Chartist), 60, 64, 147
Jones, Rev. Michael D. (politician), 104

Kay, Joseph (author), 81, 191
Kent, 37–51, 227
Kenworthy, J. M. (politician), 263
King, Peter Locke (politician), 150
Kinloss, Lady, 225
Knatchbull, Sir Edward (politician), 49
Kumar, Krishan (historian), 181

Labouchere, Henry (politician), 202
labourers, 10, 38–40, 44, 45, 74, 84–5, 117, 188–9, 193, 203–4, 229, 265
in art, 21
Irish, 46
Labourer's Friend Society, 44–5
Labour party, 14, 110, 185n23, 223–4, 231–2, 237–53
Laindon, Essex, 203
land colonies, 202–6, 208
Land and Labour League, 202
Land Law Reform Association, 264
landlordism, 1, 5, 8, 11, 12, 15, 60, 80–3, 87, 110, 121, 128–9, 137–40, 183, 190–7, 214, 230, 239–42, 263–4
landlord-tenant relations, 8, 48, 79, 93–4, 97–8, 113–16, 128–30, 131–2
in towns, 211
Land Nationalisation (1892), 242
Land Nationalisation Society, 14, 177, 212, 242–3, 263, 267
Land and the National Planning of Agriculture (1932), 241
Land and Nation League, 266
landowners
absenteeism, 93
London, 167–71
number, 81, 93
sales, 116, 138–9, 219–33, 259
scale of holdings, 2–3
landscape, 19–34, 40–1, 43, 49, 98–9
Land Tenure Reform Association, 5, 13, 82, 87
Lansbury, George (politician), 203–5, 215–16
Lansdowne, Lord, 186–7
Lattimore, Charles (farmer), 79, 84
Lavergne, Leonce de (author), 81
Law of Property Act (1925), 231, 264n22
Leasehold Enfranchisement Act (1967), 196
Leasehold Enfranchisement Association, 172, 211
Lee, Abraham (Chartist), 65
Leeds, duke of, 221, 227
Letchworth, 211, 212
Let us Face the Future (1945), 250
Lever, William Hesketh (landowner), 113–14, 212
Lewis, island of, 111, 113–14
Liberal party
England, 9–10
history, use of, 11–12
Ireland, 126–43, 260
landownership in, 172, 201
land question, 190–6
owner-occupation, 245
Scotland, 9, 109–22
taxation policy, 201–15, 221–3
Wales, 9, 97–105
Lincolnshire, 225
General View of Agriculture in (1794), 24
Lindert, Peter (historian), 168
Linton, William, J. (engraver), 61–2
Liverpool, 60, 172
Lloyd George, David (politician), 206, 208–10, 264–7
Finance Act (1910), 223
Land Campaign (1913), 12, 13, 14, 74, 176, 182, 187, 192–6, 213–14, 223–4, 232, 257–60

Lloyd George, David (politician) – *continued*
Land Campaign (1926), 259, 266
Lloyd George Fund, 266
London, 174–7
People's Budget (1909), 78, 158, 174, 186, 192, 208–10, 223, 258
Lloyd's Weekly Register, 69
Local Government Act (1894), 201
Local Government Board, 203–8, 213
Londesborough, Lord, 224
London, 167–78, 206
Equalisation of Rates Act (1894), 173
estates in, 167–71
Land Nationalisation Committee, 246
leases, 171–8
metropolitan improvements, 172–3
London County Council, 169, 173, 174, 175, 206–7, 270n22
Londonderry, marquis of, 3
London Municipal Reform League, 173
London Poor Law (1906), 205
London School Board, 173
London Working Men's Association, 69
Long, Walter (politician), 184
Lords, House of, 158, 208–9
Lowther, Claude (politician), 188
Lyrical Ballads (1802), 29

MacDonald, J. Ramsay (politician), 267–8
Mackie, John (farmer), 245
Macleod, Iain (politician), 268
Maidstone Gazette, 45, 49
Maidstone Journal, 46
Maitland, Frederic (historian), 154
Malthusianism, 62–3
Manchester Examiner, 151
'Manchester School', The, 4, 74–88
Mandler, Peter (historian), 53n35, 75
Manton, Kevin (historian), 238
Marlborough, duke of, 227
Marshall, Arthur (economist), 204
Martin, David (historian), 162
masculinity, 41–4, 46–7, 49–51
Masterman, C. F. G., 212, 259–60, 265
Matheson, Jardine, 113–14
Maylands estate, 204
McDougall, Peter (surgeon), 63
McHugh, Edward (land reformer), 111
Merioneth, 95, 99
Methodists, 63
Metropolitan Board of Works, 33
middle classes, 4, 41, 45, 87, 99, 146–62
as tenants, 172–4
Middlesex, 270n22
Middleton, Lord, 226
Miller, Thomas (poet), 6, 22–5, 27, 33–4
Mill, John Stuart (philosopher and politician), 13, 67, 75, 82, 87, 131, 133, 140, 160, 171, 258, 261
Milner, Lord, 186
Committee on Land (1912–14), 187
miners, 121–2, 241
Mingay, Gordon (historian), 19
Mitchell, John (politician), 142
Mitford, Mary Russell (author), 35n12
Monmouthshire, 221
Morgan-Grenville, Richard (landowner), 225
Morning Star, 97, 150
Morrison, Herbert (politician), 250–1
Mousehold Heath, Norwich, 23, 25
Mousley, Thomas (land agent), 96
Mowat, C. L. (historian), 259
Murdoch, John (editor), 110
Murray, Harry S. (land activist), 160

National Agricultural Labourers' Union, 147
National Agricultural Union, 183–4
National Association for the Organization of Trade, 67
National Charter Association, 59–60, 63, 64–5, 67
National Housing Reform Council, 212
national identity, 181
nationalisation of land, 14, 67–9, 70, 75, 110, 195, 241–53
nationalism
in Ireland, 110, 135–7, 141–2
and the land question, 9, 181
in Wales, 8, 97–104

National Trust, 58, 232
National Union of Agricultural Workers, 239, 248
Neesom, Charles (radical), 62
Newcastle, duke of, 221
New Liberals, 196, 211–14
Newman, J. R. B. (politician), 188
New Poor Law (1834), 41
Nonconformity, 10, 96–100, 147–9
Norfolk, 47, 170, 221–2
'Norman Yoke', 3, 43, 59–62, 157, 162, 202
Northampton, marquesses of, 171, 227, 232
Northcote, Sir Stafford (politician), 138
Northern Liberator, 59, 61
Northern Star, 61, 62
Northumberland, duke of, 227
Nostalgia, 5–6, 19–34
Nottinghamshire, 226

O'Brien, Bronterre (Chartist), 61, 63, 67–8, 69, 75
O'Connell, Daniel (politician), 60, 131–2, 142
O'Connor, Feargus (Chartist), 57, 58, 63, 67, 68
  and Land Plan, 3, 64, 75
O'Donohue, The (landowner), 147
Offer, Avner (historian), 167
O'Grada, Cormac (historian), 93
Oldcastle, Geoffrey (journalist), 43, 47
Old Corruption, 3, 59–63
'Old England', 5, 37–51, 183
O'Leary, Paul (historian), 99–100
Onslow, earl of, 186
  Land & Glebe Owners' Association, 183–4
open fields, 19–32
Open Spaces Society (formerly CPS), 33
Orme, Stanley (Labour activist), 237
Orwin, C. S. (economist), 248–9
Osney Meadow, 26, 30, 31
Ottmoor, 27, 30
Our Village (1832), 35n12
Outhwaite, R. L. (land reformer), 170
Owen, Robert (socialist), 63, 202
Oxfordshire, 20, 25–34
Oxford, University of, 147–9, 169
  Royal Commission (1922), 231

Packer, Ian, 13, 168, 176, 260
parish councils, 12, 191–2, 201
Parker, Gilbert (politician), 188
Parnell, Charles Stewart, 8, 136
Parry, J. P. (historian), 196
Passy, Hippolyte (author), 81
Past & Present (1843), 43
paternalism, 37–8, 44–5, 77, 93–7
patriotism, 5, 11, 12, 141, 181–97
Payne, Christiana (art historian), 26
Pears, Mark (landowner), 178
peasant proprietors, 80–2, 96, 128, 186–7
Peel, Sir Robert (politician), 79, 89n31
Pembroke, Lord, 225, 227
Penenden Heath, 48
Penrhyn, Lord, 97
Pickwick Papers, The (1837), 37
Pim, Jonathan (Quaker), 83
Poor Law, 203
Poor Man's Guardian, 68
Portman, viscount, 170
Portmeadow, 27–8, 30
Potter, Thomas B. (free trader), 86
Prentice, Archibald (historian), 78
Preston, Thomas (radical), 62, 69
Pretyman, E. G. (politician), 186, 259
primogeniture, 4, 47, 61, 66n20, 75, 90n63, 150, 154, 159, 191, 231, 263–4
  abolition of (1925), 231
Principles of Political Economy (1848), 67
property market, 14, 66, 113–14, 219–33, 262
  free trade in, 77–8, 86–7, 151–2, 191, 264n22
  speculation, 13, 193–4
Protestantism, 60, 114, 142
protest movements
  Crofters' War, 114
  Swing Riots, 40

Prothero, Rowland [Lord Ernle] (land agent), 176, 221, 224
Pusey, Philip (politician), 83, 98

Quinault, Roland, 13, 206

race, 43
railways, 32, 115, 160
  companies, 160, 177
Raison, Timothy (politician), 268
Raymond, Paul (landowner), 178
Readman, Paul, 11
Rebecca Riots, 107n42
recreation, 31
Reeder, David (historian), 167
Reform Acts
  1832, 39, 49
  1867, 87, 149
  1884–85, 102, 158, 185, 261
  1918, 261
Reform League, 147
resettlement schemes, 203–4
Return of the Owners of Land (1876), 2, 6–7, 110, 168, 190, 220
Reynolds's Newspaper, 153, 154
Ricardo, David (economist), 76
Richard, Rev. Henry (politician), 97–9, 100
Richardson, Reginald (Chartist), 71n15
Rickmansworth, Chartist settlement, 82
Ripon, earl of, 221
Roberts, Rev. Samuel (author), 98
Robson, Sir William (attorney general), 207
Rodney, earl, 221
Rogers, J. E. Thorold (author), 6, 10–11, 15, 86, 146–62
  British Citizen, The (1885), 157
  Cobden and Modern Political opinion (1873), 152
  Economic Interpretation of History, The (1888), 158
  Six Centuries of Work and Wages (1884), 156, 158
Rosenthal, Michael (art historian), 21
Ross, 114
Rowntree, Joseph (philanthropist), 194, 212
Rowntree, Seebohm (philanthropist), 213
Royal Commission on Land in Wales and Monmouth (1892), 9, 93, 97, 103–5
Royal Historical Society, 15
rural idyll, 40–1, 194–5
Rural Rides (1822–26), 38
Ruskin, John (intellectual), 33
Russia, 85, 246, 262
Rutland, 45
Rutland, duke of, 227

Salisbury, Lord (politician), 171, 172, 182, 184, 185
Saye and Sele, Lord, 221
Scotland, 1, 9, 60, 79, 80, 93, 97, 109–22, 168, 260–1
  Board/Department of Agriculture, 113, 118
  Crofters' Act (1886), 15, 17n24, 114, 118, 196
  Deasy's Act (1860), 135
  farming conditions, 109
  Highland land question, 113–16
  landownership in, 3, 7, 170
  Land Settlement (Scotland) Act (1919), 116
  Lowland land question, 116–19
  Royal Commissions on (1881), 117
  Royal Commissions on (1896), 110, 117
  Small Landholders Act (1911), 115–16, 118, 119
  urban land question, 119–22
Scott, Adam (author), 78
Scottish Home Rule Association (1886), 9, 116
Scottish Land and Property Federation (1906), 119, 121–2
Scottish Land Restoration League, 111, 113
Scott, Sir Walter (author), 43, 48
Selborne, Lord, 186, 187n25
Self, Peter (sociologist), 244
Settled Estates Act (1881), 12, 225
Shiel, Richard Lalor, 49

Silkin, Lewis (politician), 250
Simon, Sir John, 267
Skye, 114–16
Slater, Gilbert (historian), 11, 194, 195
Slums, 12, 119–20, 193
Smallholdings, 11, 38–9, 80–2, 142–3, 156, 185–90, 193, 197, 241
  Act of 1902, 184, 185
  Act of 1907, 182, 185, 192, 195–6, 201
  Departmental Committee, 186, 1905–6
  See also crofters
Smith, Adam (economist), 77, 82, 160
Smith W. H. (politician), 171
Snowden, Philip (politician), 240, 258, 267–8
Social Democratic Federation, 154
Socialism, 203, 237–53
Solkin, David (art historian), 21
South African War (1899–1902), 188, 197
Southampton, Lord, 221
Spencer, Herbert (intellectual), 159
Spence, Thomas (radical), 3, 69, 261
  followers of (Spenceans), 62–3, 67, 69–70, 202
sport, 110
Stamford Mercury, 24
Stanhope, Philip, 4th earl, 39, 45, 46
Stanley, W. O. (politician), 101
Stanton Harcourt, 27
Stapely, John (farmer), 48
Steel-Maitland, Arthur (historian), 188
Steere, F. W. (town planner), 212
Stoke Rochford Hall estate, Lincs, 235n35
Storing, Herbert (sociologist), 244
Stowe estate, 225–6
Strabolgi, Lord, 263
strikes, 64–5
St. Thomas' Hospital, 169
Stubbs, William (historian), 154
suburbs, 24, 33, 173, 178, 211, 213, 250
Suffolk, 170
Surrey, 40, 84, 212
Surtees, R. S. (author), 40
Sussex, 40, 84–5
Sutherland, dukes of, 2, 110n14, 227
Swing riots, 40, 44–6
Sybil (1845), 43

Tackley, 28
tariff reform, 161, 186, 205, 260
Tate Gallery, 20
taxation, 240, 258–60, 266
  income tax, 78, 208
  Increment Value Duty, 78, 158, 174, 186, 192, 208–10, 223, 258
  Land Tax, 78
  land value taxation, 4, 13–14, 193–4, 197, 264
  rates, 171–4, 206–9
  single tax, 110, 146–62, 206
  site value rating, 206–8, 210
Taxes on Knowledge, 84
Taylor, Antony, 10, 86
Taylor, Christopher (art historian), 19
Taylor, A. J. P. (historian), 259
Temple, William (Archbishop of Canterbury), 249
Tenant Right, 7–8, 82–3, 93, 98, 101, 104–5, 117, 132–7
Thompson, F. M. L., 15, 38–9, 85–6, 214
Thompson, Thomas Perronet (Benthamite), 76
Thompson, William (housing reformer), 212
Thomson, James (poet), 30
Tichaelar, Michael (historian), 238
Times, The, 65, 82, 86, 151, 173, 219, 224, 225–6, 257–60, 264–5
Tintern Abbey, 221
Tithe War (Wales), 8, 9, 102
Tollemache, Lord, 183, 221
Tosh, John (historian), 41
town planning, 211–13, 247, 250
Town Tenants League, 175
Toynbee Hall, 203
Tractarianism, 148
Trevelyan, Charles (politician), 152
Trevelyan, Sir George (politician), 173
Turner, Ben (politician), 243
Turner J. M. W. (artist), 30–2, 41n24
Turner, Michael, 12, 14, 214

Turner, William (of Oxford), 6, 22, 25–30, 33–4
Turnor, Christopher (landowner), 189

Ulster, 95, 260
Ulster Custom, 129, 130, 132, 134–5, 136
Unemployed Workmen Act (1905), 203, 205
unemployment, 13, 202–6, 215, 239, 243, 260, 266
Unionist Social Reform Committee, 186–8
Unwin, T. Fisher (publisher), 148
urbanization, 12, 44, 64, 202, 211–14

Vaughan, William E. (historian), 94
Verinder, Frederick (land reformer), 159
villages, 10, 12n26, 40, 75, 84, 157, 183, 187, 189, 191–2
Villiers, C. P. (politician), 76
Vincent, John (lawyer), 102

Waites, Ian, 6, 8, 11
Wales, 7, 48, 260–1
  Land League, 102, 223
  landowners in, 93–7, 225
  nationalism in, 97–105
  peasant mentality, 95–6
  political oppression in, 95, 99
  relations between landlords and tenants, 96–7, 99–100
  religion in, 96, 100
  urban areas, 172
  compared with Ireland, 93–5, 99–100, 101, 105
Walker, R. B. (trades unionist), 239
Wallace, Alfred Russell (naturalist), 112–13, 242
Waller, Philip (historian), 167
Walsh, Stephen (politician), 259
Wantage, Lord, 183
War, First World
  impact on land question, 176, 210, 214, 232, 257, 260
  War Agricultural Executive Committees, 247
Warwick, countess of, 227
Waugh, Evelyn, 232
Webb, Sidney, 173
Wedgwood, Josiah, 14, 15, 206, 239–40, 245, 258, 260
Wenlock, Lord, 225
Westminster, Duke of, 2–3, 110, 169–70, 171, 173, 175
Westmoreland, Lord, 221
Wheatley, John (politician), 120
Whichwood Forest (1809), 31–2
Wiener, Martin, 181, 238
Williams, J. E. (trades unionist), 240
Williamson, Tom (historian), 21
Wilson, Harold, 126
Wilson, Richard, 20
Wilson, Sir Thomas Maryon–, 33
Wilton, Lord, 221
Winchilsea
  10th Earl, 49, 51
  12th Earl, 183, 224
Wint, Peter de, 25
Wollaton Hall, Notts, 226
Wolstonecraft, Mary, 62
Woodbine, William, 43, 47
Wood, Edward (politician), 262
Wordsworth, William, 29
working classes, 6, 10, 22–5, 58, 66, 119–20, 156, 172–4, 202, 207, 211–14, 237–53
Wyndham, George, 139

Yarborough, earl of, 227
Year Book of Auction Sales, 229
yeoman, yeomen, 5, 10, 12, 37–51, 76, 86, 152n29, 185, 189, 195, 202, 231, 263
Yorkshire, 221, 225
Young, Arthur (agriculturalist), 193